# Herodotus and Religion
## in the Persian Wars

JON D. MIKALSON

*Herodotus and Religion*
*in the Persian Wars*

The University of North Carolina Press
Chapel Hill and London

© 2003 The University of North Carolina Press

Designed by Heidi Perov
Set in Minion
by Tseng Information Systems, Inc.
Manufactured in the United States of America

The paper in this book meets the guidelines for permanence and
durability of the Committee on Production Guidelines for
Book Longevity of the Council on Library Resources.

Library of Congress Cataloging-in-Publication Data
Mikalson, Jon D., 1943–
Herodotus and religion in the Persian Wars / by Jon D. Mikalson.
p. cm.
Includes bibliographical references (p. ) and indexes.
ISBN 0-8078-2798-3
1. Greece — History — Persian Wars, 500–449 B.C. — Religious aspects.
2. Herodotus. History. 3. Greece — Religion. I. Title.
BL795.W28 M55 2003
292.08 — dc21
2002154453

07 06 05 04 03    5 4 3 2 1

ὦ παῖδες Ἑλλήνων, ἴτε
ἐλευθεροῦτε πατρίδ᾽, ἐλευθεροῦτε δὲ
παῖδας γυναῖκας θεῶν τε πατρῴων ἕδη
θήκας τε προγόνων· νῦν ὑπὲρ πάντων ἀγών.

—AESCHYLUS, *Persae* 402–405

# CONTENTS

# ❧ MAPS ❧

## ❧ ACKNOWLEDGMENTS ❧

This project was begun during a most pleasant year as Whitehead Professor at the American School of Classical Studies in Athens in 1995–1996. Revisiting many of the Persian and Persian War sites under the guidance of John Camp and William Coulson gave considerable inspiration. The staff of the American School did everything to make the year productive and enjoyable. I am grateful for the helpful suggestions of John Dillery, Kevin Clinton, and Robert Garland, who read the manuscript at various stages. As always I owe most to my wife Mary, for expert editorial assistance and especially for her constant support and patience.

# ✄ ABBREVIATIONS ✄

| | |
|---|---|
| *ABSA* | *Annual of the British School at Athens* |
| *AC* | *Antiquité classique* |
| *AJA* | *American Journal of Archaeology* |
| *AJP* | *American Journal of Philology* |
| *BCH* | *Bulletin de correspondance hellénique* |
| *BICS* | *Bulletin of the Institute of Classical Studies* |
| Burkert, *GR* | W. Burkert. *Greek Religion*. Cambridge, Mass., 1985. |
| *CA* | *Classical Antiquity* |
| *CJ* | *Classical Journal* |
| *CP* | *Classical Philology* |
| *CQ* | *Classical Quarterly* |
| Farnell, *Cults* | L. R. Farnell. *The Cults of the Greek States*. 5 vols. Oxford, 1921; reprint, 1977. |
| *FGrHist* | F. Jacoby. *Die Fragmente der griechischen Historiker*. 3 vols. Berlin and Leiden, 1923–1958. |
| Fontenrose | J. Fontenrose. *The Delphic Oracle*. Berkeley, 1978. |
| *G&R* | *Greece and Rome* |
| *GRBS* | *Greek, Roman and Byzantine Studies* |
| *HTR* | *Harvard Theological Review* |
| HW | W. W. How and J. Wells. *A Commentary on Herodotus*. 2 vols. Oxford, 1912. |
| *IG* | *Inscriptiones Graecae* |
| *JDAI* | *Jahrbuch des Deutschen Archäologischen Instituts* |
| *JHS* | *Journal of Hellenic Studies* |
| *MH* | *Museum Helveticum* |
| ML | R. Meiggs and D. M. Lewis. *Greek Historical Inscriptions*. Rev. ed. Oxford, 1988. |
| Nilsson, *GGR* I³ | M. P. Nilsson. *Geschichte der griechischen Religion*. Vol. I³. Munich, 1967. |

| | |
|---|---|
| Page, *FGE* | D. L. Page. *Further Greek Epigrams.* Cambridge, 1981. |
| *PCG* | R. Kassel and C. Austin. *Poetae Comici Graeci.* 8 vols. Berlin, 1983–1995. |
| *RE* | A. Pauly, G. Wissowa, and W. Kroll. *Realencyklopädie der classischen Altertumswissenschaft.* Stuttgart, 1893–1963. |
| *REG* | *Revue des études grecques* |
| *RhM* | *Rheinisches Museum* |
| *TAPA* | *Transactions of the American Philological Association* |
| *WS* | *Wiener Studien* |
| *ZPE* | *Zeitschrift für Papyrologie und Epigraphik* |

# Herodotus and Religion
# in the Persian Wars

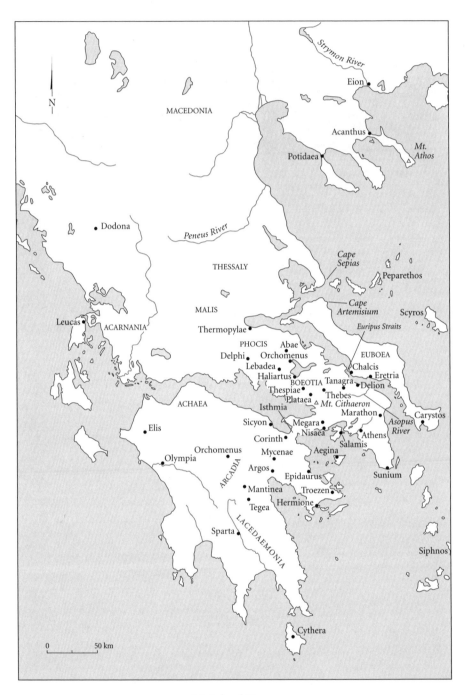

*Mainland Greece*

*Asia Minor*

The two great Persian invasions of Greece, the one ordered by King Darius and turned back by the Athenians at Marathon in 490 B.C. and the
other led by King Xerxes himself and repulsed in 480–479 by victories
of the allied Greeks at Salamis, Plataea, and Mycale, offer us our very
best opportunity from the whole of Greek antiquity to see the interplay
of Greek religion and history on a large scale. For a period of ten years,
and for somewhat longer if we include the preliminaries to the 490 invasion, we can see how the Greeks internationally, state by state, and
sometimes even individually turned to their deities and their religious
practices to influence, understand, and commemorate events that threatened their very existence. For this period we have accounts of Greeks
praying and sacrificing, making and fulfilling vows to the gods, consulting oracles, interpreting omens and dreams, believing in miracles, pon-
dering pieties and impieties, creating new cults, sanctuaries, and festivals,
and making dozens of dedications to their gods and heroes—all in direct relation to known historical events. The purpose of this book is to
collect and present the abundantly preserved religious aspects of these
critical times and thereby set Greek religion into a historical context so
as to understand better the role of Greek religion in the Persian invasions
and in Greek life in general.

Modern scholarly surveys of Greek religion, such as Walter Burkert's
*Greek Religion* and Martin Nilsson's *Geschichte der griechischen Religion*,
collect, abstract from their immediate contexts, and summarize much of
the evidence for Greek religion. They have, of course, immeasurable value
and have been the primary vehicle for organizing and analyzing this Pro-
tean subject. But there is a need also to see the human situations and
historical circumstances in which Greeks practiced their religion if we are
to understand the place religion had in their lives. The ancient sources,
written and archaeological, allow us to do this best for the period of the

Persian Wars in early fifth-century Greece. Much that we describe will be familiar to students of Greek religion, but for scholars and for non-specialists alike it may prove helpful to see these basics of Greek religion placed into social, cultural, historical, and personal contexts.

Our primary source for this study is, of course, Herodotus. His *Histories*, completed by 430 B.C. or a few years later, may reasonably be claimed to be the best and richest single source for Greek religion as it was practiced in the classical period. All who study Greek religion mine the *Histories* for discrete details about individual gods and about religious practices, cults, and institutions and for parallels to religious concepts found in other authors. Oddly, though, until very recently little attention has been paid to the whole—to the picture of Greek religion that emerges from the writings of this observer and practitioner of Greek religion in the classical period.[1] Herodotus describes Greeks practicing their religion—praying, sacrificing, making dedications, employing various methods of divination, and expressing their thoughts—on so many occasions and in such a variety of situations that one can, as I do here, weave his accounts into a general picture of religion of the time. There are, of course, significant limitations in focusing on one author, but these limitations may be counterbalanced by the opportunity to see Greek religion in human, local, and historical contexts as described by one Greek. There is even an advantage that this rich store of religious material is all the product of one man. Herodotus was certainly no ordinary Greek. He was better traveled, more cosmopolitan, more curious, more innovative, and more learned than most Greeks, and it is to these qualities that we owe the *Histories*. But when we analyze his accounts and views of Greek religion, we find that they are largely in accord with those of other contemporary and later sources for practiced religion. In our concluding chapter we attempt to discover from his writings some of his own religious beliefs and views, but with the knowledge that these were not, or most were not, peculiar to him.

Herodotus as an author is difficult to categorize. He writes an epic narrative of war, but is not a Homer. He uses some techniques and concepts of tragedy, but he is not an Aeschylus or Sophocles. Cicero terms him the "father of history," but he is no Thucydides. He is not simply a geographer, ethnographer, or historian, but he exhibits characteristics and methodologies of each.[2] He is, essentially, a category unto himself, or, put another way, he cannot be categorized. For us that is a virtue because, just as he does not fit squarely into a single genre, so he is not bound by the conventions of one genre. He does not, as Thucydides and most later historians were to do, largely exclude religious considerations from the flow of historical events.[3] Nor does he introduce the divine machinery inherent in epic or the (quite different) divine world that the conventions of tragedy dictated. So much of what we think we know of Greek religion is affected by the conventions of the genres of our sources. Very different ideas of Greek gods and religious beliefs emerge from, for example, epic, tragedy, comedy, history, or oratory, in large part because each of these genres had conventions that shaped or limited its presentation of religious material. Herodotus, it seems, stood largely outside of these conventions. We can and will find traces of some of them, but Herodotus' approach to Greek religion strikes me as less artificial, more direct, less convention-bound, and more eclectic. It may well be more the way an ordinary Greek thought about his religious world. Given the state of our sources, this is, of course, impossible to prove, but it is, I think, a hypothesis worth following to its conclusions. But even if one is reluctant to extrapolate from the *Histories* what most Greeks believed, we can at least claim to have illustrated some of what Herodotus himself apparently believed, a point to which we return in the concluding chapter.

The primary purpose of this book is to present the religious context of the Persian Wars. Herodotus explicitly and implicitly offers religious explanations of the causes and outcomes of the Persian invasions, and he gives a religious background to the major and many of the minor events of those times. These are regularly ignored, dismissed, or disparaged by both ancient and modern historians, but they are there.[4] Herodotus thought them important, included them, and integrated them into his account. They may not suit modern ideas of what is historically "important," but to assume that the Greeks would in a religious vacuum face, prepare for, fight, win, and remember a war that threatened their very existence may be to misunderstand and oversimplify classical Greek society. I do not think it solely the prejudice of a religious historian to claim that the report of a miraculous event at Delphi or unfavorable battle omens at Plataea could affect the course of events every bit as much as a general's strategy or the different styles of armor. And how the war was remembered—what Herodotus is attempting to determine and does determine in the *Histories*—is as much a matter of belief as fact, and the religious components of that memory of the war themselves then become elements of religious belief for Greeks in the future.

In tracing causation there is a natural inclination to put into separate, even opposed categories the human and the divine, the literally mundane and the metaphysical, and then to follow one of them or, at best, to follow both of them in separate if parallel lines. The former are the historians' turf; the latter are best left to the poets. In real life, however, the human and divine do often meet, and the point of contact is religious cult and religious belief. The dedications by the Greeks at Delphi after their final victory over the Persians are historical facts, no less so than the victory itself, and there were discoverable human, historical reasons for these dedications. Religious beliefs were among these reasons, and the dedications themselves, once erected, could in the future affect religious beliefs, and these beliefs would in turn become one determinant of future actions. Much, in fact most, of what we find "religious" in Herodotus' account of the Persian Wars is at this point of contact—that is, it is centered in practiced cult, and the religious beliefs underlying the cultic are as "human" and "historical" as any individual's aspirations for empire, political power, or glory. They need to be brought into the discussion of the social and cultural milieu and the causes and outcomes of these great wars.

Although I think the religious component of Herodotus' account of the Persian Wars important, I do not claim that it is Herodotus' sole or even most important explanation of the events of these years. It is one explanation among several. The interpretation of Herodotus is not a zero-sum game in which the introduction of a new set of explanations needs diminish the value of other explanations. When modern historians wish to promote the value of their own explanations, whether they be the growth of imperialism or the east-west dimensions of the conflict or some other such overarching theme, they tend to demean the importance of other factors, and religion and religious motivation are chief among these "other" factors.[5] But among all Greek prose authors Herodotus is perhaps least suited to such a zero-sum game. He presents a wide range of perspectives and methodologies. He offers numerous motivations— each to us sufficient in itself—for single major events and characters and, unlike modern scholars, rarely sees the need to choose among them.[6]

We want one answer; Herodotus provides several. The different motivations sometimes appear to us to conflict or to be otherwise inconsistent, at the very least to "overdetermine" an event, but this usually does not trouble Herodotus. The battle and Greek victory at Salamis in reality were no doubt the result of a large variety of causes, a variety that Herodotus in his wide-ranging account suggests but which we attempt to reduce to a favored few.[7] Among these causes, I would claim, were events of a religious nature and the religious beliefs of the participants. I do not claim that religious causes were the only or most important ones and that we should downplay military, political, cultural, strategic, and even geographical factors. Rather I would like to restore the religious elements to the importance that Herodotus gives them in his account of the Persian Wars, as one element among several.

Herodotus is, of course, our major source, but we can supplement his account of religious events of these times with those of later, sometimes considerably later, authors. Plutarch, Pausanias, and Diodorus Siculus each knew Herodotus' *Histories* well and sometimes simply give us abbreviated versions of Herodotus. But each also had sources of information independent from Herodotus, and they provide valuable additions to Herodotus' record. Plutarch of Chaeronea, born before A.D. 50 and living until at least 120, described in his *Lives* the activities of some of the principal figures of the Persian War period (*Themistocles*, *Aristides*, and *Cimon*), and randomly elsewhere in his voluminous writings he recounted a number of events from the time of the Persian Wars. Plutarch derives some of these from Herodotus, but others, and some especially valuable for our purposes, he draws from other, often fourth-century B.C. sources. Plutarch also did not appreciate Herodotus' portrayal of the role of his beloved Thebes in the Persian Wars, and wrote a diatribe attacking Herodotus' credibility, *On the Malice of Herodotus* (*Mor.* 854E–874C), in the course of which he offers some ill-tempered "corrections" to Herodotus' accounts. From this and from Plutarch's other writings we draw material to supplement Herodotus' account of the period.

Pausanias, from Magnesia in Lydia, toured much of mainland Greece and the Peloponnesus in the early to mid second century A.D. and wrote, in Greek, a guidebook for the sites he visited. He described Athens, Delphi, Marathon, Plataea, and many of the other places at which battles of the Persian Wars were fought or monuments were erected. Pausanias often draws upon Herodotus in his own accounts, but frequently also records stories still being told in his own time about the battles and miraculous events at these sites. His descriptions of the monuments, some mentioned by Herodotus, some not, are particularly valuable for filling in the picture of religious activities during and immediately after these wars. And, in turn, Pausanias' record of these monuments is itself often confirmed or supplemented by the discovery of some Persian War monuments in modern archaeological excavations, and these monuments will be described in their proper places.

Diodorus of Sicily, of the first century B.C., is our last major source for religious aspects of the Persian Wars. For much of the early parts of his world history he too drew from Herodotus, but he, like Plutarch, also took from other classical-period sources and preserves some important religious activities and events not to be found in Herodotus.

Plutarch, Pausanias, Diodorus, our other occasional literary sources, and even some of the inscriptions bearing on events concerning the Persian Wars are much later, even hundreds of years later than Herodotus. The accounts of these sources are often questioned by modern scholars, and we will note their objections when we introduce them. We should stress here that even Herodotus' account was not contemporary or nearly contemporary with the events he describes. The latest surely datable events in his *Histories* are from 431 and 430 B.C.,[8] and how long he had been writing by then we do not know. But clearly he did not begin writing, as Thucydides did, in the midst of the wars he was describing. If 484, the traditional date of his birth, is somewhat accurate, he was a young child at the time of the second Persian invasion. Herodotus did interview a few Greek participants in these wars,[9] but he was writing, at the least, a generation later than the events themselves, and enough time had elapsed for some facts to be lost and for legends to develop. He himself knew of Phrynichus' tragedy on the capture of Miletus in 494, he may have known of Aeschylus' production of the *Persae* in 472, and he had no doubt seen in Athens the famous painting (of the 460s) of the battle of Marathon. Herodotus is thus a "late" source for the Persian Wars, from a time when the Greeks were "constructing" their history of these wars in various media.

In this "construction" of their victory over the Persians, we must consider the possibility that the Greeks and Herodotus himself indulged in some very natural and only human exaggeration. Herodotus could be extremely precise in his use of numbers, as when he described Polycrates' tunnel on Samos,[10] but virtually no modern scholar accepts Herodotus' claims that Xerxes' invasion force included 1,700,000 infantry, 80,000 cavalry (not counting camels and chariots), 1,207 triremes, and 3,000 other ships (7.59.3–60, 87, 89.1, 97). He gives the total force, ultimately, as 2,641,610 combatants and an equal number of noncombatants (7.184–185). Herodotus anticipates objections to these numbers by describing in detail how Xerxes counted his troops at Doriscus and by listing each contingent and its commander, but the modern judgment is that these numbers are wildly exaggerated. Similar doubts are raised about Herodotus' claims that the Thasians spent 400 talents ($240 million) hosting Xerxes' army for one very sumptuous meal (7.118), that the Greeks at Thermopylae faced 3 million opponents (7.228.1), and that the Greeks at Plataea killed 230,000 of Mardonius' army of 300,000 (9.70.5). These numbers are questioned by virtually all modern scholars but not, interestingly, by ancient historians, including Thucydides. For Greeks they had clearly become part of the legend of these wars.

The question arises whether there was a similar exaggeration in religious matters. This element was, of course, shaped and constructed no less than others by Herodotus and the Greek tradition. We do not, however, see the same type of exaggeration in, for example, the number and size of victory monuments and other dedications to the gods, most of which are verified by ancient eyewitnesses and archaeological excavations. More important, though, is whether the sources exaggerated the role of the gods such as Poseidon and Apollo of Delphi in bringing victory to the Greeks. Here, of course, we are treating religious belief and not fact, and for us the real question is whether Herodotus and other sources exaggerated or misrepresented what the Greeks *believed* happened, and there is no evidence that they did. If Herodotus does not give with complete accuracy the beliefs of the actual participants in these wars, he at least represents how Greeks of the following two generations imagined them, and that has considerable value in itself. And the accounts of Plutarch, Pausanias, and Diodorus have their value in recording how these events were "remembered" many centuries afterward.

My concern is religious history, the religious events and acts associated with the Persian Wars as reported by Herodotus and other sources and the religious beliefs behind them as expressed, primarily, by Herodotus. Those who work in the political and military history of these times may well find my trust in Herodotus as a source naive, but my purposes are different from theirs. I attempt to discover what the Greeks "believed" happened and why they "believed" it happened. The political and military historians are searching for what "really" happened and for the "real" motives and causes behind these events. In so doing they often challenge Herodotus' accounts, sometimes with the help of other ancient sources but most often simply on the basis of their own sense of historical probabilities. And they devote little attention to omens, prayers, and miracles which, since Thucydides, have been largely excluded as determining events and causes in Greek history. But some religious "events" are, in fact, historical: for example, the taking of omens before the battle of Plataea and the dedications of victory at the major Panhellenic sanctuaries at the end of the wars. Historians are understandably reluctant to accept miracles or accurate oracles as reported by Herodotus. The miracles are often dismissed as tales concocted by religious personnel in the sanctuaries, and the oracles as late *ex eventu* fabrications by the oracle centers. But, whatever their origins — and at that we can only guess — these omens, miracles, and oracles were "believed in" by Herodotus and, most probably, by most Greeks of his time, and they became part of the corpus of Greek religious beliefs. That they did in fact become a part of that corpus of religious beliefs is demonstrated by Plutarch, Pausanias, and Diodorus. As such they are critical to understanding Greek religion of the time and are proper subjects for the historian of that religion. For most of these Herodotus is our sole source, and if we reject his accounts and interpretations of them, we are left with nothing but our own speculations about what the Greeks might have "believed" about the role of the gods and of cultic practices during these wars. And, finally, because so much of what Herodotus claims in religious matters can be documented or paralleled in contemporary and later sources for Greek popular religion, he earns considerable trust in those matters for which we have no other sources. All this does not mean, of course, that we accept, without discrimination, everything Herodotus tells us about Greek religion. In our discussions we will be noting Herodotus' occasional variant accounts of a religious event, his own doubts, his sometimes cautious statements about religious events, and the different "layers" of religion he introduces into his *Histories*. But, by and large, we trust Herodotus far more than do political and military historians because we are concerned primarily with "beliefs," not with the "facts" that lie behind those beliefs. It is these religious "beliefs" about the Persian Wars that Herodotus represented and no doubt in some cases shaped, and it is these "beliefs" that were part of or became part of the religion of the generations after him.

I have translated several passages from Herodotus' *Histories*, in part because Herodotus' accounts place religious matters in a larger context, and in part because I, like Pausanias (2.30.4), have no intention of rewriting "what Herodotus told well before." The prose style of Herodotus, relaxed, paratactic, and occasionally repetitious and wordy, has great charm in itself, and in my translations I have attempted to allow this style to come through, only rarely abbreviating or smoothing the flow of the original. My handling of two words requires comment. What Herodotus "tells" are called by him *logoi* (λόγοι, "things told"), whether they be short, paragraph-length accounts of brief episodes, a book-length account of Egypt, or the whole narrative of the Persian invasions. These *logoi* are by modern translators variously termed "histories," "accounts," "stories," and "myths," but to Herodotus they are all *logoi*. In my translations and discussions I avoid for *logos* "history," "story," and "myth," because each of these imposes on what Herodotus writes an un-Herodotean value judgment of its factual worth. I generally use the term "account," but also sometimes employ the transliteration *logos*.[11] *Nomos* (νόμος) is another special and important term. It and its cognates (νόμιμα, νομίζω) are frequent in the *Histories* and pose a different problem. *Nomoi* are "customs" that may or may not be institutionalized as "laws."[12] The phrase "customs/laws" sometimes used by translators for *nomoi* is cumbersome and also frequently inaccurate because many of the *nomoi* Herodotus describes remained only "customs." Depending on the context, I sometimes employ "custom," sometimes "law," and occasionally just give the transliteration *nomos*. To reduce confusion I have followed throughout the spelling of names to be found in the *Oxford Classical Dictionary*, third edition (1996), with the exception of a few deities and their epithets.

In my teaching I have long urged students—to whom terms like 10 drachmas or 3 minae or 1,000 talents have little meaning—to convert such sums to dollar equivalents at the rate of 1 drachma = $100, 1 mina = $10,000, and 1 talent = $600,000. This rate gives a middle-class Athenian an average daily wage of $100 and an annual income of about $30,000.

These dollar equivalents alert students to the vast financial resources of fifth-century Athens and also to the fact that the relative costs of certain items such as cows, clothing, and food differed greatly from what we experience today.[13] I include similar conversions throughout this study.

D. Müller in his *Topographischer Bildkommentar zu den Historien Herodots* (1987) offers maps, plans, bibliographies, and photographs of all sites mentioned by Herodotus and now in the territory of modern Greece. The photographs in particular will bring back welcome memories to those who have had the good fortune to tread many of these sites and will help others realize the intimate connections between Herodotus' accounts and the topography and monuments of the localities. For the first mention of sites important to this study I give reference to Müller's monumental work.

I give for all Delphic oracles the number assigned to them by Fontenrose (1978) in his catalog. In that catalog one will find discussion, ancient sources, and bibliography for the oracle in question. Many of the epigrams and epitaphs from the period have been attributed by ancient or modern sources to Simonides of Ceos, but few of the attributions are certain. I note the few certain ones but rather than leave the others anonymous I attribute them, as is commonly done, to "Simonides." Herodotus' *Histories* is, of course, our prime source, and references simply in the form 8.51–55 are to it. Many passages from Herodotus, Plutarch, Diodorus, and Pausanias are translated and discussed in Chapter 1 and then are referred to in later chapters, and to indicate this and to draw the reader to the initial translations and discussions I put citations of these passages in later chapters in italics (*8.51–55*). The passages in Chapter 1 may be tracked down in the Index of Passages Cited. All dates henceforth are B.C. unless otherwise noted, and, finally, Herodotus dates certain events by the number of years before "his own time." For convenience and consistency I posit "his time" to be 450.

# ✄ ONE ✄

# A Religious Account
# of the Persian Invasions

## ✄ The Prelude ✄

In 510, just twenty years before the Persians landed at the Bay of Marathon, the Athenians ousted Hippias who had succeeded his father Pisistratus as the tyrant over Athens. The elimination of a tyrannical dynasty that had ruled continuously for thirty-six years, off and on over a longer period, and the implementation, within a few years, of the democratic reforms of Cleisthenes changed fundamentally the nature of the Athenians and of their state. According to Herodotus, "When the Athenians were governed by tyrants, they were better than none of their neighbors in military affairs; but when they escaped the tyrants, they became the best by far. This shows that when they were held down, they played the cowards, as if they were working for a master (δεσπότη), but when they became free, each one was eager to work for himself" (5.78). These recently energized Athenians, again in Herodotus' judgment, were to play the key role in the ultimate defeat of the Persians (7.139). After liberation from the tyrants, there followed for the Athenians a quick succession of major battles and conflicts with neighbors, and behind these and the expulsion of the Pisistratid tyranny lies a host of religious causes and concerns, which, together, offer a glimpse into the religious environment on the eve of the Persian invasions.

In the night before the celebration of the Panathenaea in Athens, in 514, Hipparchus, Pisistratus' son and Hippias' younger brother, as reported by Herodotus, received a dream:

A tall and handsome man seemed to stand over Hipparchus and speak in a riddling way these lines:

15

"Endure, O lion, you who have already suffered unendurable things with an
   enduring spirit.
No human being who commits injustice will not pay the punishment."

As soon as day came, Hipparchus told his dream to dream interpreters,
but he rejected the dream and escorted the procession of the festival.
There he died, assassinated by Harmodius and Aristogiton (5.55–56).[1]

The words of the dream were for Herodotus "riddling" to the extent
that, contrary to his usual practice, he neither has another interpret them
nor attempts to do so himself.[2] The riddle remains unsolved for us. Was
Hipparchus the doer or the receiver of "injustice"? The first line, "Endure, O lion . . . ," would suggest the latter, but the second line, "No
human being . . . ,"—given the glory that his assassins received for their
deed—points to the former.[3] This prophetic dream, the first of many, that
we shall encounter, is uncharacteristically enigmatic. Most Herodotean
dreams are quite explicit, and *all* prove true. Hipparchus' rejection of
the dream was not a religious crime, but was a mistake, the type of mistake often made by those who were, for other reasons, guilty of impious
behavior.

At this very time the Alcmaeonidae, a prominent and rich Athenian family, were enduring the exile imposed upon them by the Pisistratidae. They
and their supporters held the fort Leipsydrion in the mountains of north-
ern Attica. They used their considerable influence and wealth to secure
from the Amphictyons of Delphi the contract to rebuild, at Delphi, the
temple of Apollo that had recently, in 548, burned to the ground. The
Alcmaeonidae in their generosity went beyond their contractual obligations, most notably by building the East facade of the temple from
marble, not from porous limestone. "And then," according to Herodotus, "as the Athenians claim, when the Alcmaeonidae were in Delphi they
bribed the Pythia to tell the Spartans, whenever they came on a public
or private oracular mission, to 'free' Athens" (5.62–64). This the Pythia
did. The oracles were "deceitful" (κιβδήλοισι μαντηίοισι, 5.91.2),[4] but the
Spartans, despite their ties of a "guest-host" relationship (*xenia*) with the
Pisistratidae, were eventually persuaded and, after an initial failed invasion, in 510 sent their king Cleomenes with a Spartan force to "free"
Athens.[5] To win the favor of Delphi with dedications or, as here, a gener-

*Attica and Environs*

ous gift was quite proper, but to "bribe" (ἀνέπειθον χρήμασι) the Pythia was quite a different matter. The same Cleomenes later corrupted Delphic officials to throw into question by oracular responses the legitimacy of the birth of his fellow king Demaratus, and, according to Herodotus, "most Greeks" gave this as the cause of Cleomenes' later madness and grisly suicide (6.66–67.1, 75.3). By contrast Herodotus offers no condemnation or punishment of the Alcmaeonidae's behavior.[6] This is our first instance in which Herodotus downplays an impiety committed by a group he admired against a tyrant or despotic power.[7] For Herodotus, in some cases at least, political objectives apparently override religious scruples.

After the Spartan expulsion of the Pisistratidae there emerged at Athens as leaders, and opponents, the Alcmaeonid Cleisthenes (perhaps the very Alcmaeonid who had bribed the Pythia [Hdt. 5.66.1]) and Isagoras. After various disputes, Isagoras, distrusting Cleisthenes' popularity and democratic reforms, called in his *xenos* Cleomenes for a second time.[8] As his reason for intervening again Cleomenes, prompted by Isagoras, charged that Cleisthenes was, as an Alcmaeonid, "polluted." Over a century earlier a certain Cylon, an Olympic victor, had attempted to establish a tyranny in Athens. He had failed and found himself with his supporters besieged on the Acropolis. He took refuge as a suppliant at the statue of Athena Polias in the temple of Athena. Cylon and his supporters were eventually removed, with the promise that they would not suffer death, but the charge was that the Alcmaeonidae and their partisans had then killed them. The murder of suppliants was clear impiety, and for it the Alcmaeonidae would be "polluted."[9] Herodotus questions the charge: "Neither Cleisthenes himself nor his friends and relatives (οἱ φίλοι) shared in the murder. These things had occurred before the time of Pisistratus" (5.70–71). Herodotus seems here, again in deference to the Alcmaeonidae, not to accept the common notion that pollution for such impiety could be passed from generation to generation.[10] But, whatever the justice of the charge, Cleisthenes fled Athens.[11]

After Cleisthenes' flight, King Cleomenes came to Athens with a small force of Lacedaemonians to assist Isagoras. He soon found himself surrounded by hostile Athenians and looked to the Acropolis for safety. Herodotus describes the scene:

When Cleomenes went up to the Acropolis, intending to take possession of it, he was entering the *adyton* of the goddess to speak directly to her.[12] Her priestess stood up from her throne before he passed through the gate, and said, "Lacedaemonian stranger, go back and do not enter the sanctuary, for it is not permitted for Dorians to enter here." Cleomenes replied, "Woman, I am an Achaean, not a Dorian."[13] (5.72.3)

Cleomenes, however, failed to heed what Herodotus considered to be a literally ominous statement (κλεηδόνι) by the priestess, "go back." Like other impious individuals in Herodotus' *Histories*, perhaps like Hipparchus, he missed or ignored a clear divine sign. Soon the priestess's word was accomplished: Cleomenes and his Lacedaemonians were thrown out of Athens again and "went back" to Sparta (5.72). The Athenians then recalled Cleisthenes and the 700 households who had been, like Cleisthenes, banished by Isagoras and Cleomenes.

In their successive, post-Pisistratid victories over the Boeotians and Chalcidians in 506 the Athenians took many prisoners, including 700 Boeotians. They eventually ransomed the prisoners of both peoples and dedicated the prisoners' chains on the Acropolis, mounting them on the fortification wall opposite the temple of Athena.[14] The chains were still there in Herodotus' time, with the wall now scorched by fire from the Persian burning of the Acropolis. Herodotus (5.77) describes the dedication the Athenians made from a tithe of the ransoms for the Boeotian and Chalcidian prisoners. It was a bronze four-horse chariot which stood to the left as one entered the Propylaea, and it bore this inscription:[15]

In deeds of war the children of the Athenians defeated
the peoples of the Boeotians and Chalcidians.
They quenched their *hybris* with painful, iron chains,
and they dedicated, as a tithe, these mares to Pallas Athena.

Throughout the Persian Wars the Greeks made dedications after victories in battle that were consistent in content, intent, and financing with these Athenian dedications of 506. The chains were actual, physical, and prominently displayed remnants and memorials of the victory, as would be the captured weapons and ships the Greeks would on later occasions dedicate in their sanctuaries.[16] For the chariot statue the Athenians used a tithe of the cash they received in ransoms, not simply donating money to Athena but in a characteristically Greek way using it to create an object of beauty that would adorn her sanctuary and the city. The tithe, one-tenth of the war booty, was the common form of offering, the "first-fruits" (ἀπαρχαί, ἀκροθίνια) of the spoils of the "victory," and one that the Greeks used regularly for dedications throughout the Persian Wars.[17]

The text of the inscription itself reveals much about the purpose and feeling behind this and later dedications. The first three lines commemorate the accomplishments of the Athenians themselves. The dedication to Pallas Athena in the last line presumes gratitude to her, although that gratitude is not explicitly expressed.[18] Most notably, there is no mention of the specific aid the goddess offered. The overall effect of the inscription is a commemoration of Athenian, human achievement. The dedication to Athena was made from one-tenth of the spoils of victory, and correspondingly nine-tenths of the dedicatory text are devoted to human efforts.[19] This combination of tithing, of rendering cash into objects of beauty, of commemorating human achievement, and of making a dedication to a deity without explicit mention of gratitude and without description of the nature of the divine aid is characteristic of all the postvictory dedications made by the Greeks throughout the Persian Wars.

Critically important to the Greek effort against the Persians would be the solidarity of the major Greek powers, among them Athens, Aegina, Thebes, and Sparta. Herodotus sees in the following religious events factors that directly threatened the necessary cooperation among these states in the years just prior to the Persian invasions.

There was, in these times, a long-standing feud between the Athenians and Aeginetans. The cause, though complex, is instructive. The Epidaurians once in the past, perhaps circa 625, were suffering a famine and sent to Delphi for help. Herodotus tells the story:

The Pythia bid them to erect statues of Damia and Auxesia and said, if they did so, things would be better for them. The Epidaurians then asked whether they should make the statues of bronze or stone. The Pythia allowed neither of these, but said the statues were to be of olive wood.[20] The Epidaurians then asked the Athenians to allow them to cut olive wood because they thought Athenian olive trees were the most sacred. . . . The Athenians said they would, on the condition that the Epidaurians each year send sacrificial victims for Athena Polias and Erechtheus. The Epidaurians accepted the terms, got what they were wanting, and made statues from these olive trees and erected them. Their land then bore fruit for them and they regularly paid to the Athenians what they had agreed upon. (5.82)

A time later friction broke out between Epidaurus and her nearby colony Aegina, and, in a raid on Epidaurus, the Aeginetans carried off the statues of Damia and Auxesia. They set them up in their own land, at a place called Oia.[21] After this, naturally, the Epidaurians stopped delivering the promised annual victims to Athenian Athena. The Athenians protested, but the Epidaurians told the Athenians to deal with the Aeginetans. The Athenians eventually demanded that the Aeginetans give the statues to Athens, but the Aeginetans refused. The Athenians, in their version of the story, then went with a shipload of citizen sailors to Aegina to reclaim forcibly the statues. "They cast ropes around the statues and were trying to pull them from their bases when, suddenly, lightning and an earthquake occurred. The sailors doing the pulling lost their wits because of this and started killing one another as if they were enemy soldiers. Only one survived and escaped back to Phaleron" (5.85.2). In the Athenian view "the divine" (τὸ δαιμόνιον) destroyed all their other men. When the survivor returned to Athens, the wives of the lost sailors, angered at his survival, stabbed him to death with their brooches, and this was to determine fashion for both Athenian and Aeginetan women. To punish these women the Athenians made all their women change from Doric to Ionic (really Carian) dress — that is, from the *peplos* to the *chiton* — so they would not be wearing brooches. But the Aeginetan women, to celebrate the event, began wearing brooches one and one-half times the normal size and dedicating these large brooches at their sanctuary of Damia and Auxesia. But no Attic products, not even the omnipresent Athenian pottery, could be brought into this sanctuary (5.82–88).[22]

Herodotus' account, anchored in the realities of the cults of major deities in each of the three cities and even in their dress fashions, offers a religious cause, and only a religious cause, for Athenian-Aeginetan hostility. Thebes, then, was to play on this hostility for its own advantage. More than a century after the Damia-Auxesia affair, the Thebans wanted to avenge their defeat at the hands of the Athenians in 506, the very defeat the Athenians commemorated on the Acropolis, and they consulted the Delphic oracle about how to do it. The Pythia, according to Herodotus, said "revenge would not happen for them from themselves, but was bidding them to discuss the matter publicly among themselves and ask 'those nearest to them' to help."[23] After public discussion and debate the Thebans decided that not real neighbors but Aeginetans were meant, because Thebe and Aegina were both daughters of their river Aso-

pus and hence Thebans and Aeginetans were closely related. The Thebans then asked the Aeginetans to send two of their heroes worshiped in
cult, the Aeacidae Peleus and Telamon, to help them, like mercenaries, in
battle against the Athenians. The Aeginetans did this, but the Thebans,
even with the Aeacidae, were again defeated. The Thebans then sent the
Aeacidae back home and told the Aeginetans they preferred to have men
instead.[24] The Aeginetans responded by starting an undeclared war on
Athens and by attacking the coasts of Attica when the Athenians were off
fighting the Thebans (Hdt. 5.79–81).[25]

Herodotus here has the Thebans, after a public debate, decide a critically important diplomatic question by reference to what we would call
a myth, that Aegina and Thebe were daughters of the Boeotian river
Asopus. To understand the import of this and that it need not be mere
poetic or historic invention, we should, perhaps, begin by urging the removal of the terms "myth" and "mythology" from this discussion and all
discussions of Herodotus' accounts.[26] Twice, and only twice, Herodotus
calls a *logos* he expressly does not believe a μῦθος. Herodotus thus had
the vocabulary and ability to designate a "silly" (εὐηθής) tale "mythical,"
but reserves it for Homer's account of Oceanus (2.23) and a Greek tale
about Heracles in Egypt (2.43–45).[27] Elsewhere all that he recounts are
*logoi*, "accounts told" or "accounts told to him." Herodotus does once
distinguish between *logoi* of "old" and "recent" events (9.26–27), but he
offers no judgment of their historicity solely on that account. He makes
no distinction, in terms of historicity, for example, between the *logoi* of
the Trojan War and of the battle of Marathon, or between the *logoi* of
the travels of Io and the revenge of Protesilaus.[28] Some "events" may be
more believable to Herodotus than others, but the older ones are not,
ipso facto, less believable. We are inclined to call his *logoi* of the older
events "myths" and "stories" and those of recent events "accounts," but
that is a distinction we, not Herodotus, make. To him they are all *logoi*.
That the *logos* of the sisterhood of Aegina and Thebe was old was no
cause for Herodotus to question its validity or appropriateness in a diplomatic discussion at the end of the sixth century. That Aegina and Thebe
were sisters was probably as much a "fact" to the Thebans as it was to the
Athenians that their Aglaurus, Herse, and Pandrosus were sisters, and
Herodotus is simply reporting that, as a *logos* and not as a *mythos*.

Peleus and Telamon, the sons of Aeacus that the Aeginetans sent to
Thebes, were heroes, that is, deceased mortals who received public cult

at their tomb. Such heroes had each done in life either some wonderfully good or frighteningly monstrous deed, or had died under such mysterious circumstances that they were thought to maintain power — for good or evil — after death. A hero's cult was usually highly localized, as that of the Aeacidae on Aegina, and was often centered on the hero's presumed tomb.[29] These same Aeacidae, Salaminian Ajax (himself the son of Telamon, and hence too an Aeacid), the Delphic heroes Phylacus and Autonous, the Athenian heroes Theseus and Echetlaeus, and others each make contributions to the Greek effort in the Persian Wars, but here, quite exceptionally in Herodotus and in Greek literature in general, the Thebans found the Aeacidae sent to them by the Aeginetans (probably as statues) ineffectual.

Aeacus, the patriarch of the heroic Aeacid clan, also played a role in the eventual settlement of Athenian-Aeginetan hostilities. When the Athenians were beginning a counterattack on Aegina, an oracle, according to Herodotus, came to the Athenians from Delphi bidding them to wait thirty years, then in the thirty-first year to build a sanctuary for Aeacus and begin the war against the Aeginetans. If they did this,

what they wished would come to them. But if they campaigned immediately, they would suffer much in the interval and also would accomplish much, and in the end would overthrow the Aeginetans.[30] When the Athenians heard this report, they built a sanctuary for Aeacus, the sanctuary that still stands in the Agora,[31] but they did not put up with hearing that they had to wait thirty years after they had suffered wrongs from the Aeginetans.[32] (5.89)

The establishment in Athens of a shrine of Aeacus, the major Aeginetan hero, might well have been an Athenian claim to ownership of Aegina,[33] a claim the Athenians eventually made good. They subdued Aegina in 457/6, and if one assumes the Delphic oracle proved completely accurate, that Athens would take Aegina in a war beginning "in the thirty-first year," the oracle must have been given after the battle of Marathon (490), not before it as Herodotus has it. But the evidence clearly indicates that these events occurred in the period between 507 and 499,[34] and so the oracle is correct in the outcome but not the timing of the end of Athenian-Aeginetan hostilities.

Threatening actions from Sparta, however, forced the Athenians to put off their planned Aeginetan campaign. The Spartans were angered at the

Alcmaeonid manipulation of the Delphic oracle (5.62–64, above), but also had in their possession ominous oracles predicting, as Herodotus tells it, that "many bad things would be for them from Athenians."[35] Before this the Spartans did not know of these oracles, but they learned of them after Cleomenes brought them back to Sparta. Cleomenes acquired the oracles from the Acropolis of the Athenians. Before that the Pisistratidae possessed them, but when they were being driven out they left them behind in the sanctuary"[36] (5.90). These newly discovered oracles strengthened the Spartans' fears of the growing power and reputation of now democratic Athens, and at just this time they attempted to convince their allies to mount a campaign to restore Hippias as tyrant of Athens.

### ≫ The Ionian Revolt ≫

In 498, for reasons that had apparently nothing to do with religious concerns, the Athenians made a small contribution to assist the Milesians and other cities of Ionia in their revolt against Persian domination and control. With twenty ships they joined a Milesian expedition to attack Persia, and one unintended by-product of that expedition was to become a dominant religious theme in the ensuing eighteen years of the Greek-Persian and Athenian-Persian conflict.[37]

The twenty ships of the Athenians joined five of the Eretrians and a force of Milesians and sailed to Ephesus. From there they went overland and found Sardis, the capital of the Lydian satrapy, largely undefended. One house in the city was set ablaze, and the fire quickly spread among the thatched-roof houses until virtually the whole city was burned to the ground. "Sardis was burned, and in it also the sanctuary of the local goddess Cybebe,[38] and the Persians later, using this as an excuse, burned in return the sanctuaries among the Greeks" (Hdt. 5.102.1). As Persian resistance mounted, the Greeks quickly retreated to Ephesus but were there overtaken by Persian forces and soundly defeated. The Athenians and Eretrians fled home and did not again heed Milesian calls for help (5.97–103). The Ionian revolt was soon put down, by the victory of the Persians at the battle of Lade in 495 and the capture of Miletus and the subjugation of Caria in 494. But the burning of Sardis, and in particular the burning of the sanctuary of Cybebe there, lived on. When King Darius first heard of it, "he took a bow, fitted an arrow to it, and shot the arrow up into the sky. As he did, he said, 'Zeus,[39] grant me to take vengeance on the Athenians,' and he ordered one of his servants to say, three times each time dinner was served, 'Master, remember the Athenians'" (5.105).[40] The burning of sanctuaries, as reprisals, would become a distinctive feature of the forthcoming Persian attacks on the Greeks for the next eighteen years, and it was in this gross impiety that Herodotus would find one of the major causes of the ultimate defeat of Persians.

Miletus' fall in 494 assured the failure of the Ionian Revolt and fulfilled an oracle of Apollo. Herodotus not only reports the oracle,[41]

Miletus, contriver of evil deeds, at that time
you will become a feast and glorious gifts for many men.
Your wives will wash the feet of many long-haired men,
and other men will concern themselves with our temple at Didyma.
(6.19.2)

but also characteristically describes in some detail how it was fulfilled: "These things befell the Milesians, when the majority of the men were killed by the long-haired Persians, and their wives and children were treated like slaves, and the sanctuary at Didyma, both the temple and the oracle, were robbed and burned" (6.19).[42] The other rebellious islands and Greek cities of Asia Minor were quickly reenslaved, one by one, and they suffered similar burnings of their sanctuaries (6.32).

The Athenian orator Isocrates in 380 claimed that

it is worthwhile to praise also the Ionians because, when their sanctuaries were burned, they laid a curse on anyone who disturbed the sanctuaries or wished to restore them to their original state. They did not lack resources to rebuild them but intended that they be for their descendants a memorial of the impiety of the barbarians and that no one ever trust those who dare such crimes against the property of the gods. (4.156)

This curse on those who might rebuild the sanctuaries and the intent to memorialize the impiety of the Persians are remarkably similar to the oath the allied Greeks later purportedly swore on the eve of the battle of Plataea (Lycurgus, *Leoc.* 80–81 and D.S. 11.29.2–4, below), and some think Isocrates may have confused the occasions.[43]

Darius' first attempt to punish Athens and Eretria, in 492, was led by his general Mardonius and was designed to follow the coast of the Aegean, from the Hellespont to Macedonia, from Macedonia to Eretria and Athens. But the Persian navy was driven by strong winds against the headland of Athos, and approximately 300 ships and 20,000 men were lost. On land the Thracian Brygoi attacked and killed many of the army and wounded Mardonius. After these losses on sea and land, Mardonius abandoned the expedition (Hdt. 6.43–45).

And then, in 490, when Athens was engaged in the continuing war with Aegina, Darius ordered his generals Datis and Artaphrenes to attack Eretria and Athens by sea, this time sailing with 600 triremes straight across the Aegean, from Samos, past Icaros, Naxos, and Delos, to Euboea and Eretria. Datis and Artaphrenes were, according to Herodotus, "to enslave Athens and Eretria and to bring back the slaves for Darius to see" (6.94.2). The Persians attacked first at Naxos, an island city-state that they had tried to master before. The Naxians fled to the mountains, and the Persians burned both the city and its sanctuaries (6.96).[44]

Before the Persians' arrival, the Delians, residents of the island sacred to Apollo and Artemis, had already fled to neighboring Tinos. Datis, according to Herodotus, sent them this message:

"Sacred men, why have you inappropriately condemned me and gone off in flight? I myself have decided, and the king has ordered me, not to harm in any way this land in which the two gods were born, neither the land itself nor its inhabitants. And, so, go back to your property and tend the island." Datis announced these things to the Delians, and later he heaped up 17,000 pounds of incense on the altar (of Apollo) and burned them. . . . After Datis left, Delos was shaken by an earthquake, as the Delians were saying, the first and last time up to my time.[45] The god, I suppose, revealed this as a miraculous sign (τέρας) to men of the evils that were to come, because in the time of Darius, son of Hystaspes, and of Xerxes, son of Darius, and of Artoxerxes, son of Xerxes, in these three successive generations more evils occurred for Greece than in the twenty generations before Darius. Some of the evils arose for Greece from the Persians, some from the Greek leaders themselves as they warred for leadership. And so it was not unfitting that Delos, untouched by earthquakes before, was shaken then. And it had been written about Delos in an oracle, as follows: "I will shake even Delos, though unshaken before."[46] (6.97–98)

This earthquake is one of several natural "marvels" (τέρατα) that we encounter in the religious history of the Persian Wars. That it should occur on previously stable Delos was unusual, but what made it truly ominous and divine was its coincidence with the arrival of Datis and the Persians. We have just previously seen Herodotus explain the details of the oracle about Miletus, but here, almost as a soothsayer, he launches into an interpretation of the omen in terms of the next sixty years of Greek history. Also noteworthy here is the Persians' respect for a major Greek religious sanctuary. Later we find Persians, under Xerxes, attempting to sack and burn Apollo's Delphi (8.35–39, below), Apollo's oracle at Abae (8.32–33, below), and countless other sanctuaries, but at moments, as here and later at Troy (7.43, below), the Persians can show proper respect for Greek deities. The Persians may here have been willing to spare Delos because this expedition was, in fact, to avenge the burning of the sanctuary of Cybebe by the Athenians and Eretrians. Delians and other Greeks were not yet involved. Accordingly, when the Persians arrived at Euboea, they went for Eretria, took it after a week's fighting, and then went into the city and robbed and burned the sanctuaries, "taking vengeance," according to Herodotus, "for the sanctuaries burned in Sardis" (6.101.3).[47]

The next target for the Persians was Athens, and at Hippias' suggestion they chose to land at the beach at Marathon.[48] Just before they marched out to Marathon to defend their country, the Athenians sent as a messenger to Sparta the "day-runner" Philippides.[49] And, as he later reported back to Athens, when he was nearing Sparta, in the region of Mount Parthenion above Tegea, he encountered the god Pan. Herodotus gives this famous account of the meeting:

> Pan shouted out Philippides' name and ordered him to deliver a message to the Athenians. "Why do the Athenians pay no attention to me, when I am well intentioned to them and have many times already been useful to them and will be so again in the future?" The Athenians believed that Philippides' account was true, and when their affairs were again in good order they established a sanctuary of Pan below the Acropolis, and now as a result of his message they appease (ἱλάσκονται) him with annual sacrifices and a torch race. (6.105)

The Athenians did in fact give Pan a cave on the north slope of the Acropolis, but no record of sacrifices or a torch race survives.[50] Pausanias (1.28.4) claims that in this encounter Pan promised Philippides "he would go to Marathon and help the Athenians fight," and that the god was "honored" for this announcement.[51] Miltiades, the victorious Athenian general at Marathon in 490, before his death in 488 erected a statue of Pan, and the dedicatory poem, attributed to Simonides (frag. 143 Diehl), would suggest that Pan had in fact assisted the Athenians at Marathon (*Anth. Pal.* 16.232):

Miltiades erected me, the goat-footed Pan, the Arcadian,
The one who was with the Athenians but against the Medes.[52]

In this account of Pan and Philippides Herodotus gives one of his few mentions of a sacrifice by Greeks to a named deity. Others include libations to Poseidon (Soter) at Artemisium (7.191–192, below), a sacrifice to the Twelve Gods at their altar in Athens (6.108.4),[53] sacrifices to the winds (7.178 and 189, below), and offerings to the hero Artachaees at Acanthus (7.117).[54] The list may appear meager, and it would be if Herodotus had intended to record all the common sacrifices of those times. But when Herodotus designates a recipient of a sacrifice, the sacrifice is usually being made as part of a new or altered cult.[55] It serves, as it were, as an explanation of later cult practice. Only then, it seems, did Herodotus think a Greek sacrifice to a specific deity worthy of record.

When the Spartans heard from Philippides the Athenians' urgent request for assistance, they wanted to help, but, according to Herodotus, "it was impossible for them to do this immediately because they did not want to break their *nomos*.[56] It was the ninth day of the month, and they said they would not go on a military expedition on the ninth when the moon was not yet full. And so they waited for the full moon," presumably about the fifteenth of the month (6.106.3–107.1). The Spartans thus arrived in Marathon the third day after the full moon, too late to share in the action and the glory of the victory over the Persians (6.120). In fact, of all the Greeks, only the Plataeans assisted the Athenians at Marathon, and for this the Athenians gave them a singular honor: "From the time of this battle, when the Athenians perform sacrifices at their quadrennial festivals, the Athenian herald prays that there be 'good things' for both the Athenians *and* the Plataeans" (6.111.2).

Plutarch, however, claims that the battle of Marathon occurred on Boedromion 6, presumably six days *after* a new moon, and attacks Herodotus' chronology and characterization of the Spartans: Herodotus is clearly shown to be telling lies against the Spartans concerning the full moon, that they waited around for it and did not go to Marathon to help the Athenians. Not only have the Spartans made countless other expeditions and battles in the first half of a month, not waiting for the full moon, but they also arrived just a little late for this battle which occurred on Boedromion 6. (*Mor.* 861E–F)

The contradictions between Plutarch's and Herodotus' accounts are numerous and complex, but most can be resolved if we accept two hypotheses: that Herodotus wrongly generalized to all Spartan months what the Spartans did for one month, that of the Carneia festival; and that Plutarch wrongly puts the battle on Boedromion 6, linking it to the date of the festival of Artemis Agrotera, which the Athenians in later years celebrated as a commemoration of the victory (Xen. *Ana.* 3.2.11–12, below).[57] With all this taken into account, the battle of Marathon was probably fought about Boedromion 15, that is, about September 1 by our calender.

Hippias, the son of Pisistratus and the deposed tyrant of Athens, in an attempt to recover his power had been urging on and helping the Persians for years. Now he was directing the Persian landing at Marathon. Herodotus tells of the dream Hippias had on the night before the landing: Hippias dreamed "he went to bed with his mother, and he concluded from this dream that he would return to Athens, recover his rule, and die as an old man in his own country." As he stood on the beach at Marathon, giving this order and that, he suffered a fit of sneezing and coughing.

Because he was an old man, many of his teeth were rattled, and one popped out and landed in the sand. He made a great effort to find the tooth, but when it did not turn up, Hippias groaned and said to bystanders, "This land, then, is not *ours* and we will not be able to subjugate it. That part of it which belonged to me, my tooth now has." Hippias concluded that his dream had come to pass in this way. (6.107–108.1)

Hippias did not, in fact, recover "his" land on this expedition, and again a dream, in a symbolic manner, predicts the inevitable future and an individual, here a tyrant unappealing to Herodotus, initially misinterprets it to his loss.

Miltiades, son of Cimon, who was soon as general to lead the Athenians to victory, was confident they would win, "if the gods made it a fair fight" (θεῶν τὰ ἴσα νεμόντων) (Hdt. 6.109.5). This phrase, "if the gods made it a fair fight," which Herodotus attributes to Miltiades, is of interest. In the Ionian Revolt the Phocaean general Dionysius had promised the Ionians victory by default or battle if only, again, "the gods make it a fair fight" (6.11.3). It is noteworthy, given the subject matter of the *Histories*, that the Greeks never, in Herodotus' whole account, pray simply for "victory."[58] They seem confident that they will win if only it be a fair fight, and we shall later see, particularly at Artemisium, the gods leveling the odds for the Greeks as they fought against an enemy with a massive superiority in numbers. All the Greeks asked of their gods was a "fair fight," and they themselves, presumably, could handle the rest.[59]

When the Athenian army was drawn up opposite the Persians at Marathon, the prebattle sacrifices were good (6.112.1),[60] and the Athenians went on to win a complete, stunning victory, killing 6,400 of the enemy while losing only 192 of their own men. That the Athenians thought gods and heroes contributed to this great victory at Marathon is overwhelmingly confirmed by the large and varied series of sacrifices, dedications, and memorials they made in the following years. First was the fulfillment of the vow they had made, before the battle, to Artemis Agrotera whose shrine, on the banks of the Ilissus, they may well have passed as they marched out to fight at Marathon. Xenophon, nearly ninety years later, tells the story:

When the Persians and those with them came with their full force to destroy Athens, the Athenians themselves dared to hold their ground and defeated them. They had vowed to Artemis that they would sacrifice to her a female goat for each enemy they killed.[61] But when, after the battle, they were not able to find sufficient goats, they decided to sacrifice five hundred goats each year, and still now they are sacrificing them. (*Ana.* 3.2.11–12)

The sixth day of every Athenian month was sacred to Artemis,[62] and these sacrifices were probably made to Artemis Agrotera at her first festival *after* the battle, that is, on Boedromion 6 of 489. The Athenians did, in fact, continue to make these sacrifices to Artemis throughout the classical and Hellenistic periods down to at least Plutarch's time in the second century A.D.[63]

Pausanias describes the memorials of the battle of Marathon still evident at Marathon in his time, nearly 700 years after the battle:

There is a tomb of the Athenians on the plain, and on it are plaques having the names of each of the men who died, tribe by tribe.[64] There is another tomb for the Plataeans of Boeotia and for slaves. Slaves for the first time fought then. And there is privately a memorial of Miltiades, the son of Cimon.[65] His death occurred later, after he failed to take Paros, and for this was tried in court by the Athenians.[66] At Marathon it is possible now to hear every night horses whinnying and men fighting. No one who has purposely attempted to hear this has benefited, but there is no danger from the *daimones* for one who accidentally and unknowingly encounters it. The Marathonioi hold in reverence (σέβονται) and term heroes (ἥρωας) those who died in the battle. . . . And, as they say, a man appeared in the battle, rustic in appearance and dress. He killed many of the barbarians with a plow and then, after the battle, disappeared. When the Athenians questioned Apollo in Delphi, the god answered nothing about him but ordered them to honor the hero Echetlaeus.[67] And, furthermore, a trophy of white marble was made.[68] The Athenians say that they buried the Medes because it is, in all cases, holy (ὅσιον) to hide in the earth the corpse of a man. But I was not able to find any tomb because there was no mound or other marker to see. The Athenians carried the Persian corpses to a trench and threw them in willy-nilly.[69] (1.32.3–5. Cf. 1.29.4 and 9.32.9)

Two items are of particular religious interest here: the tendance of the dead, and the role of heroes in the battle. The Athenians carefully and specially buried their dead in the famous common tomb (*soros*) on the battlefield, the large funeral mound that remains there as a monument today.[70] Various scholars have assigned one or the other of these two epigrams to this tomb.[71]

The Athenians, fighting for the Greeks at Marathon,
Laid low the power of the gold-wearing Medes.
(Lycurgus, *Leoc.* 109)[72]

The children of the Athenians destroyed the army of the Persians
And warded off grievous slavery from their fatherland.
(Simonides, frag. 119 Diehl)[73]

Tombs were also provided for the Plataeans and slaves who fought there.[74] The Athenians for religious reasons, because it was "holy," also buried the Persian dead, however hurriedly. Concern for the burial of the dead is persistent in accounts of the Persian Wars, and violations of burial rites are made characteristic of impious men, most notably Xerxes. The hero Echetlaeus appeared in the battle, helping the Athenians, as did also Theseus, at least according to Plutarch (*Theseus* 35.5).[75] It is noteworthy that only heroes, not gods, were seen on the battlefield. Finally, those

Athenians who fought, died, and were buried in the *soros* became, for the residents of the deme Marathon, new heroes, and centuries later Athenian youth annually made a trip to Marathon to make offerings there.[76]

As another dedication for the battle, the Athenians used, with symbolic and religious appropriateness, a marble block that the Persians had brought with them to be their trophy monument. From it the Athenians fashioned a statue of Nemesis, the goddess who punishes *hybris*. Pausanias preserves the story:

Rhamnus is about seven and one-half miles from Marathon for those going on the road along the sea to Oropus. The people have their houses on the coast, but a little inland there is a sanctuary of Nemesis. Of all the gods she is especially implacable for hybristic men. It seems that wrath from this goddess befell those barbarians who landed at Marathon. They scornfully thought that nothing stood in the way of their taking Athens, and so, as if their work was done, they were bringing a block of Parian marble for making the trophy. Phidias made from this marble a statue of Nemesis. On the head of the goddess is a crown having deer and small statues of Nike. In her left hand she holds an apple bough, in her right hand a *phiale*, and Aethiopians are engraved on the *phiale*.[77] (1.33.2–3)

Pausanias, in his description of Athens itself, describes a number of dedications made in Athens after the battle, including the famous Athena Promachos ("Forefighter") statue, which stood thirty feet tall on the Acropolis, facing the east facade of the Propylaea:

Apart from the things I have listed, the Athenians have two tithe offerings from wars—a bronze statue of Athena from the Medes who landed at Marathon, a work of Phidias. They say that Mys carved on her shield the battle of the Lapiths against the Centaurs and the other things added on, and that Parrhasion, the son of Euenor, sketched these and the rest of the works for Mys. The spear point and the helmet plume of this Athena are visible for those sailing from Sunium. The other tithe offering is a bronze chariot from the Boeotians and the Chalcidians on Euboea. (1.28.2)

This Athena was in classical times termed the "bronze Athena" but now is commonly known as Athena Promachos. Demosthenes (19.272) claimed "the city dedicated it as the prize for excellence (*aristeion*) of the war against the barbarians. The Greeks gave money for it." From this it would appear that Demosthenes imagined the Athena Promachos a dedication for both Persian Wars, paid for with the spoils divided after Plataea or even Mycale.[78] Like many of the dedications of the Persian Wars, it was constructed at least a generation or two later and eventually became associated with victory in the wars in general, not with an individual event in the wars.

Pausanias makes also a temple of Eukleia ("Good Fame") on the south slope of the Acropolis, near the later Odeion of Pericles, into a dedication of the battle of Marathon:[79]

This too is a dedication from the Medes who landed at Marathon. And I think that the Athenians took special pride in this victory. Even Aeschylus, when the end of his life was expected, made no mention of the other things, although he had attained such a reputation for poetry and had fought the sea battles at Artemisium and Salamis. He wrote (in his epitaph) only his name, his father's name, his city, and that he had as witnesses of his courage the grove at Marathon and the Medes who landed there. (1.14.5)

Aeschylus' epitaph, purportedly composed just before his death in Gela of Sicily, survives (*Vita Aeschyli*, p. 322 Page):[80]

This memorial of grain-bearing Gela covers dead Aeschylus,
    son of Euphorion, of Athens.
The grove at Marathon could tell of his famous fighting ability,
    As could the thick-haired Mede who knew it well.

Pausanias describes also a series of paintings in the Stoa Poicile in Athens, on one of which was represented the battle of Marathon.[81] The painting was variously attributed by ancient sources to Panaenus, the brother of Phidias, to Micon, and to Polygnotus, all working in Athens in the first half of the fifth century,[82] and the painting is usually dated to the 460s.

The Plataeans and the Athenian contingent go into hand-to-hand combat with the barbarians. Here the battle is evenly fought, but in the middle of the battle the barbarians are fleeing and pushing one another into the marsh. On the edge of the painting are the Phoenician ships, and the Greeks are slaying those barbarians rushing into the ships. The hero Marathon is also painted here, the hero from whom the plain is named. So too are Theseus, likened to a figure rising from the ground, and Athena and Heracles. As the Marathonians say, Heracles was recognized as a god among them first. Especially clear among those fighting in the battle are Callimachus, who had been elected *polemarchos*, Miltiades of the generals, and the hero called Echetlaeus.[83] (1.15.3)

We have other confirmation that Theseus and Echetlaeus participated in the battle, but the introduction of the heroes Marathon and Heracles and of the goddess Athena into this painting is quite likely the result of later mythologizing and romanticizing of the event.[84] The painting was not, in fact, a dedication to a deity and this, perhaps, allowed the artist greater freedom in the rendering of this, by now, epic victory.

The Athenians also memorialized their Marathon victory at Delphi, and in his tour of Delphi Pausanias records a number of these dedications. The Athenians dedicated there gold shields, probably created from spoils of the battle, on the epistyle of Apollo's temple (10.19.4),[85] and they built there, from the spoils "of those who landed at Marathon with Datis," their famous treasury (10.11.5). This treasury has been restored in modern times and a copy of a dedicatory inscription adjoining it survives:

Athenians (dedicated) to Apollo from the Medes
Firstfruits of the battle at Marathon.
(ML 19 = *IG* I³ 1463B)[86]

And, as the last of the Marathonian monuments Pausanias saw at Delphi, he describes an elaborate sculptured group on the sacred way:

There is an inscription saying that these statues were dedicated from a tithe of the battle at Marathon. The statues are Athena and Apollo and, of the generals, Miltiades. And of the so-called heroes there are Erechtheus, Cecrops, Pandion, Leos, and Antiochus who was born to Heracles from Meda, the daughter of Phylas. In addition there were Aegeus and Acamas, one of the children of Theseus. These also gave their names to the tribes at Athens in accordance with the oracle from Delphi.[87] There were also Codrus, son of Melanthus, Theseus, and Neleus, but they were not eponymous heroes. Phidias made those I have listed, and truly they are a tithe from the battle. (10.10.1)

As in the painting in the Stoa Poicile, the sculptors have apparently extended credit for the victory at Marathon beyond the circle of those originally thought involved, to include seven of the ten Athenian eponymous heroes (Oeneus, Hippothoön, and Ajax are omitted, perhaps by Pausanias' oversight), Codrus, Neleus, Athena, and even Apollo, the last perhaps as a nod to the proprietor of the sanctuary.[88] The inclusion of the general Miltiades among these distinguished heroes and deities is noteworthy.[89]

The Plataeans alone of the Greeks aided the Athenians at Marathon, and the Athenians gave them a share of the spoils. Pausanias describes how the Plataeans built a sanctuary of Athena Areia with these spoils:

The Plataeans have a sanctuary of Athena Areia. It was built from the spoils that the Athenians distributed to them from the battle at Marathon. The statue is of gilded wood, but its face, hands, and feet are of Pentelic marble. In size it is not much smaller than the bronze Athena (Promachos) on the Acropolis, which the Athenians dedicated as firstfruits of the contest at Marathon. And Phidias also made the statue of Athena for the Plataeans. . . . A statue of Arimnestus sits at the feet of the statue. In the battle against Mardonius (at Plataea) and still earlier at Marathon he led the Plataeans.[90] (9.4.1–2)

This sanctuary of "warlike" (Areia) Athena seems specially built to commemorate the victory at Marathon,[91] and Arimnestus, at the feet of Athena Areia, recalls the general Miltiades among the gods and heroes of the Athenian monument at Delphi. This same Arimnestus, ten years later when the major Greek-Persian battle was centered on Plataea, would again contribute to the Greek victory (Plut. *Arist.* 17.6–18.2, below). The Persians probably destroyed this sanctuary in their second invasion, in 480, and the Plataeans would rebuild and adorn the sanctuary with spoils from the victory in their land (Plut. *Arist.* 20.2–3, below). The statue by Phidias, commemorating the Marathon victory, was surely erected decades after the destruction of the sanctuary by the Persians in 480 and hence survived until Pausanias' time.

Two final dedications, both helmets found at Olympia, also commemorated the Athenian victory at Marathon. A bronze Assyrian-style helmet was found at Olympia in 1960, with this inscription: "The Athenians, to Zeus, having taken it from the Medes."[92] A helmet of Miltiades, also found at Olympia, may have been that worn at Marathon and later dedicated by the general.[93]

In summary, then, after the battle of Marathon the Athenians, through sacrifices and dedications, formally expressed their gratitude to Artemis Agrotera, Nemesis of the deme Rhamnus, Athena Polias (as Promachos), Apollo of Delphi, and Zeus of Olympia. The contributions of the heroes Echetlaeus and Theseus were recognized, and the Plataeans, for their part, built a new sanctuary for Athena, ultimately to be adorned with a statue by Phidias. Later tableau monuments added to these directly involved deities and heroes additional local heroes, including Marathon, Heracles, the eponymous heroes of the tribes (probably representing the Athenian demos divided into their tribal military units), Codrus, and Neleus. The Athenians and the Plataeans obviously thought that many members of the divine world had contributed to their stunning victory over the Persians at Marathon in 490, but again we note that it was only heroes, not gods, who were seen on the battlefield itself.

In the aftermath of the battle both commanders, Datis for the Persians and Miltiades for the Greeks, became involved in religious controversies, and, oddly, Herodotus has the Persian observe Greek religious traditions but has the Greek violate them and suffer death as a result. Datis, stopping at Myconos on his retreat to Asia, had a dream:

It is not said what that dream was, but at daybreak Datis made a search of the ships. He found in a Phoenician ship a gilded statue of Apollo and asked from where it had been stolen. When he learned from which sanctuary it was, he sailed on his ship to Delos. At that time the Delians had returned to their island, and Datis deposited the statue in the sanctuary and bid the Delians to return it to Theban Delion. Delion is on the coast, opposite Chalcis. . . . The Delians did not return this statue, but twenty years later the Thebans themselves, as the result of an oracle, brought it back to Delion.[94] (6.118)

Datis, in his respect for Apollo and Delos, did all the correct things, but the actions of the Delians are questionable, and they have to be compelled to do the right thing by the Delphic oracle.

Miltiades, however, now the hero of the victory at Marathon, committed a gross sacrilege. According to Herodotus, he had a personal grudge against a Parian, and he convinced the Athenians after Marathon to attack the island Paros in vengeance for Parian help to the Persians and in the expectation of rich booty.[95] Miltiades besieged the city Paros for twenty-six days, and then, according to the Parians, a Parian woman named Timo, a minor official of the cult of Demeter Thesmophoros and Kore, suggested that he could enter the city through the sanctuary of these goddesses. The sanctuary lay on a hill outside the wall. Miltiades tried the gates of the sanctuary without success.

He then leapt over the sanctuary wall and went toward the *megaron* to do something, either to disturb some things that were not to be disturbed or to do something else inside. But right at the gate a tremor of fear came over him immediately and he rushed back the way he had come. He leapt down from the wall and tore a thigh muscle or, as some say, wrenched his knee. (6.134.2)

Miltiades immediately gave up the siege and led the Athenians home.

When the Parians learned that Timo, the minor cult official of the two goddesses, had guided Miltiades, they wanted to punish her. When they were free from the siege, they sent ambassadors to Delphi. Their ambassadors were to ask if they should kill her because she had described to Miltiades how to capture their fatherland and had revealed to Miltiades sacred matters that were forbidden to males. But the Pythia was not allowing this, saying that Timo was not the cause of these things but that it was necessary for Miltiades to die not well and for Timo to appear as the guide of his evils.[96] (6.135.2–3)

When Miltiades returned to Athens, his bad leg prevented him from defending himself in a lawsuit concerning the Parian expedition. He lost the case, was fined fifty talents ($30 million), and then soon died when his injured leg turned gangrenous. So the life of the hero of Marathon ended, and his son Cimon paid the fine (Hdt. 6.132–136).[97] Sanctuaries were inviolable, and those who committed sacrilege against them, by burning them or by wrongly entering them or otherwise, suffered punishment from the gods, whether they were Persian or Greek, war heroes or not. Finally and characteristically, the Delphic oracle was called upon to rectify the difficulties caused by the impieties in both these accounts.

## ⚛ The Road to Thermopylae ⚛

For Darius the defeat at Marathon in 490 just added to the "injustices" the Persians had suffered from the Athenians, and he was all the more eager to invade Greece again. For three years men, ships, horses, food, and freighters were readied throughout the Persian Empire. But Darius was distracted by a revolt in Egypt and dissension among his sons. He solved the latter by appointing as heir to the kingship Xerxes, his son by Atossa, the daughter of Cyrus the Great who had founded the Persian Empire. But, in 486, before he could put down the Egyptians or take vengeance on Athens, Darius died.

Xerxes, now as king of the Persians, "was," according to Herodotus, "in the beginning by no means eager to campaign against Greece" (7.5.1). The desire to prove himself a worthy successor in a line of kings beginning with Cyrus, Mardonius' promises of the wealth and beauty of Greece, and various other factors influenced his ultimate decision to undertake and continue the expedition. Prominent among these "other" factors were the following ones of a "religious" nature.

Since the defeat at Marathon the Pisistratidae had remained influential at the Persian court, trying to convince the king to renew his assault on Athens and restore them to their ancestral tyranny. About 484 they introduced to Xerxes the Athenian Onomacritus, who under Pisistratus and his sons had served as a *chresmologos* and as the editor of the oracles of Musaeus. According to Herodotus, "Onomacritus had once been exiled from Athens by Hipparchus, the son of Pisistratus, when he was caught by Lasus of Hermione introducing into the writings of Musaeus an oracle that 'the islands near Lemnos would disappear into the sea.'"[98] But now the Pisistratidae called upon him again, and Onomacritus went up to Susa to Xerxes. "The Pisistratidae said reverential words about him, and Onomacritus described some of his oracles. He recited none of those that foretold failure for the king but selected out and told those most indicating success, that, for example, 'it was necessary for the Hellespont to be yoked by a Persian man.'" And so, by these and other arguments, in 484 Xerxes was persuaded to campaign against Greece (7.6.3–7.1). Onomacritus was a *chresmologos*, a collector of oracles, who, when an occasion arose, would apply oracles of his collection to the situation at hand.[99] In the spectrum of divination, *chresmologoi* seem to have ranked well below oracles, *manteis* who interpreted omens, and even dreams.[100] Here Onomacritus manipulates his oracles to make a point, and throughout the Greek tradition *chresmologoi* seem more suspect than others engaged in divination. We later see the Athenians rightly reject the interpretation by the *chresmologoi* of the famous "wooden wall" oracle (7.139–144, below), and decades later *chresmologoi* fell into even greater disfavor in Athens when they promoted the Athenians' disastrous Sicilian expedition in the midst of the Peloponnesian War (Thuc. 8.1.1).

Two years later, in 482, after he had resubjugated Egypt, Xerxes assembled select Persian leaders to lay out his plans and solicit their comments. Herodotus has him stress both the injustices and impieties the Persians thought they had suffered from the Greeks.

"I intend," Xerxes said, "to yoke the Hellespont and to march an army through Europe against Greece, to take vengeance on the Athenians for what they have done to the Persians and my father. You saw that Darius was eager to campaign against these men. But he has died, and it was not possible for him to gain vengeance. But, for him and the other Persians, I will not stop until I take and burn Athens. The Athenians began the unjust acts, against my father and me. For, first of all, they came to Sardis with Aristagoras the Milesian, our slave, and they burned the groves and the sanctuaries." (7.8.β)

First and foremost, in Xerxes' mind, was the burning of the sanctuaries, and this would motivate his own impious destruction of Greek sanctuaries.

In this conference of Persian leaders only one dared to speak out against Xerxes' plans: Artabanus, Darius' brother and Xerxes' uncle, a "wise adviser" who at various times during the invasion counseled caution, retreat, and limited objectives and whose advice was regularly proved correct by later events.[101] Here, among a host of arguments, Herodotus has him add these observations as a warning to Xerxes:

> You see how the god strikes with lightning creatures that rise above the others and does not allow them to make themselves prominent. But small creatures do not irritate the god at all. You see how he hurls his missiles always upon the greatest houses and the tallest trees. That is because the god likes to "dock" all things that rise above the others. And so even a large army is destroyed by a small one when the god, feeling *phthonos*, casts fear or lightning upon it. And in this way the soldiers perish in a way unworthy of themselves. The god does not allow anyone but himself to have "lofty thoughts." (7.10.ε)

Herodotus has Artabanus argue here, as he often does, very much in Greek terms. That lightning strikes the most prominent is a commonplace of Greek tragedy.[102] The *phthonos* that Artabanus attributes to the god is the emotion that may result when one's own prerogatives are being encroached upon by another, and it has elements of envy, ill will, self-protectiveness, and begrudgement, but allows no single English equivalent, certainly not "envy."[103] Herodotus' Solon, in his encounter with the Lydian king Croesus, describes the "divine" as *phthoneron* (1.32.1), and his Amasis, king of Egypt, views Polycrates, the wealthy and successful tyrant of Samos, as a potential victim of the *phthonos* of the divine because he rose "above the norm" (3.40–43).[104] Finally, the dislike of "lofty thoughts" that Artabanus attributes to the gods is also very Greek, associated with *hybris* and with punishment motivated by this same divine *phthonos*.[105] Divine *phthonos* is often viewed by scholars as a negative attribute of the gods, but Herodotus invokes it at other critical moments in his "religious" account of the Persian Wars, and we must reserve judgment of his view of the workings of divine *phthonos* in the Persian Wars until all the evidence is in. But, however we judge that issue, Artabanus has raised against the expedition powerful religious arguments that would resonate with a Greek audience but found no immediate acceptance with Xerxes.

In the meeting Xerxes angrily rejected Artabanus' advice and warnings, but at home that evening he realized their wisdom and decided not to campaign against Greece. He went to bed, and Herodotus describes a remarkable series of dreams which then followed:

In the night Xerxes saw, as is said by the Persians, such a dream: he thought that a tall and handsome man stood over him and said, "Are you changing your plan, Persian, so as not to campaign against Greece, after you ordered the Persians to collect an army? You do not do well in changing your plan, and no one will agree with you. But go on the same path as you planned during the day." Xerxes thought that the man, after saying this, flew away. When day came, Xerxes took no account of the dream. (7.12.2–13.1)

The next day Xerxes announced, to the delight of the assembled Persian leaders, that he was canceling the expedition.

But that night the same dream image again stood over the sleeping Xerxes and said, "Child of Darius, do you appear among the Persians after rejecting the expedition and taking no account of my words, as if you had heard them from a nobody? Now, know this well, that if you do not make the expedition immediately, the following will result: you became great and powerful in a brief time; just as quickly you will become lowly." Xerxes was terrified by the dream and dashed out of bed. (7.14–15.1)

Xerxes found Artabanus, explained the situation, and described the following plan to him: "If a god is the one sending this dream and if it is absolutely his pleasure that the expedition against Greece take place, then this same dream image will fly also to you and will give to you the same orders it gave me." To facilitate this, Xerxes bid Artabanus wear the king's clothes, sit on his throne, and sleep in his bed. Artabanus, resisting, briefly described the nature of dreams:

Son, not even these dreams are divine. I am many years older than you, and I will teach you the nature of dreams that wander their way to men. Those things which someone thinks about during the day very commonly wander their way to men as dream images. And in past days we were very occupied with this expedition. And if this dream is not as I analyze it but the divine is involved, you yourself have said everything. For let it appear also to me as it did to you, giving orders. . . . If it will take no account of me and will not think it worthwhile to appear to me, whether I wear my clothes or yours, but if it will appear to you, then we must realize this: if it will come to you repeatedly, I myself too would say it is divine. (7.16.β.2–γ.2)

When, reluctantly, Artabanus had worn the king's clothes, had sat on the royal throne, and had gone to the king's bed, the same dream image came to him.

"Are you that man persuading Xerxes not to campaign against Greece? On the grounds that you are concerned for him? But you will not get off without punishment, now and in the future, if you try to avert what must happen. It has been revealed to Xerxes himself what he must suffer if he does not heed me." Artabanus thought that the dream image was making these threats and was saying he would burn out his eyes with hot steel. He gave a cry and leapt out of bed. (7.17–18.1)

The dream was sufficient to convince Artabanus, and he said to Xerxes,

Since there is some divine impulse here, and since, as it seems, some god-driven (θεήλατος) destruction is taking hold of the Greeks,[106] I reverse myself and change my opinion. Tell the Persians what has been sent from the god, and command them to use your original orders for preparation for the expedition, and make sure that, since the god is giving us the opportunity, none of your efforts will be deficient. (7.18.3)

And so, in 482, Artabanus and, more important, Xerxes, despite lingering concerns about the dream, decided to make the expedition against Greece (7.12–18, 47).[107]

We have thus far encountered four sets of dreams, two of Greeks (Hipparchus and Hippias, Hdt. 5.55–56 and 6.107–108.1) and two of Persians (Xerxes here and Datis, 6.118). Herodotus gives great weight to Xerxes' dreams in determining the course of the Persian Wars, and we pause here to consider them in the context of dreams in general in Herodotus' *Histories*.[108] Of the eighteen dreams in the *Histories*, twelve come to Persians and Lydians, one to an Ethiopian, one to an Egyptian, and four to Greeks.[109] Why does Herodotus give most and the most elaborate dreams to the Persians? It may have been for literary reasons, but as Georges (1994.193) notes, Persian gods apparently had no voice or form (and hence no oracles), and "therefore the dream is the characteristic medium of divine communication among Medes and Persians." And Herodotus has Lydians and Persians, unlike Greeks, assume a divine origin of these dreams (1.45.2, 1.210.1, and 3.65.4).[110] Artabanus here is very concerned to prove or disprove that a god was sending these dreams to Xerxes. In his view only if they are god-sent need they be obeyed. Of course, Xerxes and Artabanus came to believe — and, given how Herodotus presents the dreams, how could they not — that the dreams were in fact god-sent and therefore must be obeyed, however great their misgivings. Also, Herodotus' dreams, with few exceptions,[111] are signs of, as for Hipparchus and Hippias, or become causes of future misfortunes for the recipients, as here for Xerxes, no matter how they might be initially interpreted. The fate they portend seems inescapable no matter what one might do.[112] As in Greek tragedy, *all* dreams prove true.[113]

Within this general context of dreams Herodotus has done everything in his narrative power to portray Xerxes and Artabanus receiving, testing, and ultimately and reasonably accepting the commands of this dream image. The net effect is that these dreams virtually forced Xerxes to renew the expedition to Greece.[114] For modern scholars, if not for Herodotus, this divine impetus complicates the calculus of Xerxes' personal and dynastic motivations for making the invasion. Was Xerxes just following divine orders? Do the dreams relieve him of personal responsibility? Was "the divine" sending Xerxes off to be punished? Was he a victim of fate?[115] The text of Herodotus, unfortunately, offers us little help in answering these and similar questions. The answers lie, I think, in the avenue of interpretation that suits also several plays of Aeschylus and Sophocles, namely that several somewhat independent and sufficient causes are presented to explain one situation. Major events, like the death of Agamemnon in Aeschylus' *Agamemnon* and the Persian Wars here, are, by modern literary standards, overdetermined.[116] The author gives several explanations, each by itself sufficient, and dreams and other forms of divination are one way of structuring the divine, metaphysical causation. But, however that may be, among the tangle of causation for the Persian invasion of 480 these god-sent dreams of Xerxes and Artabanus played a major role.

Herodotus describes how soon after this decision Xerxes had a third and final dream: "Xerxes thought he was wreathed with a bough of olive, and the branches from the olive spread over the whole earth, but then the wreath about his head disappeared." The *magoi*, the Mede priests who served the king as dream interpreters,[117] thought this referred to "all the world" and meant that "all men would be slaves to Xerxes" (7.19). The "olive wreath" was here most probably a symbol of victory and ruling power (not, as often assumed, a reference to the olive tree of Athens),[118] and what the *magoi* failed to account for was that, in the end, "the wreath . . . disappeared."

In the spring of 481/0, while Xerxes was still in Sardis marshaling his forces, and then a bit later in his expedition, troubling omens occurred, omens that, in Herodotus' account, should have dissuaded the king from the expedition.[119] The omens that Xerxes encounters here and later are of the type "contrary to nature," strange and unnatural births or a solar eclipse. Elsewhere in the *Histories* there are spontaneously boiling cauldrons (1.59.1–3), rain in usually rainless Egyptian Thebes (3.10), and earthquakes as we saw on Aegina (5.82–88) and Delos (6.97–98). The Egyptians, according to Herodotus, dismissed solar phenomena as omens (2.142.3–4), but the Persians and Greeks did not. For them celestial and other "contrary to nature" omens, both the ones here and the others we encounter later, are presented by Herodotus as "signs" that either stopped or should have stopped the recipients from intended actions or portended unavoidable disaster.[120] Like Socrates' *daimonion* in Plato's *Apology*, they serve not as advice or encouragement to do something but as a warning *not* to do it. The unnatural is what attracts notice, and it is uniformly a *bad* omen. With only one exception,[121] Herodotus does not specify the divine agents of such omens. We may think that for a thunderbolt it was Zeus (4.79.2), for the earthquake on Delos Apollo (6.97–98, above), and for the omen we shall see on the Thriasian Plain Demeter (8.65, below), but the assignment of agent is ours, not Herodotus'. The large majority of omens, whether miraculous or not, cannot be assigned to *any* specific god or divine agency.[122] Finally, and most important, to "dismiss" or to "take no account of" such omens *inevitably* led to disaster. There is no indication that to ignore such omens was "impious," but it was foolish. And in the course of the Persian Wars it was only Persians, never Greeks, who ignored omens such as these that befell Xerxes.

As Xerxes was marshaling his forces at Sardis for the invasion of Greece, "a mule bore a mule with a dual set of genitals, one male, the other female. The male set was on top." But Xerxes took no account of the omen (7.57.2). On the day of departure for the Hellespont, another omen, one that could not be ignored, occurred:

The sun left its customary position in the sky and disappeared, despite the fact that it was a clear, cloudless day, and it became night instead of day. When Xerxes saw and realized this, he became concerned and asked the *magoi* what the phenomenon meant to prophesy. The *magoi* said the god was indicating to Greeks the "eclipse" of their cities. The sun, they said, gives signs to Greeks, the moon to Persians. Delighted when he heard this, Xerxes carried on with the expedition. (7.37.2–3)

Another potentate, however, the very rich Lydian Pythius, who had eagerly joined Xerxes' army, was terrified by the eclipse and tried, unsuccessfully and tragically, to have his eldest son excused from the expedition (7.37.2–38.1).

When on his route Xerxes reached Mount Ida and proceeded into the land of Troy, during the night a great thunderstorm came up and killed many of his men (7.42.2). Xerxes then continued on to Troy itself, because "he had a strong desire to go up and see the Pergamum of Priam. When he had seen and heard about each of the things there, he sacrificed a thousand cattle to Athena Ilias, and the *magoi* poured drink offerings for the heroes. And, after they had done these things, that night, a panic fell upon the camp"[123] (7.43.1–2). Although Herodotus does not explicitly link the storm, the offerings, and the panic in the night, it may be that the storm indicated the wrath of the Trojan Athena and heroes, that the offerings were Xerxes' attempt to propitiate them, and that the panic indicated that the attempted propitiation failed.[124]

During the previous year Xerxes' engineers had been "yoking" the Hellespont at Abydos with a bridge of cables and pontoon boats, nearly one mile long. When this first bridge had been completed, a great storm came up and broke it up. Herodotus gives a vivid description of Xerxes' reaction:

When Xerxes heard of it, he thought it a terrible thing and ordered that the Hellespont receive 300 blows from a whip and that a pair of leg irons be cast into the sea. I have heard that he also sent tattooers to brand the Hellespont. And he ordered that, as they did the whipping, they were to say these barbaric and rash (ἀτάσθαλα) words: "Bitter water, your master imposes on you this punishment because you treated him unjustly when you had suffered no injustice from him. King Xerxes will cross you whether you wish it or not. And justly no human being sacrifices to you because you are a foul and brackish river." Xerxes ordered them to punish the sea in this way and to behead those who oversaw the yoking of the Hellespont.[125] (7.34–35)

This whipping, chaining, and verbal abuse of the Hellespont became Xerxes' signature impiety in the later Greek tradition. Xerxes' outburst of wrath at the Hellespont was ranked by Herodotus' Themistocles with and perhaps even above his "burning and throwing to the ground the statues of the gods," and both contributed to his eventual defeat (8.109, below). For understanding this incident one usually points out that, according to Herodotus, the Persians "especially respected rivers," not spitting or urinating into them, not washing their hands in them or allowing others to do so (1.138.2).[126] The proscriptions in Hesiod's *Works and Days* show the Greeks had similar "reverence" for rivers, with only minor differences:

Do not ever cross on foot the beautifully flowing water of ever running rivers
Until, after washing your hands with its lovely, white water,
You look into its beautiful currents and say a prayer.[127]
The gods are wrathful at a man who crosses a river
When he has washed neither his wickedness nor his hands, and afterward they
    give him griefs.
(737–741)

And do not urinate in the streams of rivers flowing
To the sea, or on their banks, but very much avoid it,
And do not ease yourself there, because this is not better for you.
(757–759)[128]

There is also good evidence that some rivers received cultic worship from the Greek peoples on their banks,[129] but these Greek and Persian cultic traditions are insufficient to explain how Xerxes' behavior at the Hellespont became and remained in the Greek tradition *the* exemplum of Persian impiety. Why should it not have been his later attack on Apollo's Delphic oracle or the destruction of the sanctuaries of Athena on the Acropolis?

These questions involve, I think, literary, dramatic, and even "poetic" purposes more than anything cultic and must be viewed from the literary tradition. These purposes can best be seen in a comparison to Aeschylus' earlier treatment of Xerxes and the Hellespont in his *Persae* of 472. Here the ghost of Darius, in the *Persae* a figure of wisdom, describes his son Xerxes:

He expected that he would restrain the flow of the holy Hellespont,
The Bosporean stream of the god, with chains as though it were a slave,
And he was trying to change its course. He threw on it
Forged chains and made it a great highway for a great army.
Being a human he thought, not wisely, that he would hold power over all the
    gods and Poseidon.
And how was my boy not suffering from a disease of the mind?
(Aeschylus, *Persae* 745-751. Cf. 723-725)

For Aeschylus there was no whipping of the Hellespont, no bitter words against it, no chains thrown *into* it. Aeschylus' chains *are* the bridge, and for him the bridging of the Hellespont was itself the irrational, impious action that challenged the gods. For Herodotus the bridge was an engineering feat worth recording in detail, not an impiety, certainly not an irrational act. But like Aeschylus Herodotus wanted to mark this critical moment, the bridging of Europe and Asia, the first attempt by one man to rule both continents, with a condemnation of the man. The Xerxes of both Herodotus and Aeschylus is explicitly made to treat the Hellespont as a master would a disobedient slave, but Aeschylus has a different focus, abstracts the action, eliminates the details, and concentrates on the theological implications. Herodotus features the details, personalizes the actions, and has Xerxes condemn himself by his own words.[130] The two presentations are significantly different, but both are powerful indictments of the impiety and irrationality of Xerxes. Aeschylus' version is, of course, more suited to the confines of a single tragedy, Herodotus' to the expanse of a prose narrative. But it is from the literary tradition, not from the cultic tradition, that Herodotus has shaped this major episode of his *Histories*. It is not simply another impiety, but an impiety of a different order and presented in a different manner from the impieties of burning sanctuaries and violating asylum.

Herodotus' use of the adjective ἀτάσθαλα ("rash") to describe Xerxes' words to the Hellespont helps confirm the "literary" nature of the account of this episode, and Herodotus will make ἀτασθαλίη into a recurrent characteristic of Persian impiety. ἀτάσθαλος is primarily poetic and archaic in tone, found especially in the Homeric epics.[131] Herodotus' use of it here places Xerxes in the company of the suitors of Homer's *Odyssey* (e.g., 23.67) and of Hesiod's Titans (*Th.* 209). With ἀτάσθαλος Herodotus elsewhere describes acts characteristic of a monarch beset by *hybris* and *phthonos* (3.80.3–4). The Persian Artaüctes reveals it when he violates the sanctuary of Protesilaus (9.116–121, below). And, interestingly, the Egyptian king Phero who cast a spear into the Nile and became blind suffered from ἀτασθαλίη (2.111.2). Later Xerxes' mutilation of the corpse of Leonidas (9.78–79, below), also an act of rage (7.238, below), is described in these same terms,[132] and, most important, Themistocles' eventual verdict on the impiety of Xerxes centers on Xerxes' ἀτασθαλίη and finds in it a cause of Xerxes' defeat (8.109, below).

In the quite different terminology of popular, practiced religion, rational error or its cause madness (μανία) leads to impiety (ἀνοσιότης), and impiety nurtures the madness, and the individual is eventually destroyed.[133] In the literary tradition *hybris* (in this context, "the failure to recognize one's place vis-à-vis the gods") or ἀτασθαλίη (mental derangement), or both in combination lead to the impious act; greater *hybris* and ἀτασθαλίη result; greater impieties are committed; and the individual similarly perishes.[134] Both the popular and literary traditions describe one cycle but through different terminology and with somewhat different theological premises. Most humans in Herodotus' *Histories* commit simple impieties and are punished for them in terms common to popular, cultic religion. But here Herodotus puts Xerxes' maltreatment of the Hellespont on a different, literary level and thereby contributes to making it his signature impiety in the Greek historical and literary tradition.

When Xerxes arrived at Abydos with his massive army in early summer, 481/0, he found a new bridge completed by a second corps of engineers. In preparation for the crossing Herodotus has him bid the Persians leaders "to pray to the gods who have obtained as their portion the Persian land," and, the next day, before dawn,

> they burned all kinds of incense on the bridges and spread myrtle branches on the roadway. When the sun was rising, Xerxes poured libations from a golden bowl into the sea and prayed to the sun that no misfortune befall him of the type that would prevent him from overthrowing Greece before he came to the boundaries

of that land. After the prayer he cast into the Hellespont the bowl and a gold wine-mixing bowl and a Persian sword. I am not able to determine for sure whether he cast them into the sea as a dedication to the sun or he regretted having had the Hellespont whipped and, in recompense for this, was giving the sea these gifts. (7.54)

When these things had been done, the Persians began the crossing, a crossing that took seven days and seven nights (7.53.2–55).[135] Herodotus here, characteristically, attempts to explain Persian behavior in terms familiar to Greeks: Xerxes' offerings of the bowls and sword were either a dedication to the sun — who was worshiped by the Persians but not the Greeks at this time (1.131–132) — or was an expiation for an impiety. Here, as again later when Xerxes has sacked the Athenian Acropolis (8.51–55, below), Herodotus tentatively assigns "second thoughts" about impieties to the Persian king. Most interesting is Xerxes' prayer to the sun that "no misfortune befall him of the type that would prevent him from overthrowing Greece before he came to the boundaries of that land." In Herodotus' narrative this is one of very few prayers that are not answered; misfortune will in fact overcome Xerxes and he will not reach the boundaries of Greece. The prayer is not, however, unanswered simply because Xerxes was not a Greek. The experience of the pious Lydian king Croesus in 547 was quite the opposite. After the Persian king Cyrus had captured Croesus at Sardis, he planned to burn him alive on a large pyre. As the fire was burning, however, Cyrus changed his mind and ordered that the fire be put out.

It is said by the Lydians that when Croesus learned of Cyrus' change of mind and saw that all the men were trying to quench the fire but could not check it, he called upon Apollo, bidding him, if he had received some pleasing gift from him, to stand by his side and rescue him from the present evil. Croesus in tears called upon the god, and suddenly clouds gathered in the clear and windless sky and a storm broke out. It rained furiously and the pyre was quenched. And so Cyrus learned that Croesus was both god-loved (θεοφιλής) and a good man.[136] (1.86–87.2)

To the extent that we know the outcomes, all of Herodotus' prayers to conventional Greek deities were answered, and all Greek prayers in the context of the Persian invasions were also answered.[137] The prayer of the pious Lydian king to Apollo is miraculously fulfilled, but that of the sanctuary-burning, Hellespont-whipping Xerxes to Helios is unsuccessful. The pattern here and throughout the *Histories* is much the same as we find in epic and tragedy: prayers of good and pious characters are answered, and those of the impious are either not answered or are answered to their detriment.[138] It is this poetic convention, I suspect, that Herodotus is following in his use of prayers in his historical narrative and especially in this prayer of Xerxes.

At the crossing of the Hellespont Herodotus takes the opportunity to have one Greek reflect, in religious terms, on the impression Xerxes and his expedition were making: "It is said that, after Xerxes had crossed the Hellespont, a Greek from the region remarked, 'Zeus, why do you, appearing like a Persian man and taking the name Xerxes instead of Zeus, want to devastate Greece, bringing with you all these men? Even without these men you could do this'"[139] (7.56.2).

Xerxes here encounters another bad, contrary-to-nature omen, one that he ignored but which Herodotus, without any doubt of its reality and with the benefit of hindsight, was ready to interpret: "When all the Persians had crossed and were starting on their way, a great, marvelous omen occurred. Xerxes took no account of it, even though it was easy to interpret. A horse gave birth to a hare. It was easy to interpret in this way: Xerxes was going to lead an army against Greece in a most stately and majestic way, but he would come back to the same place running for his life" (7.57.1).

Xerxes and his army now proceeded westward, along the north coast of the Aegean Sea. The Greek cities at suitable intervals had each been ordered, with advance notice, to provide the day's main meal for Xerxes, his retinue, and his army. For the Thasians the day's cost was 400 talents ($240 million).[140] Some cities were bankrupted by the expense, in others the citizens fled before Xerxes arrived. Abdera played the host, and after the event Herodotus has the Abderite Megacreon make the following suggestion for his fellow citizens, a suggestion that we might think was made tongue in cheek if not for the desperate realities of the situation:

The Abderitae should all go, men and women, to their sanctuaries and sit as suppliants, asking the gods also in the future to ward off half of the evils coming upon them, and they should be very grateful to the gods for what had just transpired, that Xerxes did not have the habit of dining twice a day. For if the Abderitae had been told to prepare a lunch as well as a dinner, they would have had either to flee before Xerxes came or else, remaining there, to have been ground to bits the worst of all men.[141] (7.120)

At the Strymon River, near Eion, Herodotus reports that

the *magoi* sought good omens by sacrificing white horses. They made these and many other offerings of sorcery (φαρμακεύσαντες) into the river at Ennea Hodoi (Nine Ways) of the Edonians, and then proceeded across the Strymon River on the bridges they found completed there. When they learned the place was called Ennea Hodoi, they buried alive there nine boys and maidens of the local people. It is a Persian *nomos* to bury people alive. I hear that even Amastris, Xerxes' wife, when she was old, buried alive fourteen Persian children of illustrious men. She buried them for her own sake, to return a favor to the god who is said to be beneath the earth.[142] (7.113.2–114)

The use of magic in this situation is un-Greek,[143] and Herodotus points to the un-Greek character of the human sacrifice here by labeling it a Persian *nomos*. He does not, interestingly, criticize the *nomos*; as we will see, he is very reluctant to find fault with foreign customs. He is much more likely to point to impious and wicked acts that foreigners, and especially Persians, commit in violation of their own *nomoi*. We treat the issue of human sacrifice later when we attempt to decide if Themistocles at Salamis really did have three Persians sacrificed as Plutarch (*Them.* 13.2–3, below) reports.

All of the cities, Greek or other, through which Xerxes passed with his army were forced to "Medize," to support the Persian expedition with men and/or ships. Xerxes, in addition, sent heralds throughout the Greek world, demanding from each city "earth and water" as tokens of surrender. Xerxes chose not, however, to send heralds with this request to Athens and Sparta. According to Herodotus, Darius had sent heralds with the same demand to them in 491 (6.48), and

the Athenians threw them into "the pit," while the Spartans dumped them in a well, telling them to take earth and water to the king from there. For these reasons Xerxes did not send heralds to Athens and Sparta to make the request. I cannot say what undesirable thing happened to the Athenians for having done this to the heralds, except that their land and city were devastated, but I do not think that happened for this reason. But on the Lacedaemonians fell the wrath of Talthybius, the herald of Agamemnon. There is in Sparta a sanctuary of Talthybius, and there are also descendants called Talthybiadae, and all the herald assignments from Sparta have been given to them as a privilege. After the killing of the heralds, the Spartiates were unable to get good omens in their sacrifices, and this went on for a long time. (7.133–134.2)

At last a public proclamation was made at Sparta, asking "'if any Lacedae-monian was willing to die for Sparta.' Sperthias, the son of Aneristus, and Bulis, the son of Nicolaus, both Spartiates, strong, healthy, and rich, volunteered to pay recompense to Xerxes for the heralds of Darius who had died in Sparta." Sperthias and Bulis eventually found their way to Susa and to an interview with Xerxes.

Xerxes, with magnanimity, said he would not be like the Lacedaemonians, because they in killing the heralds overthrew the *nomoi* of all men. He would not do the things for which he criticized them, nor would he, by killing Sperthias and Bu-lis, free the Lacedaemonians from their guilt. And so, for the immediate present, after the Spartiates had done this, the wrath of Talthybius stopped, even though Sperthias and Bulis returned to Sparta. But much later, as the Lacedaemonians say, the wrath was reawakened in the war of the Peloponnesians and Athenians. And this appears to me to be, in this affair, most divine (θειότατον): justice (τὸ δίκαιον) brought it about that the wrath of Talthybius fell upon heralds and did not stop until it reached its goal. Because it fell upon the children of those men who went to the king because of the wrath, on Nicolaus, the son of Bulis, and on Aneristus, the son of Sperthias . . . , it is clear to me that the event was divine (θεῖον). Nicolaus and Aneristus were sent by the Lacedaemonians to Asia as her-alds (during the Peloponnesian War, in 430) and were betrayed by Sitalces, the son of Teres, king of the Thracians. . . . They were captured near Bisanthe on the Hellespont, taken to Attica, and there put to death by Athenians.[144] (7.136.2–137)

Heralds on diplomatic missions were, by international *nomoi*, inviolate, and for the Greeks they were under divine protection.[145] Herodotus here again has the Persian king observe a religious *nomos* that the Greeks, in this case the Athenians and Spartans, violate. Herodotus seems certain that the violation will be punished. For the Spartans punishment takes the form of disruption of good relations with the gods, and hence the bad omens in sacrifices. Xerxes has no inclination to help the Spartans solve their problem, and the necessary expiation is not accomplished for fifty years, until the death of the children of the men who themselves had attempted, unsuccessfully, to expiate the impiety. The remarkable coinci-dence of the death of their children in similar circumstances proves to Herodotus the involvement of the "divine." About the Athenians' pun-ishment Herodotus is uncertain. It is unlikely, to him, that their maltreatment of heralds had caused the devastation of their land by the Persians, probably because it would seem excessive and had no thematic link—as the Spartans' punishment did—with the crime. Interestingly though, Herodotus' account here suggests that there was no commonly accepted "religious" reason for the devastation of Athens.

Pausanias, however, claims to know how the Athenians were punished for their impiety against the Persian heralds: "In Athens the wrath of Talthybius fell not on the whole people but privately on the house of one man, Miltiades, the son of Cimon, because he had been responsible for the Athenians putting to death those of the heralds that came to Attica" (3.12.7).[146] Herodotus, as we have seen, had Miltiades die because of his violation of the sanctuary of Demeter on Paros (6.132–136, above).

Herodotus reports that some cities and countries, unlike Athens and Sparta, were accepting Xerxes' demand for "earth and water":

These were some of the peoples giving these things: the Thessalians, Dolopes, Enianes, Perrhaebi, Locrians, Magnetes, Malians, Phthiotic Achaeans, the Thebans and other Boeotians except for the Thespians and the Plataeans. The Greeks who took up the war against the barbarian swore an oath against these. The oath was as follows: "Whichever Greeks gave themselves up to the Persian, if they had not been forced and their situation was good, were to pay a tithe to the god in Delphi." Such was the oath for the Greeks. (7.132)

What this tithe was meant to be is not specified, but it may have meant the total destruction of the Medizing cities, with the sale of their populations into slavery and the confiscation of all goods and lands. From the proceeds a tenth would be dedicated to the god.[147]

In Herodotus' view, "if the Athenians in fear of the coming danger had abandoned their land, or if they had not abandoned it but had stayed there and given themselves up to Xerxes, no other Greeks would have tried to oppose the king by sea." That would have meant the eventual loss of the Peloponnesus, including also Sparta. "And so Greece would have become subject to the Persians." The freedom of Greece depended upon the Athenians' decision to stay and fight, or to flee and resettle elsewhere. For Herodotus the Delphic oracle's famous "wooden wall" oracle, delivered some time before the battle of Thermopylae,[148] was a decisive factor in Athens's decision to fight and not flee the Persians, and he gives a full description of its origin, text, and interpretation at Athens.

Not even frightening oracles coming from Delphi and throwing a scare into them persuaded the Athenians to leave Greece, but they remained there and endured to receive the enemy coming into their land. The Athenians were ready, because they had sent ambassadors to Delphi to question the oracle. After the ambassadors had performed the traditional rites around the sanctuary, after they had gone into the *megaron* and sat down, the Pythia, whose name was Aristonice, prophesied the following:

> Wretched men, why do you sit here? Leave your homes
> And the heights of your circular city. Flee to the ends of the earth.
> Neither the head, nor the body, nor the feet, nor the hands
> Remain steadily, nor is anything of the midsection left,
> But they are all in an unenviable state.
> Fire and sharp Ares, driving a Syrian chariot,
> Will throw down your city.
> He will destroy also many other fortified cities, not yours alone.
> He will give over many temples of gods to raging fire.
> These temples now stand flowing in sweat, shaking in fear,
> And black blood has poured down from their rooftops
> As they see inescapable evil.
> But leave my sanctuary, and put courage as a covering over your ills.[149]

When the ambassadors of the Athenians heard this, they treated it as the greatest misfortune. As they were giving up hope because of the evil that had been prophesied, Timon, the son of Androbulus, a highly respected Delphian, advised them to take suppliant boughs and, again, to approach the oracle and, as suppliants, to question it. The Athenians were persuaded, and said to the oracle, "Lord (Apollo), respect these suppliant boughs we have come carrying and prophesy to us something better about our fatherland, or else we will not leave your sanctuary but will remain here in this place until we die." The prophetess gave them this second oracle:

> Pallas is unable to propitiate Olympian Zeus,
> Despite begging with many words and wise intelligence.
> But I, encountering what cannot be changed, will tell you this:
> All the other things which the boundary of Cecrops and
> The hollow of divine Cithaeron enclose will be taken,
> But far-seeing Zeus grants to Tritogeneia a wooden wall.
> It alone will be unsacked, and it will benefit you and your children.
> Do not quietly await the great army coming from the mainland,

The cavalry and the infantry, but turn your back and retreat.
At some time in the future you will meet that army.
Divine Salamis, you will destroy the children of women,
Either when Demeter is sown, or when she is gathered.[150]

To the ambassadors these prophecies seemed to be, and were, more kindly than the previous ones, and so, having had them written down, they departed for Athens. And when they returned, the ambassadors reported to the people. As the Athenians tried to interpret the oracle, there were many other opinions, but these two especially were opposed. Some of the older men were saying that they thought the god was prophesying that the Acropolis would survive, because long ago the Acropolis of the Athenians had been fenced in with a wooden structure. They were concluding that this was "the wooden wall." Others were saying that the god meant the ships, and they were bidding the Athenians to give up other things and prepare the ships. But those who said the ships were "the wooden wall" were being stymied by the last two lines spoken by the Pythia:

Divine Salamis, you will destroy the children of women,
Either when Demeter is sown, or when she is gathered.

On the basis of these lines the opinions of those who claimed the ships were "the wooden wall" were being confuted. The *chresmologoi* were taking these lines to mean that it was necessary for the Athenians to be defeated around Salamis if they prepared a naval battle there. One Athenian had just recently attained prominence; his name was Themistocles, and he was called the son of Neocles. He said that the *chresmologoi* did not understand the oracle correctly. "If this line has truly been said in reference to the Athenians," he said, "then he did not think it would have been prophesied in such kindly terms, but would have said 'Wretched Salamis' instead of 'Divine Salamis' if its inhabitants were going to die around it." Themistocles understood it rightly, that the oracle had been spoken by the god against the enemy, not against the Athenians. Therefore he was advising the Athenians to prepare themselves to make a naval battle, since this was "the wooden wall." As Themistocles revealed his position, the Athenians decided that his plans were preferable to those of the *chresmologoi* who were not allowing them to make a naval battle or even, in short, to lift a hand but were telling them to abandon Attica and settle in some other land. . . . And in their deliberations after the oracle the Athenians decided to meet with their ships the barbarian as he invaded Greece, trusting in the god and in those of the Greeks who were willing to help.[151] (7.139–144)

On the basis of the second oracle the Athenians thus decided to make a stand at Salamis and eventually forced the other allied Greek navies to join in a decisive battle against the Persians there. These oracles are so important to any "religious" account of the wars, are so elaborately described, and are of such intrinsic interest that they provide an excellent opportunity to consider, in somewhat broader terms, relevant aspects of Delphic oracles in general in Herodotus' account of the Persian Wars.[152] Herodotus' account of these two oracles includes most of the elements found in his many other accounts of the Delphic oracle, and we summarize them here. One either went himself to the oracle or, as here, sent *theopropoi*. *Theopropos* is the technical term for an "ambassador" sent on an oracular mission. Here the *theopropoi* went "into the *megaron*," probably the *cella* of the Apollo temple built by the Alcmaeonidae (5.62–64, above).[153] The *theopropoi* were seated, and the Pythia "prophesied" (χρᾷ) to them in dactylic hexameters. When the Athenian *theopropoi* "heard" the "wooden wall" oracle, they wrote it down and returned to Athens. There the process of interpretation began, with citizens, *chresmologoi*, and finally Themistocles contributing to the discussion.

*Theopropoi* were often used;[154] to go "into the *megaron*" was a regular feature of the procedure;[155] and others made use of local Delphians for good or ill.[156] To the Athenian *theopropoi* "the Pythia prophesied" (ἡ Πυθίη χρᾷ), but a brief look at the usual subjects and verbs of this element of the process in Herodotus' accounts is illuminating. The "giver" of the prophecy is here and most commonly the Pythia, but elsewhere it might be "the oracle" or "the god," that is, Apollo.[157] The subjects appear interchangeable, but "the Pythia" is clearly favored. The technical terms for "to prophesy" are ἀναιρεῖν, χρᾶν, and θεσπίζειν,[158] but the nontechnical verbs reveal more how oracles were viewed by their recipients. Often the Pythia quite neutrally, as here, "tells" or "says" the oracle,[159] but many times Herodotus describes the oracular statement as a command (κελεύειν) or a forbiddance (ἀπαγορεύειν, οὐκ ἐᾶν).[160] The implication in those cases is that the oracle is giving more than warnings and advice. Those are commands.

In the first of the two oracles to the Athenians the Pythia orders the Athenians to "leave *my* sanctuary," and in the second she says, "*I* will tell you this." The question here and elsewhere is who is the "I" of the oracular voice from Delphi. In some cases it is unmistakably Apollo;[161] in others, as for the "wooden wall" oracle, recipients react as though it is Apollo;[162] and in no case need we assume it is the Pythia herself. Clearly the oracular "I" is Apollo. One sought oracles (χρᾶσθαι, χρηστηριάζεσθαι, μαντεύεσθαι) from the oracle or Apollo,[163] never from the Pythia. She spoke the words, but the words were Apollo's.[164] Herodotus sometimes specifies that the oracle was in dactylic hexameter or iambic trimeter,[165] and this may suggest that not all oracles were in verse. One has also from Herodotus' accounts the impression that the Pythia herself (or the god) gave the metrical version. And only twice (here, for the "wooden wall" oracle, and 1.46–49) does Herodotus have the recipients write down the oracle, which may suggest that this was unusual. Missing in Herodotus, of course, are the machinations of the priests, the workshop of the poets, and the chasms, caves, vapors, and psychedelic mushrooms that late sources and modern scholars attempt to attribute to the Delphic oracle.[166] For Herodotus the procedure was simple and straightforward. One asked one's question, and one got one's answer, from Apollo.

The Athenians here and the Thebans earlier in their oracle "to seek those nearest them for help" (Hdt. 5.79–81, above) successfully interpret a problematical oracle. There were, however, famous cases of individuals misinterpreting such oracles and suffering for it. Croesus, the king of Lydia, when attempting to decide whether he should attack Cyrus, the king of Persia, received from Delphi the oracle that "if he campaigned against the Persians he would destroy a great empire" (Hdt. 1.53–56.1).[167] He did attack the Persians, and the empire he destroyed was his own. When he complained at Delphi, the Pythia said, "In response to the oracle that occurred, Croesus wrongly finds fault. Loxias was telling him that if he campaigned against the Persians, he would destroy a great empire. If Croesus was going to plan well, he ought to have sent again and asked whether Apollo meant his kingdom or that of Cyrus" (1.91.4–6). The Pythia here gives the essence of Croesus' failure to understand his oracle. He did not "plan well." Croesus, unthinkingly, took the oracle in the sense most favorable to his purposes. By contrast, the Athenians, faced with an oracle that seemed to predict the annihilation of their city, consulted the god a second time and then debated publicly, using all the human resources available to them. This pattern—thoughtful and wary interpretation leading to success, hasty and thoughtless interpretation leading to failure—is one Herodotus employs to explain the results of several oracles.[168] Such mistaken interpretations cause failures for the Spartans (1.65–66), the Phocaeans (1.166–167), the Siphnians (3.57–58), and King Cleomenes (6.80). Thoughtful and successful interpretations are made by Liches (1.67–68), Psammetichus (2.152), the Paionians (5.1), Cypselus (5.92.ε), and Miltiades, the son of Cypselus (6.34–36).[169]

The further question is why some individuals failed to think carefully and prudently about their interpretation of oracles. First, impiety, akin to and arising from "irrationality" and "madness," may make an individual like King Cleomenes of Sparta incapable of rational planning (6.80–82). Second, and especially prominent in Croesus' case, an inability to recognize one's place as a human being in the world may lead one to expect, unthinkingly, success in all matters and to overlook indications to the contrary. Related to this is the failure to recognize "what has to be" and to accommodate oneself to it. Any one of these can lead to a fatal misinterpretation of an oracle, a fate that the Athenians escaped by their requestioning of the oracle and their careful deliberations.

We close this digression on Herodotean oracles with a fundamental question, but one that allows no simple answer: to what extent are the oracles in Herodotus' *Histories* actual oracles given by Delphic Apollo and other oracular deities of the time? The question arises in virtually every discussion of the Delphic oracle and has been the focus of the studies by Parke and Crahay. It involves examination of each of the hundreds of oracles individually, and that is impossible here. But for our purposes Fontenrose (1978) provides a complete and convenient example of the approaches to the question, with references to most prior studies, and his results are representative of the more conservative approach to the historicity of the oracles. Fontenrose labels virtually all the Delphic oracles in Herodotus *quasi-historical* (Q), by which he means "those which were allegedly spoken within historical time, i.e., after the legendary period, but which are, to our knowledge, first attested by a writer whose lifetime was later than the accepted or supposed date of the response. . . . The prefix *quasi* must be given its exact Latin meaning: it means that these responses are recorded *as if* spoken in historical times (i.e. after 800); it is not intended to reflect in any way on the authenticity of these responses. Some are obviously authentic; others are obviously not; many others are questionable" (1978.8). Clearly each oracle must be examined individually, and in his book *The Delphic Oracle* Fontenrose does this, primarily, by comparing and contrasting their features to oracles he terms *historical* (H), oracles "which appear in contemporary records; that is, the accepted probable date of the response fell within the lifetime of the writer who attests it, or of the earliest writer when several attest it, or not long before the date of the inscription which records it"

(p. 7). Fontenrose then labels, sometimes after discussion in the text, each quasi-historical oracle as "authentic," "not genuine," "doubtful," "possibly genuine," or "probably genuine."

Of the forty-nine Herodotean Delphic oracles we encounter in this study, Fontenrose judges none "authentic." Q157 of 8.121–122 (below) is "probably genuine," 148 of 7.178 (below) "possibly" so, and 146–147 (those concerning the "wooden wall") are, in Fontenrose's judgment, "doubtful." The remaining forty-five are deemed "not genuine," and among the many casualties are the "Halys River" oracle to Croesus (1.53–56), Apollo's response to the Delphians that he could protect his own property (8.35–39, below), and many others most would be sorry to lose.[170] "Not genuine" may, of course, mean a number of things—for example, that Delphi never issued such an oracle, or that it did not issue the oracle in the form Herodotus gives it.[171] Fontenrose tends not to make these distinctions, but they are of great import for those wanting historical accuracy. Evidence is, however, lacking. Significantly more important for religious history is the question whether Greeks of the time *believed* that Delphi issued these oracles, and, quite simply, there is no evidence that they did not.[172] None, in classical times, is rejected as a forgery. Whatever their origins, however they may have been revised or reshaped, the Delphic oracles seem to have been accepted by the Greeks after Herodotus as Herodotus presented them.[173] And if so, they become part of the corpus of Greek religious beliefs, whatever fact or fiction lies behind them.

An inscription (ML 23) of the early third century records what purports to be a copy of the decree proposed by Themistocles (Hdt. 7.144.3) for the evacuation of Athens and for naval forces to be sent to Artemisium and Salamis. It was discovered in Troezen, the city to which many of the Athenian women and children were evacuated. Since its original publication by Jameson (1960), this text has raised a host of issues concerning its purposes, date, the chronology of Athens's plans for evacuations, and, generally, Herodotus' whole account of the time from Artemisium to Salamis.[174] Whatever the sources and purposes of this text of Themistocles' decree, parts of it were widely known and quoted from the late fourth century on.[175] These parts of the inscription refer to religious activities:

Themistocles, son of Neocles, of the deme Phrearrhioi proposed to [entrust][176] the city to Athena who protects Athens[177] and to all the other gods to guard and [to ward off the barbarian] for the sake of the land. . . . [The treasurers] and the priestesses are to remain on the Acropolis[178] [guarding the property of the gods].

Half the fleet is to sail to Artemisium and half to Salamis, and among the final arrangements for departure "the Boule and generals are to sacrifice an appeasement offering (ἀρεστήριον) to Zeus [Pancrates], Athena, Nike, and Poseidon Asphaleios."[179] Such appeasement offerings were usually made when significant changes were made in cult buildings, cult statues, votive gifts, and such things,[180] and may have been required here because the Athenians were removing sacred objects from their sanctuaries for evacuation from Attica.

As the Persians were approaching, the Greek allies sought desperately to enroll other Greeks on their side. Among those Greeks who might have been willing to help against the Persians were the Argives and the Cretans. But both refused, and Herodotus offers religious motives and the Delphic oracle as among the causes of their refusals.

For their part, the Argives give the following account: they right at the beginning learned of the undertakings of the barbarian against Greece, and they recognized that the Greeks would attempt to take them along as allies against the Persian. They therefore sent ambassadors to Delphi to ask the god "what they should do for the best result." Very recently (494) six thousand of their men had died at the hands of the Lacedaemonians and Cleomenes, the son of Anaxandrides, and for that reason they sent to Delphi. The Pythia, they said, answered the following to their question:

> Hated by your neighbors, dear to the immortal gods,
> Keep your spear at home. Sit, protect yourself, and
> Protect your head. And the head will save the body.[181]
> (7.148.2–3)

Despite their fear of this oracle which "forbade them to make an alliance with the Greeks" against Xerxes, the Argives said they would ally with the Greeks if they could assume one-half of the command and if they could have a thirty-year treaty with Sparta.[182] These terms were refused, and Argos did not join the alliance. Other accounts suggested collusion between Persia and Argos. Xerxes, as one widespread account went, made a special arrangement of friendship and neutrality with the Argives because Perses, the eponym and ancestor of the Persians, was the son of Perseus, himself the ancestor of the Argives. The Argives and Persians were thus blood relatives and should not fight one another (7.148–151).[183]

When the Cretans were asked to join the Greek alliance, they "sent ambassadors to Delphi to ask the god 'if it would be better for them if they helped Greece.' The Pythia replied, 'Do you fault the tears that Minos in his wrath brought to you as a result of your help to Menelaus? The Greeks did not help Minos avenge his death in Camicus, but you helped the Greeks avenge the woman who had been stolen from Sparta by a barbarian man.'"[184] Minos in his search for Daedalus had come to Sicily and died a violent death in Camicus three generations before the Trojan War. The Cretans had then come to Sicily and unsuccessfully and tragically tried to avenge his death. And after the Trojan War, Crete suffered famine, plague, and depopulation. "The Pythia reminded the Cretans of these events and stopped them, despite their wishes, from helping the Greeks" (7.169–171).

## ≭ Artemisium and Thermopylae ≭

The allied Greek forces eventually decided to meet the invading Persians at Thermopylae by land and Artemisium by sea. These places were close together and so communications between infantry and navy would be good. Both, and especially Thermopylae, afforded a narrow, restricted area, which would benefit the smaller Greek forces. But, before either battle, the gods began to help make it a "more fair fight." Just at this time, when the Greeks were coming to Thermopylae and Artemisium, Herodotus reports that

the Delphians, in fear for themselves and Greece, were consulting the god, and an oracle was given to them "to pray to winds, because winds would be great allies to Greece."[185] The Delphians accepted the oracle and first announced to those Greeks wanting to be free what had been prophesied to them. For having made this announcement to the Greeks who were terribly frightened of the barbarian, the Delphians stored up undying gratitude. And afterward the Delphians established an altar for the winds in Thyia where there is a sanctuary of Thyia, the daughter of Cephisus.[186] The land Thyia is named after her, and there the Delphians with sacrifices were seeking winds. The Delphians, on the basis of this oracle, still even now appease the winds. (7.178)

When the two navies were in their anchorages, the Persians on and about Cape Sepias near Artemisium and the Greeks at Euripus, the very narrow straits separating Euboea from the mainland, a violent wind storm arose on a previously clear and windless day.[187] Herodotus tells of the religious appeals the Athenians had made to Boreas, the north wind:

A story is told that the Athenians had summoned Boreas after an oracle came to them "to summon their son-in-law." According to the account of Greeks, Boreas has a Greek wife, Oreithyia, the daughter of Erechtheus (who was once a king of Athens). As the account goes, the Athenians on the basis of this marriage tie concluded that Boreas was their son-in-law, and when, lying in wait at Chalcis of Euboea, they learned that the wind storm was strengthening, or even before that, they sacrificed and summoned Boreas and Oreithyia to help them and to destroy the ships of the barbarians just as they had also before around Athos.[188] I cannot say if for these reasons Boreas fell now upon the barbarians at anchor, but the Athenians say that Boreas had helped them before and then accomplished these things. After the Athenians departed, they founded a sanctuary of Boreas (in Attica) alongside the Ilissus River.[189] (7.189)

For three days the Persians in their more exposed position suffered the brunt of the storm. And finally, according to Herodotus,

the *magoi*, making sacrifices and shouting chants at the wind and also sacrificing to Thetis and the Nereids, on the fourth day stopped the wind, or else in some other way the wind itself of its own will abated. The *magoi* were sacrificing to Thetis because they heard from the Ionians the story that she had been snatched from this place by Peleus and that all Cape Sepias belonged to her and the other Nereids. (7.191.2)

By conservative estimates the Persians lost no less than 400 of their 1,327 ships to this storm. When the Greeks learned of the Persian losses, "they prayed and poured libations to Poseidon Soter (Savior) and rushed back as quickly at they could to Artemisium. . . . And from that time until now they have named Poseidon 'Soter'" (7.192). Some days later, at the time of the final battle of Thermopylae, a similar storm hit Persians ships sailing at night around Euboea. Several ships were destroyed, and "everything was being done by the god to make the Persian force equal in size to the Greek and not much larger" (8.13).[190]

This violent storm off Artemisium is the best and most developed example of such divinely motivated phenomena that Herodotus offers for the Persian Wars and is a splendid example of Greek polytheism in practice.[191] The Delphians had been told by Apollo to pray to the winds and no doubt did this. They erected an altar for the winds in Thyia where they later continued to appease the winds. The Athenians sacrificed and summoned Boreas and said that he brought about the storm. Afterward the Athenians, who evidently did not share Herodotus' uncertainty about Boreas' role, founded a sanctuary for him in Attica. The other Greeks, when they learned of the Persian losses, poured libations to Poseidon Soter. The beneficial storm at Artemisium was—as we should expect in Greek pluralism and polytheism—attributed to different deities by different people: to the winds at Thyia by the Delphians, to their Boreas and Oreithyia by the Athenians, and to Poseidon by other Greeks. Each credited the deity to whom they had prayed and performed offerings.

This sequence of prayer, fulfillment of the prayer, and expression of gratitude surrounding the storm at Artemisium illustrates what we might term "cultic logic": if one prayed to a deity that something occur, and that event did occur, one then naturally believed that the deity caused it and therefore expressed one's gratitude to the deity. The proof of the deity's effectiveness lay in the accomplishment of the prayer.[192] The Athenians prayed to Boreas and Oreithyia for winds, the beneficial winds came, and the Athenians expressed their gratitude. The Delphians established a cult of the winds at Thyia, sacrificed to them for winds, benefited from the storm, and thereafter maintained the cult. It is also noteworthy that in both instances a new sanctuary, altar, and sacrifices were established. The other Greeks, so far as we hear, did not make prior prayers for a storm, and so they credited and expressed their gratitude in a Panhellenic setting to Poseidon, the generalized Greek god of the sea. All this makes perfect sense in "cultic logic."

The epithet Soter ("Savior") given to Poseidon by the Greeks also is of interest. Here, for the Greeks, "safety" was apparently their primary concern. When the battle or personal danger is over, the victors make an offering to their Soter, whether it be a river (8.138.1) or, as here, a god. "Safety," of course, usually resulted from "victory," and we may be making too much of the distinction between the two, but nowhere in prayers, dedications, or sacrifices does Herodotus have the Greeks ask, thank, or give the gods credit explicitly for "victory" in battle. With the omens favorable, with a "saving" god watching over them, when the fight was fair, these experienced soldiers and sailors apparently thought the "victory" itself was in good part their own work.

On the other side, even the Persians appealed to Greek divinities to stop the storm, although Herodotus seems reluctant to attribute success to this endeavor. Perhaps the storm just stopped of its own accord. But for the Greek side Herodotus does state confidently that by the storm at Artemisium "everything was being done by the god to make the Persian force equal in size to the Greek and not much larger." The god, again, was trying to make it a "fair fight" for the Greeks.

There were also, after the storm, skirmishes at sea at Artemisium, and the Athenians later erected a dedication there. Plutarch (*Them.* 8.2–3) describes the sanctuary of Artemis at Artemisium, the dedication, and the elegiac poem, often attributed to Simonides, inscribed there:[193]

Artemisium has a small temple of Artemis Proseoa ("Facing the East"). Trees grow around it and plaques of white stone have been set in the ground in a circle. When the stone is rubbed with the hand, it gives off the color and fragrance of saffron. On one of the plaques this elegiac poem was inscribed:

> The children of the Athenians on this sea
> Once defeated races of all sorts of men from Asia
> In a sea battle. When the army of the Medes perished,
> The Athenians erected these memorials for the maiden Artemis.[194]

The poem, like the dedications after Marathon, is directed primarily to the accomplishments of the Athenians and seems intended as a memorial of them.

Individuals, too, might choose to commemorate their personal accomplishments in battle, and, if we accept Herodotus' location of this event (8.11.2), we have an example from the battle of Artemisium.[195] According to Plutarch, the Athenian trierarch Lycomedes was the first to capture an enemy ship, and "he cut off the emblems of the ship and dedicated them to Apollo Daphnephoros at Phlya" (*Them.* 15.2). Lycomedes no doubt chose this sanctuary in part because it was in his home deme in Attica.

In the meantime the Persian army from the north and the Greeks from the south were coming together at the narrow, one-wagon-wide pass of Thermopylae.[196] The Greek army included Spartans, Tegeans, Mantineans, Orchomenoi and others from Arcadia, Corinthians, Phleiasians, and eighty Mycenaeans. From the mainland came the Thespians, Thebans, Opountian Locrians, and 1,000 Phocians. The following argument, based on the difference between men and gods, convinced, according to Herodotus, the Phocians to participate:

The Greeks had summoned the Phocians, telling them through messengers that "they themselves had come in advance of the full army, and the rest of the allies were expected daily. The sea was being guarded by the Athenians, Aeginetans, and others assigned to the navy. There was nothing for the Phocians to fear. The person invading Greece was not a god but a human being. And there was and would be no mortal who did not have in his life, right from birth, some misfortune. The greatest men had the greatest misfortunes. And so the invader was obliged, since he was a mortal, to fall short of what he expected." The Phocians heard this and went to help. (7.203)

The Spartans had sent 300 Spartiates to Thermopylae with their king Leonidas, "so that the other allies seeing these might join the campaign and not Medize." But, as at Marathon (6.106.3, above), religious festivals prevented the full participation of the Spartans and other Greek allies.

The Carneia[197] prevented the Spartans from sending more, but they were intending, after having celebrated their festival and having left guards in Sparta, quickly to come to help with their whole army. And so also the rest of the allies intended to do, because the Olympia festival coincided with these events.[198] For this reason they were sending only an advance force, not expecting that the war at Thermopylae would be decided so quickly. (Hdt. 7.206)

Leonidas, his 300 Spartiates, and a still large force of allies were positioned to defend the pass, but they were betrayed by a Malian who led a contingent of Persians on a little-known path over the adjoining mountain to surround them. Herodotus has both a prophet and a Delphic oracle determine the course of action at this moment. "The prophet Megistias, after looking at the sacrifices, first indicated to those of the Greeks at Thermopylae that death would come to them with dawn, and then deserters announced that the Persians had them surrounded." Leonidas saw that his allies were frightened and despondent, and sent them off.

It was not good for Leonidas himself to leave, but if he remained, there was for him great fame and the prosperity of Sparta would not be wiped out. For it had been prophesied to the Spartiates by the Pythia about this war, just when it began, that either Lacedaemon was to be devastated by the barbarians or their king was to die. This is the oracle of the Pythia, in hexameter verse:

Inhabitants of Sparta with its broad dancing areas,
Either your great and glorious city will be destroyed by Persian men,
Or else not that, but the land of Lacedaemon will grieve
For a dead king of Heracles' race.
The strength of neither bulls nor lions will stop the barbarian,
Because he has the strength of Zeus. Nor do I think the Persian
Will stop until he destroys one of these two things completely.[199]

Leonidas, taking into account these lines and wanting to establish the fame of the Spartiates alone, dismissed the allies. (7.220.2–4)

The Spartans were left to fight and die, joined by the Thespians alone.

When Xerxes later, as victor, visited the battlefield at Thermopylae, he came upon the corpse of Leonidas. Herodotus recounts that

Xerxes ordered that Leonidas' head be cut off and affixed to a pole. There is lots of other evidence, but this incident especially makes it clear that King Xerxes felt a greater wrath at the living Leonidas than he did at any other man. For otherwise Xerxes would not have violated traditions in this way in regard to his corpse, since among the peoples I know Persians traditionally honor especially men who are good in military affairs. (7.238)

This act of Xerxes was again a clear impiety, one that violated Greek and, as Herodotus notes, Persian *nomoi*. Pausanias gives an account of what later became of Leonidas' corpse and of the Spartans' monument to their dead from Thermopylae:

Opposite the theater (in Sparta) is a memorial of Pausanias who commanded at Plataea. The other monument is Leonidas'. Every year the Spartans make speeches over them and hold a contest, a contest in which only Spartiates may compete. Pausanias (grandson of the hero of Plataea) recovered the bones of Leonidas from Thermopylae forty years after the battle. There is also a plaque recording the names and fathers of those who endured the struggle against the Medes at Thermopylae.[200] (3.14.1)

These war heroes later commemorated at Sparta were originally buried by the Persians at Thermopylae (Paus. 9.32.9), and, according to Herodotus, their tomb and those of other Greeks who died there were later adorned by the Amphictyons with these epigrams inscribed on plaques:

Four thousand men from the Peloponnesus
Once fought three million men in this place.[201]

That was inscribed over them all, but specifically over the Spartans,

Stranger, report to the Lacedaemonians
That here we lie, obeying their commands.[202]
(7.228.1–2)

Strabo (9.4.2) reports that the following epitaph was inscribed on the first of the five plaques at Thermopylae. It honors the Locrians of Opous.

The Opountian metropolis of right-lawed Locrians
Longs for these men who died for Greece against the Medes.[203]

Soldiers of Thespiae also fought and died at Thermopylae (7.222 and 8.25.1), and this epigram by Philiades of Megara may be from their memorial there:[204]

These men once dwelled beneath the peaks of Helicon,
And Thespiae with its broad dancing places boasts of their courage.
Philiades, frag. 1 (Page, *FGE*)

For the last of the epitaphs of the dead of the battle of Thermopylae we turn to Herodotus' description of the death of Leonidas' loyal and accurate *mantis*, Megistias of Acarnania. On the night before the final battle, Megistias had realized from his sacrifices that death was coming to the Greek defenders.

The Acarnanian Megistias, said to be descended from Melampus, was following the army, the *mantis* who from the sacrifices had said how things were going to turn out for them. Leonidas openly tried to send him away so that he would not perish with them. Megistias himself, despite being ordered away, did not leave but sent off his only son who was campaigning on the expedition. (7.221)

Megistias died at Thermopylae, and his *xenos* Simonides composed and had inscribed on his tombstone there this epitaph:

This is the memorial of glorious Megistias.
    The Medes killed him after they crossed the Spercheius River.
He was a *mantis* who, though he clearly knew then that the spirits of death were
    coming upon him,
    Did not dare abandon the commanders of Sparta.[205]
(7.228.3–4)

For those investigating Greek religious views, these epigrams, epitaphs, and other contemporary epitaphs[206] are remarkable for their lack of any mention of an afterlife, of the gods, or of anything we might term "religious."[207] They are almost exclusively "this-worldly," and, like the dedications, primarily memorialize the virtues and accomplishments of these warriors. About their existence after death there is not a word.

Simonides, who composed the epitaph for Megistias, also wrote this encomium of the dead at Thermopylae (frag. 531 Diehl). The occasion of performance is not known,[208] but the song provides a fitting conclusion to our account of the battle of Thermopylae.

> The Fortune of those who died at Thermopylae
> Is glorious, and their fate is beautiful.
> Their tomb is an altar, their lament their memory, and
> Their death their praise.
> Neither mold nor all conquering time
> Will make such a tomb offering fade away.
> This sanctuary of good men has taken the honor of Greece as its inhabitant.
> Leonidas, the king of Sparta, serves witness;
> He left behind the great adornment (κοσμόν) and eternal fame of his virtue.
> (D.S. 11.11.6)

In this song Simonides alludes to the glorious Spartan war dead as heroes with a sanctuary, altar, and perhaps hymns in their honor. So too were the Athenian casualties at Marathon worshiped in later times as a special class of heroes, a class between established cultic heroes and the common dead.[209] And so too will be honored the Greek war dead after the battle of Plataea (Plut. *Arist.* 21.2–5, below).

## ⚞ Salamis: Prelude and Battle ⚟

The Greek forces that Xerxes' army eventually defeated at Thermopylae (the 300 Spartiates and the Thespians) and the various allied contingents dismissed before the final battle were only "advance troops." The Greeks, however, never sent the promised full forces (Hdt. 7.206, above), and, in Herodotus' account, Xerxes soon learned why and was offered an unwelcome lesson in how Greeks differed from Persians.

A few deserters from Arcadia came to the Persians, in need of food and wanting to be part of the action. The Persians took them to the king and asked what the Greeks were now doing. . . . The Arcadians said the Greeks were holding the

Olympic festival and were watching athletic and equestrian contests. The Persian then asked what prize they were competing for. And the Arcadians said the prize given was a wreath of olive. At this point Tritantaechmes, the son of Artabanus (and a Persian general), expressed a very noble opinion but one for which he incurred a charge of cowardice from the king. For when he heard that the prize was a wreath and not money, he could not keep silent and said for all to hear, "Alas, Mardonius, against what kind of men did you lead us to fight, men who compete not for money but for virtue?" (8.26)

During the battle at Thermopylae the Greek naval force, with 271 triremes, was in position at the Euripus straits, deciding whether to stay and fight or retreat. A loss at Thermopylae and retreat of the navy would expose to immediate Persian attack all those cities and areas lying between Thermopylae and Athens. The Euboeans, hoping to secure time to evacuate their children and households, with Themistocles' connivance persuaded the Greeks to stay and fight. In the ensuing battle off Artemisium and Euboea, some of the Persian ships, as we have seen, were destroyed by god-sent storms (Hdt. 7.191–192 and 8.13, above) and in combat the Greeks won a narrow victory. But, given their losses and the news of Leonidas' defeat at Thermopylae, the Greeks decided to retreat to the Bay of Salamis off Attica. The Euboeans were forced into an emergency evacuation. They had, according to Herodotus,

disregarded the oracle of Bacis, as if it said nothing, and so did not gather their things or store them up for the coming war. As a result they brought about a sudden reversal in their affairs. Bacis' oracle about these matters is,

> Be mindful, when the non-Greek speaker casts a papyrus yoke onto the
> Sea, to keep your much bleating goats from Euboea.

The Euboeans made no use of these words in the troubles then present and expected, and now they faced disaster in the things most important to them.[210] (8.20)

Bacis is a somewhat mysterious figure, perhaps a Boeotian *chresmologos* whose career antedated the Persian Wars and whose collection of oracles was widely circulated.[211] Two other oracles from Bacis play a role in the religious events of this invasion (8.77 and 9.42–43, below), one of which so impressed Herodotus that he expressed his confidence in all such oracles (8.77, below). Here the Euboeans did not misinterpret their oracle but simply ignored it, a not uncommon cause for misfortune in Herodotus' *Histories*.[212]

The Phocians alone of the Greeks in this region were not Medizing, mostly because of their hatred of the Thessalians, their Medizing and traditional enemy to the immediate north. Led by the Thessalians, the Persians overran Phocis and continued their policy of destroying the sanctuaries of cities that opposed them. Herodotus reports that

everything the Persians took they burned and cut down, burning the cities and the sanctuaries. Proceeding along by the Cephisus River they were ravaging everything, and they burned down Drymus, Charadra, Erochus, Tethronium, Amphicaea, Neon, Pedies, Trites, Elateia, Hyampolis, Parapotamii, and Abae. At Abae there was a wealthy sanctuary of Apollo, adorned with many treasures and dedications. Then there was an oracle there, and it is there now too. They robbed and burned this sanctuary.[213] (8.32.2–33)

As the Persian army now moved south with little opposition, one contingent split off west to take Delphi, "to rob the sanctuary in Delphi and deliver the property to King Xerxes."[214] What transpired, as described by Herodotus, is the most remarkable series of "miracles" in these wars, miracles that lived long in Delphi lore.

As I hear, since many people were always talking of them, Xerxes knew all the noteworthy things in Delphi—especially the dedications of Croesus, son of Alyattes[215]—better than the property he had left at home. As the Delphians heard of this, they became terribly frightened, and in great terror they sought an oracle about Apollo's sacred property, whether they should bury it or take it to another land. But the god did not allow them to disturb it and said that he himself was capable of protecting his own property.[216] After the Delphians heard this, they started thinking about themselves. They sent their wives and children across to Achaea, and most of the men climbed up to the peaks of Parnassus and retreated to the Corycian cave. . . .[217] And so all the Delphians left the city, except for sixty men and the *prophetes*.[218] And when the barbarians were near and were seeing the sanctuary in the distance, the *prophetes* saw, lying in front of the temple, the sacred weapons. These weapons, which it was unholy for any human to touch, had been brought out of the *megaron*. He then went to report this marvel (τέρας) to the Delphians there. In the meantime the barbarians were rushing along, and when they reached the sanctuary of Athena Pronaia, even greater marvels than this happened to them. For the previous one was certainly a marvel, that the weapons of their own accord appeared lying in front of the temple. But the marvels that occurred after this are, among all marvels, especially worth marveling at. For when on their march the barbarians were at the sanctuary of Athena Pronaia, at this moment lightning bolts fell upon them from the sky, and two peaks broke off from Parnassus and came crashing down and caught many of them. And from the sanctuary of Pronaia there was shouting and wailing. All of these things happened together, and a panic fell upon the barbarians. When the Delphians realized the Persians were fleeing, they attacked and killed a multitude of them. And the survivors fled straight to the Boeotians. Those of the barbarians who escaped, as I hear, said that they saw also other divine things (θεῖα). Two hoplites, larger than humans, pursued and killed them. The Delphians say these were their two native heroes, Phylacus and Autonous. They have sacred precincts near Apollo's sanctuary, Phylacus by the road above the sanctuary of Pronaia, Autonous near the spring Castalia under Hyampia peak. The boulders that fell from Parnassus were preserved still into my time, lying in the sanctuary of Pronaia.[219] (8.35–39)

The divine involvement in these "miracles" is characteristic. Apollo's efforts in defense of his sanctuary were recognized by their effects, but the god Apollo was not actually seen in action. Only the heroes themselves were seen on the battlefield.

According to Diodorus (11.14.4),

The Delphians wanted to leave behind for later generations an undying memorial of the appearance of the gods and erected a trophy monument beside the sanctuary of Athena Pronaia. On it they inscribed this elegiac poem:

> The Delphians who drove back the city-sacking ranks of the Medes
>> And protected the bronze-crowned sanctuary
> Erected me as a memorial of man-warding-off war
>> And as a witness of the victory,
> Showing gratitude (χαριζόμενοι) to Zeus and Phoebos.[220]

This brief epigram, as well as its treatment by scholars, raises an important question. How did the Greeks think that the gods contributed to their victories? The difference between modern and ancient expectations is nicely exemplified in modern attempts to "improve" the text of the dedication. Valckenaer and some other modern scholars emend the text so that it reads as follows:

> The Delphians erected me as a memorial of man-warding-off war
>> And as a witness of the victory,
> Showing gratitude to Zeus and Phoebos who drove back
>> The city-sacking ranks of the Medes
> And protected the bronze-crowned sanctuary.

With a few touches of the modern pen and with slightly awkward Greek, primary credit for driving off the Persians is transferred from the Delphians to Zeus and Apollo. But on such monuments did the Greeks give primary credit to the gods? Did they imagine such immediate intervention by the gods? The other dedications that we have seen thus far, that for the Athenian victory over the Boeotians and Chalcidians in 506 (Hdt. 5.77, above), that for the battle at Artemisium (Plut. *Them.* 8.2–3, above), and the original of this Delphic dedication suggest not. These and similar dedications of the time[221] give the clear impression that even in these offerings to the gods, foremost in the writers' minds were the efforts and successes of the humans, of the Delphians, the Greeks, the Athenians, or the individuals. Gratitude might occasionally be formally expressed, as in this Delphic dedication, and is certainly implied in dedicating the monument to a deity, but little attention is paid to the deity and the deity's specific role is never described.[222] Without excluding a sense of gratitude, we still may see, from the texts themselves, these dedications primarily as memorials of human achievement, prominently displayed in sanctuaries for all visitors to see.[223]

The Athenians, the target of Xerxes' expedition, asked the Greek navy, as it was leaving Artemisium, to put in at the Bay of Salamis so the Athenians could evacuate their wives and children from Attica. Herodotus tells of another imposing omen in the religious heart of Athens, an omen that removed any doubt whether the Athenians should evacuate their homeland.

After their arrival, the Athenians made a proclamation to rescue children and members of households to wherever one could. Most sent them to Troezen, but some to Aegina, others to Salamis. They were eager to do this because they wished to serve (ὑπηρετέειν) the ("wooden wall") oracle, and, not least of all, for the following reason: the Athenians say a large snake lives in the sanctuary (of Athena) as a guard of the Acropolis.[224] They say this, and they put out monthly offerings to it as if it really exists.[225] These offerings are honeycakes. In earlier times this honeycake was always consumed, but on this occasion it was untouched. After the priestess revealed this, the Athenians even more eagerly abandoned the city because they thought that the goddess had left the Acropolis. (8.41)

According to Plutarch (*Them.* 10.1), the priests, following Themistocles' lead, explained the disappearance of the snake as a sign that Athena "had left the city and was leading the Athenians to the sea."[226] The Athenians took with them on their evacuation the cult image of Athena Polias[227] whose gorgon image was, at least for a time, lost (10.4 = Cleidemus, *FGrHist* 323 F 21).

Plutarch also reports how Cimon, the son of Miltiades, the hero of Marathon, made a dramatic gesture, in the religious realm, to convince the Athenians that they should fight at sea, not on land.

When the Medes were approaching, Themistocles was trying to convince the (Athenian) people to give up their city, leave their land, and to take up weapons in their ships before Salamis and to settle the contest at sea. Most were astonished at this bold maneuver, but Cimon took the lead. He was seen going cheerfully through the Ceramicus onto the Acropolis with his friends, and there he took and dedicated a horse's bridle to the goddess, thinking that the city at that time had need not of a cavalry force but of fighting seamen. He dedicated the bridle and took one of the shields hanging around the temple. After a prayer to the goddess, he went down to the sea and for many (of the Athenians) became a source of confidence. (*Cimon* 5.2–3)

One did not exchange dedications in a sanctuary, a bridle, as it were, for a shield. A dedication to a deity was the permanent property of the deity, and in other, less desperate times, Cimon's removal of the shield would be an impiety, but given the circumstances Plutarch finds no fault with it.

The Athenians thus evacuated their land, and Herodotus gives a full description of how the Persians took the Acropolis and of the resulting destruction of sacred monuments, with impieties on Xerxes' part and a miracle on the Athenian side.

The Persians took the city deserted, and in the sanctuary (of Athena) they found a few of the Athenians, the treasurers of the sanctuary and some poor men.[228] These men had fenced off the Acropolis with wooden doors and were trying to ward off the attackers. In part they did not evacuate to Salamis because of their poverty, but they also thought they had discovered the meaning of the oracle which the Pythia had prophesied to them, that "the wooden wall" would not be taken. This, and not the ships, was, in their view, the place of refuge according to the oracle. The Persians took up a position on the hill opposite the Acropolis, the hill the Athenians call the Areopagus. From there they were besieging them. They attached hemp to arrows, lit it, and shot it into the fence. Here the Athenians, besieged, still were defending themselves, even though they had come into extreme suffering and had been betrayed by their fence. They did not accept the proposals of the Pisistratidae for a truce, and in their defense devised other countermeasures and even hurled down boulders on the barbarians as they approached the gates.

And so Xerxes, unable to take the defenders, for a long time was at a loss. But, at length, a way out of their difficulties appeared for the barbarians, because it was necessary (ἔδεε), according to the oracle, for all Attica on the mainland to become subject to the Persians. In front of the Acropolis, but behind the gates and the ascent, where no one was either keeping guard or expecting that any man would climb, here some Persians climbed up, at the sanctuary of Cecrops' daughter Aglaurus, even though this place is a sheer cliff.[229] When the Athenians saw that the Persians had climbed up there, some hurled themselves down from the wall and perished. Others were fleeing into the *megaron* (of Athena's temple). The Persians who had made the ascent turned to the gates, and after opening these they killed the suppliants (in Athena's sanctuary).[230] After all their opponents had been laid low, the Persians robbed and burned all the Acropolis.[231] When Xerxes had complete control of Athens, he sent a messenger on horseback to Susa to announce to Artabanus his present success. On the second day after the sending of the messenger, Xerxes summoned the Athenian exiles (accompanying his expedition) and bid them, following him, to climb the Acropolis and make sacrifices in the Athenian way. He ordered this either because he had had a dream or because he became worried that he had burned the sanctuary (of Athena). And the exiles of the Athenians did what was ordered. I will tell you why I mentioned all of this. On this Acropolis there is a temple of Erechtheus who is said to have been "earth-born." In it there is an olive tree and a sea.[232] The story from the Athenians is that Poseidon and Athena, after they had contested for possession of this land, established these as proof (of their contest). It happened that this olive tree was burned down by the barbarians together with the rest of the sanctuary. But on the second day after the burning, when those of the Athenians who had been ordered to sacrifice by the king climbed up to the sanctuary, they saw that a one and one-half foot sprout had run up from the trunk of the olive tree.[233] (8.51–55)

The sprouting of the olive tree, sacred to Athena and the token of her patronage of Athens, represented, of course, the eventual revival of Athens, an interpretation so obvious that Herodotus need not give it. Xerxes, after his capture of the Acropolis, had good reason to be troubled. Herodotus, attempting to explain this in Greek terms, suggests he may have had a dream—as Persians often did—or that "he became worried that he had burned the sanctuary (of Athena)." The offering he had his Athenian sympathizers make would then be an "appeasement offering" (ἀρεστήριον) for his impieties. But Xerxes also had had the Athenians taking refuge in Athena's temple killed, and in Herodotus' *Histories* and throughout Greek literature the killing of a suppliant in a sanctuary is a gross impiety that almost always results in punishment for the perpetrator.[234] Those who took asylum in the sanctuary of a deity became, essentially, property of the deity for the time they were there, and to remove suppliants forcibly was "not holy."[235] The Spartan king Cleomenes with his usual disdain of religious law killed Argive suppliants, and the Argives thought that was the cause of his grisly suicide (6.75 and 79). The Cymaeans even consulted the oracle at Didyma about giving up their suppliant Pactyes, and after some prompting Apollo reasserted the sanctity of suppliants (1.157–160).[236] About 490, rich Aeginetans incurred both pollution and the anger of Demeter for violently violating the asylum of a suppliant in her sanctuary, and they were never able to appease the goddess (6.91).[237]

By violating asylum one angers the deity and incurs pollution.[238] One must then attempt both to appease the deity and to "sacrifice away" the pollution, and, if we go beyond Herodotus, this may have been, in part, why Xerxes had sacrifices made to Athena. He, like the Aeginetan plutocrats, was ultimately unsuccessful. He had committed two of the most blatant impieties, the destruction of a deity's sanctuary and the murder of those having asylum in that sanctuary, and a Greek reader of Herodotus would not have been sanguine about Xerxes' future.

The Persians then systematically destroyed Athens and Attica, and Pausanias and Plutarch give some isolated accounts of sacred objects damaged or carried off. In Pausanias' time, in the second century A.D., some statues of the Athena herself that had been damaged by the Persians still stood on the Acropolis: "There are also old statues of Athena. They have lost no parts, but they are rather dark and too frail to sustain a blow. The fire caught them when the (Persian) king took the city which was deserted of soldiers after the Athenians had embarked on their ships" (1.27.6). Xerxes carried away from the Athenian Agora the statues of Harmodius and Aristogiton, the slayers of Pisistratus' son Hipparchus in 514. The "tyrannicides" were killed immediately by supporters of the Pisistratids, but were probably given a hero cult very soon after the expulsion of Pisistratus' other son Hippias in 510. According to Pausanias (1.8.5), "Antenor sculpted their old statues, but Xerxes, when he took Athens and the Athenians abandoned the city, carried off these statues as booty. Antiochus (one of the successors to Alexander) later returned them to the Athenians."[239] Xerxes also took the statue of Artemis Brauronia from the deme Brauron and later, to punish the Milesians for deserting him at the battle of Salamis, carried off the bronze statue of Apollo from their oracle of Apollo at Didyma. Later Seleucus, king of the Seleucid Empire from 321 to 281, sent this statue back to the Milesians (Pausanias, 8.46.3. Cf. 1.16.3).[240]

After the war Themistocles, the hero of the battle of Salamis, personally was involved in repairing some of the damage caused by Persians in Athens. Plutarch (*Them.* 1.3) reports that the "initiation hall" (*telesterion*), probably of Demeter, in the deme Phlya was burned by the Persians. It was the property of the Lycomid family, and Themistocles, a Lycomid, himself "later repaired it and adorned (ἐκόσμησε) it with paintings."[241] Plutarch also offers a touching vignette of how Themistocles, somewhat later,

when he went to Sardis (in his exile from Athens) and had leisure, was looking at the furnishings of the sanctuaries and the multitude of dedications there. In the sanctuary of Meter he saw the bronze girl, called the "water carrier," three feet high, which he himself had dedicated when he was overseer of the waterworks in Athens. He had convicted those who were stealing and diverting water, and from their fine he made and dedicated the statue. At Sardis he either felt sorrow at the "enslavement" of the dedication or else wanted to show to the Athenians what honor and power he now had in the affairs of the king. He therefore spoke to the satrap of Lydia, asking him to send the girl back to Athens. (*Them.* 31.1)

Herodotus reports a miracle that, just before the battle of Salamis, was witnessed on the Thriasian Plain lying between Athens and Eleusis[242] by two Greek followers of Xerxes—Dicaeus, an Athenian, and Demaratus, the renegade Spartan king. Dicaeus, who knew the Eleusinian cult well, thought it an omen of Xerxes' danger in the event of a sea battle.

Dicaeus, the son of Theocydes, was an Athenian exile held in high regard among the Persians. He said that at this time, when Attica was being ravaged by Xerxes' infantry and was empty of Athenians, he happened to be in the Thriasian Plain with Demaratus, the exiled Spartan king. They saw a dust cloud coming from Eleusis, a dust cloud like one caused by 30,000 men. They marveled at what men caused the dust, and straightway they heard a sound. The sound seemed to be the Iacchos-cry of the Mysteries.[243] Demaratus knew nothing of the rites at Eleusis, and so he asked Dicaeus what this sound was. And Dicaeus said, "Demaratus, it is not possible that there will not be some great harm for the army of the king. For it is clear, since Attica is deserted, that the sound is divine (θεῖον) and is coming from Eleusis to help the Athenians and their allies. And if this cloud falls upon the Peloponnesus, the king and his army will have danger on land, but if it turns toward the ships on Salamis, the king will run the risk of losing his naval force.

This festival the Athenians hold every year for the Mother and Kore, and whatever Athenian or Greek wishes is initiated. And the sound that you hear is the Iacchos-cry they use in this festival." And Demaratus replied, "Keep quiet and do not tell this story to anyone else. If your words are reported to the king, you will lose your head. Neither I nor anyone else will be able to save you. Keep quiet. The gods will take care of this expedition." Demaratus so advised Dicaeus, and from the dust cloud and sound came a regular cloud. It rose up and moved toward Salamis, toward the camp of the Greeks. And so Demaratus and Dicaeus learned that Xerxes' naval force would perish. This was the story of Dicaeus, son of Theocydes, and he took Demaratus and others as witnesses.[244] (8.65)

Plutarch offers two dates, seven months apart, for the battle at Salamis, Boedromion 20 (*Cam.* 19.6) and Mounichion 16 (*Lys.* 15.1 and *Mor.* 349F).[245] The former, Boedromion 20, fell in the midst of the Eleusinian Mysteries, and the omens that Herodotus here describes would then have been a miraculous procession of the Mysteries at its proper time. But it is quite probable that Plutarch or his source dated the battle just on the basis of these miraculous occurrences. Plutarch's other proposed date, Mounichion 16, was linked by him to the festival of Artemis Mounichia: "The Athenians consecrated Mounichion 16 to Artemis, the day on which the goddess as a full moon shone on the Greeks as they won their victory around Salamis" (*Mor.* 349F).

Mounichion 16 was probably the festival day, the Mounichia, of Artemis long before the battle of Salamis, and by the late second century Athenian ephebes annually held a regatta as part of the Mounichia, no doubt commemorating the victory at Salamis.[246] Artemis' full moon may have facilitated the Greeks' efforts, during the night, to put the finishing touches on their victory. Others (e.g., Garland, 1992.72) think the full moon may have helped the Greeks make their observations and plans on the night before the battle. It is also quite possible that the battle did not in fact occur on Mounichion 16, but that the Athenians later chose the festival as an appropriate occasion to commemorate the victory, not as its anniversary.[247] In much the same way, as we have seen, Plutarch probably wrongly put the battle of Marathon on Boedromion 6, linking it directly to the date of the festival of Artemis Agrotera, which the Athenians later celebrated as a commemoration of that victory (*Mor.* 861E–F, above).[248]

At Salamis the Greek admirals debated whether to stay and fight there or to retreat to the narrow Isthmus joining the Peloponnesus to the mainland. Themistocles argued for Salamis, and Herodotus has him introduce, among others, religious arguments: "'(Salamis is) the place where,' he said, 'there is even an oracle that we will overcome our enemies. If men plan reasonable things, they generally occur. But if men plan unreasonable things, not even the god is willing to support their plans'" (8.60.γ).[249] According to Plutarch (*Them.* 12.1), Themistocles' argument was supported by a favorable omen, an owl, the bird of Athena, flying by on the right side of the ships: "It is said by some that when Themistocles was holding a discussion about these matters from the deck of his ship, an owl was seen flying by from the right of the ships and alighting on the masthead. And for this reason especially the others joined Themistocles' side in the argument and made preparations to fight at sea."

After the Greeks had decided to fight the naval battle at Salamis, the next day, according to Herodotus, "at dawn, an earthquake occurred both on land and at sea. The Greeks decided to pray to the gods and to summon the Aeacidae as allies. So they decided, and they did the following: after they prayed to all the gods, they summoned Ajax and Telamon from Salamis, and they sent a ship to Aegina for Aeacus and the other Aeacidae" (8.64). The Aeginetan Aeacidae later arrived, just moments before the battle began (8.83.2).[250] The Aeacidae, about twenty-five years earlier, had proved to be of little help to the Thebans (Hdt. 5.79–81, above), but Plutarch attests to their contribution during the battle at Salamis: "Some thought they saw phantoms of armed men from Aegina holding their hands in front of the Greek ships. They conjectured that these were the Aeacidae who had been summoned for help with prayers before the battle" (*Them.* 15.1).

On the eve of the battle the Persians drew up the western wing of their navy from Cynosura to the Mounichia promontory, the site of the sanctuary of Artemis Mounichia. Herodotus reports here an oracle of Bacis which he found to be so strikingly confirmed that he took the occasion to state his general faith in such oracles:

When I look at events like this, I cannot say that oracles are not true because I do not wish to try to put down those that speak clearly.

But when they bridge with ships the holy headland of golden-sword Artemis
And Cynosura on the sea, having sacked gleaming Athens in crazy hope,

Divine Justice will quench mighty Koros,[251] the son of Hybris,
Terrible, raging Koros who thinks he will lead everyone astray.
Bronze will meet bronze, and Ares will redden the sea with blood.
Then far-seeing Zeus and Lady Nike will bring on Greece's day of freedom.

I do not myself dare to argue against, nor do I accept from others arguments against Bacis concerning oracles when he speaks so clearly in such matters.[252] (8.77. Cf. 8.96.2)

Just moments before the battle of Salamis three Persians were killed by the Greeks, according to Plutarch, as human sacrifices:

Three prisoners were brought to the commander's ship as Themistocles was making the prebattle sacrifices for omens.[253] They were very handsome to look at, and they were adorned distinctively by their clothes and gold jewelry. They were said to be children of Artaüctes and Xerxes' sister Sandauce. The prophet Euphrantides saw them, and when at the same moment a large and widely seen fire flashed out from the sacrificial victims and a sneeze on the right gave a sign,[254] Euphrantides grasped Themistocles' hand and ordered him to sacrifice the young men and to consecrate them all, with a prayer, to Dionysus Omestes (Eater of Raw Flesh). For so, he said, there would be safety and victory for the Greeks. Themistocles was astonished because the prophet's pronouncement was great and terrible, a type that is common only in great struggles and difficult troubles. But the majority there, expecting that their safety would come more from what lay beyond reason than from good plans, together, with one voice, were invoking the god. They took the prisoners to the altar and forced that the sacrifice be made just as the prophet ordered. Phanias of Lesbos, a philosopher and not inexperienced in historical writings, has told this story. (*Them.* 13.2–3. Cf. *Pelop.* 21.3 and *Arist.* 9.1–2)

This episode has occasioned great debate among scholars. Did the Greeks, even once, actually sacrifice human beings? Did Themistocles and the Greeks sacrifice three young Persian noblemen during the battle of Salamis? Herodotus says nothing of it and attributes human sacrifice to Greeks only of legendary times. The Achaeans made it a threat for Athamas and his descendants (7.197),[255] and, according to the Egyptians, Menelaus, after enjoying Egyptian hospitality and recovering Helen, sacrificed two Egyptian children to secure favorable winds to leave the country. This was, to Herodotus, "an unholy act" (πρῆγμα οὐκ ὅσιον) of an "unjust man" (ἄδικος, 2.119.2–3).[256] Elsewhere Herodotus has only foreigners perform human sacrifices: of war prisoners to Ares by the Scythians (4.62), of the Persian Oiobazus by the Thracian Apsinthians to their local god Pleistorus (9.119.1), and of shipwrecked men and other Greeks to Iphigenia by the Taurians (4.103).[257] In their invasion of Greece, at Ennea Hodoi near the Strymon River, as we saw, the Persians "buried alive nine boys and maidens of the local people. It is a Persian custom to bury people alive." Even Xerxes' wife had it done (7.113–114, above). And in early skirmishes near Artemisium the Persians selected from the first captured Greek ship the most handsome sailor and slaughtered him, considering him a "good omen" (7.180).[258] If Themistocles did have three Persians "sacrificed" at Salamis, it is hardly conceivable that Herodotus would not have known of it. It either did not happen, or Herodotus suppressed it as an "unholy" and un-Greek act. Either alternative raises problems.[259] Plutarch is obviously aware of the special, non-Herodotean character of this story and takes care to give the name and credentials of his source.[260] In other *Lives* he treats it as a report or fact (*Pelop.* 21.3 and *Arist.* 9.1–2). On balance, because the reasons Herodotus might exclude it seem more compelling than the possible reasons Phanias might invent it or Plutarch accept it, I would tend to think that it happened. It was a "great and terrible thing," but these were also "great struggles and terrible troubles."

In the course of the battle at Salamis a series of remarkable, miraculous events favored the Greek cause. Herodotus reports that, at the very beginning of the naval battle, when the Greeks were showing a disinclination to fight, "it is said that an apparition of a woman appeared to them. When she appeared, she gave orders so loudly that all the navy of the Greeks heard her. But first she criticized them as follows: 'Gentlemen, how long still do you row your ships backward?'" (8.84.2). Pausanias also tells of the intervention of the hero Cychreus, as a snake. On Salamis "there is a sanctuary of Cychreus. It is said that when the Athenians were fighting against the Medes a snake appeared among the ships. The god in an oracle told the Athenians that this was the hero Cychreus" (1.36.1. Cf. Plut. *Thes.* 10.3).[261] Lastly, Herodotus gives the Athenian version of how the Corinthians were stopped in their flight from the battle:

The Athenians say that Adeimantus, the Corinthian general, right at the beginning, when the ships were just entering battle, lost his wits and was terrified.[262] He raised the sails and went off in flight. When the Corinthians saw their general's ship in flight, they did the same. And when in their flight they were near the sanctuary of Athena Sciras on Salamis, a cursor, by divine escort (θείη πομπῇ), came upon them. No one appeared to have sent it, and it approached the Corinthians when they knew nothing of what was happening with the fleet. And they concluded that the event was divine (θεῖον) in the following way: when the cursor was near their ships, the crewmen from the cursor said, "Adeimantus, you race off, turning your ships to flight and betraying the Greeks. But the Greeks are winning the complete victory over their enemies for which they were praying." When they said this, Adeimantus did not believe them, and so they spoke again: "We ourselves can be taken as hostages, to die if the Greeks do not appear to be winning." And so Adeimantus and the Corinthians reversed course and arrived at the camp to find the action finished. Such is the story about them from the Athenians.[263] The Corinthians themselves, however, do not agree but think that they were in the forefront of the naval battle, and also the rest of Greece attests to that for them. (8.94)

We have thus the mysterious woman appearing to the Greek forces, the hero Cychreus appearing as a snake, and the crew of the mysterious cursor, "by divine escort," giving advice to the Corinthians. Here again, no specific deity, only a hero, is identified aiding the Greeks in person on the battlefield.

The Greeks, led by the Athenian navy, won, of course, a decisive victory in the battle of Salamis. Much of the Persian navy was destroyed or captured, and the remnants fled back toward the Hellespont. There would be more battles for the Greeks to fight, at Plataea by land and at Mycale by sea and by land, but the victory at Salamis was the turning point. Xerxes himself fled back to Persia. The defeat of his navy made it nearly impossible to keep his huge army supplied by sea. The Persian army, under Mardonius' command, would, for a time, retreat from Athens to Boeotia and then would return to Athens with a smaller but still large force of 300,000. It is in planning sessions immediately after the victory at Salamis that Herodotus has Themistocles give to his fellow Athenians this assessment of the victory: "Not we but the gods and heroes accomplished this. They begrudged (ἐφθόνησαν) one man who was unholy and rash (ἀνόσιόν τε καὶ ἀτάσθαλον) to be king of Asia and Europe. He treated holy and profane things alike, burning and throwing to the ground the statues of the gods. He even whipped the sea and hurled leg irons into it" (8.109.3).

This judgment, put by Herodotus into the mouth of the leading Greek of this time, is a critical element in Herodotus' account of the religious aspects of the Persian Wars and requires some detailed attention. In short, Themistocles views the Greek victory as the result of actions by the gods and heroes against the impieties of the Persian king. The king was both "unholy and rash" (ἀνόσιόν τε καὶ ἀτάσθαλον), and the two elements and the specific terms used suggest two somewhat different aspects of "impiety" in the Greek tradition. We have previously described both the archaic, poetic character of ἀτάσθαλος and the popular, cultic nature of ἀνόσιος. Herodotus had previously termed Xerxes' verbal attacks on the Hellespont ἀτάσθαλα (7.34–35, above), and we suggested there that Herodotus framed his description of this signature impiety of Xerxes in literary, not cultic, terms. Here, in Themistocles' verdict, "unholiness" (ἀνοσιότης) and "rashness" (ἀτασθαλίη) are both present, the former indicating, in this context, violation of religious law and traditions, the latter a loss of rational balance leading to reckless behavior. The logic and rhythm of Themistocles' summary suggest that with ἀνοσιότης are associated the desecration of the statues of the gods and with ἀτασθαλίη the whipping and chaining of the Hellespont. If we are not overinterpreting the passage, we have here two levels or two somewhat different conceptual patterns for the interpretation of "religious" matters. The first would be popular, prosaic, and, in a literal sense, mundane: it is "unholy" to rob, burn, and destroy sacred property. The second is more literary, poetic, and theoretical in conceptual terms: that ἀτασθαλίη leads powerful, unrestrained individuals to offend the divine. The former stands at the beginning of a prose tradition that will be continued in Thucydides, Xenophon, and the Attic orators. The latter is at or near the end of a poetic tradition exemplified by Homer and Hesiod. Together they may represent a dichotomy in how Herodotus explained religious matters, a topic we explore later in our general survey of the religious views of Herodotus.

Finally, what the gods felt toward Xerxes for his impieties was *phthonos*, the emotion that results when one's prerogatives are threatened. It is the combination of envy, ill will, self-protectiveness, and begrudgement that we described in connection with the *phthonos* that Artabanus, in his advice to Xerxes, attributed to the gods (7.10.ε, above). There we left open the question whether, for Herodotus, divine *phthonos* is a negative attribute of the gods. Artabanus had warned Xerxes that "the god gives a taste of the sweet life but then is found to be *phthoneros* in it" (7.46.2–4). From the Persian perspective, "the gods," "the god," or "the divine" provided, on the favorable side as it at least initially appeared, help in establishing and expanding their empire (7.8.α.1); the birth, rescue, and success of Cyrus, the founder of the empire (1.118.2, 124.1, 204.2, and 209.4); the downfall of Lydian Croesus and his "enslavement" to Cyrus (1.89.1);[264] a dream to Cambyses revealing a conspiracy against him (3.65.4); and the dreams that induced Xerxes to continue the expedition (7.12–18, above). On the negative side the "divine" would contribute to the defeat at Plataea (9.16.4) and here, in Themistocles' judgment, to the loss at Salamis. "The divine" can thus give both good and evil, success and failure.

In very general terms we have in Herodotus' *Histories* winners (the Greeks) and losers (Lydians and Persians), and Herodotus employs, from the very beginnings of the contest between Greeks and barbarians, Greek religious language and concepts characteristic of his time to explain success (for the Greeks) and failure (for the barbarians). Among the Greeks only the exceptionally successful Polycrates (3.40–43) and the excessively vengeful Pheretima (4.205) are victims of *phthonos*. Elsewhere *phthonos* of the divine assails only non-Greeks, and of them the two who lost the most were Croesus and Xerxes. *Phthonos* is, fundamentally, one of Herodotus' religious explanations for failure, and it is generated in "the divine" either by extraordinary successes (Polycrates and Croesus) or by impiety in the form of a lack of respect for the gods and their property (Xerxes).[265] Herodotus uses it primarily to explain the great Persian losses. For him the Greeks were neither so consistently successful nor so consistently impious as to suffer from the *phthonos* of the divine. And, finally, *phthonos* in Herodotus is attributed only to the divine collective, never to an individual god or hero.[266] It is a product of generalizing thought about "the divine," not of cult or religious practice. It is a religious-moral framework for understanding the failure of the Persian attempt to subjugate the Greeks, from Solon's early, programmatic warning to Croesus to these later reflections of Themistocles on the Greek victory at Salamis. The same *phthonos* that undid the Persians brought success to the Greeks, and thus, from the Greek perspective, the *phthonos* of "the divine" in the Persian Wars was a good thing. That "the divine" could be *phthoneron* need not lead us to think that Herodotus' gods were unjustly or amorally evil, hostile, or malignant.[267] In Herodotus divine *phthonos* could and did serve good purposes: it brought Greeks victory in the decisive battle at Salamis.

After Salamis, as after Marathon, dedications were made to the gods for the victory. Plutarch, who is at great pains to defend the Corinthians against the "Athenian" story of their flight from battle (8.94, above), reports two dedications erected by Corinthians after the victory.[268] "Diodorus was one of the Corinthian trierarchs and had this inscribed on the dedications in the sanctuary of Leto":[269]

> The sailors of Diodorus dedicated to Leto these weapons
> Taken from hostile Medes, as memorials of the sea battle.
> (*Mor.* 870F)

The second is unique in many aspects, a dedication made by the sacred prostitutes at Corinth fulfilling a vow that they had included in their (presumably successful) prayers to their Aphrodite to cast "passion" into Corinthian men for the fight against the Persians:

> The Corinthian women alone of the Greek women prayed that beautiful and remarkable (δαιμόνιον) prayer, that the goddess (Aphrodite) cast into their men a passion (ἐρῶτα) for the battle against the barbarians. . . . This was much talked about, and Simonides (frag. 104 Diehl) wrote an epigram for the bronze statues erected in the temple of Aphrodite, the temple they say Medea founded. . . . This is the epigram:
>
>> These women stand here, after their remarkable vow to Aphrodite on
>>     Behalf of the Greeks and their straight-fighting citizens.
>> Divine Aphrodite did not contrive to betray to the bow-bearing Medes
>>     The acropolis of the Greeks.
>> (*Mor.* 871A–B)

Athenaeus (13.573C–D), citing earlier authorities, provides the background for this dedication:

> As Chamaeleon of Heraclea writes in his *On Pindar*, there is an old custom in Corinth that when the city prays to Aphrodite about great things, as many as possible of the courtesans (τὰς ἑταίρας) participate in the supplication. They too pray to the goddess and later are present at the sacrifices. And when the Persian was leading his expedition against Greece, as Theopompus (*FGrHist* 115 F 285) and Timaeus (566 F 10) write, the Corinthian courtesans went into the temple of Aphrodite and prayed for the safety of the Greeks.

Athenaeus adds that the dedications were paintings (not sculptures) of the women.[270] It may well be relevant to understanding this whole episode that the statue of Aphrodite on Acrocorinth was "armed" (Paus. 2.5.1).

The major dedications of the allied Greeks, however, were made when the fleet had returned to Salamis after punishing Andros and a few other Aegean islands that had Medized, and they are described as follows by Herodotus:

First they selected firstfruits for the gods, other things, and three Phoenician warships—one to dedicate at the Isthmus, which was still there in my time; one for Sunium;[271] and one for Ajax there on Salamis.[272] After this they divided up the booty and sent firstfruits to Delphi, and from those was made a statue (of Apollo) holding the stern ornament of a ship in his hand.[273] It is eighteen feet high and stands where the gold statue of the Macedonian Alexander stands.[274] After the Greeks sent those firstfruits to Delphi, they jointly asked the god if he had received complete and satisfying firstfruits. He said that he had from the other Greeks, but not from the Aeginetans.[275] He was asking from them the prize they had received for excellence in the naval battle at Salamis.[276] When the Aeginetans heard this, they dedicated gold stars, those three stars which are mounted on a bronze mast in the corner of the sanctuary, very close to the crater of Croesus.[277] (8.121–122)

So, after their naval victory at Salamis the Greeks as a group made their dedications of captured ships to Poseidon of the Isthmus, to the Athenian Poseidon whose sanctuary stood nearest to the battlefield, and to the Aeacid hero who resided on the island around which the battle was fought. Then, from the booty taken from the Persians, they dedicated to Apollo of Delphi a statue of himself holding the stern ornament of a Persian ship. In each case the divinity had contributed to the victory, and the form of the dedication is symbolically appropriate.

Plutarch, again in his effort to defend the Corinthian role in the battle of Salamis, gives three of their epitaphs (*Mor.* 870E). The original of one, in Corinthian letters, has been found on Salamis (ML 24 = *IG* I³ 1143):[278]

Stranger, once we lived in the well-watered town of Corinth,
    But now Salamis, the island of Ajax, holds us.
Here we took Phoenician ships and Persians and Medes,
    And we rescued holy Greece.

There was also, according to Plutarch, this inscription on a cenotaph of Corinthians at the Isthmus:

We lie here after having rescued with our lives
All Greece when she stood on the razor's edge.[279]

And, finally, the epitaph of the Corinthian general Adeimantus who was charged by the Athenians with fleeing the battle (Hdt. 8.94, above):

This is the tomb of glorious Adeimantus.
Because of him all Greece put on the crown of freedom.[280]

## ✄ The Battle of Plataea ✄

After the Greek victory at Salamis Xerxes decided to return home to Persia but to leave his general Mardonius in Greece with an army of 300,000 men to attack the Peloponnesus. First, though, Mardonius was to escort Xerxes at least part of the way to the Hellespont. Herodotus relates how, on route, in Thessaly, they encountered a Spartan herald.

An oracle had come from Delphi to the Lacedaemonians, bidding them to ask Xerxes for recompense for the death of Leonidas and to accept whatever Xerxes gave.[281] The Spartiates sent a herald as quickly as possible, and he overtook the Persian army when it was still in Thessaly. He went before Xerxes and said, "King of the Medes, the Lacedaemonians and the descendants of Heracles from Sparta[282] ask you for recompense for murder, because you killed their king when he was protecting Greece." Xerxes laughed and paused a lengthy time. Mardonius happened to be standing at his side, and Xerxes pointed at him and said, "Well, then, Mardonius will pay to them the recompense they ought to have." The herald accepted what Xerxes said and departed.[283] (8.114)

In a few months Mardonius would pay to the Spartans recompense, by his own death and that of hundreds of thousands of his soldiers at Plataea, and in his description of that occasion Herodotus explicitly points to the fulfillment of this oracle (9.64.1, below). Here Herodotus typically, the good storyteller that he is, does not anticipate the fulfillment of the oracle. He makes the reader wait until the fulfilling event. Such is his treatment of most Delphic oracles. By contrast he introduces the oracles of Bacis immediately *after* the events they describe. Events on Euboea (8.20, above) and off Mounichia of Attica (8.77, above) are referred to Bacis' oracles, but simultaneously and retrospectively. The explanation may be that Bacis' oracles had been around for years in oracle collections and the original circumstances in which they were given were unknown. Only later would they be associated with the events by the *chresmologoi* who were expert in such collections. The Delphi oracles, however, were being given as events unfolded and each had a historical occasion of its own.[284] Herodotus perhaps wished to preserve for Delphic oracles the occasion of both the oracle and its fulfillment and not diminish the significance of the former by combining it with the latter, or to put out of its historical place the latter by combining it with the former. Herodotus' treatment of the Delphic oracles also, of course, creates the suspense and anticipation — since all knew these oracles would come true — essential to good storytelling.

Artabazus, another Persian general, with 60,000 men took up Mardonius' role of escort and delivered Xerxes safely to the Hellespont. On his leisurely return to Mardonius, Artabazus decided to attack and re-subjugate the Potidaeans who had revolted from the Persians after the battle of Salamis,[285] and Herodotus in his description of the results offers one of his strongest assertions of miraculous divine assistance to the Greeks:

When Artabazus had been besieging Potidaea for three months, a great and long-lasting ebb tide occurred. The barbarians saw that the sea had become just a lagoon there and began crossing it. When two-fifths of them had crossed and three-fifths (who were supposed to cross over and get into the city) remained behind, a great flood tide occurred, a tide the size of which, as the natives say, seldom is seen. The barbarians who did not know how to swim perished, and the Potidaeans sailed up to the others in boats and killed them. The Potidaeans say the cause of the tide and of the Persian loss was that those Persians who were killed by the sea had committed an impiety (ἠσέβησαν) against the temple and statue of Poseidon in the suburbs of the city. When they give this as the cause they seem to me to be right. Artabazus led the survivors back to Thessaly to Mardonius. (8.129)

As Apollo had miraculously defended his sanctuary at Delphi (8.35–39, above), so here the Potidaeans and Herodotus are convinced that Poseidon miraculously avenged impieties committed against his sanctuary. Again the Persians commit impieties against a Greek sanctuary and are punished for it.

While Mardonius was wintering in Thessaly with his Persian army, he consulted Greek oracles in the general region, probably wishing, according to Herodotus, to understand better the present circumstances:

He sent to the oracles a man of Europus, Mys by name, and he ordered him to use every oracle he could try anywhere. I cannot say why Mardonius ordered this and what he wished to learn from the oracles. That is nowhere said. But I think he sent him to learn about the current situation and nothing else. This Mys appears to have come to Lebadea and, after bribing one of the locals, to have gone down to Trophonius.[286] He also went to Abae of the Phocians, to the oracle. And when he went to Thebes he first inquired of Ismenian Apollo—it is possible to divine there from the sacrificial victims, just as at Olympia[287]—and there he persuaded a foreigner (and not a Theban) with money and slept in the sanctuary of Amphiaraus. . . .[288] And then the Thebans tell what is the greatest marvel to me. As the Europan Mys toured all the oracles, he came also to the sanctuary of Apollo Ptoös. This sanctuary is called Ptoön.[289] It belongs to the Thebans, but lies above the Copaic Lake, on the mountain very near the city Acraephia. When Mys went into this sanctuary, three select local citizens from the community followed him to write down what the god would prophesy. But the prophet straightway spoke in a foreign language! The attendants of the Thebans were astonished when they heard a foreign language instead of Greek, and they did not know how to cope with the situation. But the Europan Mys snatched from them the tablet they were carrying and wrote on it what was being said by the prophet. Mys said the prophet was speaking Carian! He wrote the prophecy down and went back to Thessaly.[290]

Mardonius pondered what the oracles were saying and afterward sent as a messenger to Athens Alexander, son of Amyntas, a Macedonian. . . . Mardonius thought he would in this way win over the Athenians. He had heard that they were a populous and valorous people, and he knew that they especially had caused the misfortunes that had happened to the Persians at sea. He was hoping that, if they joined him, he would easily control the sea—which would have happened—and he thought he was much stronger on land. And so he reasoned that he would be superior to the Greeks. But perhaps also the oracles were prophesying this to him, advising him to make the Athenians his ally. And trusting in the oracles he sent Alexander to Athens. (8.133–136)

That Mardonius should consult available Greek oracles is not surprising because, as we have seen, Datis made offerings at Delos (Hdt. 6.97–98, above), Xerxes made sacrifices to gods and heroes at Troy (7.43, above), and the Persians appealed to Thetis to stop the winds at Artemisium (7.191.2–192, above). Delphi is not on Mardonius' list for obvious reasons, given the previous unsuccessful Persian assault on the sanctuary

(8.35–39, above), and one wonders what reception his emissary received at Abae, which, just months before, had been burned and robbed by the Persians (8.32.2–33, above). It is of interest but probably not significant that Mardonius consulted two of the oracles that had failed Croesus' test of oracles (1.46–49), that of Trophonius and that at Abae. Herodotus can only guess why Mardonius turned to these oracles and what he learned. Elsewhere in his account of these invasions Herodotus has no Greek god or oracle give any help to the Persians, and the most that he grants here is the possibility that the oracles recommended that the Persians try to win the support of the Athenians, an attempt that proved to be futile.

At Mardonius' request the Macedonian king Alexander went directly to Athens, and Herodotus has him report to the Athenians Mardonius' own words:

A message has come to me from King Xerxes, saying as follows, "For the Athenians I forgive all their sins (ἀμαρτάδας) against me. Now, Mardonius, do this: give back to them their land, and let them choose another land in addition to theirs, whatever land they wish. And let them be autonomous. If they are willing to come to terms with me, restore all their sanctuaries which I burned."[291] (8.140.α.2)

So Herodotus had Xerxes, through Mardonius and the Macedonian Alexander, promise Athens, with an emphasis on restoration of the sanctuaries. Alexander thought that Xerxes' "power was beyond that of a human being," and urged the Athenians to accept the terms (8.140.β.2). The Athenians replied to Alexander,

Announce to Mardonius that the Athenians say that as long as the sun goes on its current path we will never come to terms with Xerxes. In our defense we will attack him, trusting in the gods and heroes as our allies, the god and heroes for whom Xerxes had no respect and whose buildings and statues he burned. (8.143.2)

The Spartans had previously gotten wind of what Mardonius would offer the Athenians, and they were frightened because "they remembered oracles that they and the other Dorians must be expelled from the Peloponnesus by Medes and Athenians."[292] They therefore had sent ambassadors to be present when Alexander conveyed the Persian proposals (8.141.1). To the Spartans the Athenians offered this reassurance:

Many great things prevent us from doing this, even if we want to. First and greatest are the statues and buildings of the gods that have been burned and destroyed. We must, to the greatest extent possible, avenge these rather than come to terms with the one who did these things. Second is "our Greekness" (τὸ Ἑλληνικόν), being of the same blood and language, and with shared sanctuaries of the gods, sacrifices, and similar customs. It would not be good for Athenians to become traitors of these.[293] (8.144.2)

Somewhat later the Athenians phrased these concerns a little differently: "We did not accept (Xerxes' offer) because we respected (αἰδεσθέντας) Zeus Hellenios and we thought it a terrible thing to betray Greece" (9.7.α.2). And finally, according to Plutarch, the Athenians sealed their decision to reject Mardonius' offer with this curse proposed by the Athenian statesman Aristides:

"As long as the sun continues on its course, the Athenians will fight the Persians because of their devastated land and because of the sanctuaries that have been impiously treated and burned." And, in addition, Aristides proposed that the priests put curses on any man who made peace overtures to the Medes or abandoned the alliance of the Greeks. (*Arist.* 10.5–6)

These Athenian responses to Mardonius' offer of reconciliation, virtually identical on four separate occasions, from two different ancient sources, effectively reprise the critical elements of Themistocles' evaluation of the victory at Salamis (8.109, above): the Athenians trusted in the gods and heroes as their allies, and by burning their sanctuaries and statues Xerxes had shown no respect for these gods and heroes. The Athenians could never come to terms with the perpetrator of such impieties. Rather, they must avenge them. First and foremost in their decision, as represented by Herodotus, were their religious concerns. Second to their private religious concerns was their unwillingness to betray all that was Greek, but in "Greekness" too lay religious elements: common sanctuaries and sacrifices and Zeus Hellenios, the Zeus common to all Greeks.[294]

With Mardonius still in Thessaly the Athenians asked the Spartans to send an army so that together they might meet Mardonius in battle in Boeotia. The Spartans were slow in coming, however, as they had been at Marathon (6.106.3–107.1, above) and again because of a religious festival. They were, according to Herodotus, "celebrating a festival—it was the Hyacinthia—and they thought it most important to perform the rites of the god" (9.7.1).[295] That and the completion of the wall across the Isthmus of Corinth were foremost in the Spartans' minds now, and they even put off for ten days Athenian messengers pleading for help. By then Mardonius had reoccupied Attica, and the Athenians were expecting the battle to be in Attica. At last the Spartans realized that without the Athenian navy their wall across the Isthmus would be of little use, and they sent 5,000 Spartiates and 35,000 helots.[296] The Spartans and other Peloponnesians united forces at the Isthmus, where the omens were good, as they were also when the combined army reached Eleusis (9.19.2).

In the midst of these events Mardonius made a brief incursion into the Megarid (Hdt. 9.14), and Pausanias reports Artemis' assistance to the Megarians against part of Mardonius' force:

They say that men of Mardonius' army, after they had made an incursion into the Megarid, wanted to return back to Mardonius in Thebes, but, by Artemis' plan, night came upon them as they were traveling. They missed the road and turned into a mountainous area. They shot some arrows, testing to see if an enemy army was nearby. The nearby cliff, when hit, groaned, and the Persians shot their arrows again with more eagerness. In the end they used up their arrows, thinking they were shooting at the enemy. Day then appeared, and the Megarians attacked. Because they were fighting armed against those who were unarmed and did not have a supply of arrows, they killed most of the Persians. And because of this the Megarians made a statue of Artemis Soteira ("Savior"). Strongylion made this Artemis.[297] (1.40.2–3)

Herodotus describes how Mardonius, when he learned that the Peloponnesian forces were approaching, retreated from Athens toward Boeotia, but only "after burning Athens and razing and destroying any still-standing piece of the walls, of the buildings, or of the sanctuaries" (9.13.2).[298] Pausanias describes how some Persians committed sacrilege against even a shrine of their Boeotian allies and then paid the penalty for it: "Of those of Xerxes' expedition who were left behind in Boeotia with Mardonius, some went into the sanctuary of the Cabiri, probably in the hopes of finding great wealth, but more, I think, in disrespect toward the divine. These men immediately went mad and perished by hurling themselves into the sea or down from the cliffs" (9.25.9).[299]

Various sources report a series of oaths and vows that the allied Greeks and the Athenians swore in the weeks and days before the great land battle against the Persians at Plataea. According to Diodorus (11.29.1),

"[T]he counselors of the Greeks decided to help the Athenians, to go with all their forces to Plataea to fight for freedom (ἐλευθερίας), and to vow to the gods that if they won the Greeks would celebrate together on that day each year the Eleutheria and would hold the agonistic games of Freedom (τὸν ἐλευθέριον ἀγῶνα) in Plataea"—a vow they fulfilled after the Greek victory at Plataea (Plut. *Arist.* 21.1, below).

A fourth-century Athenian inscription records what appears to be an Athenian version of an oath which all the Greek allies swore at Plataea before the hostilities with the Persians began:

The oath that the Athenians swore
when they were going to fight against the barbarians.

"I will fight as long as I live, and I will not make living more important than being free (ἐλεύθερος). I will not abandon my *taxiarchos* or *enomotarchos*[300] when he is living or dead, and I will not leave unless the leaders lead the way, and I will do whatever the generals order. I will bury those who die fighting with me as allies in the same place, and I will leave no one unburied. When I have defeated the barbarians in battle, I will 'tithe' the city of Thebes,[301] and I will not uproot Athens, Sparta, Plataea, or any of the other cities that fought with me as an ally. Nor will I overlook it when they are being held by famine, nor will I restrict the free flow of their water whether they are friends or enemies in war. If I keep the provisions in this oath, may my city be free from disease; if I do not, may it have disease. If I keep this oath, may my city be unsacked; if not, may it be sacked. If I keep this oath, may my city be fruitful; if not, may it be unfruitful. If I keep this oath, may the women bear offspring like their parents; if not, may they bear monsters. If I keep this oath, may the herd animals bear offspring like herd animals; if not, may they bear monsters." After swearing these things, they covered the sacrificial victims with their shields and, at the sound of the trumpet, made a curse that, if they transgressed any of the things sworn and did not keep the things written in the oath, pollution should come upon those themselves who swore the oath.

Lycurgus (*Leoc.* 80–81) and Diodorus (11.29.2–4) summarize this oath, but add one further provision: "Nor will I rebuild any of the sanctuaries that have been burned and razed, but I will leave them as a memorial for our descendants and as a memorial of the impiety of the barbarians." Finally, Pausanias (10.35.2) describes some ruined buildings that remained in his time, nearly 700 years later, as the result of these oaths not to rebuild sanctuaries destroyed by the Persians: "Those of the Greeks who opposed the barbarian decided not to restore the sanctuaries that were burned down but to leave them for all time as memorials of their hatred. And for this reason the temples in the land of Haliartus and, for the Athenians, the temple of Hera on the Phaleron road and the temple of Demeter at Phaleron still remain half burned even in my time."[302]

Scholarly controversy has surrounded the historicity of each of these oaths. For the vow promising the establishment of the Eleutheria festival and its games as reported by Diodorus, the difficulty is that the games are not attested until the fourth century.[303] The Athenian oath, one of the fullest and most solemn surviving from antiquity, is questioned especially because it was denounced as a forgery by the fourth-century historian Theopompus of Chios (*FGrHist* 115 F 153). It also, like the equally disputed decree of Themistocles on the evacuation of Athens, first appears relatively late, this one on a fourth-century inscription. Several scholars have accepted Theopompus' verdict, but others have offered strong support of the oath's historicity.[304] But even Siewert, the strongest defender of the Athenian oath, rejects as a genuine provision of the Athenian oath the promise not to rebuild the sanctuaries, as reported by Lycurgus and Diodorus.[305] But archaeologists in particular emphasize how well it serves to explain why the Athenians waited so long to rebuild sanctuaries on the Acropolis in the decades after the Persian destruction. To them, if such an oath were not recorded, one would have to hypothesize something like it to understand later Athenian building policy.[306]

There are no sure answers to the various questions about these oaths, but, as we will see below, the Eleutheria and its games may in fact have been celebrated immediately after the victory at Plataea. And, in terms of religious history, it is clear from the inscription and from Lycurgus that Athenians in the fourth century at least accepted the Athenian "oath of Plataea" as one taken by their ancestors, as did later sources such as Diodorus and Pausanias. The solemnity and language of that oath certainly suit the historical crisis and desperation of the times before Plataea, and the provision not to rebuild the sanctuaries echoes the vow Isocrates attributes to the Ionians under similar circumstances (4.156, above). It may offer the best explanation why the Athenians waited so long after the war to rebuild their major religious monuments on the Acropolis. If one accepts these oaths as genuine, they offer not only a valuable supplement to Herodotus' religious account of the events surrounding the battle of Plataea but also striking instances of the correlation between, on the one hand, a vow and the establishment of a festival and, on the other, an oath and later public policy. If not genuine, they at least reveal how Athenians and Greeks of the fourth century and later viewed these events.

For Herodotus and Plutarch religious events were also decisive in determining both the place and the timing of the Plataean battle itself. The massive Greek (110,000 men) and Persian (300,000+) armies took up positions facing one another, on opposite banks of the Asopus River.[307] Herodotus reports the activities of the *manteis*: "There, on the second day, both sides were making sacrifices" (9.33.1). Tisamenus, an Iamid from Elis,[308] a man whom Delphi had said would win five of the greatest contests,[309] served as *mantis* for the allied Greeks. "For the Greeks (the omens of) the sacrifices were good if they defended themselves, but not if they crossed the Asopus and began the battle. Mardonius was eager to begin battle, but (the omens of) the sacrifices were not suitable, although they were good for him too if he only defended himself. Mardonius was using Greek sacrifices, and he had as his *mantis* Hegesistratus, also an Elean, a leading Telliad,"[310] a man who had been badly treated by the Spartans and was also looking to earn some money. The Greeks fighting on the Persian side had their own *mantis*, Hippomachus of Leucas, and for them too the omens were bad for beginning the battle (9.36– 38). And so the Greeks and Persians waited—for ten days. Then, on the eleventh, Mardonius decided to begin the battle as soon as possible, before more Greeks gathered against him. He chose "to dismiss the sacrifices of Hegesistratus and not to try to force well-omened ones, but to use the Persian way and to fight" (9.41.4).[311] When he reached this decision,

Mardonius sent for the commanders of his companies and the generals of the Greeks fighting on his side. He asked them if they knew of any oracle that the Persians would perish in Greece. Those summoned kept quiet, some because they did not know the oracles. Others knew them well but were afraid to speak. Then Mardonius said, "Since you either do not know of any or do not have the courage to speak, I, knowing this well, will speak. There is an oracle that it is necessary for the Persians to come to Greece, to pillage the sanctuary in Delphi, and then after the pillaging, for all to perish. We know this, and therefore will not go to the sanctuary or attempt to pillage it, and we will not perish for this reason.[312] And so rejoice, all of you who are well intentioned to the Persians, because we will overcome the Greeks." After he had said this, he bid them a second time to ready and arrange everything because the attack would take place at dawn the next day. (9.42)

At this point Herodotus intervenes in his own narrative, pointing to Mardonius' mistaken interpretation of the oracle and giving an oracle of Bacis, which did in fact refer to the battle at Plataea:

I know that this oracle, which Mardonius said referred to the Persians, really was made in reference to the Illyrians and the expedition of the Encheledae,[313] not to the Persians. But there are lines referring to this battle (at Plataea) written by Bacis:

> The gathering of the Greeks and the barbarian-sounding wailing
> At the Thermodon and the grassy Asopus,[314]
> Here many of the bow-bearing Medes will die
> Beyond their lot and time, when the destined day comes.

I know that there are these lines and other similar ones of Musaeus relating to the Persians. (9.43)

Mardonius has, at this critical juncture in the action, committed two grave errors: he has disregarded the battle omens reported by his *mantis* and, as Herodotus takes pains to explain, misinterpreted an oracle.

By contrast, the gods were giving, through an oracle and a dream, their assistance to the Greeks, who were heeding both, as in fact they heeded their *manteis*. Plutarch reports that, just before the battle, the Athenian Aristides sent a last-minute question to the oracle:

After Aristides sent to Delphi, the god responded that the Athenians would defeat their enemy if they prayed to Zeus, Hera Cithaironia, Pan and the Sphragitid Nymphs, and if they sacrificed to the heroes Androcrates, Leucon, Pisander, Damocrates, Hypsion, Actaeon, Polyidus,[315] and if they fought the battle in their own land, in the plain of Demeter Eleusinia and Kore.[316] When this oracle came, it caused difficulty for Aristides. The heroes to whom the god bid him to sacrifice were founding heroes (ἀρχηγέται) of the Plataeans, and the cave of the Sphragitid Nymphs is on a peak of Cithaeron, facing the west. . . .[317] But the plain of Demeter Eleusinia and the statement that the Athenians were granted victory if they fought in their own land called them back to Attica and were changing the place of the war. At this time Arimnestus, the general of the Plataeans, thought that in a dream he was asked by Zeus Soter what the Greeks had decided to do. He responded, "Master, tomorrow we will lead the army away to Eleusis, and we will fight the barbarians there in accordance with the oracle." Then Zeus said that the Greeks missed the whole point; the places prophesied were there around Plataea, and if they investigated they would discover it to be so. After this dream had appeared clearly to Arimnestus, he awoke and very quickly summoned the eldest and most experienced of his citizens. Discussing the matter with them and sharing his difficulties, he discovered that at the foot of Cithaeron near Hysiae there was a very old temple said to be of Demeter Eleusinia and Kore.[318] Straightway he took Aristides and led him to the place, a place most suitable for those inferior in cavalry to array an infantry force, because the foothills of Cithaeron made the edges of the plain and the part next to the sanctuary unfit for horses. Near to it was also the heroön of Androcrates, encircled by a grove of thick, shady trees.[319] And so that the oracle might lack nothing concerning the hope of victory, Arimnestus proposed and the Plataeans voted to take up their boundary stones on the side of their country toward Attica and to give the land to the Athenians. And so the Athenians could fight on their own land for Greece's sake in accordance with the oracle.[320] (*Arist.* 11.3–8)

By combining Herodotus' account of the oracles and the warnings of the *manteis* and Plutarch's account of Aristides' oracle and Arimnestus' dream, we have an exceptionally clear contrast between Persian and Greek dealings with the divine on one important occasion. While Mardonius, the sacker of sanctuaries, rejects his *mantis*' advice and misinterprets an oracle, the Athenian Aristides receives a puzzling oracle from Apollo and Arimnestus, the Plataean hero of Marathon (Paus. 9.4.1–2, above), receives a helpful dream from Zeus Soter. Then the two statesmen, with the help of local citizens, thoughtfully and carefully work out the solution and, in addition, do what must be done to bring the oracle to fulfillment. The gods help the Greeks here, but wise and wary Greeks use their skills to make that help a reality.

After various maneuvers Mardonius did in fact lead his army across the Asopus first (Hdt. 9.59.1). Herodotus tells how the Spartans, as they were about to enter into combat against the Persians opposite them, made the usual prebattle sacrifice: "But the victims were not good for them." As his soldiers were being killed and wounded by Persian arrows, the Spartan general Pausanias "looked toward the Plataean Heraion and invoked the goddess, asking that the Spartans not be deprived of what they hoped for.[321] As he was making this invocation, the Tegeans led the way and attacked the barbarians, and immediately after Pausanias' prayer the victims became good for the Spartans as they sacrificed," and they too joined the assault on the Persians (9.61.3–62.1). And in the fierce battle that ensued near the sanctuary of Demeter, the Spartans and Tegeans killed Mardonius and routed the Persians. Plutarch offers a more detailed and graphic account of this same episode.[322]

When Pausanias was sacrificing and not obtaining favorable omens, he ordered the Lacedaemonians to put their shields down before their feet, to sit quietly, and to pay attention to him. They were not to fight off the enemy. Pausanias himself again sought favorable omens, and the Persian cavalry was attacking. And now a missile reached them and one of the Spartiates was hit. . . . The suffering was terrible, and the self-restraint of the men was astounding. They did not fight off the enemy, but despite being pelted and falling in the ranks they awaited the right moment from the god and their general. Some say that Pausanias was a little distant from the line of battle, sacrificing and praying. Some Lydians attacked him suddenly and scattered the sacrificial implements. Pausanias and those with him did not have weapons, but struck the attackers with staffs and whips. And for this reason still even now are performed, as remembrances of that assault, the whippings of the ephebes around the altar in Sparta, followed by a procession of the Lydians. Pausanias was much distressed by the situation, and while the *mantis* was killing one sacrificial victim after another, Pausanias in tears turned his gaze toward the Heraion. He raised his hands and prayed to Hera Cithaironia and other gods who held the Plataean land, that if it was not destined for the Greeks to win, they at least grant them to suffer after they had accomplished something and, by their action, had shown to the enemy that they campaigned against good men who knew how to fight. As Pausanias was calling on the gods, at the same moment as his prayer, the omens appeared good and the *mantis* announced victory. (*Arist.* 17.6–18.2)

To Herodotus "it is a marvel that although they were fighting alongside the grove of (Eleusinian) Demeter, not even one of the Persians appeared to have gone into the sanctuary or to have died there. Most fell in the profane area around the sanctuary. And I think—if it is necessary to 'think' (δοκέειν) anything about divine actions (περὶ τῶν θείων πρηγμάτων)[323]— that the goddess herself was not taking them in because they had burned the *anaktoron* in Eleusis" (9.65.2).[324]

These various "religious" episodes at the beginning and in the course of the battle at Plataea—the taking of battlefield omens by the *manteis*, the appeal to Delphi for assistance, and the sacrifices and appeals to Plataean deities and heroes—are firmly grounded in cultic conventions and in local Plataean deities and sanctuaries. All rings true to a historian of Greek religion, and it is highly improbable that Herodotus, Plutarch, or their sources concocted such accounts out of thin air. The account may have been later dramatized, as in Plutarch, but many of the heroes were local, known previously only to Plataeans, and the gods involved are linked to real Plataean sanctuaries. The overall effect is more than one of verisimilitude; it is that such events actually happened and were thought by Plataeans and other Greeks to have affected the course of the action of this critical battle. Again we find the gods helping the Greeks with an oracle and a dream, answering a prayer for a Greek, and then taking vengeance on the Persians for burning a sanctuary. Finally, we note, too, that on the battlefield the *manteis* for all three parties, for the Persians, for the Greeks, and for the Greeks allied with the Persians, proved accurate in Herodotus' account.

The victory of the Greek forces over the Persians and their allies at Plataea was complete. If we can believe Herodotus here, more than 230,000 of the barbarian troops were killed. To Herodotus Mardonius' death fulfilled the oracle given to the Spartans that told them to ask Xerxes for recompense for the death of Leonidas and to accept whatever Xerxes gave. Xerxes, as we saw, said that Mardonius would pay this recompense (8.114, above). Herodotus then elaborates this account to have Pausanias, the Spartan commander, elegantly contrast Greek and particularly Spartan behavior in these matters to impious, unholy, and rash (ἀτάσθαλα) acts of the Persians. "Now, according to the oracle, the Spartiates exacted justice from Mardonius for the death of Leonidas, and Pausanias, son of Cleombrotus, grandson of Anaxandrides, won the finest of all victories we know" (9.64.1). But Lampon of Aegina wanted more vengeance for Leonidas, and proposed to Pausanias

a most unholy plan. In great seriousness Lampon said the following to Pausanias: "You have accomplished a deed extraordinary in its size and beauty, and god (θεός) has granted you, in protecting Greece, to win the greatest fame of the Greeks whom we know.[325] And now do what remains so that you may have an even greater fame and so that hereafter no barbarian will do rash acts (ἔργα ἀτάσθαλα) against the Greeks. When Leonidas died at Thermopylae, Mardonius and Xerxes cut off his head and impaled it on a pike (Hdt. 7.238, above). If you give a similar punishment to Mardonius, you will be praised, first of all by all the Spartiates, and then also by the other Greeks. For by impaling Mardonius you will be avenging your uncle Leonidas." Lampon was saying this, thinking he was winning favor. But Pausanias answered with such words: "Aeginetan friend, I admire you for being well intentioned and looking to my interests, but now you do not have a good idea. You raised high me, my country, and my deed, but you cast them down into nothingness when you advised me to mutilate a corpse and when you say that, if

I do these things, I will have a better reputation. It is fitting for barbarians more than for Greeks to do these things, and we loathe those barbarians. Let me not, for this, please the Aeginetans or others who like these things. I am content to please the Spartiates, to do holy things and to say holy things. I say that Leonidas, whom you bid me to avenge, has been greatly avenged. He and the others who died at Thermopylae have been honored by the countless lives (of the barbarians who died here)."[326] (9.78–79)

In their total victory over the Persians the allied Greeks took the Persian camp and acquired vast amounts of war booty, and, as after the battles of Marathon and Salamis, they dedicated a portion of this to the gods, some in the sanctuaries of their homelands and some in the international religious centers. In the early stages of the battle the Tegeans had captured the richly furnished tent of Mardonius. They took "the other things from it and the manger of the horses, the manger that was solid bronze and worth seeing. The Tegeans dedicated Mardonius' manger at the temple of Alea Athena (in Tegea),[327] and the other things they captured they collected into one place for the Greeks" (Hdt. 9.70.3).

Pausanias, commander in chief of the Greek forces, had the helots collect the rest of the immense booty from the battlefield and the Persian camp. What the helots did not steal and sell (mostly to the Aeginetans) was distributed. From this booty the Greeks made their joint dedications to the Panhellenic deities who had helped them in driving the Persians from Greece. According to Herodotus, the Greeks

set aside a tithe for the god in Delphi, and from this was dedicated the gold tripod on the bronze three-headed snake which stands near the altar.[328] They set aside a portion also for the god in Olympia, and from it they dedicated a bronze Zeus, fifteen feet tall. And there was a portion for the god at the Isthmus, and from it came a ten and one-half foot bronze Poseidon.[329] After they had set these aside, they divided the rest of the booty and each contingent received what it deserved, including the concubines of the Persians, the gold, silver, other property, and the pack animals. (9.81.1)

Nothing more is known of the bronze Poseidon at Isthmia, but the dedication of the gold tripod at Delphi caused an uproar.[330] According to Thucydides (1.132.2–3) and Plutarch (*Mor.* 873C–D), the Greek commander Pausanias had the Delphic gold tripod inscribed as follows:

Pausanias, commander of the Greeks, after he destroyed the army
Of the Medes, dedicated this memorial to Phoebos.[331]

Other Greek cities protested, no doubt because Pausanias was apparently laying personal claim to the victory and dedication, and the Spartans had the monument reinscribed. Its new text, according to Diodorus (11.33.2), was,

The saviors of Greece with its broad dance floors dedicated this,
  After they saved their cities from hateful slavery.[332]

The names of the thirty-one cities that contributed to the war effort were inscribed on the coils of the three intertwined snakes, including first Sparta, second Athens, third Corinth, then the others.[333] Seven hundred years later the bronze snake-stand still stood in Delphi, but the gold tripod had been carried off by the Phocians in the Third Sacred War of 357–346 (Paus. 10.13.9). Today the three intertwined bronze snakes, with the inscribed names of the Greek allies, may be seen in the Hippodrome in Istanbul. The bronze statue of Zeus at Olympia was attributed to the sculptor Anaxagoras of Aegina, and its dedicatory inscription also recorded the allied Greek cities, a list very similar to that on the gold tripod at Delphi. The statue faced east, perhaps toward the defeated enemy (Paus. 5.23.1–3).[334]

The contributions of Apollo and Poseidon to the war effort against the Persians are by now obvious, and the following perhaps explains Zeus' presence among the three Panhellenic divine champions honored by the joint Greek dedications. As we have seen, before the battle at Plataea the Greeks had vowed "to the gods that if they won the Greeks would celebrate together on that day each year the Eleutheria and would hold the agonistic games of Freedom in Plataea" (D.S. 11.29.1, above). We learn the rest of the story of the founding of Zeus' Eleutheria from Plutarch's life of Aristides: after the battle, in a general assembly of the Greeks, the Athenian statesman

Aristides proposed that each year counselors and *theoroi* from Greece come together to Plataea and that they hold the quadrennial games of the Eleutheria . . . and that the Plataeans be left inviolable and sacred as they sacrificed to the god for Greece.[335] (21.1. Cf. Thuc. 2.71–74)

When the Greeks asked about the sacrifice, the Pythian god responded that they should found an altar of Zeus Eleutherios, but they should not sacrifice until they had quenched the fire throughout the land because it was polluted by the barbarians. They should kindle pure fire from Delphi, the common hearth (of all Greeks).[336] The rulers of the Greeks then went out immediately and were compelling those using fires to quench all of them. Euchidas, one of the Plataeans, went to Delphi, promising that as quickly as possible he would bring the fire from the god. At Delphi he purified his body and sprinkled it with holy water and put on a crown of laurel. He took the fire from the altar and ran back to Plataea. He arrived back before sunset on the same day, having traveled 125 miles. After greeting his fellow citizens and handing over the fire, he straightway collapsed and shortly died. The Plataeans in their admiration for him buried him in the sanctuary of Artemis Eukleia[337] and wrote this on his tomb: "Euchidas ran to Delphi and back on the same day." (20.4–5)

The new altar of Zeus was inscribed as follows:

The Greeks, after driving away the Persians
By the power of Nike and the work of Ares,
Founded for a free Greece (ἐλευθέρᾳ Ἑλλάδι)
This common altar of Zeus Eleutherios.[338]

They fought this battle on Boedromion 4 according to the Athenian calendar . . . , and on this day still now the Greek assembly gathers in Plataea and the Plataeans sacrifice to Zeus Eleutherios for the victory.[339] (19.6–7)

Pausanias reports that both the statue and altar of Zeus Eleutherios were marble and that the Eleutheria featured foot races in armor (9.2.5–6).[340]

In a simple sense the cult of Zeus Eleutherios and his festival the Eleutheria were founded as the fulfillment of a vow.[341] The Greeks promised to Zeus the essentials of the cult and festival if they should win. They did win, and Aristides proposed and the Greeks accepted the fulfillment of that vow. The festival was an occasion of prayer and sacrifice, and the prayers and sacrifices the Plataeans made were, in Plutarch's words, "for Greece" (ὑπὲρ τῆς Ἑλλάδος, *Arist.* 21.1) or "for the victory" (ὑπὲρ τῆς νίκης, 19.7). "The victory" clearly looks backward and suggests commemoration and gratitude.[342] So may "Greece" here. Nothing in the descriptions indicates that Zeus Eleutherios is henceforth to be worshiped as a promoter, in the future, of "freedom" or "victory" or even "Greece." The festival appears primarily commemorative, and in this regard it is characteristic of other festivals whose foundation Herodotus describes. During the rule of the Corinthian tyrant Periander (ca. 627–587), the Samians created a new *heorte* for their Artemis:

Periander, the son of Cypselus, was sending to Alyattes in Sardis 300 children of leading Corcyraeans to be castrated. When the Corinthians taking the children put in at Samos, the Samians learned the reason why the children were being taken to Sardis. They first instructed the children to "lay hold of the sanctuary of Artemis," and afterward did not allow the Corinthians to drag the suppliants from the sanctuary. When the Corinthians tried to keep food from the children, the Samians created (ἐποιήσαντο) a festival (ὁρτήν), which they still now hold in the same way.[343] (3.48.2–3)

Again without denying other religious aspects of these festivals, we see a primary emphasis in Herodotus on the commemorative nature of these festivals, and this is also very apparent in the founding of the Eleutheria after Plataea.[344] Festivals whose origins we best know appear in some good part commemorative, and, apart from their origins, this is important in understanding the purposes for which and the celebratory mood in which Greeks held them. These festivals termed *heortai* were, of course, religious occasions with solemn moments of sacrifice and prayer, but they were also characterized by a joyful atmosphere, in most cases with dancing, singing, eating, drinking, and partying.[345] In Herodotus' *Histories* women wore their finest clothes to a Hera festival in Corinth (5.92.η.1–4), feasted at her festival in the Argive Heraion (1.31. Cf. 3.48), and danced at the festival of Damia and Auxesia on Aegina (5.83.2–3, above). The Athenians, before Plataea, complained that the Spartans were "playing" (παίζετε) at the Hyacinthia when there was a war to be fought (9.11.1. Cf. Plut. *Arist.* 10.7). Such no doubt was the atmosphere of the new Eleutheria for Zeus, a festival that commemorated and celebrated the great victory over the Persians at Plataea.

When after the battle the Spartans and Athenians were vigorously contending for the "best warriors" prize of the battle, a Corinthian found the solution, and the result was a windfall for the Plataeans.[346] Plutarch reports that the Corinthian

made a proposal that pleased and surprised all, on behalf of the Plataeans. He advised that the Greeks eliminate the contention by giving the prize to the Plataeans, and that neither the Spartans nor Athenians be angered that the Plataeans were being honored. And when this was proposed, Aristides first yielded for the Athenians and then Pausanias for the Lacedaemonians. And so, reconciled, they set aside eighty talents ($48 million) for the Plataeans, and with that money the Plataeans rebuilt their sanctuary of Athena, erected a statue, and adorned the temple with paintings. The paintings remain, up to now, in top condition. And the Lacedaemonians and Athenians, separately and privately, set up trophies.[347] (*Arist.* 20.2–3)

If we combine the report we saw earlier from Pausanias (9.4.1–2, above) with this account from Plutarch, we may, in fact, have a rather complete history of this Plataean sanctuary in its early times. It was probably originally founded as a victory dedication from the spoils of Marathon after 490, destroyed by the Persians in the invasion of 480, and now rebuilt, again as victory dedication, with spoils from Plataea. The new statue in the rebuilt sanctuary Plutarch describes may well be Phidias' gilded statue of Athena Areia, which Pausanias views as a dedication from the victory at Marathon. Plataea had the honor, if that is the right word, of being a principal in the battles of both Marathon and Plataea, and the history of the Plataean Athena Areia cult reflects the complexities of that dual involvement.

As they had after the battle of Marathon, after the battle of Plataea the Athenians apparently dedicated gold shields at Delphi. They are first mentioned in the mid-fourth century by Aeschines, and he gives the dedicatory inscription (3.116):

The Athenians, from the Medes and Thebans
When they were fighting against the Greeks.[348]

Themistocles, according to Pausanias, was remarkably unsuccessful in making what apparently was a private dedication at Delphi to celebrate the victory:

It is said that Themistocles arrived at Delphi bringing some Persian spoils for Apollo. He asked if he should place the dedications inside the temple, but the Pythia ordered him to take them entirely out of the sanctuary. So this part of the oracle goes:[349]

Do not deposit the very beautiful Persian spoils in my temple.
Send them back home as quickly as possible.

I was surprised that the Pythia thought it unworthy to accept Persian spoils from only Themistocles. Some believed that Apollo would similarly have rejected all spoils from the Persian if others, like Themistocles, had asked him before they made their dedications. Some said that Apollo knew that Themistocles would (later) become a suppliant of the Persian and for this reason did not wish to accept the gifts. A dedication by Themistocles would have made the Persian's hatred toward him unending.[350] (10.14.5–6)

This was not Themistocles' only misadventure with what would seem a simple pious gesture, making a dedication. As overseer of the waterworks before the war he dedicated, as we have seen, a bronze statue of a "water-carrying" girl (Plut. *Them.* 31.1, above). And after the war, presumably as victor, he made another apparently private dedication of a temple of Artemis Aristoboule ("Of Best Counsel") in Athens.[351] About this Plutarch reports that

Themistocles annoyed the people when he founded the sanctuary of Artemis, to whom he gave the epithet Aristoboule because he had devised the best plans for the city and the Greeks. He built the sanctuary near his house in Melite, the place where now the public servants throw out the bodies of executed men and dispose of the garments and nooses of those who commit suicide. And still in our time there was a statue of Themistocles in the temple of Aristoboule. He appears to have been someone heroic not only in soul but also in appearance.[352] (*Them.* 22.1–2. Cf. *Mor.* 869D)

Each dedication occasioned some trouble and ill will. The bronze girl was carried off by Xerxes to Sardis, and Themistocles' later attempt to recover it, whether from motives of piety or pride, got him into political trouble in Persia. His establishment of the sanctuary of Artemis Aristoboule after the war did not find favor with the Athenian people, and during the war his offer to place dedications *in* the temple of Apollo at Delphi was rejected by the god himself. Apollo's rejection of Themistocles' dedications mystifies modern scholars as well as Pausanias. Pausanias' attempts at explanation are not compelling. The salient point is, perhaps, that Themistocles was not only making dedications but wanted them set up in the prime place of honor, *in* the temple.[353] Apollo addresses that very point, and he may have found Themistocles to be presumptuous in making this request. In these various cases, it appears, Themistocles was thought to be promoting himself unduly through his dedications, as his Spartan counterpart Pausanias did in his inscription on the gold tripod at Delphi after the victory at Plataea (Thuc. 1.132.2–3 and Plut. *Mor.* 873C–D, above).

According to Pausanias, some spoils of the battle of Plataea found their way into the Erechtheum in Athens:

Of the dedications worthy of notice . . . are spoils from the Medes, the breastplate of Masistius who at Plataea led the (Persian) cavalry and a dagger said to have been Mardonius'. I know that Masistius was killed by Athenian cavalry, but Mardonius fought opposite the Lacedaemonians and was killed by a Spartiate.[354] Athenians would not have gotten the dagger to begin with and likewise the Peloponnesians would not have allowed them to carry it off.[355] (Paus. 1.27.1)

Demosthenes (24.129) mentions as dedications on the Acropolis not only Mardonius' dagger but also a "silver-footed footstool" that reportedly had belonged to Xerxes.[356]

According to Plutarch, "of the Greeks who fought for Greece (at Plataea), 1,360 died. Fifty-two of these were Athenians, all from the Aiantis tribe, as Cleidemus says (*FGrHist* 323 F 22), men who fought very well. And for this reason the members of the Aiantis tribe used to make a Pythian-ordained sacrifice, for the victory, to the Sphragitid Nymphs. They recovered the costs (of the sacrifice) from the public treasury" (*Arist.* 19.5). These sacrifices by the Aiantis tribe to the Sphragitid Nymphs, whose sanctuary was on a west-facing peak of Mount Cithaeron, were no doubt associated, perhaps as the fulfillment of a vow, with the prayer to these nymphs that Apollo through his oracle urged on the Athenians before the battle (Plut. *Arist.* 11.3–8, above).[357]

The Greeks, in their oath before Plataea, had vowed to bury any of their number who died in the battle. They fulfilled this vow, and Herodotus describes the arrangement of the tombs:

After the Greeks had divided up the spoils in Plataea, they were burying their own dead, each group separately. The Lacedaemonians made three tombs. In one they buried the twenty-year-olds, among whom were Posidonius, Amompharetus, Philocyon, and Callicrates. These twenty-year-olds were in one tomb, and in another the rest of the Spartiates, and in the third the helots. So the Spartans buried their dead, and the Tegeans separately buried all their men together. The Athenians also buried theirs together, and the Megarians and Phleiasioi buried those who had been killed by the Persian cavalry. The tombs of all these were full. There are tombs of other Greeks too at Plataea, but I hear that these Greeks, ashamed at their absence from the battle, each heaped up empty mounds for their descendants' sake. There is, for example, at Plataea the so-called tomb of the Aeginetans, but I hear that a Plataean, Cleades, the son of Autodicus, the *proxenos* of the

Aeginetans,[358] heaped it up ten years after the battle at the Aeginetans' request.[359] (9.85)

Pausanias reports that Simonides composed epitaphs for the Athenian and Lacedaemonian tombs (9.2.5), and, though the attribution is uncertain, Page (*FGE*, 197–200) is inclined to follow Bergk in assigning the following epitaphs to these tombs:

These men cloaked their dear fatherland in undying fame,
    But put on themselves the dark cloud of death.
Though dead, they have not died, since their virtue,
    Glorifying them, raises them from the house of Hades.
(Simonides, frag. 121 Diehl)

If dying well is the greatest part of virtue,
    Fortune gave it to us above all men.
For in our eagerness to clothe Greece in freedom,
    We lie here, enjoying ageless good repute.
(Simonides, frag. 118 Diehl)

The Greek dead of Plataea were thus buried on the battlefield, far from their homelands, and, according to Plutarch, the Plataeans took on the responsibility of providing the tomb cult for these war heroes, a responsibility that they were still fulfilling in Plutarch's time, 700 years later:

The Plataeans took it upon themselves to make, each year, offerings to those of the Greeks who had fallen and were buried there. And still up to now they do it in the following way. On Maimakterion 16 (which is Alalkomenios 16 among the Boeotians), they hold a procession. A trumpeter, giving the battle signal, leads out the procession at dawn, and wagons full of myrtle and garlands follow. There is also a black bull, and freeborn young men carry drink offerings of wine and milk in jugs and pitchers of olive oil and perfume. No slave may participate in anything concerning that service because these men died for freedom's sake. The archon of the Plataeans is in charge of the whole. At other times he may not touch iron or wear any but a white garment, but then he puts on a dark garment, takes a water pitcher from the state archives, and armed with a sword leads the way through the middle of the city to the tombs. Then, after taking water from the spring, he himself washes the tombstones and anoints them with perfume. Onto the pyre he slaughters the bull and, with a prayer to Zeus and Hermes Chthonios,[360] invites to dinner and the bloodletting those good men who died for Greece. He then mixes a bowl of wine and water and, pouring it out, says, "I offer this drink to the men who died for the freedom of the Greeks." The Plataeans still even now maintain these rituals.[361] (*Arist.* 21.2–5)

These Plataean offerings differ in more than scale from usual offerings to the dead. The Plataeans honor — and this is exceptional — more than their own dead; they perform these rites at the tombs of Spartans, Athenians, and other Greeks as well as Plataeans. This is a counterpart to the also exceptional Eleutheria, which united around the Plataeans these same Greeks. Second, the dead being honored were the war dead, a "special category" of the dead, falling between ordinary dead and cultic heroes such as Phylacus and Theseus who were worshiped as deities at their tombs.[362] It is as war dead that the Greek dead of Marathon, Thermopylae, and Plataea, at home and abroad, received elaborate annual offerings and sometimes even games.[363] This account also offers the fullest description we have of the founding and performance of such tomb cult, and we note some of its features. Each year the tombs were cleaned, made to smell good, and decorated with abundant myrtle garlands.[364] The sacrificial victim was black and male because it was intended for the male dead. The ritual had two peculiarities: only freemen could participate, and, for this occasion only, the Plataean archon wore black and carried a sword. From inscriptions and various sources we know hundreds of such local "peculiarities" in Greek rituals, but rarely do we understand, as here, the reason for them. Only freemen participated because the dead "died for freedom's sake." And, so obvious that Plutarch need not tell us, the archon wore black for mourning and carried the sword because these rites were for the war dead. Such logical explanations, if only we knew them, surely lay behind or were contrived to explain most peculiarities of Greek rituals.

## ⚜ The Battle at Mycale ⚜

On the same day in 479 that the Greek land forces defeated Mardonius and his army at Plataea, the Greek naval forces encountered the Persian navy at Mycale on the coast of Asia Minor opposite Samos. The Samians had secretly sent an embassy to Leotychides, the commander of the Greek navy, to plead for help in their revolt against the Persians. According to Herodotus, the Samian ambassador Hegesistratus ("Leader of the Expedition") "invoked the gods they shared[365] and was urging them to rescue Greek men from slavery and to ward off the barbarian." After Hegesistratus had made his arguments, "Leotychides asked, either wishing to learn it for the sake of an omen or just by chance, with a god causing it (θεοῦ ποιεῦντος), 'Samian friend, what is your name?' And he said, 'Hegesistratus.' And Leotychides preempted further talk, if Hegesistratus started to say something, and said, 'I accept the omen'" (9.90.2–91).[366] Here the spoken word, in special circumstances, becomes an omen (κληδών), as it should have for King Cleomenes of Sparta when he was entering Athena's temple on the Acropolis (5.72, above) and as it did for the Greeks when, as we see next, they heard at Mycale the report of the victory at Plataea.

The Persians sought to evade naval battle and beached their ships where they would be protected by the 60,000 Persian troops on land, "near the sanctuary of the Potniae at Gaeson and Scolopoeis of Mycale,[367] where there is a sanctuary of Eleusinian Demeter. Philistus, son of Pasicles, founded this sanctuary when he followed Neileus, son of Codrus, for the foundation of Miletus" (Hdt. 9.97).[368] As at Plataea, the battle was to occur near a sanctuary of Demeter Eleusinia, and Herodotus considered this coincidence one of several "divine elements" (τὰ θεῖα) involved in the battle at Mycale: after the Greek sailors landed and were beginning their march against the Persians,

a herald's staff appeared lying in the edge of the surf, and a report "flew upon" the whole army. The report passed among them that the Greeks were fighting and defeating the army of Mardonius in Boeotia. The divine elements (τὰ θεῖα) of these affairs are clear from many pieces of evidence, if the day of the (Persian) loss at Plataea and that of the one about to occur at Mycale were the same, and if the report came to the Greeks at Mycale, a report that caused the Greek army to become much more courageous and to be willing to face the danger more eagerly. And there was this other coincidence, that sanctuaries of Eleusinian Demeter were close to both battles. For at Plataea the battle took place right beside the sanctuary of Demeter, as I said before (9.65.2), and at Mycale it was going to be the same way. The report turned out true that there had been a victory at Plataea of the Greeks with Pausanias, for the battle in Plataea occurred early in the day, but the one in Mycale around evening time. And not much later, when they inquired, it became clear that the battles happened to occur on the same day and in the same month. And before the report came, (the Greeks at Mycale) were frightened, not so much about themselves as about the Greeks, that Greece might suffer defeat in the Mardonius battle. But when this omen in speech (κληδών) "flew" to them, all the more and all the more quickly they were making their attack. The Greeks and the barbarians were eager for battle since the prizes of victory were both the islands and the Hellespont.[369] (9.100–101)

The Greeks won a total victory at Mycale, destroying the large part of the Persian army and navy that had stayed to face them. They also began the liberation of Ionia, and the Athenians brought the Samians, Chians, Lesbians, and other islanders who had campaigned with them into a military alliance, an alliance secured by oaths (9.106.4). The Greek force then sailed north, intending to destroy Xerxes' bridges over the Hellespont. When they found the bridges already down, the Spartans under Leotychides sailed home, but the Athenians and their allies undertook to liberate cities of the Chersonesus and put in at Sestus. Herodotus, now in the final pages of his *Histories*, describes an incident at Sestus that is unimportant in military and political terms but serves as a final, strong illustration of the divine punishments that come to those who, like Xerxes, rashly commit sacrilege against sanctuaries of the gods.[370]

Xerxes' governor Artaüctes was ruling this region as a tyrant, a Persian, a terrible and rash (ἀτάσθαλος) man. He had even deceived King Xerxes when Xerxes was marching against Athens, by stealing from Elaeus the property of Protesilaus, son of Iphicles.[371] For in Elaeus of the Chersonesus there is a tomb of Protesilaus and a sanctuary around it, and in it there was much property and golden and silver bowls, bronze, garments, and other dedications. These Artaüctes stole when the king allowed it. He misled Xerxes by saying, "Master, this is the house of a Greek man who campaigned against your land and justly died. Give me his house so that everyone may learn not to campaign against your land." By saying these things he was easily going to persuade Xerxes to give him the man's house, because Xerxes suspected nothing of what Artaüctes had in mind. . . . And when his request was granted, Artaüctes gathered up the property from Elaeus and took it to Sestus and had the sanctuary sown and pastured, and whenever he went to Elaeus, he had intercourse with a woman in the *adyton*. But now, not prepared for a siege and not expecting the Greeks, Artaüctes was being besieged by the Athenians. (9.116)

After the siege and the flight of the Persians, the Greeks captured Artaüctes and his party and brought them to Sestus.

The Chersonesitae say that for one of the guards, when he was frying dried fish, the following marvel (τέρας) occurred: the dried fish lying in the fire were leaping around and quivering as fresh caught fish do. The men crowded around and were astonished at this, but Artaüctes, when he saw the miracle, called the man roasting the fish and said, "Athenian friend, do not fear this miracle. It did not give a revelation to you, but Protesilaus in Elaeus indicates to me that, even when dead and a fish, he has from gods (πρὸς θεῶν) power to punish the man who treated him unjustly. Now I am willing to impose upon myself this recompense: for the things that I took from the sanctuary I will deposit one hundred talents ($60 million) with the god, and, if I survive, for myself and my child I will pay two hundred talents ($120 million) to the Athenians." But he did not persuade the (Athenian) general Xanthippus by promising these things.[372] The people of Elaeus, seeking vengeance for Protesilaus, were asking that Artaüctes be killed, and the general himself was thinking in these terms. They led Artaüctes to the headland where Xerxes yoked the Hellespont—some say to the hill above the city Madytus—nailed him to a plank, and suspended him in the air. Before his eyes they stoned his son. When they had done this, they sailed back to Greece, bringing with them the other things and the bridge equipment, to dedicate it at the sanctuaries.[373] (9.120–121.1)

Herodotus' report of bridge equipment and "other things" the Greeks dedicated in their sanctuaries after the victory at Plataea is supplemented by the accounts of Pausanias and Plutarch of other monuments the Greeks gave to the gods to celebrate their victory. There was, still in Pausanias' time, in Athens "a building near the sanctuary of Dionysus and the theater. It is said that it was built in imitation of Xerxes' tent. This was the second one, because Sulla the general of the Romans burned the old one when he took Athens" (Paus. 1.20.4). This was probably the Odeion of Pericles, because, according to Plutarch (*Per.* 13.5), that Odeion was modeled after Xerxes' tent. Vitruvius (5.9.1) claims that masts and spars of Persian ships were built into its roof.[374] In his description of Sparta Pausanias reports that at Sparta

the most illustrious part of the *agora* is the stoa which they call "Persian." It was made from the Persian spoils. Over time they remodeled it into its current size and decoration. On the columns are Persians sculpted from white marble, others and Mardonius, the son of Gobryas. An Artemisia was also made, the daughter of Lygdamis, queen of Halicarnassus. They say that she willingly campaigned against Greece with Xerxes and was effective in the sea battle around Salamis.[375] (3.11.3)

At Delphi "the Epidaurians in the Argolid erected one of the statues of Apollo from (the spoils of) the Medes. . . . And there is a cow of the Plataeans from when they with the other Greeks warded off Mardonius, the son of Gobryas, in their land" (Paus. 10.15.1). This and a similar cow and calf sculpture of the Carystians "the Plataeans and Carystians dedicated because they thought that after having driven off the barbarian they acquired other prosperity (εὐδαιμονίαν) and their land now free to plow" (10.16.6).[376] Also at Delphi has been found the statue base of a Peparethian dedication, by the Athenian sculptor Diopeithes, with this inscription:

The Peparethians, after capturing two ships of the Carians in battle,
Erected this as a tithe offering to far-darting Apollo.[377]

And, finally, among the dedications after the war, Pausanias tells that at Troezen "they seem reasonably to have built an altar of Helios Eleutherios because they escaped slavery from Xerxes and the Persians" (2.31.5).

After the final victories of the Persian Wars, the Athenians, according to Diodorus, "adorned (ἐκόσμησε) the tombs of those who died in the Persian War, and then for the first time held the funeral games (τὸν ἀγῶνα τὸν ἐπιτάφιον) and made it a custom for select orators to speak encomia over those who were being buried at public expense" (11.33.3).[378] Some scholars doubt Diodorus' claim here, but if he is correct,[379] this was the beginning of a tradition that reached its pinnacle in the funeral oration that Thucydides (2.34–46) has Pericles deliver fifty years later over the Athenian war dead in the Peloponnesian War. The practice of giving such funeral orations then would, with the funeral games, continue into the Hellenistic period.[380]

We close our account of the religious aspects of the Persian Wars not with one of the great dedications or monuments of the most powerful Greek states, but with the epitaph, still preserved on stone, that the rather humble Megarians composed for their soldiers who had died in various battles of this great Panhellenic victory:

Eager that the day of freedom wax for Greece and Megarians,
    We received our portion of death,
Some below Euboea and Pelion, where is famed
    The sanctuary of pure, bow-bearing Artemis,
Some on the mountain of Mycale, some before Salamis,

And some on the Boeotian plain, those who dared
    To engage cavalrymen in hand-to-hand combat.[381]
Our citizens erect for us this common honor, around the navel,[382]
    In the people-receiving *agora*, overlooking Nisaea.[383]
(*IG* VII 53)

# ✻ TWO ✻

## *Greek Gods, Heroes, and the Divine in the Persian Invasions*

As we have seen, individual Greek gods, heroes, and the "divine" contributed to the Greek victories over the Persians at critical moments. In this chapter we survey, again largely from Herodotus' perspective, their contributions, deity by deity, and, to understand them and their roles better, we also offer some background on their cults and on conceptions of them at the time of and just before these great wars.

## ✻ The Gods ✻

After the battle of Plataea, the final victory in Greece to end the Persian attempt to "enslave" the mainland, the Greeks

set aside a tithe for the god in Delphi, and from this was dedicated the gold tripod on the bronze three-headed snake which stands near the altar. They set aside a portion also for the god in Olympia, and from it they dedicated a bronze Zeus, fifteen feet tall. And there was a portion for the god at the Isthmus, and from it came a ten and one-half foot bronze Poseidon.[1] (Hdt. *9.81.1*)

Apollo, Zeus, and Poseidon, each of a specific cult site, were the gods whom the Greeks as an international group judged deserving of a share of the spoils of victory, and we begin with them, giving priority in account if not in gratitude to Zeus.

### ZEUS

Zeus was for Herodotus and for all Greeks the bringer of rain (2.13.3; 3.124.1 and 125.4) and the paradigm of superlative prosperity and power (5.49.7; *7.56* and *220.4*). The Zeus of Olympia whom the Greeks honored with their tithe is noted especially for his grand temple (2.7.1)[2] and the games held at his quadrennial festival, games that the Eleans administered (2.160). Competition in them was limited to Greeks, and the acceptance of Alexander (I), son of Amyntas, as a competitor, probably in 476, gave to the Macedonian royalty the coveted status of being Greeks (5.22). The celebration of the Olympic games in the summer of 480 caused the Greeks to send initially only a small force to Thermopylae (7.206) and occasioned the famous response of the Persian general Tritantaechmes (8.26): "Alas, Mardonius, against what kind of men did you lead us to fight, men who compete not for money but for virtue?"

That aspect of Zeus, or, perhaps more precisely, that aspect of Zeus Olympios most credited with helping the Greeks to become or remain "free" from Persian slavery was Eleutherios ("Of Freedom").[3] The role of Zeus Eleutherios in contemporary Greek life is illustrated in the founding of his cult on Samos by the successor to Polycrates in 522, as described by Herodotus:

Maeandrius, the son of Maeandrius, was holding the power over Samos, having received that rule as a trust from Polycrates. . . . After the death of Polycrates was announced (ca. 522), Maeandrius did the following: first he erected an altar of Zeus Eleutherios and marked out around it the sanctuary that still now is outside the city. And afterward, after the sanctuary had been created, he assembled all the townsmen and said, "As you know, the scepter and all the power of Polycrates have been entrusted to me, and I now have the opportunity to rule you. But I, so far as it lies in my power, will not myself do those things for which I criticize my neighbors. For I was not pleased with Polycrates ruling men who were the same as he, nor with anyone else who does such things. Polycrates has fulfilled his fate, but I now give the rule to the people and announce an equality-before-law for you. I think, however, that I deserve for myself the following prizes of honor: that six talents ($3.6 million) from Polycrates' money be set aside for me, and that I take in addition to the money the priesthood of Zeus Eleutherios for myself and my descendants. I myself founded his sanctuary, and I am giving freedom (ἐλευθερίην) to you."[4] (3.142.1–4)

The cult of Zeus Eleutherios thus could betoken and commemorate the establishment of political freedom from despotism and tyranny,[5] and so the god could be associated with the Greek victory over the despotic Persians. The oracle of Bacis had predicted such a victory for the battle at Salamis: "Then far-seeing Zeus and Lady Nike will bring on Greece's day of freedom" (8.77). And it was for this Zeus Eleutherios that, after their victory, the Greeks, at Delphi's bidding, established at Plataea a sanctuary with a marble altar and statue and with a quadrennial festival, the Eleutheria, which included athletic games, especially footraces in armor.[6] The altar was inscribed:

The Greeks, after driving away the Persians
By the power of Nike and the work of Ares,
Founded for a free Greece (ἐλευθέρᾳ Ἑλλάδι)
This altar of Zeus Eleutherios.

This festival continued to be celebrated into Roman times on Boedromion 4, the day of the battle by the Athenian calendar (Plut. *Arist. 19.6–7*).

For the Athenians the Pythia in the famous "wooden wall" oracle may have laid the foundation for their association of Zeus with the victory at Salamis. The oracle gives, uncommonly in Herodotus,[7] a glimpse into divine politics. Athena was unable to persuade her father, Zeus Olympios, to spare Athens from occupation by the Persians,

But far-seeing Zeus grants to Tritogeneia a wooden wall.
It alone will be unsacked, and it will benefit you and your children.[8]
(Hdt. *7.141.3*)

According to one tradition, the Athenians established for Zeus Eleutherios in commemoration of these services a sanctuary in the Agora, the stoa of which was built about 430–420.[9] There, in later centuries, honors were paid to Athenian soldiers who had excelled or fallen defending the *eleutheria* of the Athenian people against foreign enemies.[10] This Zeus Eleutherios of Athens had also the epithet Soter ("Savior"),[11] and the Zeus Soter who before the battle of Plataea appeared in a dream to Arimnestus and helped him interpret Aristides' oracle (Plut. *Arist. 11.5–8*) may have been Zeus Eleutherios. Thus it is quite probable that in Athens, at Plataea, and among the Greeks in general it was Zeus Olympios in his guise as Eleutherios/Soter who was credited with assistance during the Persian invasions.

## POSEIDON

Poseidon was recognized by Thessalians, Greeks, and Herodotus as the "earth-shaker" (*7.129.4*), but it was for his contributions at sea that he received for his cult at the Isthmus the bronze statue from the Greeks. The storms at Artemisium and off Euboea that caused so much damage to the

Persian fleet were credited to the winds by the Delphians, to Boreas and their Oreithyia by the Athenians, but to Poseidon by the other Greeks. In gratitude those Greeks prayed and poured libations to the god and gave him the epithet Soter ("Savior") (7.192). And after the victory at Salamis and some mopping-up operations in the Aegean, Herodotus reports that the Greeks "selected firstfruits for the gods, other things, and three Phoenician warships, one to dedicate at the Isthmus . . . , one for Sunium, and one for Ajax on Salamis" (8.121.1). The Phoenicians were the core of the Persian naval force, and their captured ships were a most appropriate dedication to the Greek god of sailors. And, befitting the nature of the battle, one went to his Panhellenic sanctuary on the Isthmus and one to his Athenian cult at Sunium.[12] And later the Greek generals sailed to the Isthmus to place their ballots for the "best warrior of the war" award on Poseidon's altar. The winner, though not undisputed, was Themistocles, the founder of Athenian sea power and hero of the battle at Salamis (8.123).[13] In one final blow, Poseidon of Potidaea with a timely and unusually large flood tide helped the Potidaeans in 479 massacre a besieging force of Persians under Artabazus (8.129). Here the god of the sea with the resources under his control saved the city named for him and avenged an impiety directed specifically against him. And that all made perfect sense to Herodotus.[14]

For the invasion itself, Poseidon's cults at the Isthmus and Sunium were prominent, and that at Potidaea played a small part. Most significant for Ionia was his cult center, the Panionion, at Mycale on the Asia Minor mainland opposite the island Samos.[15] It had been founded jointly by the twelve Ionian cities, and they kept it to themselves (1.143.3). The Panionia of Poseidon Helikonios there was their communal festival (1.148).[16] The Ionians gathered there also for counsel in times of crisis (1.141.4 and 170.1). It served again as their place of meeting in 495 when they were making the plans that led to the battle of Lade, the sea battle that ruined their chances of success in the revolt from Persian domination (6.7).

## APOLLO

In the list of deities to whom the Greeks gave a tithe of the spoils of Plataea, Apollo stands first, and that reflects the importance Herodotus gives to the god of Delphi in the success of the Greeks over the Persians. His sanctuary, unlike that of Zeus of Olympia or Poseidon of the Isthmus, stood in the path of the invasion and had its own direct encounter with Persian soldiers, but Apollo's interest was much broader and deeper than the protection of his own property. We begin with Delphic Apollo and a survey of the precious dedications given in gratitude to him by both Greeks and non-Greeks before and during the Persian Wars. In the sanctuary itself these dedications would have illustrated for Herodotus and other visitors the power and range of the deity, and we attempt, however inadequately, to recreate that experience for readers.

From the spoils of the Persians at Marathon, Pausanias reports, the Athenians dedicated at Delphi gold shields and a treasury building. They also dedicated a monument with statues of Apollo, Athena, Miltiades, the heroes Codrus, Neleus, and Theseus, and their eponymous heroes. Phidias sculpted the statues, and hence the monument was constructed a least a generation after the battle. But it was still, in Pausanias' time, associated with the victory at Marathon (*10.10.1–2, 11.5*, and *19.4*). After the battle of Salamis Apollo received, from the Greeks, a statue of himself, eighteen feet tall, carrying in his hand the stern ornament of a ship. With this, however, the god was not content. He wanted also from the Aeginetans "the prize they had received for excellence in the naval battle at Salamis," and the Aeginetans duly gave him three gold stars mounted on a bronze mast (Hdt. *8.122*). From the spoils of Plataea the Greeks gave a tithe to Delphic Apollo, and from this tithe was made the gold tripod, so appropriate to his cult, supported on three intertwined snakes. The monument rose at least thirty feet, and on the coils of the snake were inscribed the names of the thirty-one Greek cities that had defeated "the barbarian" (*9.81.1*). The Athenians may again have dedicated gold shields (Aeschines *3.116*). The Epidaurians also dedicated a statue of Apollo, and the Plataeans, Carystians, and Peparethians also had monuments there (Paus. *10.15.1* and *16.6*).

These dedications from the Persian Wars would have joined the famous series of early Phrygian, Lydian, and Persian dedications that were still standing at Delphi in Herodotus' time. Midas, king of Phrygia, was the first barbarian to make a dedication at Delphi. He, the legendarily just judge, gave "the royal throne upon which he sat when he judged cases" (Hdt. *1.14.2–3*). Gyges, who took the kingship of Lydia from Candaules about 680, after the Delphic oracle confirmed his kingship, "sent to Delphi not a few dedications. Of all the silver dedications at Delphi, most are owed to Gyges. And apart from the silver, he dedicated a vast amount of gold, other gold, and also that which most deserves mention, six gold craters.[17] These now stand in the treasury of the Corinthians and weigh 1,710 pounds" (1.14.1–2).[18] Alyattes, the third Mermnad successor to the throne of Lydia after Gyges, in gratitude for escaping a disease, dedicated at Delphi a large silver crater and what especially attracted Herodotus' attention, an iron crater-stand fashioned by welding (1.25.2). But these Phrygian and early Lydian dedications must have paled in comparison to those sent by Croesus to win Apollo's favor just prior to 547. When he had assured himself of the accuracy of Delphic Apollo's oracle (1.46–49),

Croesus was trying to win over (ἱλάσκετο) the god in Delphi with great sacrifices. He sacrificed 3,000 victims of all kinds, and he heaped on a great pyre and burned silvered and gilded couches, golden *phialai*, and purple himatia and chitons, hoping that he would more "acquire" (ἀνακτήσεσθαι) the god by these offerings. . . . And after the sacrifice he melted down a vast amount of gold and forged ingots 18 inches long, 9 inches wide, and 3 inches in height. There were 117 ingots in all, 4 of pure gold, 142.5 pounds each; and the others of white gold, 114 pounds each. He had made also a 570-pound statue of a lion, of pure gold. When the temple in Delphi was burning (548 B.C.), this lion fell from the ingots and now sits in the treasury of the Corinthians and weighs 370.5 pounds, because 199.5 pounds of it were melted away in the fire. After Croesus had these made, he sent them to Delphi, and also the following other things: two large craters, one gold, one silver. The gold one sits to the right as one enters the temple, the silver one to the left. These were moved when the temple was burned, and the gold one now is in the treasury of the Clazomenians, weighing 495.75 pounds. The silver one sits in the corner of the pronaos and holds 5,737.5 gallons. It is used by the Delphians for mixing wine at the Theophania. The Delphians say it is the work of the Samian Theodorus, and I think it is, because the work is above average.[19] Croesus sent also four silver *pithoi* which now sit in the treasury of the Corinthians, and two *perirrhanteria*, one gold, one silver. . . . And Croesus sent in addition many other uninscribed dedications, including round silver bowls and a 4½ foot tall gold statue of a woman. The Delphians say it is a representation of Croesus' cook.[20] And, in addition, Croesus dedicated his wife's necklaces and belts.[21] (1.50–51)

To these Phrygian and Lydian dedications we may add those given to Delphi before the war by Greeks, including the statues of Cleobis and Biton dedicated by the Argives (1.31.4).[22] Less beautiful but useful for the sacrifices were the many iron "bull piercing" spits stored between the altar of the Chians and the temple at Delphi. These the famous Thracian courtesan Rhodopis dedicated as a tithe of the fortune she had made plying her trade in Egypt (2.135.4).[23] In the treasury of the Corinthians, in Herodotus' time, was also the censer (*thymiaterion*) dedicated circa 538 by King Euelthon of Cyprian Salamis (4.162.3). From a victory over the Thessalians just before the Persian invasion, the Phocians had sent to Delphi 2,000 Thessalian shields and some large statues which encircled the tripod in front of the temple (8.27.4–5).[24] Buildings, too, were, in essence, dedications, such as the ornate treasury which the Siphnians built, circa 535, with a tithe of the income from their gold and silver mines (3.57.2).[25] But the largest and most complex "dedication" was the very temple of Apollo, the temple that replaced the one destroyed by fire in 548.[26] The new temple was contracted for 300 talents ($180 million), one-fourth of which the Delphians put up. For the rest they sought contributions. King Amasis of Egypt gave 1,000 talents of alum and the Greeks living in Egypt one-third of a talent in coin ($200,000) (2.180). We have already seen how the exiled Alcmaeonidae obtained the contract for building this temple, and, beyond the terms of the contract, enhanced the building with a facade of Parian marble (5.62.2–3).

The buildings and other dedications described by Herodotus formed only a part, perhaps not the largest in quantity but a most conspicuous part, of the wealth and beauty of Apollo's Delphic sanctuary in the historian's time. These offerings in their various ways commemorated and expressed gratitude for victories in battle, health, economic prosperity, and, most often, helpful oracles.

The oracles, the "oracular wisdom" of Apollo, play the single greatest "religious" role in Herodotus' account of the Persian Wars, and to understand Apollo's contribution to the Greek cause we offer here a brief survey of the Delphic oracles that, according to Herodotus, affected the course of events.

In the years just prior to the war the Pythia, bribed by the Alcmaeonidae according to Herodotus, by frequent advice persuaded the Spartans to expel the sons of Pisistratus from Athens (5.63.1–3). This led quickly to the establishment of democracy in Athens, and the escape from tyranny, in Herodotus' judgment, was the key factor in the sudden rise and power of Athens (5.78). This newfound power and energy, no doubt, led to Athens's involvement in the Ionian Revolt, brought on thereby the hatred of the Persians, and allowed Athens to compete for leadership of the Greeks against the Persians on land and sea.

The affairs of newly democratic Athens became entangled with Aegina, in part as a result of two oracles. In 506 the Thebans took a Delphic oracle to mean that they should ally with Aegina against Athens (*5.79–81*). In the course of these hostilities the oracle advised Athens to hold off from any war with Aegina for thirty years.[27] Then, the oracle promised, in the thirty-first year the Athenians would "overthrow the Aeginetans." Actions prior to that would result in some victories and some defeats. The Athenians nonetheless made some attempts on Aegina, but soon diverted their attention to the Spartans and Persians. Athens in 458/7 finally got control of Aegina (*5.89*).

The Argives received at Delphi an unusual double oracle, one part concerning them, the other the Milesians. The second part predicted defeat for the Milesians and slavery for their wives. Herodotus saw the fulfillment of this oracle in the Persian capture, pillaging, and enslavement of Miletus in 494 (*6.19*).

Demaratus, the former Spartan king, served as a useful and wise counselor to Xerxes throughout his expedition, and the Delphic oracle played a role in his flight from and bitterness toward the Spartans. Cleomenes, the other Spartan king, was among those calling into question Demaratus' paternity and hence legitimacy as king. Delphi was consulted, and Cleomenes worked through a prominent Delphian to have the Pythia reply that Ariston was *not* Demaratus' father. Demaratus thus fled the country and became a valuable ally to Xerxes. Soon thereafter, in 490, Cleomenes committed suicide in a particularly grisly manner "because, as most Greeks say, he had persuaded the Pythia to say those things about Demaratus" (*6.75* and *84.3*).

To Herodotus the freedom of Greece depended upon and ultimately resulted from the decision of the Athenians to stay and fight the Persians. And "not even frightening oracles coming from Delphi and throwing a scare into them persuaded the Athenians to leave Greece, but they remained there and endured to receive the enemy coming into their land." The Athenians had consulted Delphi and received, in fact, a frightening oracle: the Persians would destroy their city as they would many cities in Greece; Athenians should "leave their homes and the heights of their circular city" and should "flee to the ends of the earth."[28] Flight and resettlement were an option open to them, one that the Athenians did not choose, fortunately in Herodotus' judgment, because it would have meant the enslavement of all Greece. The Athenians, grief-stricken at the oracle, demanded that Apollo "prophesy to them something better about their fatherland." The Pythia, in a second oracle, repeated that Attica would be taken by the Persians, that the Athenians should retreat, but added the "something better," the unsacked "wooden wall" and the role of Salamis in a future battle with the Persians. After considerable discussion, the large majority of Athenians, at Themistocles' promptings, interpreted the "wooden wall" to be the ships of the navy and the reference to "divine Salamis" to be in their favor. "And in their deliberations after the oracle the Athenians decided to meet with their ships the barbarian as he invaded Greece, trusting in the god and in those of the Greeks who were willing to help." In hindsight these two oracles, as interpreted by the Athenians, proved accurate. The Athenians did evacuate Attica; Xerxes did destroy Athens and Attica as he did other cities;[29] and with the "wooden wall" and at Salamis the Athenians did engage and defeat the Persians.[30] The Athenians ignored only one piece of Delphic advice, to "flee to the ends of the earth," and this saved Greece (7.139–144).

Less than helpful to the Greek war effort were the oracle's responses to the Argives and the Cretans.[31] The Argives, weakened by the loss of 6,000 men in a war with the Spartans in 494, asked Delphi "what they should do for the best result" during the Persian Invasion. Delphi told them to stay at home, and that is what they ultimately chose to do (7.148–152). The Cretans "sent ambassadors to Delphi to ask the god 'if it would be better for them if they helped Greece.'" The Pythia reminded them of the past when the Greeks had not helped them, and "stopped them, despite their wishes, from helping the Greeks" (7.169–171). Such responses at this time were certainly not promoting the Greek cause, but whether they turned out to be in the best interests of the Argives and Cretans themselves is more difficult to decide.[32]

On a far more positive note, Apollo bid his Delphians to pray to the winds for help against the Persian navy, "because winds would be great allies to Greece." The Delphians reported the oracle to the Greeks, and for this they "won the undying gratitude of the Greeks." The Delphians themselves prayed to the winds, and the Athenians, advised by yet another oracle, prayed to their in-law wind, Boreas. The winds did come and destroy hundreds of Persian ships off Artemisium and Euboea. This was evidence, in Herodotus' judgment, that the gods were beginning to make it a more fair fight (7.178, 189, 191–192, and 8.13).

The death of Leonidas at Thermopylae fulfilled, in a way favorable to the Greek effort, a recent Delphic oracle, that either Sparta or one of its two kings would fall to the Persians. Leonidas, according to Herodotus, took this oracle into account in his decision to dismiss the allies and with Spartans alone to die fighting in the final battle (7.220).

Two Herodotean Delphic oracles played out at Plataea. The *mantis* serving the Greek army there, Tisamenus of Elis, had received an oracle that he would win "five of the greatest contests."[33] After Tisamenus' failed attempt as an Olympic athlete, the Spartans realized that the oracle referred to military contests, and after tough negotiations hired him to serve as their *mantis* in the encounter with Xerxes. The battle of Plataea was Tisamenus' first victory; the fifth and last came twenty-two years later at Tanagra (9.33–35). Finally, in the weeks just prior to the battle of Plataea, an oracle came "from Delphi to the Lacedaemonians, bidding them to ask Xerxes for recompense for the death of Leonidas and to accept whatever Xerxes gave." Xerxes laughed at their request. "Mardonius happened to be standing at his side, and Xerxes pointed at him and said, 'Well, then, Mardonius will pay to them the recompense they ought to have.'" Mardonius soon paid the recompense, by his death and those of his hundreds of thousands of soldiers at Plataea (8.114).

Plutarch in his biography of Aristides reports two Delphic oracles concerning Plataea. At Aristides' inquiry, Apollo told the Greeks what gods they should pray to, what heroes they should sacrifice to, and where they should fight the battle (Plut. *Arist.* 11.3–8). After the Greek victory Apollo directed them to establish the altar of Zeus Eleutherios but not to sacrifice on it until they had put out the fires polluted by the Persians and fetched new fire from Delphi (Plut. *Arist.* 20.4–5).

Apollo's Delphic oracle was thus, to some degree, involved with all the major battles and events of the Persian invasion, except for the battle of Marathon.[34] As positive contributions to the Greek cause, it assisted Athens's rise to power; it recommended the strategically wise evacuation of Athens, the dependence on the navy, and Salamis as the site of battle; it urged prayers to the winds, prayers that resulted in the destruction of a large part of the Persian navy; it designated the specific site at Plataea for the battle; it brought the lucky Tisamenus there; and, quite indirectly, it set up Mardonius for disaster. In more neutral terms it predicted correctly the fall of Miletus, Athens's ultimate control of Aegina, the devastation of Athens and many other Greek cities, and the death of Leonidas. But some Delphic pronouncements also worked counter to Panhellenic interests. One cost the Greeks the support of the Argives and Cretans; one was manipulated to lose for them the services of the able and wise Spartan king Demaratus; and, finally, by its advice to "flee to the ends of the earth" and by its dire (though accurate) predictions, one nearly frightened the Athenians into abandoning the Greek cause, and that, in Herodotus' judgment, would have meant loss to the Persians and the enslavement of the whole of Greece. But despite these negatives the dedications after Salamis and after Plataea clearly indicate that for the Greeks of the time the contributions of Delphic Apollo remained foremost in their minds.[35] Not until modern scholarship do we find criticisms of Apollo's behavior in the Persian Wars coming to the fore.[36]

Herodotus has, as we have seen, Delphic Apollo act powerfully and successfully through his oracle and through a variety of miracles to protect his own sanctuary and property against the Persians (8.35–39). It is the fullest and most graphic description of divine action in the *Histories*; when combined with the equally full and graphic description of the dedications at Delphi it creates for the reader a clear sense of the awesome power of the deity. Apollo's defense of his own sanctuary may be imagined as a purely parochial effort, but that Apollo's role in the defeat of the Persians was much greater, that he in fact was the religious focal point of the Greek effort, is indicated by the oath that all Greeks took at an early stage in the invasion: "Whichever Greeks give themselves up to the Persians, if they have not been forced and their situation is good, are to pay a tithe to the god in Delphi" (7.132).[37] During the invasion, Apollo of Delphi was the deity singled out to represent the Greek side. Only later did he share the honors of victory with Zeus of Olympia and Poseidon of the Isthmus.

Delian Apollo stood alongside Darius' sea route to Attica in 490 as Delphian Apollo did alongside Xerxes' land path in 480. Datis, Darius' general, by his own inclination and on Darius' instructions, did not harm "the land in which the two gods were born." He landed at nearby Rhenea, and on Apollo's altar on Delos he made an offering of 17,000 pounds of incense. After the Persians departed for Marathon, the god by an earthquake, a highly unusual event on Delos, "gave a miraculous sign to men of the evils that were to come, because in the time of Darius, son of

Hystaspes, and of Xerxes, son of Darius, and of Artoxerxes, son of Xerxes, in these three successive generations more evils occurred for Greece than in the twenty generations before Darius" (6.97–98). And Datis on his return after his defeat at Marathon showed no less respect for Delian Apollo. From a dream he learned that one of his Phoenician ships was carrying a gilded statue of Apollo stolen from Delian Apollo's sanctuary at Delion. Datis recovered it and deposited it for safekeeping in the god's sanctuary on Delos (6.118).

Of the three Apollo sanctuaries near Thebes, two escaped the general destruction that the Persians brought to the region. The sanctuary of Apollo Ismenios at Thebes housed the oracle of Amphiaraus, the one oracle in addition to Delphi that passed Croesus' test of oracles worldwide (1.49). At the time of the invasion the sanctuary was adorned with the gold shield and spear that Croesus had dedicated (1.52). Herodotus notes also a gold tripod dedicated by Croesus (1.92.1), a tripod that would have joined the three very old tripods from the time of Laios, Oedipus, and Oedipus' grandson Laodamas (5.59–61).[38] Amphiaraus' oracle there was also one of at least four Greek oracles that Mardonius consulted between the battles of Salamis and Plataea (8.133–136). Mardonius' Carian agent Mys also visited Apollo's oracle at Ptoön, and from it received, to the astonishment of all, an oracle in the Carian language, intelligible only to Mys. Mys traveled also to nearby Phocian Abae. "At Abae there was a wealthy sanctuary of Apollo, adorned with many treasures and dedications" (8.33). Among the dedications were one-half of the 4,000 Thessalian shields captured in battle by the Phocians and also statues made from the tithe of the spoils (8.27.4–5).[39] Apollo's oracle at Abae had failed Croesus' test and a few months before Mys' visit had been robbed and burned by the Persians (8.33). One wonders what Mys' reception must have been.

Delphic Apollo, as we have seen, offered no oracular help directly to the Persians against the Greeks, and even Herodotus has no good information on what Mardonius wanted to learn or did learn from Apollo Ismenios, Ptoös, or Abaios (8.133). Herodotus guesses that these oracles advised him to make Athens his ally (8.136.3). In this, however, as in the battle at Plataea, Mardonius met failure. Despite his consultations, Apollo gave him and the Persians no help.

Apollo of Delphi, Zeus of Olympia, and Poseidon of the Isthmus were each, despite association with one major sanctuary, Panhellenic deities whose festivals had long served a Panhellenic audience. Athena's role in the Persian invasion is, by contrast, local. The Greeks as a group direct no prayers to her and give her no dedications.[40] She receives such elements of worship only from a citizen group, usually at its own local sanctuary. The Athenians, for example, included an Athena in a statue group they dedicated at Delphi to Apollo after the battle of Marathon (Paus. *10.10.1*) and in a painting representing that battle (Paus. *1.15.3*). The Tegeans dedicated to their Alea Athena the bronze horse manger of Mardonius, which they carried off when they ransacked his tent at Plataea (Hdt. *9.70.3*). The Plataeans with their share of the spoils from the battle of Marathon constructed a monumental wood and gilded statue of Athena Area (Paus. *9.4.1–2*). And after the victory at Plataea the Greeks, according to Plutarch (Plut. *Arist. 20.2–3*), awarded the prize for valor of a city to the Plataeans, and with it "the Plataeans rebuilt their sanctuary of Athena, erected a statue,[41] and adorned the temple with paintings." But the Panhellenic altar and festival that the Greeks established at Plataea to commemorate the victory were for Zeus Eleutherios.

The Greek Athena does wax large in the account of Herodotus, but primarily in her role as patroness of Athens. Athens's role in the war was great, and because much is told from an Athenian point of view, the Athenian Athena comes to the fore. For Athenian Athena one must begin with Herodotus' famous, not to say notorious, account of Pisistratus' restoration to power in Athens circa 556:

Those who had driven out Pisistratus were again at odds with each other. Megacles, who was being battered by this strife, asked Pisistratus if, on the condition of recovering the tyranny, he would be willing to take Megacles' daughter as his wife. After Pisistratus accepted this proposal and agreed on these terms, they devised for Pisistratus' return what I find to be by far the most naive (εὐηθέστατον) action—at least it is the most naive action since the Greek people were separated out from the barbarian people of long ago, and the Greek people were more clever and more removed from foolish naiveté. And it was naive especially if they devised such a thing among the Athenians who are said to be the first of the Greeks in wisdom. There was a woman in the deme Paeania, Phye by name, five feet ten inches tall and otherwise good-looking.[42] They dressed this woman up in full armor, put her on a chariot, and gave her a general appearance that was going to be most eye-catching. They drove her into the city after they had sent ahead messengers who, when they came to the city, proclaimed what they had been ordered to say: "Athenians, with good will receive Pisistratus. Athena herself has honored him especially among men and brings him back to her Acropolis." The messengers were going about saying these things, and immediately the report reached the demes that Athena was bringing back Pisistratus. The people in the city believed that the woman was the goddess herself and were praying to the woman and were welcoming Pisistratus. After recovering his tyranny in the way I have described, Pisistratus according to his agreement with Megacles married his daughter.[43] (1.50–51)

There is a certain irony, then, that about forty-two years later Pisistratus' son Hipparchus was assassinated as he oversaw the procession of the Panathenaea, Athena's greatest festival and one that had been enhanced and promoted by the Pisistratidae themselves (5.55–56).[44] Another four years later Cleomenes, a king of Sparta, motivated by the Pythia (5.62–65), ousted Hippias, Pisistratus' surviving son, seized Athens briefly, and had an unhappy and ill-omened encounter with the goddess and her priestess on the Acropolis (5.72). And in 506 the Athenians dedicated to their goddess, as the firstfruits of one of their first military victories as a "free people," a bronze four-horse chariot. They also mounted on the Acropolis wall the chains with which they held the hundreds of prisoners taken in that war (5.77).

From the spoils at Marathon the Athenians later had Phidias sculpt the towering Athena Promachos on the Acropolis, visible even for those sailing from Sunium to Piraeus (Paus. 1.28.2). The goddess was also depicted in the famous painting of the battle of Marathon in the Stoa Poicile (Paus. 1.15.3). From the battle of Plataea the Athenians later kept in the Erechtheum the breastplate of Masistius and what they claimed was the dagger of Mardonius. Also to be seen on the Acropolis were a footstool of Xerxes and, perhaps, some of the equipment the king had used for his bridge over the Hellespont (Paus. 1.27.1). Some modern scholars think the early Parthenon, the temple under construction when destroyed by Xerxes in 480, was intended as a commemoration of the battle of Marathon.[45]

In the second invasion, according to the "wooden wall" oracle from Delphi (Hdt. 7.141), Athena attempted unsuccessfully to prevent the occupation and devastation of her city, but did win as a concession from Zeus the unsackable "wooden wall," which proved to be the key to the Athenian and Greek victory over the Persians. In the face of the Persian occupation of Attica in 480 Athena herself joined the evacuation: the large snake that lived in the sanctuary of Athena ceased to eat the monthly offerings put out for it, and the Athenians concluded she had left the city (Plut. *Them. 10.1*). But in the first days of the occupation another element of Athena's cult, her sacred olive tree, miraculously gave to Xerxes and his few pro-Persian Athenian supporters an indication of the future: on the second day after the burning of the Acropolis Athena's olive tree sent up a one and one-half foot sprout (Hdt. *8.55*). On the eve of the battle of Salamis, an oracle of Bacis came into play, assuring the Athenians that "far-seeing Zeus and Lady Nike will bring on Greece's day of freedom" (*8.77*). Zeus is here Zeus Eleutherios, and Lady Nike is quite probably Athena Nike, whose cult was already established on the bastion of the Acropolis.[46]

The lack, for the next generation, of major Athenian monuments for Athena or other gods commemorating divine assistance in the Persian Wars is noteworthy. The general devastation of Athens and Attica was, no doubt, a factor. Also contributing may have been clauses of the oath which the Athenians with the other Greeks purportedly swore before the battle of Plataea (Lycurg. *Leoc. 80–81*): "Nor will I rebuild any of the sanctuaries that have been burned and razed, but I will leave them as a memorial for our descendants and as a memorial of the impiety of the barbarians."[47] When the Athenians finally did turn their attention to the repair of the Acropolis, under Pericles, they lavishly devoted their funds and efforts to honoring their Athena with the Parthenon, the temple of Athena Nike, and the Erechtheum. Clearly, rebuilding sanctuaries that the barbarians had burned down was part of the rationale of the Periclean program (Plut. *Per.* 17.1). And the Athena Nike temple represented on its south frieze Greeks fighting and defeating Persians.[48] One may see in the Periclean rebuilding of the Acropolis in its totality of buildings, dedications, and particularly iconography a theme of, as Hurwit (1999.230) puts it, "*Nike* (Victory) — Victory Personified, Victory Commemorated, and Victory Represented." The greatest victory and that which probably initially inspired the whole was that over the Persians, particularly at Marathon.[49]

## DEMETER

The Greek Demeter was, of course, the giver of grain, and this association was so familiar that Herodotus and Apollo could use her name as metonymy for that crop (*1.193.2–3; 4.198.2; 7.141.4*). In cult the Demeter who was worshiped in much but not all of the Greek world for this gift was Thesmophoros, and Herodotus has her rituals introduced from Egypt to the Peloponnesus in the time of Danaus (2.171.2–3). Herodotus illustrates the power of Demeter Thesmophoros by two incidents that occurred shortly after the battle of Marathon.[50] On the island Paros, Miltiades, the hero of the Athenian victory at Marathon, violated the goddess's sanctuary. In the sanctuary he was seized by a panic, wrenched his knee while fleeing, and soon thereafter died from the injury (6.132–136). And at about the same time a party of rich Aeginetans during a civil war violated the asylum of their sanctuary of Demeter:

The rich men suffered a pollution (ἄγος) that they found impossible "to sacrifice away," and eventually they were exiled from their island before they appeased the goddess, because after they had captured 700 of the common people, they were leading them off to kill them, but one escaped his bonds and fled to the doorway of Demeter Thesmophoros. He took hold of the doorposts and held on. When the rich Aeginetans were not able by pulling to drag him away, they cut off his hands and then took him away. But those hands still clung tightly to the doorposts.[51] (6.91)

The cult of Demeter at Athens was centered at Eleusis, the home of the Eleusinian Mysteries. "This festival the Athenians held every year for the Mother and Kore, and whatever Athenian or Greek wishes is initiated." The Iacchos cry and the procession of her festival, during the Persian occupation, were heard and seen in the dust cloud by Dicaeus and Demaratus and gave an omen of Persian defeat at sea (8.65). And near a sanctuary of Demeter Eleusinia the major battle of Plataea was fought. Miraculously, in Herodotus' view, no Persians, dead or alive, were found in the sanctuary after the battle. "And I think . . . that the goddess herself was not taking them in because they had burned the *anaktoron* in Eleusis" (9.65.2). Among the "divine" coincidences of the battle of Mycale, as at Plataea, was a nearby sanctuary of Demeter Eleusinia, a sanctuary founded centuries earlier by the Athenian Philistus (9.97 and 101.1). From Herodotus' account it would seem that Demeter's interest in defeating the Persians arose largely from her desire to punish the sacrilegious treatment of her own property, as it was also in the cases of Miltiades and the Aeginetans.

Herodotus, though familiar with the major sanctuaries of Greek Artemis at Ephesus (1.26 and 92.1; 2.148.2), Samos (3.48), and Delos (4.34.2), assigns to these goddesses no role in the invasion. In Attica, Artemis Agrotera had a sanctuary at Agrae on the Ilissus River, near the route the Athenians would have taken on their march from Athens to Marathon in 490. Before the battle the Athenians vowed "that they would sacrifice to her a female goat for each enemy they killed. But when they were not able to find sufficient goats (for the 6,400 Persians killed), they decided to sacrifice 500 goats each year." The Athenians probably made these sacrifices on Artemis' first sacred day after the battle and then continued them well into the Roman period (Xen. *An. 3.2.11–12*).[52] Artemis Agrotera regularly received, at least from the Spartans, a prebattle goat sacrifice (Xen. *Hell.* 4.2.20), but the unique vow by the Athenians before Marathon may have been motivated by the proximity in time of the battle to the goddess's festival.[53]

Artemisium itself was named after the goddess whose sanctuary was prominent there (7.176.1), and the Athenians made a large dedication to her after the Greek victory there (Plut. *Them. 8.2–3*). Chance location, too, gave fame to the Athenian Artemis Mounichia, opposite whose sanctuary near Piraeus the Persians drew up their ships for the battle of Salamis. This in turn brought fulfillment of an oracle of Bacis, but even in the oracle not Artemis but Dike, Zeus, and Lady Nike were to bring the "day of freedom" (*8.77*). Artemis' association with the battle remained long in the Athenians' minds, however, and four centuries later they were still holding, at Artemis' festival Mounichia, a regatta celebrating the victory.[54] After Salamis and before Plataea, Artemis Soteira helped the Megarians kill some Persians in their territory, and the Megarians dedicated two bronze statues to her (Paus. *1.40.2–3*). Plutarch records Themistocles' private foundation of a cult of Artemis Aristoboule ("Of Best Counsel") near his home after the war. He did this, Plutarch claims, "because he had devised the best plans for the city and the Greeks" (*Them. 22.1–2*. Cf. *Mor.* 869D).

## HERA

In the initial stages of the encounter at Mycale, when the Greeks were still on their ships, the Greek commander Leotychides sailed past the

Persians and their Greek, mostly Ionian, allies encamped on the shore. Speaking in Greek so as not to be intelligible to the Persians, he called to the Ionians to assist their fellow Greeks in the forthcoming battle, and he gave them the Greek password, "Hera" (Hdt. 9.98.3).[55] Why "Hera" was chosen we are not told. It may have been because the Greeks had recently stopped at the Samian Heraion near Calami (9.96.1).[56] More probably it is a reflection of the major role Hera played in the civic cult of Samos and the region. Because Mycale was less than one mile by sea from Samos and the Samians were largely responsible for bringing the Greek fleet to Ionia at this time, the Samian Hera may have been selected for this "honor." Whether this was the case or not, we take the opportunity for a Herodotean-style digression on Hera's internationally famous cult there.

Samian Hera's temple was, according to Herodotus, "the largest of all the temples we have seen" (3.60.4. Cf. 2.148.2).[57] The sanctuary was filled with precious dedications. Amasis, pharaoh of Egypt (570 to circa 525), gave two wooden statues of himself out of his friendship with Polycrates. In Herodotus' time they still stood in the temple, behind the doors (2.182). The Samian Maeandrius dedicated there the furniture from Polycrates' living room, probably after the tyrant's death (3.123.1). Mandrocles, the Samian architect who designed Darius' bridge over the Bosporus circa 516, gave the sanctuary a painting of the bridge, Darius, and the Persian army (4.88). Some Samian merchants, after huge financial success from a voyage into the Atlantic, gave six talents ($3.6 million), one-tenth of their profits, and from that was made an Argive-style bronze crater, with griffin heads around its rim and supported by three kneeling bronze statues, each over ten feet high (4.152.4). Also in Hera's sanctuary stood the large bronze, sculptured crater that Samians had stolen or bought from the Spartans, a gift originally intended for Croesus (1.70).

### APHRODITE

From Plutarch and other non-Herodotean sources we hear that Aphrodite, the major deity of Corinth, at the request of her courtesans inspired the Corinthian men for battle. The courtesans later erected a dedication in her temple because "she did not contrive to betray to bow-bearing Medes the acropolis of the Greeks"—that is, Acrocorinth (Plut. *Mor. 871A–B*).

Such were the Olympian deities who contributed to the Greek war effort against the Persians. Ares, Hephaestus, Dionysus, and other Olympians also make appearances in the pages of Herodotus, but the historian gives them no credit for the Greek victories. The Greeks as a group expressed their gratitude to the three Olympians whose cults and worship were Panhellenic: Apollo of Delphi, Zeus of Olympia, and Poseidon of the Isthmus. Each had already established Panhellenic festivals, and each acted in this war beyond local concerns for their sanctuaries. The other Olympians, by contrast, benefited and were honored by individual cities and peoples: Athena of Tegea, Plataea, and Athens; Demeter Eleusinia of Eleusis and affiliated cults; Artemis of Artemisium, Artemis Soteira of Megara, and Artemis Mounichia and Agrotera of Athens; Hera of Samos; and Aphrodite of Corinth. The participation of this second group of Olympians was largely a geographical happenstance: because the cities or lands they protected became the sites of battle or were immediately threatened, they were acting from parochial motives.

## ❧ The Heroes ❧

Even more locally bound, by cult and conception, were the cultic heroes of the time.[58] They were dead mortals who, for a variety of reasons, after their deaths received state cult at their tombs.[59] They, too, contributed to the Greek victories. After the battle of Salamis, Herodotus has Themistocles say, "Not we but the gods and heroes accomplished this" (*8.109.3*). The hero Ajax received one of the three Phoenician ships the Greeks dedicated in commemoration of and gratitude for the victory—the two others went to cults of Poseidon at Sunium and the Isthmus (*8.121.1*). The Athenians also later expressed their trust "in the gods and heroes as their allies, the gods and heroes for whom Xerxes had no respect and whose buildings and statues he burned" (*8.143.2*).

The Athenian Cleisthenes in 508, as part of his democratic reforms, remodeled the Athenian tribal system, limiting the role of the four Ionian tribes and creating ten new tribes. And to each of the ten he assigned an eponymous hero.[60] According to Herodotus, "Cleisthenes named them after local heroes, except for Ajax. Ajax (whose cult was on Salamis) he added, even though he was a foreigner, because he was a neighbor and an ally (5.66.2).[61] Ajax was an Aeacid, a grandson of the Aeginetan hero

Aeacus. The importance of Aegina in and before the war and of Salamis during the war brought Aeacus, Ajax, and the other Aeacidae (Aeacus' sons Peleus and Telamon) into the conflict. When the Thebans and Aeginetans allied against Athens in 506, the Thebans asked the Aeginetans to send two of their cultic heroes, the Aeacidae Peleus and Telamon, to help them, like mercenaries, in battle against the Athenians. The Aeginetans did this, but the Thebans, even with the Aeacidae, were again defeated. The Thebans then sent the Aeacidae back home and told the Aeginetans they preferred to have men instead (*5.80.2–81.1*). In this same conflict the Athenians were told by Delphi that, if they waited thirty years and built a sanctuary for Aeacus, they would "overthrow the Aeginetans." They did build the sanctuary, which was still standing in the Agora in Herodotus' time (*5.89*).[62] And on the day before the battle of Salamis, "the Greeks decided to pray to the gods and to summon the Aeacidae as allies. So they decided, and they did the following: after they prayed to all the gods, they summoned Ajax and Telamon from Salamis, and they sent a ship to Aegina for Aeacus and the other Aeacidae." The Aeacidae arrived just at the beginning of the battle (*8.83.2*). Ajax must have contributed to the victory because, as we have seen, he received one of the three Phoenician ships dedicated by all the Greeks after the battle (*8.121.1*). If the Aeginetan Aeacidae contributed or if, as for the Thebans, they disappointed, we are not told by Herodotus, but Plutarch (*Them. 15.1*) reports that some saw them protecting the Greek ships. For the Athenians Ajax remained, even centuries later, cultically associated with the victory at Salamis.[63]

Other cultic heroes played relatively minor, local roles. Echetlaeus and Theseus assisted the Athenians at Marathon (Paus. *1.15.3, 32.5* and Plut. *Thes. 35.5*), and the Delphian Phylacus and Autonous chased down and killed some of the Persians attacking Delphi (Hdt. *8.38–39.1*).[64] One such local hero, Protesilaus of Elaeus, in the closing days of the Persian invasion protected and avenged his sanctuary against an impious Persian, and Herodotus gives heightened importance and a programmatic character to the story by placing it, emphatically, as the penultimate *logos* of his *Histories* (*9.116–121*). Protesilaus, like the other Greek cultic heroes, had the power to defend himself and his property, and this cautionary tale we are given in the last pages of Herodotus' *Histories*.

As an interesting footnote to the role of heroes in the Persian Wars, one Persian became a hero worshiped in a Greek city.

When Xerxes was in Acanthus, it happened that Artachaees, his overseer of the channel (across Athos), died of disease. Artachaees was highly esteemed by Xerxes and was an Achaemenid. He was the largest of the Persians, about eight feet tall, and he had the loudest voice of any man. Xerxes considered his death a great misfortune and held a very beautiful funeral procession and burial ceremony for him. All the army poured offerings on his tomb. And as the result of an oracle the Acanthians sacrifice to this Artachaees as a hero, calling him by name.[65] (7.117)

## ⚞ The Divine ⚟

Herodotus commonly assigns to "the divine" (τὸ θεῖον), "the gods," "god," "the god," "the *daimon*," or "the *daimonion*" events not obviously tied to a specific sanctuary or ritual sequence. This practice is characteristically Greek, found in all genres of poetry and prose.[66] In Greek polytheism, especially from the Panhellenic viewpoint that Herodotus often assumes, any number of individual gods or heroes might be responsible for a specific event, and it would be difficult to identify the correct deity and perhaps even dangerous to give credit to the wrong one. It was wiser and more pious, if one was unsure, to hedge one's bet and to name τὸ θεῖον or "divine fortune" (θείη τύχη).[67] We should not view Herodotus' attributions of such events to θεῖον instead of to specific gods or heroes as a sign of disbelief or skepticism.[68] It was the normal and usual thing for a Greek to do.[69]

"The divine" itself may also have, as a collective, a unity,[70] and Ivan Linforth (1928.218) well described that unity and its relationship to individual gods as found in Herodotus:

But when [Herodotus] has occasion to refer in any way to the relation between men and gods, it is his general habit to attribute divine activity not to particular named gods, but to gods in general or to particular gods about whose identity he ventures no opinion. The impression which one receives from his manner of expression is that he recognized the existence of numerous gods who may act as individuals on particular occasions, or who may be thought of as something like a unified group with a racial solidarity contrasting them with the race of men. This divine race, godkind, set over against mankind, is very real, and its part in the affairs of men and the universe is plain for all to see. One can detect its influence in the world with more or less certainty, and one can form opinions concerning its general character; but little can be known about it from within. Men have discerned certain individual members of the race and know them by name. These individuals are believed to be active in certain more or less well defined phenomena, and in the particular places where cults have been established for their worship. But of their relations among themselves we can know nothing, and in the extremely complicated and diversified phenomena of human history and experience it is seldom possible to see the hand of a particular known god. The result is that though the multiplicity of gods is never called into question, there is a disposition to speak of the divine element in the world *as if* it were characterized by the indivisibility of the god of the pure monotheist.

If we isolate the activities of τὸ θεῖον not explicitly or implicitly associated with specific deities, and if we take—as has been amply demonstrated in modern scholarship—τὸ θεῖον, τὸ δαιμόνιον, "the gods," and sometimes even "god" or "the god" all to refer to the "divine,"[71] we are in a position to assess the role Herodotus gives this collective "divine" in the Persian Wars.[72] We begin with Themistocles' comments to fellow Greeks after the victory at Salamis: "Not we but the gods and heroes accomplished this. They begrudged (ἐφθόνησαν) one man who was unholy and rash to be king of Asia and Europe. He treated holy and profane things alike, burning and throwing to the ground the statues of the gods. He even whipped the sea and hurled leg irons into it" (*8.109.3*). The Athenians expressed much the same confidence, but looking to the future rather than the past, in response to Mardonius' overtures of alliance before the battle of Plataea: "Announce to Mardonius that the Athenians say that as long as the sun goes on its current path we will never come to terms with Xerxes. In our defense we will attack him, trusting in the gods and heroes as our allies, the gods and heroes for whom Xerxes had no respect and whose buildings and statues he burned" (*8.143.2*).[73] Herodotus, too, sees the contributions of the gods to Athenian and Greek success in the war:

If someone should say that the Athenians were the saviors of Greece, he would not miss the truth. For whichever side, Greek or Persian, they turned to was going to prevail. They chose that Greece should survive free, and they were the ones who, second only to gods (μετά γε θεούς), gathered together all the rest of the Greek world . . . and repulsed King Xerxes.[74] (*7.139.5*)

The assistance that "the divine" gave to the Athenians and the Greeks against the Persians took a variety of forms. "Divine" was the appearance of the cursor that, in the Athenian version, put an end to the Corinthian flight from Salamis (*8.94*). "Divine," too, was the herald's staff (and the resulting announcement of the victory at Plataea) that inspired the

Greeks to their final, successful assault on the Persians at Mycale (*9.100–101*). In a more particular way the Aeginetan Lampon claimed that "a god" granted to Pausanias, the commanding general at Plataea, his rescue of Greece and the resulting fame (*9.78.1–2*).[75] And in the aftermath of Mycale, the Greek gods as a group (θεοὶ Ἑλλήνιοι) could be invoked in pleas to liberate Ionia from Persian slavery (*9.90.2*).[76] In battle, interestingly, it was not necessary for the divine to *give* the Greeks victory but to make it a "fair fight."[77] In the Ionian Revolt the Phocaean general Dionysius promises the Ionians victory by default or battle if only "the gods make it a fair fight" (6.11.3). At Marathon Miltiades was confident the Athenians would win, again "if the gods made it a fair fight" (θεῶν τὰ ἴσα νεμόντων) (*6.109.5*). The storm at Artemisium and later off the coast of Euboea led Herodotus to the conclusion that "everything was being done by the god to make the Persian force equal in size to the Greek and not much larger" (*8.13*). Given their opponents' massive superiority in numbers, all the Greeks needed from their gods was a fair fight.

The "divine," specific gods, and specific heroes each helped the Greeks, against overwhelming odds, defeat the invading Persians. As Herodotus tells it, the "divine" and some gods may have helped the Persians as a group and as individuals in earlier times,[78] but when the conflict became one between Persians and Greeks, the divine world conceived of as a whole or in parts stood completely and solely behind the Greeks.[79] We need not review here the many instances detailed in this and the previous chapter of how the "divine," the gods, and the heroes helped the Greeks on land and at sea, by oracles and omens, by personal appearances and apparitions. We rather note some characteristic features of this help. Only heroes, for example, appear themselves assisting the Greek soldiers in battle, like Echetlaeus and Theseus at Marathon (Paus. *1.32.5* and Plut. *Thes. 35.5*) and Phylacus and Autonous at Delphi (*8.38–39.1*). Greek gods do not, à la Homer, make an epiphany in battle (or anywhere else) in Herodotus' *Histories*,[80] and the historian labels Pisistratus' self-serving attempt to stage a divine epiphany a "naive action" (*1.60.3–5*).[81] This distinction—heroes occasionally and personally participating in historical battles, gods never—is not peculiarly Herodotean. It is characteristic of prose history accounts of Greek warfare in the classical period.[82]

Second, divine participation is determined largely by locale. Herodotus' Athena, Demeter, Artemis, and Hera became involved in the Persian

Wars because their own sanctuaries were in the field of combat. They are the Athenian Athena and Artemis, the Artemisian and Megarian Artemis, the Plataean Demeter, and the Samian Hera. Had the conflict played out elsewhere, in the Peloponnesus, for example, we would find quite different deities involved, and this is all in accord with the local and regional character of Greek religious cult. Only the Panhellenic deities, deities already Panhellenic *in cult*, participated beyond local and state boundaries: Zeus Olympios, Poseidon of the Isthmus, and Apollo of Delphi. Only they, at the conclusion of the whole war, received gratitude and dedications from *all* the Greeks ( *9.81.1*). Local deities may help in nearby battles, like Ajax and Poseidon of Sunium at Salamis (*8.121.1*), but for the whole effort the Greeks thank the acknowledged Panhellenic gods.

Recognition of the local concerns of the participating deities raises the question of motivation. Why did the gods, in the Herodotean view, support the Greeks and oppose the Persians? The answer, somewhat surprisingly, may be that the gods were interested primarily in protecting their own sanctuaries and punishing the Persians for violation of these.[83] As Herodotus presents it, giving support to devoted worshipers or fellow countrymen was not the gods' foremost concern. He has Themistocles say after Salamis, "Not we but the gods and heroes accomplished this. They begrudged one man who was unholy and rash to be king of Asia and Europe. He treated holy and profane things alike, burning and throwing to the ground the statues of the gods" (*8.109.3*). The heroes Phylacus and Autonous chased the Persians from Delphi, the site of their sanctuaries. Apollo drove the Persians from Delphi, "capable," as he had promised, "of protecting his own property" (*8.35–39*). Protesilaus took vengeance on the Persian Autaüktes for the desecration of his sanctuary ( *9.116–121*), and, in Herodotus' view, Demeter Eleusinia at Plataea denied Persians asylum because they had burned her sanctuary in Athens ( *9.65.2*).

These individual events are but a part of the dominant religious theme of Herodotus' Persian Wars, the burning and destruction of the sanctuaries of gods and heroes. In 498 the Athenians with their Ionian allies captured Sardis, the capital of the Lydian satrapy, and in the aftermath the sanctuary of the goddess Cybebe was burned, accidentally according to Herodotus' account. When King Darius learned of it, "he took a bow, fitted an arrow to it, and shot the arrow up into the sky. As he did, he said, 'Zeus, grant me to take vengeance on the Athenians.'" It was the burning of Cybebe's sanctuary that the Persians used as an excuse for burning sanctuaries throughout the lands of hostile Greek cities for the next eighteen years (*5.101–105*).[84] These included, after the Ionian Revolt, Apollo's temple and oracle at Didyma and the sanctuaries of *all* the Ionian cities and islands of Asia Minor except Samos (*6.19* and *6.25*). Later Datis on his way to Marathon in 490 burned the sanctuaries of Naxos (*6.96*) and Eretria (*6.101.3*). In the second invasion Xerxes destroyed the sanctuaries in twelve Phocian cities, including Abae (*8.32–33*). Finally, with their occupation of Attica Xerxes and Mardonius fulfilled the vengeance demanded by Darius. They leveled and burned, so far as we know, all the sanctuaries of Athens and Attica (*7.8.β* and *140*, *8.53.2–55*, and *9.13.2*). It was for this sacriligious treatment of the deities' property that Herodotus has the Athenians later express confidence that the gods and heroes have helped them and would help them against the Persians (*8.109.3* and *143.2*). In the face of this onslaught of an unholy, impious man the gods and heroes acted. They took the Greek side, primarily, to judge from Herodotus, to protect their own sanctuaries and, if unsuccessful in that, to avenge their loss. Only the Greek gods already Panhellenic in cult, Zeus of Olympia, Poseidon of the Isthmus, and Apollo of Delphi, had concerns beyond their own sanctuaries and property.

## ✣ THREE ✣

# Some Religious Beliefs
# and Attitudes of Herodotus

The discussions and the Herodotean passages in the preceding pages derive, I hope, in good part from and in turn exemplify aspects of Herodotus' own religious beliefs. But given the varying purposes of the accounts,
the multiplicity of events, the foreign peoples introduced, and the Greek
historical personages represented, it may be helpful here to focus attention on Herodotus himself and survey components of his personal religion as he expressly states them or as they emerge unmistakably from
the ways he presents or shapes some of his accounts. We will, of course,
scarcely scrape the surface of knowing and understanding Herodotus'
personal religious world, but we can at least collect and study what he
chose to reveal in his *Histories*.[1]

To begin at the beginning, we give the three most basic beliefs of ancient Greek religion as Herodotus' contemporaries and later especially
Plato formulated them: "the gods exist," "the gods pay attention to the
affairs of men," and "there is reciprocity between men and gods."[2] That
Herodotus personally shared these beliefs requires no demonstration. A
reading of but a few pages of what precedes or, better, of the *Histories*
themselves suffices. We rather move onward to ask Herodotus, "What
kind of gods are these who exist," "to which affairs of men do they pay
attention," and "what are the forms of reciprocity that exist between men
and gods?"

In a statement that we analyze in some detail in the Appendix, Herodotus claims that 400 years before his own time Hesiod and Homer
gave the Greek gods their epithets, genealogies, offices, skills, and appearances (2.53). To conclude from this that Herodotus, as a Greek, personally
believed his gods to be such or only such as Hesiod and Homer estab-

lished them would be easy but simplistic. It would also be easy to assume that he was particularly devoted to the cults and deities of his native Halicarnassus. He may in fact have been so, but we can prove nothing of all this. And we must remember that Herodotus was a widely traveled, cosmopolitan individual with, for his or any time, great interest and wide personal experience in various religious systems of his world. What he personally believed when he was writing the *Histories* may have reflected that.

Herodotus does on occasion explicitly express his own views on the activities and powers of the gods. Casually and in passing he, as virtually all Greeks would, credits Zeus with giving rain (2.13.3; 3.124–125) and Demeter with grain (1.193.2–3 and 4.198.2). He also accepts the common association of Poseidon with earthquakes, and his account of the Peneus River gorge reveals his reasoning. The Peneus River flowed from the Thessalian plain through a magnificent gorge in the mountains to the Aegean Sea.[3] It was a stunning sight, and Xerxes sailed south from Therme along the coast just to see it. Herodotus was also impressed and, after describing it, gives an account of how it was formed: "The Thessalians themselves say that Poseidon made the channel through which the Peneus flows, and they are saying reasonable things (οἰκότα λέγοντες). For whoever thinks that Poseidon shakes the earth and that partings (of the earth) from an earthquake are the products of this god, would say, if he saw that gorge, that Poseidon made it because the parting of the mountains, as it appeared to me, is the product of an earthquake" (7.129.4).[4]

With considerably less scholarly qualification Herodotus accepts the Potidaeans' account of how the Persians there were killed by an unusual flood tide for violating the sanctuary of Poseidon (*8.129*). And in his final comment on the storms at Artemisium and off Euboea, Herodotus, not as a Delphian or as an Athenian but as one of the Greeks, seems to conclude that Poseidon was the cause: "Everything was being done by the god to make the Persian force equal in size to the Greek and not much larger" (*8.13*). Herodotus asserts with only minimal qualification ("I suppose") that "the god," no doubt Apollo, caused the unprecedented earthquake on Delos "as a miraculous sign to men of the evils that were to come" (*6.98*), and the historian is confident that the punishment (the wrath of the hero Talthybius) that befell the Spartans for maltreating Persian heralds was "divine" (*7.133–137*).

Herodotus also sees as "reasonable" the following structuring of the natural world by "the divine": "And somehow the foresight of the divine τοῦ θείου ἡ προνοίη), as is reasonable, since it is wise, made creatures that are edible and cowardly in soul all have many offspring so that they may not become extinct by being eaten. But it made those creatures that are tough and causers of distress have few offspring." Herodotus then offers hares and lions as examples of each type (3.108.2–4).

And in the Persian Wars, in addition to Poseidon's efforts at Artemisium, Herodotus himself concludes, "if it is necessary to think anything about divine actions," that Demeter excluded the Persians from her sanctuary at Plataea "because they had burned the *anaktoron* in Eleusis" (9.65.2). Each of the demonstrations of divine power introduced thus far receives explicit acceptance by Herodotus.[5] As we move farther afield, he has the Athenian Dicaeus attribute the miraculous dust cloud at Eleusis to "the divine" (almost certainly Demeter) (8.65), and only an incorrigible skeptic would question Herodotus' belief in the power that Apollo demonstrated in saving his sanctuary (8.35–39) or that the hero Protesilaus showed in punishing the violator of his cult (9.116–121). It was Herodotus' own view that the Athenians, "second only to gods," gathered together all the rest of the Greek world and repulsed King Xerxes (7.139.5), and that inclines us, not unreasonably, to see Herodotus' own beliefs behind what he has Themistocles say after the victory at Salamis: "Not we but the gods and heroes accomplished this." The gods, with their power, defeated the "unholy and rash" Xerxes (8.109.3).[6]

The preceding discussion includes all of Herodotus' explicit statements about the activity and power of Greek deities as well as a few of the more obvious implicit beliefs. Many more of the latter could be added, but interpretation would become increasingly subjective. Clearly, though, in several cases "it is reasonable" to Herodotus that Poseidon, Apollo, Demeter, and some heroes did what they were said to have done, and, importantly, in each case such action is tied to a sanctuary or venue specific to that deity. In all these cases the deities have limited spheres of activity—most often their own sanctuaries. "It is reasonable" might not seem to be a ringing declaration of faith, but Christian-style faith and strong pronouncements of it were not features of classical Greek religion. I have argued elsewhere that "reason" and "common sense" were major components in Greek religious belief,[7] and to say that something in the religious realm was "reasonable" is as strong a statement of belief in it as we can expect to find. The Greek language of religious belief was cognitive, not emotional, and we must allow for that in determining what Herodotus "believed."

Scholars have occasionally found in Herodotus' use of "the divine," "the gods," or "some god" instead of a specific deity an indication of disbelief or skepticism. This is erroneous. As discussed in Chapter 2, the use of these terms in describing divine events not obviously tied to a specific sanctuary or ritual sequence is characteristically Greek. It was the usual and normal thing to say, and it tells us nothing about the writer's personal beliefs except that he is following normal practices. Similarly Herodotus has heroes but not gods personally appear on the battlefield and elsewhere assisting their worshipers. This does not mean that Herodotus "believed in" heroes but not gods. That distinction between the epiphany of heroes and the nonappearance of gods is characteristic of Greek prose (vs. poetic) accounts of warfare and probably reflects common popular beliefs. Except in dreams (and only rarely then), Greek gods did not appear to their worshipers.[8]

Finally, to make a Socratic distinction, Herodotus in his explicit statements tells us what he thinks or accepts that gods *do*, not what they *are*. The best evidence for the latter may be his theory of the origins and development of Greek religion. In the Appendix I attempt to reconstruct that view from comments scattered throughout the *Histories*, and in very brief form it is this: the gods exist everywhere, but each society creates for itself its particular conceptions and worship of them; the pre-Greek Pelasgians living in what was to be Greece gave the gods Egyptian names; and Hesiod and Homer gave these gods their genealogies, offices, crafts, outward appearances, and distinctive epithets. From at least Pelasgian times gods received sacrifice and prayer, but in later times Greeks took up the Egyptian customs of giving the gods altars, processions, offering bringings, temples, and statues. Herodotus may have "thought" all of this, but to label it his "religious belief" is probably to misunderstand both the nature of religious belief and the nature of Greek historical and philosophical inquiry. Herodotus, I imagine, would cling rather tenaciously to the belief that Apollo could and did defend his sanctuary at Delphi, but with new evidence he could have been quite readily convinced that, for example, not Egypt but some other country gave to Greece the custom of holding religious processions. Herodotus' views of the origins of Greek religion are a theory to be tried, tested, and improved; his ideas about the existence and power of the gods are more what we would, I think, call religious "belief."

As we have seen, largely from his own words, Herodotus credits his gods with some real and important powers: to bring rain, produce grain, cause earthquakes, protect and avenge their own sanctuaries, and decide the outcome of a world war. These are some aspects of the gods' side of their reciprocal relationship with men. From the divine world also come oracles, and Herodotus accepts them in principle as divine but is fully aware of the caution necessary in judging each one.[9] Individual oracles might be vague, misleading, misinterpreted, or corrupted by human agents. But the oracles of Apollo at Delphi and of Amphiaraus at Thebes passed Croesus' exacting test (1.46–49), and the fulfillment of Bacis' oracle about events in the battle of Salamis led Herodotus to conclude that "when I look at events like this, I cannot say that oracles are not true because I do not wish to try to put down those that speak clearly" (8.77).[10] Herodotus sees as completely fulfilled or explains the fulfillment of Apollo's oracles to Croesus (1.53–56, 91); to the Milesians about the destruction of their city (6.19); on the earthquake on Delos (6.98), if it is Apollo's oracle; to the Delphians about praying to the winds (7.178); to the Spartans about the death of their king (7.220); to Tisamenus about his victories (9.33–35); of Bacis and Musaeus about the battle of Salamis (8.77 and 96.2); and, most famously, to the Athenians on the "wooden wall" (7.139–144).[11]

Omens were no doubt a greater part of an individual's daily life than oracles, and Herodotus consistently accepts their validity: "[S]igns somehow customarily appear when great evils are about to befall a city or people," and, in the case of the Chians, "the god showed these signs to them" (6.27). The omens Cleomenes received at the Argive Heraion proved accurate (6.82.2). The god sent the omen of the earthquake to the Delians, and here Herodotus serves as our *mantis* to explain that it predicted the evils that were to come to Greece from Darius, Xerxes, and Artoxerxes (6.98). He also offers his own interpretation of the horse-bearing-a-hare omen to Xerxes at the Hellespont (7.57) and, slightly less coherently, of the omens the Greeks received at Mycale (9.100–101). All these omens proved accurate, and so did virtually all those interpreted by others, like Hegesistratus' *kledon* at Mycale (9.91), Artaüctes' fish at

Sigeum (*9.10*), and the dust cloud on the Thriasian Plain (*8.65*). The battlefield omens Herodotus has both sides take at Plataea all proved accurate, for the winners as well as the losers (*9.36–38, 41, 61.2–62.1*).

Whether dreams come from "the divine" is the topic of intense discussion between Xerxes and Artabanus (*7.15.3–18*). Herodotus gives no credit for a Greek dream to a Greek god but attributes a dream of Cyrus and one of Cambyses to a *daimon* (1.210.1 and 3.65.4). He himself interprets Cyrus' dream for us, as he does also the dream of Polycrates' daughter (3.124.1–125). Most of the dreams Herodotus reports give signs of failure or disaster and what they predict is inescapable.[12]

*Manteis* were intermediaries between humans and omens. The Egyptians thought that the mantic art was possessed by no man (2.83),[13] but Herodotus clearly respected the work of the Greek practitioners of this art. He presents Megistias, Leonidas' *mantis* at Thermopylae, as professionally skilled and personally heroic (*7.219.1, 221,* and *228.3–4*). To judge by the outcome, the three *manteis* employed by the opposing forces at Plataea all judged the omens correctly (*9.36–38, 41, 61.2–62.1*). *Chresmologoi*, interpreters and collectors of oracles, might be right or wrong. Lysistratus' oracle proved true at the battle of Salamis (8.96.2),[14] but other Athenian *chresmologoi* were in error in their interpretation of the "wooden wall" oracle from Delphi (*7.143.3*). In Onomacritus Herodotus has a *chresmologos* manipulate his oracles to achieve a political end (*7.6*). Herodotus' *manteis*, however, were accurate and honest, and their accuracy, as well as that of most oracles, omens, and dreams in the *Histories*, may reflect Herodotus' personal beliefs but may well also find its basis, as will be discussed later, in a poetic convention.

Humans were obliged as part of their reciprocal relationship with the gods to render the gods "honor" (τιμή) through prayer, sacrifice, and dedications. We have numerous descriptions of each of these acts of worship in Chapter 1, and Herodotus never pauses to give his personal thoughts about these religious acts so familiar and routine to his intended audience. We can pick up only a few hints—for example, that he considers sacrifices to be a sign of a well- and justly governed society (2.129.1) and believes that, in desperate circumstances, a prayer could be instantly answered (*9.61.2–62.1*).[15] His telling of the *logos* of Croesus on the pyre suggests that a pleasing gift to the god followed by a prayer could bring lifesaving help (1.87.1–2). That all the prayers Herodotus has made to Greek gods were answered may be relevant, but may also result from the historian adopting a poetic convention. One should be hesitant to argue from what Herodotus does *not* say, but he does introduce prayers, sacrifices, and a multitude of dedications into his account of the Persian Wars, and nowhere does he call into question or leave in question their efficacy. It would seem reasonable to conclude that he treats them as normal religious activities that contributed and responded to the success of the Greeks over the Persians.

The gods thus do "pay attention" to prayers, sacrifices, and dedications, and Herodotus unmistakably thinks they attend also to violations of things under divine protection. These include the rights of asylum, oaths, *xenia*, respect for the dead, and, especially relevant in the Persian Wars, the gods' own sanctuaries and property. On such noncontroversial topics Herodotus rarely has need to judge, but several accounts show obvious acceptance of their sanctity as well as of the punishments of those who violate them. Apollo of Branchidae, with some prompting, asserted the protection of a suppliant with asylum (1.157.3–160), the Aeginetans suffered lengthy pollution for violating it (6.91), and for the same reason King Cleomenes may have committed his grisly suicide (6.75). Herodotus has Apollo of Delphi affirm the sanctity of oaths and the destruction of the family of perjurers, and the case of Glaucus illustrates the point (6.86). It is the historian's personal opinion that the sufferings of the Trojans were the result of Alexander's violation of Menelaus' *xenia* and the gods' punishment of that (2.120). He obviously abhors maltreatment of the dead, whether by Cambyses (3.16.2 and 37.1) or Xerxes (*7.238* and *9.78–79*). His disapproval of the impiety of robbing, burning, and desecrating sanctuaries has already been abundantly discussed and forms a major theme of his whole work, but we note the emphasis he gives it, in his final pages, with the account of the desecrations and punishment of the Persian Artaüctes (*9.116–120*).

Harrison (2000.102–121), under the chapter heading "Divine Retribution," has an extensive discussion of the gods' punishment of human beings for various kinds of misbehavior in all of the *Histories*. His examples, as all the examples given previously, can be interpreted as punishments for impieties. Impiety, however, was one form of injustice,[16] and to this degree the punishments for impiety were for injustice as well. The gods can be enforcing "justice" in their punishments of acts that were "unjust" as well as "impious." Harrison asserts, but does not prove (esp. 108–109), that the "category of actions likely to receive [divine] retribution is broader (potentially at least) than just the narrow class of acts of sacrilege." The distinction is important, because Harrison would have Herodotus' gods concerned with justice in general and beyond matters of impiety, whereas in fact all examples of divine intervention to punish individuals in the *Histories* can be seen to arise from impieties. Herodotus' gods are concerned with actions that affect them and their property and specific human institutions under their protection. They do not, in broader terms, attend to all matters of justice among human beings.

As we describe man's side of the reciprocal relationship with the gods, we find ourselves involved in questions of piety and impiety. As Herodotus presents it, the impious individual treated "holy and profane things alike" (*8.109.3*), could be beset by *atasthalia* and madness (2.111.2; 3.16 and 37–38.2; *7.34–35*; *8.109.3*; *9.78* and *116.1*), and had "no respect" for gods and heroes (*8.143.2*). He exhibited an evil "daring" (1.183.3). Such a person violated asylum, oaths, *xenia*, the dead, and divine property. He was also likely to misinterpret the import of oracles, omens, and dreams. The flagrantly and repeatedly impious like Cambyses, Cleomenes, Artaüctes, and Xerxes were punished severely, usually with death. Glaucus (6.86) and Miltiades (*6.132–136*) might suffer the same for a single impiety. An interesting exception to the rule, perhaps revealing Herodotus' own bias, is that impious acts directed against a tyrant or tyrannical authority were left unpunished by the historian (5.18–21, 36.3–4, 46.2, and 63).

Herodotus himself expresses (3.38) and exhibits considerable respect for the "customs" (νόμιμα) of others, however strange they might seem.[17] He describes without pause or snicker foreign goat-faced and ram-faced gods, but, however open-minded, he cannot silently accept sexual intercourse in religious settings. The ritual prostitution of their women by the Babylonians is their "most shameful" custom (1.199); he does not like it that non-Greeks and non-Egyptians have, like animals, sexual intercourse in sanctuaries (2.64);[18] and he is not willing to accept that a Zeus in Babylon or Egyptian Thebes spent the night in a temple with a mortal woman (1.181.5–182).[19] He is, of course, following Greek traditions in this attitude,[20] and we need not psychoanalyze him to find the reasons for it.

Herodotus is also reluctant to reveal "sacred *logoi*" (ἱ ροὶ λόγοι), some of which he apparently knew.[21] He seems to have known who was mourned at Isis' festival in Egypt (2.61.1); the mysteries and who was buried in the special tombs at Sais (2.170–171.1); and who gave his name to Egypt's most elaborate embalming procedure (2.86.2), but he thought it "not holy" (οὐκ ὅσιον) to tell. There were also sacred *logoi* about the Egyptian lamp festival of Athena (2.62.2)[22] and why Orphics and Bacchics could not be buried in woolen garments (2.81.2). Herodotus knows why Egyptians sacrifice pigs only to Dionysus and Semele but will not reveal the *logos* (2.47.2), nor will he describe the Greek ritual of the Thesmophoria (2.171.2–3) or the sacred *logos* of the Mysteries at Samothrace (2.51.2–4). There was also a sacred *logos* explaining the form and movements of the Egyptian Dionysus puppets (2.48). Why Herodotus chose not to tell the ἱροὶ λόγοι probably varied from *logos* to *logos*. In some cases he may not have known them, in some (as we know of the rituals of the Thesmophoria) they may have been secret.[23] Often it may be just as Herodotus claims, that it was "not holy" to reveal the *logos*.[24] Occasionally it does not suit his taste (οὐ ἥδιον, 2.46.2) or his sense of decorum (οὐκ εὐπρεπέστερός ἐστι λέγεσθαι, 2.47.2).

Why Herodotus did not tell ἱροὶ λόγοι is a different matter from his twice expressed reluctance to describe "divine activities" (θεῖα πρήγματα)[25] in his account of Egypt. "I am not eager to describe the explanations of divine activities that I heard, except only for the names, because I think all men have equal knowledge about them. I will mention whatever divine activities I do only when forced to do so by my narrative" (2.3.2). About sixty chapters later — many devoted to Egyptian gods and religious practices[26] — he restates this reluctance in identical terms, this time concerning why animals are sacred in Egypt (2.65.2). First, it must be noted that Herodotus asserts this reluctance only in his account of Egypt, but, properly understood, it seems to reflect his practice throughout.[27] Second, if we take θεῖα πρήγματα etymologically and very literally as "actions done by the gods," as "divine activities," then Herodotus' claim is generally true.[28] He certainly gives far more than their names, but we learn almost nothing of what *in a mythological sense* these gods are said or thought "to have done."[29] θεῖα πρήγματα are apparently mythological accounts of the *deeds* of the gods — the kind of accounts Hesiod and Homer created for the Greek gods. "All men have equal knowledge about them" because, like the Hesiodic and Homeric accounts, they have been equally "created" by each society. In all probability, Herodotus did not describe them because, unlike cult activities in which humans participated (τὰ ἀνθρωπήια), they were unverifiable by the historical methods he used.[30]

Herodotus simply did not believe that Babylonian Zeus spent nights in his temple there, no matter what the priests said (1.182.1), and this is one of the relatively few instances where the limits of Herodotus' credulity are reached in religious matters. He likewise does not believe that the statues of Damia and Auxesia were originally sculpted standing but in the commotion surrounding their theft fell to their knees and remained in that posture (5.86.3). He also does not accept the *logos* that the Neuroi of Scythia become werewolves once a year (although his sources swore it was true, 4.105.2), and he is hesitant to believe that in rites of Egyptian Demeter (Isis) wolves lead a blindfolded priest two and a half miles to and from the goddess's sanctuary (2.122.2–123.1).[31] Nor, finally, does he believe the Egyptian account of the sacred phoenix, that it envelops its father in a myrrh egg and carries it from Arabia to the sanctuary of Helios in Egypt for burial (2.73).[32]

In each case Herodotus rejected the *logos* despite what his sources "said" or "swore." Herodotus could thus explicitly reject "what was said," or could waffle, saying he neither believed nor disbelieved it, as of the *logos* of Salmoxis of the Getae (4.96. Cf. 7.189).[33] Such examples should make us wary of assuming that when Herodotus, instead of giving an account on his own authority, introduces actively ("they say") or passively ("it is said") another source, he means to cast doubt on the story.[34] Unless he explicitly questions his source,[35] we should think that he is simply reporting, not judging.[36] He can tell us when he is judging if he wishes to. To say that Herodotus is "reporting, not judging" is not to claim that he "accepts" every account he "reports."[37] That, for example, his account of Philippides and Pan (6.105) is presented in indirect discourse with the passive-type presentation of the source should *not* incline us to assume that Herodotus did not accept the story.[38] Herodotus could easily and on occasion did mark what he did not believe.

Herodotus exercised his independent judgment also in a range of other religious matters. He sometimes let stand alternative explanations of religious phenomena:[39] why the winds abated at Artemisium (7.191–192, 8.13); why Xerxes had sacrifices performed on the Acropolis in Athens (8.54); and whether the Corinthians were urged back to the battle of Salamis by the miraculous ship and crew (8.94). But he also might choose among various possibilities: there were three impieties for which King Cleomenes may have been punished, and at the end of his account of this king Herodotus chooses one among them (6.75 and 84.3).[40] In his account of the founding of the oracle at Dodona, Herodotus gives the Egyptian and Dodonaean versions, but then offers a third, separate version of his own (2.54–57). And, as in the case of the origins of Dionysus, Heracles, and Pan (2.145–146), Herodotus could offer a solution that would reconcile apparently discordant versions. Generally when he chooses among variants, Herodotus prefers the less miraculous, the one more reasonable (κατ' οἰκότα).

Between descriptions of religious phenomena as facts and outright rejections of them lies, as we have seen, a broad range of modalities—among them attribution to named or unnamed sources, variant versions, and the use of indirect statement. These are all forms of what Gould (1994.92–96) terms the "cautionary mode of narrative" that is particularly appropriate to discussions of divine and supernatural topics.[41] Poets can create a world in which divine action and responsibility are confidently described and assigned. But that is a luxury the historian did not enjoy. He had to infer from events what causes, human and divine, might lay behind them. The "cautionary mode" does not betoken disbelief, just that some uncertainty attends what is being described.[42] It is, as Gould (94) puts it, "no more than the expression of a universal (and among Greeks universally accepted) implicit acknowledgement of the limitations of human knowledge in such areas," and it is what we would expect from a historian working carefully and thoughtfully.[43]

Like most Greeks of his time, Herodotus can interpret omens, as that of disaster for the Chians (6.27) or of victory for the Greeks at Mycale (9.100–101). He knows well, of course, the Delphic oracles and is willing to hazard a guess at what Mys' oracles told Mardonius (8.136.3). He points explicitly, from his knowledge, to Mardonius' misinterpretation of another oracle (9.42–43).[44] He gave a detailed analysis of the dream of Polycrates' daughter (3.124–125). And, on a different kind of issue, he ventures an opinion, almost as an Athenian expert on matters of pollution and murder, of who was and was not "polluted" by the sacrilegious murder of Cylon (5.70–71). The historian also expresses what are explicitly or implicitly his views of immoral, impious behavior: of Alexander's violation of *xenia* and the punishment of the Trojans for that (2.114 and

120.5); of Cambyses' numerous impieties (3.16.2); of Pheretima's punishment of the Barcaeans (4.205); of the Aeginetan violation of asylum (6.91); of Spartan and Athenian maltreatment of Xerxes' heralds (*7.133–137*); and of Xerxes' mutilation of Leonidas' corpse (*7.238*).

There is also a "scholarly" side to Herodotus' treatment of religious matter: a correction of a detail in the *logos* of Euenius (9.95), the identification of Egyptian Aphrodite Xenia with Helen of Troy (2.112.2), and a reference to a mythical variant in a play of Aeschylus (2.156.6). But of vastly greater significance is his scholarly and historical approach to the history of Greek religion. He does not treat the subject systematically or comprehensively and never intended to do so, but in the Appendix we see his personal attempts to bring chronological, cultic, and even mythographical order to variant Egyptian, Phoenician, Libyan, and Greek accounts of the gods. Finally, in what may be his most important contribution to the topic, he claims that it is his own view that Hesiod and Homer "created a divine genealogy for Greeks, gave their epithets to the gods, distributed their offices and crafts, and marked out their outward appearances" (2.53.2).

Herodotus does often, as he himself says of his Egyptian account, simply "write what is said by each of the peoples" he encounters (2.123.1. Cf. 7.152.3). But the preceding selections from the many possible examples of various types reveal that he is willing in religious matters to use his own knowledge and to make personal judgments. He does so in a rather gentle manner, and in his respect for local customs he rarely challenges or questions them. One of his strongest such challenges, to the "foolish story that Greeks tell about Heracles," he ends with perhaps characteristically temperate and pious caution: "May there be goodwill from the gods and heroes as we say such things about these matters" (2.45).

Important elements of Herodotus' outlook on life are commonly treated as "religious" and have occasioned a great deal of scholarly discussion. Whether we think them properly "religious" or not depends, of course, on how we conceive of and define Greek religion. For the purposes of this book I concentrate on Greek religion as it was practiced in cult, that is, on the prayers, vows, sacrifices, dedications, and other religious acts that were intended to bring a favorable response from the gods and to express gratitude to them. I include as well omens, oracles, and even miracles, all of which were features of Greek cultic religion. By this admittedly restricted definition of Greek religion, the following interrelated elements of Herodotean thought, including a fatalistic notion of "what must happen," the idea of a cycle of the "reversal of human fortunes," and finally the concept of divine *phthonos*, would not be "religious" because they are unaffected by human prayer, sacrifice, dedications, and other forms of worship. They each, I argue, derive from a tradition of poetic speculations about the nature of the "divine," not from the cultic tradition of Greek religion. But they have their place, an important place, in relation to Herodotus' concepts of cultic religion because they offer him explanations for some of the evils that befall human beings.

Let us begin with events that Herodotus reports "had" to happen, that were, in some undefined way, "destined."[45] Foreigners could be affected: things "had" to turn out badly for Candaules, king of Lydia (1.8.2); for King Apries of Egypt (2.161.3); and for the Scythian king Scyles (4.79.1). "It was necessary" (ἔδεε) that the Naxians not be taken in Megabates' expedition of 499 (5.33.2), and, in the last few pages of his *Histories*, evils "had" (ἔδεε) to befall Xerxes' mistress and her family (9.109.2). Finally, the dream image that had previously appeared to Xerxes warned Artabanus not to attempt to prevent the king's expedition against the Greeks. It was "what must happen" (τὸ χρεὸν γενέσθαι, *7.17.2*), and it, too, turned out to be a disaster. Greeks, too, might encounter a similar "necessity": that evils "sprout up" for Corinth from Eëtion's family (5.92.δ.1); that Demaratus' origins be revealed and he lose his kingship in Sparta (6.64); that, in the words of the Pythia, Miltiades "die not well" (*6.135.3*); and that the Hellespont "be yoked by a Persian man" (*7.6.4*). Why it "was necessary" that all these things happen we are not told, but it is noteworthy that each event in its own context is treated as a misfortune or disaster.[46]

Herodotus occasionally has oracles report such "necessity": the Spartans had oracles that they "must be (χρεόν ἐστί) expelled from the Peloponnesus" (*8.141.1*), and the Athenians that they must (δεῖ) found Siris in Italy (8.62.2). Herodotus does not introduce such "oracular" necessity for events of the Persian Wars, with one important exception: "it was necessary (ἔδεε), according to the oracle, for all Attica on the mainland to become subject to the Persians" (*8.53.1.* Cf. *7.140–141*). These "necessary" events reported in oracles are also mostly evil from the point of view of those to whom the oracles are directed.

Only once does Herodotus appear to suggest a direct connection between an oracle and the god's will that an event happen. Cleomenes thought he discovered from the oracles and omens concerning the taking of "Argos" "everything that Apollo wanted to happen" (6.82). But the most common relationship between oracles and "what must happen" or "what will happen" in the *Histories* is more complex and less explicit. When an oracle predicts, without any limiting conditions or alternatives, "what will happen," it is predicting in all essentials "what must happen" and "what, eventually, does happen."[47] From Herodotus' perspective, looking back as a historian, these events are the "Given of History" (die Gegebenheiten des Geschehenen) as J. Kirchberg (1965.28) terms them. In her study Kirchberg gives a convincing demonstration that Herodotus has numerous oracles describe (*not* prescribe) "what will and has to happen," and then has individuals and states either "learn" (μανθάνειν) from the oracle "what must happen" and adapt to it or misinterpret, ignore, or forget the oracle and thereby act counter to "what must happen." They do not affect the predicted event but bring needless grief and destruction upon themselves. From her many examples we select these: to the Lydian Gyges it was predicted by the Delphic oracle that in the fifth generation punishment would come on his family for his murder of Candaules and assumption of his power (1.13.2), and in the fifth generation his descendant Croesus paid that punishment and lost his empire to the Medes, "in accordance with the oracle" (1.86.1 and 91.1–3); the destruction of Miletus was predicted, and it happened, "according to the oracle" (*6.18–19*); and Apollo predicted that all Attica would be occupied and destroyed by the Persians (*7.140–141*), and so it happened, "according to the oracle" (*8.53.1*).

In terms of human responsibility one has the "freedom" to fit one's life into the framework of "what must happen" as best one can. First, of course, one must correctly interpret the often obscure or even misleading oracle. To do this successfully, as did the Thebans in *5.79–81* and the Athenians in *7.139–144*, one must proceed thoughtfully, prudently, and warily. Haste, forgetfulness, overeagerness for one's plan, or a lack of awareness of a human being's changeful fortunes may cause error in interpretation and then destruction, as they did, for example, for Croesus (1.53–56 and 90–91) and Cleomenes (6.80–82).

Kirchberg variously terms the force behind "what must happen" as "The Plan of Divinity" (der Plan der Gottheit), "The Will of the Gods" (die Götterwille), and "Fate" (das Schicksal), but Herodotus gives no name to this "force."[48] Most important, he does not associate it with the gods or a god, and, in fact, on the one occasion where the two are linked, in 1.91.2–3, he has the god subject to it. In a sense this "determiner" of "what must be" is not an element of Greek religion because it pays no heed to sacrifice or prayer or to human wishes. I, like Herodotus, give no name to this "force" because virtually any name selected, even one as bland and un-Greek as "Fate," introduces connotations not present in Herodotus' account.[49] It is simply "what will happen" and "what does in fact happen." Proper nomenclature or avoidance of nomenclature is essential here because it determines whether we view the "what has to happen" and "what will be" phenomena as fundamentally religious or not. Finally, in virtually all cases "what has to happen," whether predicted by an oracle or not, is bad for the individual or state concerned. Herodotus uses this concept almost exclusively to "explain" evils, in much the way that other, especially later Greek authors use "fortune" (τύχη), which also, etymologically, is simply "what happens."[50]

Herodotus offers a related but not identical explanation for the evils some men suffer in the principle, announced in the "second" preface (1.5.3–4) and vividly and programmatically detailed in the Solon-Croesus encounter (1.29–33), of the "reversals of human fortune" — namely, the small become great and, much more commonly in the *Histories*, the great become small. One can judge the quality of a person's life only at the end because "a human being is, in every regard, chance" (συμφορή, 1.32.4). Harrison (2000.33–63) has shown in full detail how this principle is an underlying pattern in the careers of Croesus, Cyrus, Polycrates, Xerxes, and a number of other once powerful individuals in the *Histories*. Like the "what must happen" phenomenon, it seems more prescriptive than descriptive in several accounts, but, unlike "what must happen," it is sometimes explicitly attributed to the action of "the divine." The divine, in Solon's formulation, is φθονηρόν and ταραχῶδες ("full of *phthonos* and disruptive," 1.32.1) and might at any time assail a prosperous man, and that is why one cannot judge a man's life until he sees a happy end. The source of this view enounced by the Herodotean Solon and endorsed by Herodotus himself is, as Harrison has shown (36–40), the poetry of the real Solon, and it is echoed in poetry from Solon's to Herodotus' time.

For our purposes of delineating the role of practiced Greek religion in the Persian Wars, three points are critical for understanding the role Herodotus gives to this principle of the reversal of human fortunes. First, it is occasioned by "the divine" (τὸ θεῖον, 1.32.1, 3.40.2. Cf. 3.42.4), by "some divine impulse" (δαιμονίη τις ὁρμή, 7.18.3), or by "the god" (ὁ θεός, 1.32.9; 7.10.ε, 18.3, and 46.4. Cf. 1.34.1 and 127.2), never by a named god of cult. It is the product of speculation about the divine in general, not about the deities of cult. Second, the progress of these reversals seems unaffected by prayer, sacrifice, and dedications—the cultic acts of worship of the Greeks.[51] That is, in part, because it is associated with no specific deity, only with the generalized "divine," and the Greeks did not sacrifice or pray to or worship the generalized "divine." Finally, this principle of the reversal of fortunes and the ideas associated with it are products of the poetic tradition and seem restricted to it,[52] as are components of it such as *phthonos* and *nemesis*. It was from the poetic, not cultic tradition that Herodotus borrowed it, and he used it almost exclusively, as he did the "what must happen" phenomenon, as one among many explanations of the evils that beset men and countries.

In our discussion of *7.10.ε* in Chapter 1 we saw how Herodotus had Artabanus use the concept of *phthonos* of the divine to explain human failures to Xerxes. *Phthonos* is a factor, too, in the undoings of Croesus (1.32), Xerxes (*8.109.3*), and Polycrates (3.40–43). Divine *phthonos* is also a concept favored by some poets (e.g., Solon, Pindar, and Aeschylus) prior to or contemporary with Herodotus, and it is often a component of the "reversals of fortune" principle. Herodotus employs it as one explanation for the disasters of a few major figures, but not for major or minor events of the Persian Wars or for other characters. He introduces *phthonos*, I think, when he wants to give a fuller account of misfortune than his and other Greeks' more usual appeals to "necessity" or "the reversals of fortune" would allow. For featured individuals, for the great kings and tyrants, he uses not the "mythological," Homeric-style explanation of the desires and hostilities of individual deities, but the more abstract concept of *phthonos* of the "divine" in general, a concept most fully developed in the poetry of Solon.

To grasp the place of "necessity," "the reversals of fortune," and divine *phthonos* in Herodotus' world view, we need to reassert that Greeks in practiced religion seem reluctant to assign responsibility for evil and misfortune to individual gods. This is, I would claim, a fundamental difference from religion as depicted in much of epic and tragedy.[53] The divinely bestowed "goods" that come to the Greeks in the Persian Wars are owed to gods of cult, Apollo of Delphi, Isthmian Poseidon, Demeter Eleusinia, and Artemis Mounichia. For the cause of evils, whether for Greeks or Persians, Herodotus turns elsewhere, to "necessity," "the reversals of fortune," *phthonos*, or to voluntary human actions in combination with one of these three "poetic" principles. And then, in what may be a particularly Herodotean twist, these usual poetic causes of failure and misfortune bring disaster primarily to the Persian Xerxes in the Persian Wars and thereby help save the Greeks. Herodotus has thus taken common Greek explanations of failure, has applied them to Xerxes (and his paradigm Croesus), and has them ultimately become part of the explanation of the success of the Greeks. If we were to ask if Herodotus "believed" in "the reversal of human fortunes," in divine *phthonos*, and that some events simply "had" to happen, the answer would probably be affirmative, but with two important caveats: he does not use them to explain all or most situations to which they could reasonably be applied, that is, they are not part of a consistent theology;[54] and for him they proved ultimately good, just, and helpful to the Greeks. They contributed, as did the gods of cult, to the Greek victories in the Persian Wars.

I have suggested that Herodotus' presentation of *manteis*, omens, oracles, and dreams (that they are virtually all accurate and fulfilled) and of prayers to Greek gods (that they are all answered) may also be influenced by poetry, but here not by specific concepts taken from poets but by a poetic convention. By a poetic convention I mean the way religious topics, here divination and prayer, were consistently treated in earlier and contemporary poetic literature, specifically the Homeric epics and early Athenian tragedy. In these genres virtually all prayers to Greek gods by pious individuals are answered, and those of the impious are either not answered or are answered to their disadvantage.[55] So, too, in Herodotus. In tragedy virtually all *manteis*, oracles, omens, and dreams are eventually found to be accurate,[56] and so, too, in Herodotus.[57] Such treatments of prayers and of divination both presume and require careful shaping of the material by individual poets, but the uniformity of presentation in this regard between genres (epic and tragedy) and among poets suggests that it was more than an individual poet's preference—it was a poetic convention of the time, and I think that these aspects of Herodotus' presentation of divination and prayer can best be explained as an adoption of these poetic conventions in his prose history.[58]

Such are the primary "poetic" elements I see in the religious world of Herodotus. But one perhaps is not allowed to leave this topic without commenting on two poetic features most strikingly *not* in Herodotus' *Histories*: the explicit description of impieties as *hybris* directed against the gods; and, second, the Homeric-style gods and divine machinery. Of Herodotus' thirty-eight uses of *hybris* terms (ὕβρις, ὑβρίστης, ὑβρίζειν, περιυβρίζειν, and καθυβρίζειν), only one appears linked with human impieties.[59] The tyrant Pheidon of Argos committed great *hybris* (ὑβρίσαντος μέγιστα δὴ Ἑλλήνων ἁπάντων) when he drove the Eleans from Olympia and seized control of the Olympic games (6.127.3), but even here the *hybris* may be the wrong done to the Eleans, not to Zeus, and there is no mention of divine punishment.[60] These *hybris* terms, surprisingly, are not to be found in Herodotus' accounts of the religious behavior of those individuals whose actions were notoriously impious or religiously problematic: Croesus, Cambyses, Darius, Xerxes, Artaüctes, and Cleomenes.[61]

That the *hybris* terms do not occur in such contexts does not, of course, preclude the presence of underlying *hybris* concepts such as the punishment of a hybristic individual by the gods, but discussion of this requires an agreed-upon definition of *hybris*. The traditional definitions of *hybris* are conveniently collected by Fisher (1992.2–3): that *hybris* is "essentially an offence against the gods . . . ; it is the act, word, or even thought whereby the mortal forgets the limitations of mortality, seeks to acquire the attributes of the gods, or competes with the gods, or boasts overconfidently; or it is any act or word by which a man incurs the hostility of the gods, or even arouses their jealousy . . . ; or it is any 'excessive' act or word contrary to the spirit of the Delphic Oracle's pronouncements; it may even be no more than the possession of great good fortune, which in itself offends the gods." By most of these definitions, of course, examples of *hybris* can be found throughout the pages of Herodotus. Fisher points to the inadequacies of these definitions and offers a substitute that seems to cover better the actual range of *hybris* words in Greek religious and secular life: "[H]ybris is essentially the serious assault on the honor of another, which is likely to cause shame, and lead to anger and attempts at revenge." If the "another" whose honor is assaulted is a deity, then we have what we might term "religious *hybris*" (vs. "secular *hybris*"),[62] and by applying his own definition Fisher (345–365) finds a few examples of "religious *hybris*" in Cambyses and other impious individuals. Cairns (1996) stresses the "dispositional" (vs. "behavioral") aspect of *hybris* and, for example, directly equates "thinking big" with *hybris*, and he can thus label Xerxes hybristic on the basis of passages such as 7.8.γ.1–2, *10*, and 16.α. One can, then, by one's own definition of *hybris* find various examples of "religious *hybris*" in Herodotus, but at best the examples are isolated and do not form a pervasive theological causality.

There are abundant assaults by men on gods' property and honor in the *Histories*, and there is the occasional talk about the dangers of "thinking big," but the question remains: why does Herodotus choose not to define such assaults and behavior explicitly in terms of *hybris*? The answer is, I think, that in avoiding explicit discussions of *hybris* against the gods in this way, Herodotus is following popular (not poetic) religious convention. The term *hybris* apparently was not used in the context of Athenian practiced religion of the fifth and fourth centuries. In lawcourts, for example, religious malefactors were charged with impiety, not *hybris*,[63] and so, too, in Herodotus' *Histories*. Although Herodotus occasionally uses language associated with concepts of *hybris*, as he does also with *phthonos*, he much more commonly describes religious matters in cultic, not poetic terms.

A similar preference for cult realities over poetic conceptions may explain Herodotus' exclusion of the Homeric-style gods and divine machinery from his accounts, even of the Trojan War. Herodotus can, for example, in various places give accounts of important elements of the *logos* of Alexander, Helen, and the Trojan War without once introducing an individual god. In his accounts of the theft of Helen (1.3 and 5.94.2), of her stay in Egypt (2.112–117), and of the outcome of the war (2.120), Herodotus introduces no Homeric gods, no owl-eyed Athena or white-armed Hera—in fact, no Athena or Hera at all. Only "the divine (τὸ δαιμόνιον) who was arranging it so that the Trojans, having been completely destroyed, might make it clear to human beings that the punishments from the gods for great injustices are great" (2.120.5). He has given a Homeric *logos*, but he has removed from that *logos* the genealogies, epithets, offices, crafts, and outward appearances of the gods that he himself expressly says Homer (and Hesiod) "created" (2.53.1–2).[64] By removing the divine machinery, he puts perhaps even greater emphasis on the religious cause of the war in a cultic sense, the violation of *xenia* by Alexander and the divine's punishment of that.

We are not told why Herodotus removed from his *logoi* of "old events" the gods associated with them in poetry along with their Homeric gene-alogies, attributes, and appearances. It may have been, in part, his cos-mopolitanism. These gods were appropriate to the Greek version of the war, but in his travels Herodotus also learned Persian and Egyptian *logoi* about events of the Trojan War (1.3; 2.112–117). These Persian and Egyptian accounts would hardly have featured the gods as the Greek poets imagined them, and familiarity with such non-Greek accounts of this and other ancient events may have made it more conceivable and easy for Herodotus to disassociate such "old events" from the divine machin-ery the Greek poets put around them. It may also be that, because he thought the poets "created" the genealogies, epithets, crafts, honors, and appearances of the gods, he then concluded that the gods *in that form* were a poetic fiction, or in good part a poetic fiction, irrelevant to his expressed purpose of preserving "what came to be from human beings" (τὰ γενόμενα ἐξ ἀνθρώπων, 1.preface). Truly relevant to "what came to be from human beings" in near or remote history are the gods with whom human beings actually interacted in real life, and these were the gods of cult. The gods of cult do, as we have seen, appear throughout Herodotus' *Histories*, and interestingly do so more in recent than in remote events, more — *we* might say — in historical than in mythological times. In a para-doxical way, given the literary tradition before him, Herodotus has Greek gods considerably more involved in recent historical events than in re-mote, to us "mythical" events.[65] That, I think, results from a conscious break with the Homeric-Hesiodic tradition, a turn away from the "fic-titious" divine world of the poets to the gods of cult. He has chosen to find explanations in the gods and heroes of practiced religion, not in the gods "created" by Hesiod and Homer. In so doing he took an impor-tant step in developing the anthropological and historical approaches to understanding and describing human affairs.

Herodotus' religious interests and experiences ranged far beyond the Greek, of course, and as we investigate his religious thought, it may be worthwhile to see how he describes foreign religions.[66] In particular it will be useful to see how Greek he made foreigners or, more precisely, upon which aspects of a foreign religion he imposed the *Graeca interpre-*

*tatio.* To treat fully the whole subject and all the peoples that Herodotus introduces would require a separate book,[67] but, I think, satisfactory and representative results emerge from what Herodotus has to say about one people, the Persians. The Persians are the one foreign people whose leaders Herodotus has most "talk" among themselves and most interact with the Greeks, and Persian religious attitudes and practices, as Herodotus understood them, were most critical to the Persian Wars.

The Persians are among the first of peoples for whom Herodotus gives a description of distinctive religious practices. He has them *not* erect statues, temples, and altars or use libations, flutes, garlands, or barley corns in their sacrifices. The *magos*, a priest type inherited from the Medes, must attend their sacrifices and sing a theogony. The Persian prays for "good things" for all Persians and the king, not specifically for himself. The Persian Zeus is the sky, and Persians sacrifice to him on mountaintops. In addition to Zeus they sacrifice to the sun, moon, and earth and to fire, water, and the winds. And they do not believe as Greeks do that the gods have human form (1.131–132). Herodotus designates only the last item as un-Greek, but what Herodotus tells us Persians did *not* do is implicitly un-Greek.[68] And it may well be that much of what he has them do—for example, sacrifice to the sun, moon, and earth and to fire, water, and the winds—is in part or in combination distinctively Persian and for this reason caught Herodotus' attention.

Most of what Herodotus attributes to the Persians are practices, not the beliefs lying behind them.[69] The important exception is again the last item, anthropomorphism: "The Persians do not have the custom of erecting statues and temples and altars, and they impute folly to those who do because, I think, they do not believe as the Greeks do that the gods have human form" (1.131.1).[70]

Elsewhere Herodotus gives additional details of Persian religious customs: that they bury people alive as offerings to the gods (*7.114*) and that they do not cremate their dead because, to them, fire is a god and they do not wish to give a corpse to a god (3.16.3). Herodotus labels as "barbaric" both Xerxes' maltreatment of Leonidas' corpse (*7.238* and *9.79.1*) and his verbal attack on the Hellespont (*7.35*) but makes them un-Persian as well as "barbaric." The king's chariot of Zeus with its eight horses (7.40.4), sacred horses (1.189.1 and 7.40.2–3), and horse sacrifices (*7.113.2*) all were Persian. Xerxes' offerings and prayers to the rising sun (*7.54.2* and 223.1), though not unparalleled in the Greek tradition,[71] reflect that god's importance to the Persians, as does leprosy as a punishment for sinning against him (1.138.1). Finally, that Persians reportedly intentionally had the corpses of the dead mangled by birds and dogs before burial would have shocked a Greek audience (1.140.1).[72]

Such are the religious beliefs and practices of the Persians that Herodotus describes, explicitly or implicitly, as un-Greek. But Herodotus has, on several occasions, these same Persians acting and thinking in very Greek ways and even participating in and using the cults of Greek gods and heroes. Darius orders that Delos, the birthplace of Apollo and Artemis, be respected, and his general Datis made a large offering on Apollo's altar there (6.97.2). Xerxes' consultation with the Athenian *chresmologos* Onomacritus was, according to Herodotus, among the factors that led him to undertake his expedition against Greece (7.6.3–5). When he reached Troy, Xerxes made a magnificent sacrifice to Athena Ilias and, in appropriate Greek ritual, had offerings poured to the Greek heroes, though without great success (7.43.2). In Achaea he protected and visited the shrine of Athamas (7.197.4). And amid the storms at Artemisium the *magoi*, the priests serving the Persians, sacrificed to Thetis and the Nereids, and the winds stopped (7.191.2). After the battle of Salamis, after his king had fled Greece, the Persian general Mardonius used Greek divination extensively. He sent Mys to the nearby Greek oracle of Trophonius and to the oracles of Apollo at Abae and Ptoön and of Amphiaraus at Thebes (8.133–136). In the battle of Plataea Mardonius used and for a good time heeded a Greek *mantis* (9.37–38 and 41.4) and, at a decisive moment, he questioned his Greek generals about oracles they might know. He even ventured (unsuccessfully, in Herodotus' judgment) to interpret an oracle he had heard himself (9.42–43).

Herodotus also gives to his Persians a number of religious practices that, if not explicitly Greek, are identical to the Greek. Mardonius used a Greek *mantis* at Plataea, but Herodotus has Persians using Greek-style divination from the time of Darius: as Darius was leading six conspirators against two rebellious priests, "seven pairs of hawks appeared chasing two pairs of eagles, tearing out their feathers and scratching them. After they saw these things, the seven conspirators all approved Darius' plan and, encouraged by the birds, went to the palace" (3.76.3).[73]

In the very early stages of his expedition Xerxes ignored bad omens that were remarkable but of a type common in the Greek tradition, for example, a hermaphroditic mule or a horse giving birth to a hare (7.57). He was misled in the interpretation of an eclipse by the *magoi* who, among other duties, played the role of *manteis* for Persian kings (7.37.2–3). His taking of omens before crossing the Strymon River can be paralleled by Spartan practices (6.76.1), but the sacrifice of horses there is probably uniquely Persian (7.113.2).[74] And in the last pages of his history Herodotus has the Persian Artaüctes and his Greek guards all recognize the miracle of the revivified fish (9.120.1–2). The Persians would appear from Herodotus to have had no indigenous oracles. Cambyses used that of Leto in Egypt (3.64.4), and, as we have just seen, Mardonius canvassed the Greek oracles.

A dream induced the Persian general Otanes to refound Samos (3.149); Datis, a Mede general serving Darius, to attempt to return a statue of Apollo to Delion (6.118); and, perhaps, Xerxes to have traditional Athenian sacrifices made on the Acropolis after he captured it (8.54). We learn the content of none of these dreams, but the dreams of Astyages concerning the founder of the Persian Empire are more characteristic of the dreams Herodotus elsewhere gives to his Persians:

A daughter by the name of Mandane was born to Astyages. Astyages in a dream thought that she urinated so much that she filled his city and flooded even all of Asia. He referred the dream to the dream interpreters of the *magoi*, and he was terrified when he learned from them the details. When Mandane was of marriageable age, in fear of the dream he gave her as wife to no one of the Medes who were worthy of himself, but to a Persian whose name was Cambyses. He discovered that Cambyses was of a good family and a peaceful disposition, but far inferior to the average Mede. And when Mandane was living with Cambyses, in their first year Astyages saw another vision. He thought that a vine grew from the genitals of his daughter and encompassed all of Asia. After he saw this and referred it to the dream interpreters, he had his daughter, now pregnant, sent to him from the Persians, and he watched over her when she arrived. He intended to kill her baby because the dream interpreters of the *magoi* from the vision indicated to him that the son of his daughter would become king in his place. (1.107–108.2)

The dreams proved true, and despite Astyages' concerted efforts, Mandane's son Cyrus became king and the founder of the Persian dynasty.

Cyrus himself later had a similarly complex and accurate dream about Darius (1.209–210), as did the later Persian king Cambyses about the revolt of "Smerdis" (3.30.2–3). Such elaborate dreamings, simply coming true or, as in Cambyses' case, coming true in an unexpected way, are characteristic of dreams in Greek poetry, particularly tragedy. The closest parallel, in subject, time, and setting, is the elaborate dream Aeschylus gives to Xerxes' mother in the *Persae* (176–199).[75] Most important for the Persian Wars were, of course, the dreams that urged, virtually forced Xerxes to undertake the expedition (*7.12–18*). These dreams and the debate about them between Xerxes and Artabanus are very Greek, no less so than the famous "Greek" debate about the ideal constitution among the Persian leaders Darius, Otanes, and Megabyzus (3.80–82).[76]

In Herodotus Greek-style oaths are a common feature of international dealings. Cyrus has a sworn treaty with the Milesians (1.141.4, 143.1, and 169.2), Otanes with some Samians (3.144), and Darius with the Milesian Histiaeus (5.106.6), the last being by Persian, not Greek gods. The rebellious *magoi* put a Persian fellow conspirator under oath (3.74.2). The Greek physician Democedes had Xerxes' mother Atossa swear an oath that, if he healed her breast cancer, she would do for him whatever he wanted (3.133.2). In a similar situation, recalling the oaths of the Spartans Agetus and Ariston (6.62–63.1), Xerxes swore an oath to his mistress that he would give her whatever she wanted (9.109.2). Such open-ended promises secured by oaths invariably, of course, brought misfortune to the unwary person who made them. The Persians in all these cases, as Greeks were expected to do, remained true to their oaths even in the face of disaster. Herodotus even has the Persian king Cyrus decry the casual perjury of Greek merchants in the marketplace (1.153.1–2).

Finally, Herodotus has his Persians do a number of very traditionally Greek things in the religious realm. They make tithes (1.89.3), libations (*7.54.2* and 223.1), offerings in return for being saved (1.118.2 and 8.99.1), and tomb offerings at a funeral (7.117), and they show respect for rivers (1.138.2), *xenia* (7.27–29 and 39.2), and heralds (*7.133–137*). In the case of the heralds Xerxes upheld Greek traditions better than did the Spartans and Athenians.

In terms of religious beliefs and practices, Herodotus makes his Persians very Greek. He struggles, for example, to make Cyrus' putting of Croesus and fourteen Lydian children on a pyre intelligible in terms traditional to Greek religion: "Cyrus intended to make them firstfruit offerings to one of the gods, or to pay a vow, or else he put Croesus on the pyre because he had heard that Croesus was god-respecting and wanted to know if one of the gods would rescue him from being burned alive" (1.86.2). And it was Herodotus' opinion that Cambyses' impieties showed that he was mad (3.37–38). In both cases we have Herodotus' own suggestions for understanding the events, but in the following cases the historian has the Persians themselves talking very much as Greeks would. Just before the battle of Plataea an unnamed Persian says to a fellow, Greek banqueter, "It is impossible for a human being to avert what must come to be from the god" (9.16.4). Cyrus, the founder of the Persian dynasty, said that "the gods took care of him and revealed to him ahead of time all things that were coming" (1.209.4). His birth was, he claimed, by "divine fortune" (θείη τύχη) (1.126.6),[77] and the Persian Artembares told Cyrus that Zeus gave "hegemony (of nations) to Persians, but leadership of men" to Cyrus (9.122.2).[78]

It is, however, the wise Artabanus, uncle and counselor to Xerxes, who is most thoroughly and consistently Greek, giving voice to many Greek sentiments:

In a life so short no human being is completely happy, no one of these or other men. To each of them will come, many times and not just once, the wish to die rather than to live. Misfortunes and diseases befall them and disturb their lives and make their lives, though short, seem long. Life is then burdensome, and so death becomes a most desirable refuge from it for a human being. The god gives a taste of the sweet life but then is found to be *phthoneros* in it. (7.46.3)

You see how the god strikes with a thunderbolt all living things that rise above the norm and does not allow them to show themselves off, but the small things do not irritate him at all. And you see how he hurls his thunderbolt always against the biggest buildings and trees. The god likes to dock all things rising above the norm. And so even a large army is destroyed by a small one in the following way, when a god, feeling *phthonos*, casts panic or thunder on it and because of that the soldiers are destroyed in a manner unworthy of themselves. For the god does not allow anyone other than himself to be proud. (7.10.ε)

These and occasional other comments by Artabanus ("Misfortunes rule men, not men misfortunes," 7.49.3) are quintessentially Greek and find their parallels in the Greek poetic tradition, particularly in lyric and Athenian tragedy.[79] Through Artabanus Herodotus has the plans of the Persian king criticized and opposed by a wise and foresighted adviser who is nominally Persian—hence his allegiance to the king—but philosophically and temperamentally a Greek.[80] And so we receive through Artabanus a running Greek commentary on Xerxes' major decisions about the Persian Wars.

King Croesus was, of course, a Lydian, not a Persian, but he is so featured and so interesting in Herodotus' *Histories* that we can hardly pass up the opportunity to investigate the "Greekness" of his religious world.[81] In so doing we find, in fact, that apart from his two comments about "the god(s) of the Greeks," there is hardly a hint of Lydian or other foreign religious beliefs or practices. Quite to the contrary, Herodotus has made Croesus so fully Greek in religious matters, and in such conventional Greek terms, that a review of Croesus' involvement with the gods and his comments about them offers a somewhat surprising way to conclude this whole treatment of the religious views of Herodotus, a way to return from what he attributed to foreign peoples to what Greeks and probably Herodotus himself "believed."

Herodotus' Croesus consulted the Delphic oracle four times: in the famous test of oracles (1.46–49); to decide whether to launch an expedition against the Persians and, if so, which Greeks to take as allies (1.53–54); to discover if his kingship would be long-lasting (1.55–56.1); and to help his son who could not speak (1.85). Except for the testing, the occasions are those common to the Delphic oracle in poetic accounts. The offerings he made after learning of Delphic Apollo's accuracy, in the attempt to "win over" or "acquire" the god, were Greek in nature if not in quantity: 3,000 animals, silver and gilded couches, golden libation bowls, and clothing. To sacrifice and burn all or parts of sacrificial animals was Greek, but Croesus' burning of the furniture, clothes, and precious objects was not. If Croesus had acted as a Greek here, he would have sent them along with his many other offerings of gold and silver objects to Delphi as dedications to adorn the sanctuary (1.50–51).

For his dedications Croesus received, as many did after him, special privileges at the oracle, including, if he had chosen to assume it, the right to become a Delphic citizen (1.54.2). Alcmaeon, the Athenian who assisted Croesus in his Delphic affairs, was so richly rewarded with gold by Croesus that he established the fortune of one of Athens's leading families, the Alcmaeonidae (6.125). The oracles Apollo gave to Croesus all proved true, as the Pythia later argued and Croesus himself accepted (1.91), even the oracle that Croesus would rue the day that his mute son spoke (1.85).

Croesus thus, through his test, recognized the special powers of Delphic Apollo and attempted to "win him over" with gifts, gifts that were, given Croesus' position, on a grand scale. The oracles he received in return were, at first glance, favorable to his purposes, and Croesus must have thought his efforts highly successful. But then his world collapsed. His forces were defeated, his city Sardis was captured, and he himself faced imminent death on a burning pyre. At this critical moment Herodotus has the Lydian Croesus invoke the Greek Apollo in very Greek terms: "He called upon Apollo, bidding him, if he had received some pleasing (κεχαρισμένον) gift from him, to stand by his side and rescue him from the present evil." Croesus appeals, for safety and protection, to the χάρις relationship established by the giving and receiving of "pleasing favors" that he had established with the god.[82] If he had stored up χάρις with the god by his gifts, he was asking for a return of that χάρις now. The god did respond, sending a rainstorm that quenched the fire and saved Croesus' life. To Cyrus, who had heard that Croesus was god-respecting (θεοσεβῆ), this proved that Croesus was also god-loved (θεοφιλής) (1.87.1–2).

In similar, Greek terms Herodotus has Croesus later complain about the oracles that Apollo had given him. First, to Cyrus: "You will do me a favor if you allow me to send (to Delphi) the chains (I wore) and to ask the god of the Greeks, whom of the gods I especially honored (ἐτίμησα), if it is his custom (νόμος) to deceive those who treat him well" (1.90.2). Croesus then bid his Lydian emissaries to go to Delphi, to place the chains on the floor of Apollo's temple — as sarcastic firstfruits (ἀκροθίνια) of his failed expedition — and "to ask if it is customary (νόμος) for the Greek gods to be without χάρις (ἀχαρίστοισι)" (1.90.4). He is challenging Apollo with failing to uphold his side of the fundamental relationship of χάρις between gods and men. The Pythia then responds in the same terms, claiming that, by delaying the capture of Sardis three years, Apollo gave to Croesus all the χάρις he could (ἐχαρίσατο) within the constraints that the Moirae imposed upon him.[83] He also, she adds, saved him from the burning pyre (1.91.1–3). She then patiently explains the true meaning of each oracle, and Croesus finally and completely accepts that the error was his, not Apollo's (1.91.4–6).

This nexus of respect for the gods (θεοσέβεια), honoring (τιμᾶν) of the gods through sacrifices and gifts, the bond of χάρις between gods and men, and the expectation of help from the god on the basis of that relationship, is here, both in concept and details of language, quintessentially Greek, and nowhere else in classical Greek literature is it set forth quite so fully and explicitly. And, most remarkably, Herodotus lays it out through the predicament and from the mouth of a Lydian king.

In other, minor ways Herodotus also makes Croesus appear Greek: in casual turns of phrase, such as "The gods (or Zeus) gave me as a slave to Cyrus" (1.89.1 and 207.1), or that "the gods might give an idea" to his enemies (1.27.3);[84] in his concern for a strange omen, though with Telmessian *exegetai*, not Greek *manteis* (1.78); in his suggestion to Cyrus that booty be collected from pillaging soldiers on the excuse of making a tithe to Zeus (1.89.3); in attributing evil to a *daimon* (1.87.4); and in his eventual acceptance of the Solonian scheme of *tyche* and fortune — "If you know that you are a human being and you rule other human beings, then first of all understand that there is a cycle of human events, and this cycle in its circular course does not allow always the same men to be successful" (1.207.2).

We conclude this account of Croesus' Greekness in religious matters with Herodotus' account of the death of Croesus' son Atys, an account that closes with one of the most revealing statements we have about Greek religion from any source. A dream indicated to Croesus that Atys, his one healthy son and obvious heir, would be killed in his youth by an iron spearpoint. Croesus naturally attempted to shelter his son, removing even the spears hanging on the walls of the house. Soon thereafter a Phrygian named Adrastus arrived, having been banished from his home for having accidentally killed his brother. Croesus welcomed him and purified him of the pollution of murder. He did this very much as a Greek would because, as Herodotus tells us here, Lydian and Greek purification rites were very similar. Croesus treats Adrastus as a *xenos*, as Croesus later explicitly terms this very Greek form of relationship.

Later some Mysians came to Sardis to ask Croesus' help in ridding their country of a rampaging and destructive wild boar. At his son's urging and despite his own reservations, Croesus sent Atys on the boar hunt, with the precaution that Adrastus be present to protect him. During the hunt Adrastus by an errant cast of his spear killed Atys, and Croesus recognized that the dream was fulfilled (1.34–43). All up to this point of the *logos* is fully Greek, of a type that we might expect to find in a Greek tragedy. And so, too, is Croesus' reaction upon hearing of the death of his son:

Croesus was terribly aggrieved at the misfortune, and he invoked Zeus Kathar-sios ("Of Purifications"), calling upon him to witness what he had suffered from his *xenos*, and he invoked Zeus Epistios ("Of the Hearth") and Hetaireios ("Of Comrades"), naming this same god. He was invoking him as Epistios because he received the *xenos* into his house and did not realize that he was feeding the mur-derer of his son. And he was invoking him as Hetaireios because after he sent Adrastus as his son's guard he found him to be his greatest enemy. (1.44)

Herodotus not only has Croesus utter Greek sentiments here but has him offer some of the best evidence we have for how Greeks conceived of the different aspects of a deity to whom they assigned the same name. The god is Zeus, but as Katharsios he oversees purifications, as Epistios mat-ters of an individual's hearth, home, and family, and as Hetaireios an individual's relationship to close but not kindred friends. The epithets and roles might be divided up slightly differently by different authors and in different locales. Aeschylus, for example, quite probably would have introduced a Zeus Xenios here,[85] but Croesus' conception of Zeus with those specific epithets and functions and with the individual epi-thets matching individual functions is entirely Greek.[86] Perhaps because Croesus is a Lydian, Herodotus has him express basic Greek religious concepts, both here and in his dealings with Apollo, more completely and with more detail than Greeks themselves do elsewhere in the surviv-ing literature. In this sense Herodotus' Croesus has become more Greek than a Greek.

We may now, after reviewing how Herodotus presents the Persians and Croesus, draw some conclusions about his *Graeca interpretatio* of foreign religions. The fundamental distinction is between practices and beliefs. He describes, sometimes in great detail, practices and rituals that caught his attention for being un-Greek, but only rarely, as in 1.131.1, does he probe the beliefs underlying these differences. He has foreigners such as Xerxes, when they are at the sites of Greek cults, occasionally respect or even participate in their rituals, a not improbable occurrence in this non-exclusive religious world. Herodotus' Persians and Croesus share, with only minor differences, the Greek use of omens, oracles, prophets, oaths, tithes, libations, and dedications. But it is in the area of beliefs, of who the gods are, what they do, and how they interact with men that Herodotus has most fully Hellenized his foreigners. In terms of Cambyses' impieties, of Artabanus' conception of fortune and divine *phthonos*, of Croesus' religious attitudes, and of miscellaneous details, these foreigners speak as Greeks. They are kings and royalty, and the religious conceptions and sentiments Herodotus attributes to them appear to come from, and are paralleled from, similar royal figures in Athenian tragedy.[87] In creating the religious personalities of the great foreign kings, especially Croesus and Xerxes, Herodotus has turned, as he did for the infallibility of oracles, omens, *manteis*, and dreams, to models of poetic literature. There is much of popular religion in Herodotus' *Histories*, as we have attempted to show throughout, but particularly in creating religious *personae* for featured foreign characters Herodotus has looked elsewhere. And this, I think, accounts in part for the dual nature of "religious" material in the *Histories*. One part, the much smaller part, involves the Solonian cycle of fortune, *phthonos* of the gods, *atasthalia*, and perhaps even *hybris*. The other, much larger part concerns individual cultic deities, sacrifices, dedications, and prayers. The first part, which I would term the "poetic" conception, Herodotus employs primarily but not exclusively for remote times or places for which he has little if any "historical" information or sources or even monuments to offer a cultic context. The second part, that of popular, practiced religion, is present throughout but comes to dominate when Herodotus describes events close to his own time, events for which he had better information and sources, events for which he was less dependent on his own imagination, that is, for the events of the Persian Wars themselves.

# ✄ APPENDIX ✄
## Herodotus on the Origins of Greek Religion

Herodotus offers some of our earliest, fullest, and perhaps best information on what Greeks, or at least some Greeks, thought to be the origins of their religion. Herodotus, of course, never intended his *Histories* to be a treatise on the origins of Greek religion, and here we are forced to collect bits and pieces that Herodotus introduces in passing and casually, often as familiar comparanda to foreign practices or deities. Once, however, in his account of Egyptian religious practices Herodotus does linger on the beginnings of Greek religion, and we use this as a rather solid foundation to begin our discussion.

The names of almost all the gods have come to Greece from Egypt.[1] I have heard that the names have come from foreigners and I find it to be so, and I think they have come especially from Egypt. Except for Poseidon, the Dioscuri . . . , Hera, Histia, Themis, the Charites, and the Nereids, the names of the other gods have always existed for the Egyptians in their land. Those (Greek) gods whose names the Egyptians say they do not know were, I think, named by the Pelasgians, except for Poseidon. The Greeks learned of him from the Libyans, because no peoples except the Libyans possessed the name of Poseidon from the beginning, and the Libyans have always honored this god. And the Egyptians do not believe in heroes at all.

From the Egyptians the Greeks have established these and other traditions which I will indicate. But they have not learned from the Egyptians to make the statues of Hermes have erect genitals. The Athenians first of all the Greeks took this from the Pelasgians, and then the others took it from the Athenians.[2] The Pelasgians were dwelling in their land with the Athenians who already at that time were counted among the Greeks, and as a result the Pelasgians began also to be considered Greeks. And whoever has been initiated into the rites of the Cabiri, the rites which the Samothracians took from the Pelasgians and now perform, knows what I mean.[3] These Pelasgians who came to dwell with the Athenians inhabited Samothrace in previous times and from them the Samothracians took the rites. And so the Athenians first of the Greeks learned from the Pelasgians and made the statues of Hermes have erect genitals. And the Pelasgians told a sacred story about this, a story that has been revealed in the mysteries on Samothrace. In previous times the Pelasgians used to make all their prayers and sacrifices to the gods, as I know from what I heard in Dodona, but they created no epithet or name for any one of them. That is because they had not yet heard them. And the Pelasgians named them "gods" (θεοί) from the fact that the gods "had put" (θέντες) in order and controlled all things and all distributions. After much time had passed the Pelasgians heard the names of the other gods that had come from Egypt, but much later they heard the name of Dionysus. And after a time they consulted the oracle at Dodona about the names, because this was thought to be the oldest of the oracles in Greece and was, at this time, the only one.[4] When they consulted the oracle in Dodona if they should take up the names that had come from the foreigners, the oracle bid them to use them. And from this time on the Pelasgians were sacrificing using the names of the gods. And the Greeks later received the names from the Pelasgians.

From where each of the gods came to be, or if all always were existing, and how they look, the Greeks did not know until recently, just yesterday so to speak. For I think that Hesiod and Homer were older than I by four hundred years and no more, and they are the ones who created (ποιήσαντες) a divine genealogy for Greeks, gave their epithets (ἐπωνυμίας) to the gods, distributed their "offices" (τιμάς) and their "crafts" (τέχνας), and marked out their outward appearances (εἴδεα). The poets who are said to be earlier than Hesiod and Homer were, I think, in fact later.[5]

The priestesses at Dodona tell the first part of this account, but I say the latter things that refer to Hesiod and Homer. (2.50–53)

We begin our examination of this critically important passage by removing the exceptions and the usually welcome, very Herodotean digressions. In very early pre-Greek times on mainland Greece, the Pelasgians prayed and sacrificed to deities for whom they established the generic term θεοί. They had, however, no names for their individual deities. After a long time the Pelasgians heard the gods' names that were coming from Egypt. They asked at the one oracle then existing in Greece, that is, at Dodona, if they should use these names, and they were told to do so. The Pelasgians then employed these Egyptian names for their gods. Later, when the Greeks arrived and expelled or assimilated with the Pelasgians, they took over these gods' names from them. The Greeks had, at this stage, gods, a generic term (θεοί) for them devised by the Pelasgians, and individual names for them taken, via the Pelasgians, from the Egyptians. But it was not until circa 850 that Hesiod and Homer gave these gods genealogies, epithets, offices, crafts, and traits of outward appearance.

Before continuing, let us be sure of our terms. The Pelasgians were to Herodotus the pre-Greek, non-Greek-speaking, Ur-people inhabiting mainland Greece.[6] In various ways they were assimilated, subjected, or driven into exile by the Greeks. And, concerning Hesiod's and Homer's contribution to the Greek pantheon, the "genealogies" were the theogonies, the stories of the gods' births and families, a major component of divine and sacred "mythology"; the "epithets" were those adjectives associated with a god's name, such as "cloud-gathering" for Zeus, or "white-armed" for Hera, or "owl-eyed" for Athena; the τιμαί of the gods were those "offices" for which they were held in "honor" (τιμή), for Zeus his rule over the sky, for Poseidon his rule over the sea, and for Hades his lord-

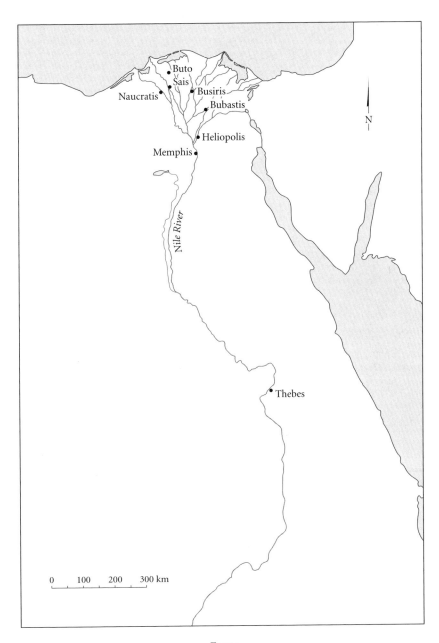

*Egypt*

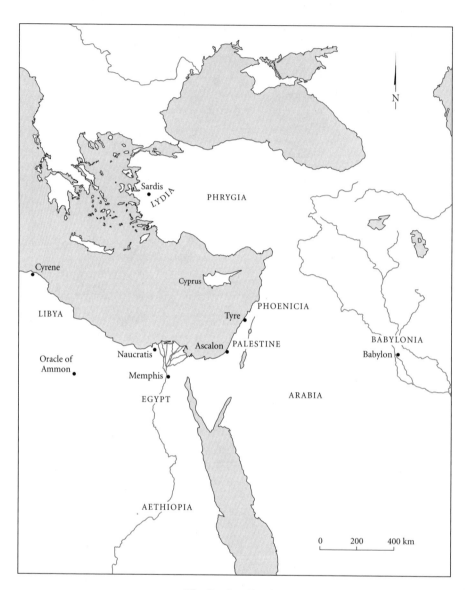

*The Persian Empire*

ship of the underworld; their τέχναι were their skills and crafts, for Hephaestus his smithing, for Athena her weaving, for Apollo his lyre playing. And, finally, Hesiod and Homer indicated the gods' appearances, no doubt their individual physical features, clothing, and equipment. The poets may, in fact, have first "made" the gods anthropomorphic.[7]

In the conclusion to this passage Herodotus forthrightly states that it is his own claim that Hesiod and Homer contributed such things to the gods of Greek religion. Others would apparently assign them to earlier poets. But for the Pelasgian adoption of the Egyptian names for the gods Herodotus' source is the priestesses at Dodona. And, as Herodotus goes on to explain, the involvement of Zeus' oracle at Dodona in this affair was not by chance. He offers three possible versions of the founding of the oracle, one Egyptian, one of the Dodonaeans, and one his own (2.54–57). All three agree in making the oracle at Dodona and the one of (Zeus) Ammon in Libya sister oracles, both founded at the same time from the oracle of Egyptian Zeus at Egyptian Thebes. The Zeus of Dodona is thus the Egyptian Zeus of Thebes.[8] And so, when the Pelasgians asked the god of Dodona if they should use for their gods the Egyptian names they were hearing, the positive response was logical and predictable.

To understand the import of 2.50–53 it is essential to recognize that the Pelasgians imported, according to Herodotus, *only* the names of the gods from Egypt, not the gods themselves.[9] The Pelasgians had their own nameless gods to which henceforth they applied Egyptian names. The Greeks took over these names, and later Hesiod and Homer gave the gods the many specifying attributes.[10] No one, in this account, imports or creates a *new* god. The gods seem to be there throughout:[11] first they receive prayer and sacrifice, then the generic name θεοί, then Egyptian names, and, finally, from Hesiod and Homer their distinguishing attributes.

It is also important, for following Herodotus' arguments, to realize that he nowhere has the Greeks "invent" a god's name. If none is invented by the Greeks, then the origin of each must be foreign. Most are, of course, Egyptian, but if the Egyptians did not have such a god, as in the case of Poseidon, Herodotus looked for the origin of the name elsewhere, in Poseidon's case in Libya.[12] And it was the Pelasgians who named the Dioscuri, Hera, Histia, Themis, the Charites, and the Nereids.

From the Egyptians the Greeks took thus only the names of the Egyptian gods, but even this simple claim is complicated by the rest of Herodotus' account of the Egyptians. To limit ourselves to the Olympian gods, Herodotus says that Demeter is the Greek name of the Egyptian Isis (2.59.2 and 156.5), Dionysus of Osiris (2.42.2 and 144.2), Apollo of Horus (2.144.2 and 156.5), Artemis of Bubastis (2.137.5 and 156.5), and Zeus of Amun (2.42.5). Why, if the names of the Greek gods are Egyptian, is the goddess Demeter in Greece but Isis in Egypt?

Why is the god Apollo in Greece but Horus in Egypt? This type of question has long bedeviled the understanding of what Herodotus means in 2.50–53,[13] and there is no satisfying solution. The fundamental point, though, is that by all appearances Herodotus is here writing of real *names*.[14] If one accepts this point, as I do, then the question is how Herodotus could reconcile that Egyptian priests claimed, for example, that "Zeus" was in origin an Egyptian name *and* his own claim that "the Egyptians call Zeus 'Amun'" (2.42.5). The two claims stand in separate discussions and separate contexts but remain contradictory, the type of contradiction that modern scholars cannot abide in ancient authors.

I am inclined to let the contradiction stand rather than do violence to the Greek. It may have originated from a habit of Herodotus' sources, Greek and perhaps even Egyptian, of regularly giving these Egyptian gods Greek names for a Greek audience.[15] The initial impression would have been that these were the Egyptian gods' real names, and because Egyptian culture long antedated Greek, the Greeks must have taken these names from the Egyptians, not vice versa.[16] Only a deeper level of inquiry, of the ethnological type in which Herodotus specialized, would reveal that, in fact, the Egyptians had another, different name for each of these gods. In 2.50–53 all the conclusions are drawn from this initial impression, and the Egyptian names of 2.42.5 and elsewhere result from further inquiry. The results are contradictory, but it is a contradiction that Herodotus either did not recognize or chose not to deal with. This solution is neither pleasing nor satisfying, but modern attempts to obviate it create no fewer difficulties.[17] For our purposes it is important that Herodotus in his conception of the early development of Greek religion builds on the initial impression, that the *names* of most Greek gods — for example, Zeus, Apollo, Artemis, and Athena — are Egyptian in origin.

The gods for whom the Pelasgians and Greeks used Egyptian names were without genealogies, epithets, offices, crafts, and physical features. Hesiod and Homer gave these to the gods and thereby made them distinct individuals with separate histories and characteristics. They did so mostly outside the Egyptian tradition,[18] and thus the "new" Hesiodic/Homeric deities need have little or nothing except names in common with their Egyptian namesakes.

In the divine world of Herodotus the gods, seemingly, remain essentially unchanged. Humans "learn of" them,[19] give them a generic name (θεοί), then individual names, then the full characterization known to us from the Greek epics. The resulting god, the end product, may differ significantly, of course, from its beginning. For us Homeric Zeus is greatly, generically different from a nameless, formless, characterless Pelasgian deity who receives only prayer and sacrifice. But where we see differences, the cosmopolitan and polytheistic Herodotus tends to emphasize similarities and continuities. The differences are, for him, the result of human discovery and invention. It is humans who "learn," "adopt," or "make up" the gods' individual names, functions, and characters. Furthermore, in Herodotus' polytheistic world, there is no single and exclusively "correct" name, or office, or appearance for a deity. The Hesiodic/Homeric scheme of the pantheon is millennia younger than the Egyptian, but to Herodotus it is apparently no better or worse, no more or less valid. It is simply different, with two cultures coming to different characterizations and representations of what is in origin the same divine world. The deities of Herodotus' world are culturally determined, but the "divine," in essence, is not.[20] To foist our deductions further upon Herodotus, the recognition that throughout the world the divine is essentially the same but that the local deities are culturally determined may have inclined the historian to search out and record similarities—some seemingly farfetched to us—among the deities of Greeks and foreigners, and to overlook some major differences in identifying foreign with Greek deities.[21] In our discussion of individual Greek deities we will see several examples of the emphasis of similarities at the expense of differences. The cause is the premise that underlying the diversity there is a fundamental unity of the divine.

Do the individual peoples "discover" or "invent" these gods and their attributes? That is, how does a society know about the gods when it has not "learned" or "heard" about them from another culture but itself from itself develops them? For Herodotus the independent part of the Greek tradition began with Hesiod and Homer, "who 'created' a divine genealogy" and other distinguishing features for the Greek gods. They "created" (ἐποιήσαντο) the genealogy,[22] "gave" (δόντες) the epithets, "distributed" (διελόντες) the offices and crafts, and "marked out" (σημάναντες) their outward appearances (2.53.2).[23] Herodotus has his poets (ποιηταί) "make" the Greek gods, not "discover" their true nature. The Homeric gods are, in this sense, the products of men. At 4.79.3 Herodotus has the Scythians criticize the Greeks "for the celebration of Bacchic rites (τοῦ βακχεύειν πέρι), because, they say, it is not reasonable to 'invent' (ἐξευρίσκειν) a god who incites men to go mad." In Herodotean usage ἐξευρίσκειν may mean "search out" or "invent," but the logic of this passage requires "invent."[24] In short, Herodotus has the Scythians claim that Dionysus is a Greek invention. And, as we will soon see, the Greeks learned of Dionysus' name from the Egyptians but then "genealogized his birth" (γενεηλογέουσι τὴν γένεσιν, 2.146.2), that is, they made him the Greek Dionysus. The Greeks did not discover his genealogy; they created it. But that the Greek Dionysus was "invented" makes him a no less real or powerful deity, as the king of these same Scythians could attest (4.79.2).

In Herodotus' scheme, then, Homer and Hesiod essentially made Greek these Pelasgian gods with Egyptian names. In giving them their genealogies, offices, crafts, and outward appearances they did not discover a hitherto unknown truth but rather invented a poetic truth about the nature of the gods. Such poetic creations might be acceptable or not—Herodotus rejects, for example, Homer's account of Oceanus (2.23)—but he does not (unlike the tragedians and philosophers) call into question the Hesiodic/Homeric depiction of the divine world.[25] To the cosmopolitan Herodotus the Hesiodic/Homeric scheme was just one set, a Greek set, of traditions about the gods, one set among many other sets in the peoples he knew. Each was locally created. There were similarities between the sets, and one set might borrow from another, but no one set was superior or "more true." Each set deserves respect. "Each people thinks that its own traditions are by far the best. Therefore no one but a madman ought to laugh at such things" (3.38.1–2).

The Greek gods, therefore, are in Herodotus' world view just one system among many other systems of conceiving of and dealing with the universal "divine." This divine was defined by Greek poets in the context of Greek culture as it was by Egyptian priests in their culture. And, remarkably for us, to Herodotus, a Greek, the Greek system was not better or the best. It was simply different.[26] In fact, a feature of Greek religion is that its devotees seem not to have claimed that their gods were superior to gods of other peoples or of other Greek states. Whether Herodotus is merely a product of this Greek religious egalitarianism or whether he contributed significantly to it, we cannot judge.

Finally, to state a truism, the gods Hesiod and Homer defined were the Hesiodic and Homeric gods, that is, the gods we know from their poems. But a great many Greek gods, and some of the most important in family and state cult, never appear in these poems. Who then defined these? If we apply the Herodotean model to these, we would see them initially just as "deities" with no names and no personal definition, just the recipients of cult acts. Over time they would be defined, virtually "invented," within the culture to which they belonged—in these cases not the Panhellenic culture of Homer and Hesiod but that of the individual city-states. In establishing that definition, the Athenians, for example, could, like the Pelasgians, borrow "foreign," that is, non-Athenian, names. The Pelasgians borrowed the Egyptian names they heard; the Athenians, perhaps, borrowed the Homeric names they were hearing. For their deity with distinctive rituals for the maturation of young women, the Athenians could use, for example, the Homeric name Artemis but could keep their Attic Artemis distinct with an epithet of their own locale, Brauronia. With the Homeric name might come various Homeric features, but the distinctive and often unique characteristics of the local goddess and her rituals would persist also. The product would be an amalgam of Hesiodic/Homeric and local traditions, and that product, in its totality, would be unique to that city, as Artemis Brauronia was to Athens. There would be similarities to the Homeric Artemis, and there would be similarities to other cults in other cities, but the specific blend would be unique to Athens. Such would be the origin and development, if we extend Herodotus' model, of the thousands of quite distinct local deities with Homeric names we find throughout the Greek world.

For our next question—When did the Greek gods come to be?—we can leave behind Herodotean-style speculation and return to what the historian actually wrote.[27] Hesiod and Homer established the canons of the Greek pantheon no more than 400 years before Herodotus' time, about 850 (2.53). Individual Greek deities appeared considerably earlier, however: Pan, the son of Penelope and Hermes, 800 years before Herodotus, that is, 1250; Heracles, son of Alcmene, 900 years before Herodotus, 1350; and Dionysus, son of Semele, 1,000 years before Herodotus, 1450.[28] And, Herodotus tells us, the Greeks learned of their names later than those of other gods, and so, by Herodotus' reckoning, most Greek gods must have acquired their names before circa 1500 (2.145.4–146).

Herodotus offers further welcome incidental information on the "dates" of these gods through their human descendants. He has his contemporary Hecataeus make the claim that his family went back sixteen generations to a god (2.143.1). Because Herodotus here gives, for purposes of rough estimates, 100 years to three generations (2.142.2) and since we place Hecataeus about 500, Hecataeus' unnamed divine ancestor consorted with a woman about 1030. Similarly the Spartan king Leonidas was the twenty-first descendant of Heracles, and that places Heracles 840 years before 480, or about 1320 (7.204).[29] Through these genealogies the Greeks put such divine activities about the time of the Trojan War,[30] a war in which several children of divinities (e.g., Achilles, Aeneas, Sarpedon, and Helen) played a major role. Clearly those were fruitful times for Greek gods, goddesses, and heroes.

By their nature the heroes of Herodotus, unlike his gods, are generated fully defined. Being born originally as humans, they have birthdays and their cults begin at their deaths or soon after, and both events can be given, at least in theory, absolute dates in the framework of human history.[31] The births of gods in the Hesiodic/Homeric genealogies, however, have only relative dates, with almost no correlation to human history. The heroes' genealogies, offices, skills, and physical appearances are also, again in theory, those that they had as living men or women. The poets did not have to "invent" them. Herodotus tells us of no "development" of these heroes as deities or of their cults, no contribution by poets to their identity, certainly no Egyptian influence (except for the binatured Heracles) because the Egyptians did not believe in heroes (2.50.3).[32]

Orestes of Tegea and later Sparta (1.67–68), Talthybius of Sparta (7.133–137), Protesilaus of Elaeus (9.116–120), and Ajax of Salamis (8.121.4) are all familiar figures of Trojan War legend, the last two playing roles later as religious heroes in the Persian Wars. Some heroes were of the generations immediately preceding the Trojan War: Ajax' father Telamon and grandfather Aeacus (5.79–81 and 8.83.2); Peleus; Adrastus of Sicyon; and Melanippus of Thebes (5.67), the latter three all involved in the expedition of the Seven against Thebes. Herodotus makes Pan the most recent of all his gods, first appearing after the Trojan War, in 1250 (2.145.4), but his heroes continued to "come to be" right down to his own time: Lycurgus, by some accounts the founder of the Spartan way of life (1.66.1); the founders of colonies Timasius of Abdera (1.168) and, just shortly before the Persian Wars, the Athenian Miltiades, uncle of the general of Marathon, for the Chersonesus (6.36–38); Cyrnus by the Phocaeans in exile during Croesus' reign (1.167.4); Philippus of Croton, an Olympic victor, at Egesta (5.47); about 497 Onesilus of Salaminian Cyprus, for the Amathusians (5.114); and as late as 480 Artachaees the Persian for the Acanthians (7.117).[33]

Hero cult was thus an expandable and (slowly) expanding element of Greek religion in the time of the Persian Wars. It would continue to expand, with, for example, Cimon bringing Theseus' bones from Scyros to Athens in 476 and instituting or elaborating a festival there in his honor.[34] But, in contrast, the Greek set of gods, the Greek pantheon, was by the time of the Trojan War virtually complete. No new Greek gods appear. Only a few foreign ones would come later, and they would be imported, not newly born.[35]

As we turn from the deities to cult practices, we give first Herodotus' most detailed account of Greece's debt to the Egyptians.

I heard also other things in Memphis when I talked with the priests of Hephaestus.[36] I turned also to both Thebes and Heliopolis because I wanted to know if they would agree with what was said in Memphis. The Heliopolitans are said to be the Egyptians most knowledgeable in history.[37] I am not eager to describe the explanations of divine affairs which I heard, except only for the names, because I think all men have equal knowledge about them.[38] I will mention whatever divine affairs I do only when forced to do so by my narrative. . . . The priests were saying that the Egyptians first established the custom of epithets (ἐπωνυμίας) of the twelve gods,[39] that the Greeks took up the custom from them, and that the Egyptians first assigned altars, statues of gods, and temples to the gods and first sculpted living figures on stones. (2.3–4.2)

Here we must take care to give credit to the Egyptians for only what Herodotus credits them. He does not say here that the Greeks followed the Egyptians in assuming twelve gods or that the Greeks received the names of the gods from the Egyptians—the latter claim was made elsewhere, in 2.50. If we take Herodotus' ἐπωνυμίας literally here as "epithets,"[40] the Egyptians first developed the custom of giving epithets to the gods, a practice that the Greeks took from the Egyptians. The Greek epithets were not themselves Egyptian, only the custom of assigning epithets to the gods, a practice then implemented by Hesiod and Homer (2.53.2). Herodotus then links this custom with cult practices, the giving of altars, statues of gods, and temples. We have here the transference of customs, but not of the concrete forms those customs took in each society. The Egyptians had altars for their deities. The Greeks, too, had altars, and, in Herodotus' argument, it is the custom of having altars that the Greeks received from the Egyptians, not the shape or necessarily even the purpose of the altars.[41] As so often is the case in Herodotus, the underlying argument is *post hoc ergo propter hoc* ("after this, and therefore because of this").[42] The Egyptians *first* had epithets, altars, statues of the gods, and temples, and each succeeding people who had them must have taken these customs from the Egyptians. Finally, we should remember that these are the claims of Egyptian priests. Herodotus was free, of course, to reject priests' claims and occasionally did.[43] When he does not, we might assume that he found nothing shockingly illogical or improbable about the claim being made.

In similar fashion, "the Egyptians are the first of men to have made festivals (πανηγυρίας), processions (πομπάς), and 'offering bringings' (προσαγωγάς), and the Greeks have learned of them from the Egyptians.[44] And the following is my proof of this: the Egyptian ones appear to have been made for a long time, but the Greek ones were made only recently. And the Egyptians hold festivals not once a year, but have several, especially and most eagerly for Artemis at Bubastis, secondly for Isis at Busiris" (2.58–59.1). The deities the Greeks inherited from the Pelasgians received only prayer and sacrifice (2.52.1). In cult, after their adoption, the Greeks gave these gods altars, temples, statues, festivals, processions, and formal presentations of offerings, all major Greek cult practices, all going back, according to Herodotus, to much earlier Egyptian customs. Although the Greeks may have put their own stamp on each of these customs and a Greek festival might be very different from an Egyptian festival, the practices themselves were, according to Herodotus, Egyptian. Here again the argument is *post hoc ergo propter hoc*. Herodotus offers no thoughts about the dating of these major innovations in Greek religion except that, in terms of Egypt's long history, they are "recent." If in fact in 2.4.2 Herodotus is speaking of "epithets" and not "names" of the gods,[45] the one correspondence is here. Epithets are an Egyptian custom (2.4.2), Hesiod and Homer gave the Greek gods their epithets, and these poets are to be dated no earlier than 850. Whether Herodotus imagined altars, temples, statues, processions, and festivals beginning at that same time, we do not know, but it would place them at the very beginnings of many characteristic features of Greek culture.

Herodotus' attention is often caught by unusual sexual practices or customs around the world, and the Greeks share the following religious prohibition, quite properly in Herodotus' view, with the Egyptians.

The Egyptians are the first who maintained the religious provision not to have sexual intercourse with women in sanctuaries and not to enter sanctuaries unbathed after intercourse with women. Almost all other human beings except the Egyptians and Greeks have intercourse in sanctuaries or go unbathed after intercourse into a sanctuary. They think humans are just like the other animals, because they see all the animals and birds having intercourse in the temples and precincts of the gods. (They say) that if this were not acceptable (φίλον) to the god, the animals would not be doing it. They raise such considerations, but they are doing things that do not please me.[46] (2.64)

The Greeks owe virtually all their imported cult practices to the Egyptians, but Herodotus credits to the Libyans the "wail" made at the moment of sacrifice: "I think that also the wail (ὀλολυγή) over sacrificial victims first occurred in Libya, because the Libyan women certainly practice it and do it well.[47] The Greeks also learned from the Libyans how to yoke together four horses" (4.189.3)

We save for later the Egyptian origins of individual deities, including Heracles, Dionysus, Demeter Thesmophoros, and Zeus of Dodona. But it was through Zeus of Dodona that the Greeks owed to Egypt the art of prophecy (2.54–57). Herodotus knew also of astrology and puts it among the Egyptian inventions: "And these other things have been invented by the Egyptians: to which of the gods each month and day belongs, and what kinds of things a man born on a certain day will encounter, and how he will die, and what kind of person he will be. Those of the Greeks engaged in poetry made use of these"[48] (2.82.1). Astrology was not a feature of archaic or classical Greek religion, and Herodotus is apparently referring to Hesiod's *Works and Days* and perhaps some Orphic poetry. Orphic too may be the unnamed Greek followers of Egyptian theories of the transmigration of souls:

Egyptians are the first who told also this *logos*, that the soul of a human being is immortal, and that when the body wastes away, the soul goes into another living creature that is being born. And when the soul passes through all the creatures of land, sea, and sky, it goes again into the body of a human being, and it makes this cycle in 3,000 years. There are Greeks who made use of this *logos*—some earlier, some later—as if it were their own. I know their names but do not write them down.[49] (2.123.2–3)

With astrology and transmigration of souls we have moved a good distance from mainline archaic and classical Greek religion, but both practices, as Herodotus could not know, would have a long and important later history in Greek philosophy and in the Western tradition.

We turn now to individual foreign deities to whom Herodotus gives Greek names and who, on occasion, he claims lie at the origin of a Greek cult. Our interest is not in understanding the foreign deity—a very worthwhile enterprise in itself—but in seeing how Herodotus connects the foreign deity to the Greek deity. What does it mean when Herodotus names Isis Demeter? Is, for him, Isis really Demeter, or is he simply giving the closest parallel he can find to make this deity intelligible to his Greek audience? It is important to remember at the outset that Herodotus may have been inclined to emphasize similarities over differences and, second, that on the Greek side he was primarily using the genealogies, offices, crafts, and outward appearances of the gods as, in his view, Hesiod and Homer had created them. It is in these Hesiodic/Homeric genealogies and attributes that Herodotus finds similarities to the foreign deities.[50]

## Zeus

A brief summary of the Scythian pantheon gives an initial glimpse of how freely Herodotus was willing to associate Greek gods with foreign gods.

The Scythians appease (ἱλάσκονται) only these gods: Histia especially, and also Zeus and Ge, and they think that Ge is the wife of Zeus. And, in addition, they worship Apollo, Aphrodite Ourania, Heracles, and Ares. All the Scythians believe in these, but the "royal" Scythians sacrifice also to Poseidon. And in the Scythian language Histia is named Tabiti, Zeus is called—most correctly in my opinion—Papaios, Ge Api, Apollo Goitosyros, Aphrodite Ourania Argimpasa, and Poseidon Thagimasadas. But the Scythians are not accustomed to make statues, altars, and temples except for Ares. (4.59)

"Histia" and Ares were the major deities, "Zeus'" wife is "Ge," and of them all only Ares has the usual Greek cult apparatus.[51] The Scythians claim to be descended from "Zeus" and a daughter of the river Borysthenes, but Herodotus does not believe it (4.5.1. Cf. 4.127.4).

The links between the Greek Zeus and the major Persian deity are far more apparent. He was "the whole circuit of the sky" and was worshiped on mountaintops (1.131.2), both easily assimilated to the cult of the Greek Zeus. It may be significant that Herodotus does not reveal this god's Persian name, Ahura Mazda. The effect of being given the deity's foreign name, at least for this reader, is to "distance" that society, for example, the Scythians, from the Greeks, to emphasize by the un-Greek name the un-Greekness of the people. But Herodotus often Hellenizes his Persians, and to call their sky god Zeus and only Zeus would contribute to that.

The Carians worshiped their own Zeus, at Mylasa (1.171.6) and, with the epithet Stratios ("Of the Army"), at Labraunda (5.119.2). Here the Greek epithet suggests that the cult was already Hellenized, and Herodotus from nearby Halicarnassus would have known it well.[52] He finds it noteworthy that in Athens the family members of Cleisthenes' rival Isagoras sacrificed to "the Carian Zeus" (5.66.1).

The Ethiopians at Meroë worshiped only Zeus and Dionysus, and Zeus' oracle there bid them when and where to campaign (2.29.7).[53]

Herodotus describes in detail the spectacular and multitiered temple of Zeus Belus at Babylon. He never gives the god's Babylonian title Bel or name Marduk, but he marks him by the foreign epithet Belus. This male patron of a city with his towering temple and statue would have invited comparison with Zeus by Herodotus and no doubt other Greeks before him. The priests claimed that the god spent his nights in the temple sleeping with a mortal woman, but Herodotus, who does not like sexual activity in sanctuaries, does not believe it (1.181–183).

"The Egyptians call Zeus Amun" (2.42.5).[54] This simple statement serves as a timely reminder of two equally simple points. Whatever the relationship of Greek and Egyptian gods' names may have been circa 1450, in Herodotus' time "similar" Greek and Egyptian gods have different names. Second, Herodotus is describing all of this from the Greek perspective: "The Egyptians call (our) Zeus Amun," not "We call Amun Zeus." Amun's cult center was Egyptian Thebes, and he was worshiped only by Egyptians from that district (2.42.1–2). He, reputedly, like Zeus Belus spent his nights in his temple with a mortal woman (1.182). From a tale of his encounter with Heracles his Egyptian devotees represent him in sculpture as ram-faced and do not sacrifice rams except at his festival (2.42.3–6). The Ammonians, part Egyptian, adopted this Theban Zeus and likewise represent him as ram-faced (2.42.4 and 4.181.2).[55] Both the Theban and the Ammonian "Zeus" had oracles, and, as we have seen, this is the link to the Greek Zeus of Dodona. The oracle at Dodona was founded from the Theban cult (2.54–57), and Zeus of Dodona (though certainly not all Greek Zeuses!) is the only god to whom Herodotus gives a direct and uncontested Egyptian origin.[56] The god of Dodona, in Herodotus' scheme, predated all identifiable Greek gods, providing divination to the Pelasgians even before their gods had names. The Egyptian Zeus of Dodona would be, in Herodotus' program, the very earliest "Greek" god.

## Apollo, Artemis, and Leto

I have already mentioned many times the oracle (of Leto) in Egypt, and I will give an account of it because it deserves one.[57] This oracle is the sanctuary of Leto and is situated in a large city at the Sebennytic mouth of the Nile as one sails inland from the sea. Buto is the name for this city where the oracle is. . . . And there is in Buto a sanctuary of Apollo and Artemis. The temple of Leto, in which the oracle is, is large and has a gateway sixty feet in height. And I will tell you what of the visible things gave me the greatest wonder. In this precinct of Leto there is a temple made of stone, a square, in width and height sixty feet. Another stone lies on top as the covering of the roof, with an overhang of six feet. And so the temple is the most wondrous of the visible things concerning this sanctuary.

But in the second group (of wondrous things) is the island called Chemmis. It is in a deep and flat lake beside the sanctuary in Buto, and the Egyptians say this island is floating. I myself did not see that it was floating or moving, and I am astonished if an island is truly floating. And on this island there is a large temple of Apollo, and three altars have been erected, and on the island grow many date palm trees and many other trees, both fruit trees and others.

The Egyptians say Chemmis floats, telling this *logos*. On this island, which before was not floating, Leto, one of their eight first gods and dwelling in Buto where the oracle is, received Apollo as a deposit from Isis, protected him, and hid him on the island now said to be floating. She did this when Typhon came searching everything, wanting to find the child of Osiris. They say that Apollo and Artemis are children of Dionysus and Isis, and that Leto became their nurse and savior. In the Egyptian language Apollo is Horus, Demeter Isis, and Artemis Bubastis. From this *logos* and no other Aeschylus, son of Euphorion, alone of the earlier poets made Artemis a daughter of Demeter. Because of all of this, the island became a floating island. So the Egyptians say. (2.155–156)

Herodotus gives here a version of the Egyptian Isis myth, with Dionysus as Osiris and Apollo as Horus.[58] The key to Herodotus' Hellenization of the myth is of course Leto, now not the mother but the savior and nurse of Apollo and Artemis. The oracle (Leto's, not Apollo's)[59] gives Herodotus links to Delphic Apollo, and the floating island Chemmis and its date palms add a Delian coloring. But all the ties with the Delian triad of Apollo, Artemis, and Leto are quite superficial and most, importantly, result from the "late" Hesiodic/Homeric genealogizing of the Greek gods.

## Demeter

"The Egyptians hold festivals not once a year but have several, especially and most eagerly for Artemis at Bubastis and secondly for Isis at Busiris.[60] In this city there is the largest sanctuary of Isis, and this city has been established in the middle of Egypt's delta. In the language of the Greeks Isis is Demeter" (2.59.1–2). Isis with Osiris (Dionysus) was worshiped by all Egyptians (2.42.2), and the pair was thought to rule the underworld (2.123.1).[61] She and Osiris were, as we have just seen (2.156.5), the parents of Horus (Apollo) and Bubastis (Artemis). By the Egyptians Isis was sculpted as a woman with cow's horns, "just as the Greeks paint Io," and all Egyptians equally held in reverence (σέβονται) female cattle (2.41.2).

The Egyptians said that their king Rhampsinitus while living made a descent to the place which the Greeks consider to be Hades and there played dice with Demeter.[62] In some games he defeated her, and in others he lost to her, and then he came back up, having as a gift from her a golden kerchief. And they said that as a result of Rhampsinitus' descent, when he came back, the Egyptians put on a festival, and I know that they are still performing it up to my time, but I cannot say if they hold the festival for these reasons. (2.122.1–2)

Isis' festival at Busiris was characterized by ritual acts of grieving by thousands of men and women, but Herodotus will not tell for whom they grieve (2.61).[63]

The Greek women of nearby Cyrene evidently adopted the cult of Isis: "The women of the Cyrenaeans do not think it right to eat female cattle because of Isis in Egypt, but they even have fasts and festivals for her" (4.186.2).

Within Herodotus' account the points of comparison between Demeter and Isis are few (both female, both "mother" figures, both associated with the underworld), but the differences are legion (Isis cult practiced by men as well as women, features of the festivals, genealogy, outward form, etc.). The degree of identity for Demeter/Isis is of particular concern because Herodotus claims that the Thesmophoria, the rites of Demeter Thesmophoros, a goddess widely worshiped in Greece and a contributor to the Greek victory in the Persian Wars, had Egyptian origins:

About the ritual of Demeter that the Greeks call the Thesmophoria, let me keep a pious silence (εὔστομα κείσθω), except for how much of the ritual can be piously told.[64] The daughters of Danaus were the ones who brought this ritual from Egypt and taught the Pelasgian women. And when the whole Peloponnesus was depopulated by the Dorians, the ritual perished. But the Arcadians alone, the only ones of the Peloponnesians who were left behind and did not evacuate, preserved it. (2.171.2–3)

With Danaus and his daughters the Danaids we reach the early strata of human mythology, a time when Greeks and foreigners are scarcely differentiated.[65] Danaus becomes the eponym of the Danaoi (a Homeric term for Greeks), his brother Aegyptus the eponym of the Egyptians, and his brother-in-law Phoenix the eponym of the Phoenicians. The story of the flight of the Danaids from Egypt to Greece to escape the sons of Aegyptus is the theme of an Aeschylean trilogy, of which only the *Suppliants* survives. There the fleeing Danaids were received in Argos by king Pelasgus. Aeschylus' Danaids claim Greek descent from Io who had fled generations earlier from Argos to Egypt. His Danaids were thus Greek, but in this myth the distinction between Greek and Egyptian is, as it were, premature; the Danaoi and Aegyptii are still close blood relatives. For our purposes the distinction is, in any case, not relevant because whether the Danaids were "Greek" or "Egyptian," Herodotus claims they brought the Thesmophoria from Egypt. Furthermore, we see in Aeschylus' king Pelasgus a reflection of the Danaids giving these rites to the Pelasgians.

From all of this we might conclude that the rites of Demeter were based on those of Egyptian Isis and were introduced into the pre-Greek, Pelasgian world of the Peloponnesus. They survived the Pelasgian expulsion only in Arcadia, that region of the Peloponnesus not occupied by the Dorians. From there they presumably spread over the rest of the Greek world. This all occurred, in the Herodotean scheme, long before the Greek gods were differentiated by office, skills, genealogies, and appearances. The rituals of the Thesmophoria, not the goddess Demeter, were brought to "Greece" from Egypt. This is not, in itself, impossible. Herodotus does not describe Isiac rituals similar to the Greek Thesmophoria, but both were, of course, secret and of a type Herodotus would not reveal. We cannot validate or refute the "Egyptian" origin of the Thesmophoria, but six centuries later Plutarch, a student of Egyptian religion, thought the idea, like so much of Herodotus' history of Greek religion, outrageous (*Mor.* 857C).

## Dionysus

The Arabians named Dionysus Orotalt and (Aphrodite) Ourania Alilat and worshiped only them. They say that they, like Dionysus, cut their hair short all around and shave off their sideburns (3.8.3). The Thracians worship only Dionysus, Artemis, and Ares (5.7), and in the mountains Dionysus provides to one of their tribes an oracle with a Pythia-type prophetess (7.111.2). The Ethiopians of Meroë "honor" only Dionysus and Zeus (2.29.7),[66] and those around "sacred Nysa" celebrate festivals for Dionysus (3.97.2).

For Herodotus, however, it was the Egyptian "Dionysus," Osiris, who influenced Greek religion and became, in a sense, the Greek Dionysus. In his account of Dionysus we see Herodotus struggling—as does every serious student of Greek religion—with problems of chronology, locale, and migration of cult. As we have seen, Isis is Demeter, Osiris is Dionysus, and their children are Horus (Apollo) and Bubastis (Artemis) (2.156.5). Isis and Osiris rule the underworld (2.123.1) and, unlike most Egyptian gods, were worshiped by all Egyptians (2.42.2).

Herodotus treats quite separately the Dionysiac rites and the god himself, and in so doing makes (in practice, not in theory) a distinction at the core of most modern studies of ancient religion, a distinction between ritual (τὰ δρώμενα, "what is done") and the cult stories and myths about the deity (τὰ λεγόμενα, "what is said"). For Demeter and the Thesmophoria Herodotus gives only the ritual side; here, for Dionysus, we have both sides. Let us begin with the "Dionysiac" ritual.[67]

Each Egyptian on the eve of the festival slaughters in front of his house a pig for Dionysus, and then he gives it back to the swineherd who sold it to carry it off.[68] Except for choral dances,[69] the Egyptians hold the rest of their festival for Dionysus in almost all the same ways the Greeks do. But instead of phalluses they have invented puppets about one and a half feet tall, on strings. Women carry them about the villages, and the genitals, which are not much smaller than the rest of the body of the puppet, bob up and down.

A flute leads the way, and the women follow, singing of Dionysus. There is a sacred *logos* told about the puppet, why it has too large genitals and why the genitals alone move.

I think that Melampus, son of Amytheon,[70] was not unaware of this sacrifice but was experienced in it. Melampus is the one who described (ἐξηγησάμενος) to Greeks the name of Dionysus, the sacrifice, and the procession of the phallos. He revealed the whole *logos* to the Greeks but did not comprehend it exactly. Wise men (σοφισταί) after him revealed more, but Melampus is the one who described the sending of the phallus for Dionysus, and after learning it from him the Greeks do what they do. I say that Melampus, a wise man, devoted himself to the art of prophecy (μαντικήν) and both learned and introduced to Greeks many other things from Egypt and the things concerning Dionysus and changed few of them. For I will not say that the rites for Dionysus in Egypt and those among the Greeks coincided by chance, because then the rituals would be like Greek rituals and would not be recently introduced. Nor will I say that the Egyptians took either this or any other custom from Greeks. I think Melampus learned the Dionysiac things from the Tyrian Cadmus[71] and those who came with Cadmus from Phoenicia to the land now called Boeotia. (2.48–49)

The Greek seer Melampus thus learned some characteristic Dionysiac rituals in Boeotia from Cadmus, the founder of Greek Thebes. Cadmus himself had immigrated to Greece from Phoenician Tyre, a city that serves for Dionysiac ritual as a halfway station between Egypt and Boeotia. Dionysus was Cadmus' grandson and first appeared in Greece 1,000 years before Herodotus, that is, circa 1450 (2.145.4, but see discussion of date below), and thus Dionysiac ritual first appeared in Greece circa 1500. It should be noted that Herodotus puts them at the place and time, if not in the fashion, that Euripides has them in the *Bacchae*.

Herodotus' rather careful method of concluding that the rites came from Egypt to Greece should be noted. Because there were similar rites in the two countries, there were three possibilities: they coincided by chance; the Egyptians took them from the Greeks; or the Greeks took them from the Egyptians. Herodotus offers reasons for excluding the first two and is left with the third. And he then provides a mechanism to explain the spread of the rites from Egypt to Greece. Whatever we may think of the reasons he gives for excluding the other possibilities, the methodology is sound.[72]

Of the god Dionysus himself and of Heracles and Pan, all "younger" gods with Egyptian origins, Herodotus gives this account.

Among the Greeks the youngest of the gods are thought to be Heracles, Dionysus, and Pan, but among the Egyptians Pan is the oldest, one of the so-called first eight gods, and Heracles is one of their second group, the twelve.[73] Dionysus is of their third group, those who were descendants of the twelve. I revealed before how many years the Egyptians say there were from Heracles to King Amasis (17,000 years, 2.43.4). And for Pan there are said to be still more years, but the fewest for Dionysus. For him 15,000 years are reckoned until King Amasis. The Egyptians say they know these things with certainty because they always reckon and record the years.

For the Dionysus said to be the son of Cadmus' daughter Semele, there are about 1,000 [or 1,600] years to my time, and for Heracles, the son of Alcmene, about 900 years. Pan, the son of Penelope (Pan is said by Greeks to have been the son of her and Hermes), is more recent than the Trojan War, about 800 years to my time.

Concerning both (the Egyptian and Greek dates for these gods) one may use whatever accounts he will more believe, but I have revealed my opinion about them. For if Dionysus, the son of Semele, and Pan, the son of Penelope, too, had appeared and grown old in Greece like Heracles (see 2.43-45), someone might say that they, too, were born men and took the names of those earlier (Egyptian) gods.[74] But the Greeks say that right after Dionysus was born Zeus sewed him into his thigh and carried him to Nysa which is beyond Egypt in Ethiopia. They are not able to say where Pan was raised after he was born. It is clear to me that the Greeks learned the names of these deities later than those of the other gods. And they give a genealogy to each from the time when they learned of him. (2.145-146)

Osiris appeared to the Egyptians about 15,500 years B.C., one of their younger gods. The Greeks learned of Dionysus' name much later than they learned of most other gods' names (2.52.2), and they gave him a genealogy from the time they learned of his name, that is, the genealogy as son of Semele and grandson of Cadmus. And when was this? In the Greek text of 2.145-146 it was 1,600 years before Herodotus, or circa 2050. But that date is one of the few wildly inconsistent dates in Herodotus. It would suit neither the usual "mythical" time of Cadmus nor Dionysus' status, with Heracles and Pan, as a relatively late arrival to the Greek pantheon. I have therefore accepted the common emendation of the text to give, for the appearance of Dionysus' name, 1,000 years before Herodotus,[75] that is, 1450 B.C., 100 years before Heracles, 200 years before Pan. If the emended dating is correct, Dionysus' "name" appeared about 1450, but not necessarily his genealogy, offices, skills, and attributes. Those might still be assigned to Hesiod and Homer, some 600 years later. If we take 2.48-49 and 145-146 together, the net result may be that in Herodotus' scheme Dionysiac-type rituals were practiced in Greece some 600 years before the god Dionysus fully emerged in the form we think we know him from sources such as Euripides' *Bacchae*.[76]

## Heracles

Heracles especially interested Herodotus, and the historian made particular efforts to sort out the chronology and details of his cult. He tells of the Egyptian, Tyrian, Thasian, and other Greek cults of the deity, and he leaves the impression that his name was everywhere Heracles.

About Heracles (in Egypt) I heard this *logos*, that he was one of the twelve gods.[77] But nowhere in Egypt was I able to hear about the other Heracles, the one whom the Greeks know. The Egyptians did not take Heracles' name from the Greeks, but rather the Greeks, and especially those among the Greeks who gave to Amphitryon's son the name Heracles, took the name from the Egyptians. I have many other pieces of evidence that this is so, among them the following. The parents of this Heracles, Amphitryon and Alcmene, were both in ancestry from Egypt.[78] Also, the Egyptians say that they do not know the names of Poseidon or the Dioscuri, and these gods have not been received by them among their other gods. If the Egyptians had taken the name of some *daimon* (like Heracles) from the Greeks, then certainly they were going to remember Poseidon and the Dioscuri if at that time the Egyptians sailed and if there were some of the Greeks about as sailors. So I expect and so my opinion inclines. And so the Egyptians would know the names of Poseidon and the Dioscuri more than than that of Heracles.

But Heracles is an old god for the Egyptians. As they themselves say, it has been 17,000 years up to King Amasis (ca. 550 B.C.) since the twelve gods, of whom Heracles was one, were born from the eight gods. And wishing to know something clear about these things from those from whom it was possible (to learn), I sailed also to Tyre of Phoenicia because I heard that in that place there was a holy sanctuary of Heracles.[79] And I saw a sanctuary richly equipped with many other dedications, and in it were two plaques, one of pure gold, the other of an emerald so large that it made the nights shine. I talked with the priests of the god there and asked how long ago the sanctuary was founded. And I found that not even they agreed with the Greeks. For they said that the god's sanctuary was founded when Tyre was founded, and 2,300 years had passed from when Tyre was founded. I saw in Tyre also another sanctuary of Heracles, and he had the epithet "Thasian." And so I went to Thasos where I found a sanctuary of Heracles founded by Phoenicians who, in their search for Europa, sailed out and founded Thasos.[80] And these things were five generations before Heracles, the son of Amphitryon, was born in Greece. My inquiries now reveal clearly that Heracles is an old god. I think that those Greeks act most correctly who have established and possess two kinds of sanctuaries of Heracles and who sacrifice to the one as an immortal with the epithet "Olympios" and make offerings to the other as a hero.[81]

The Greeks say many other things without reflection, and there is also this foolish story (μῦθος) that they tell about Heracles. They say that he came to Egypt, and the Egyptians put garlands on him and led him off in a procession to sacrifice him to Zeus. He kept quiet for a while, but when they were making the preliminary offerings at the altar, he turned to force and slew them all. In saying these things the Greeks, I think, are completely inexperienced in the nature and customs of the Egyptians. For the Egyptians it is not holy to sacrifice even herd animals except for sheep and male cows and calves— whichever ones are pure—and geese. And how would they sacrifice men? And how is it natural for Heracles, being alone and a man, to slay—as they say—thousands upon thousands? May there be goodwill from the gods and heroes as we say such things about these matters.[82] (2.43–45)

Herodotus recognizes three Heracleses: (1) the very old Egyptian god, 17,100 years before Herodotus, with a sanctuary near the Canobic mouth of the Nile, an oracle, and a site for asylum (2.83 and 113.2–3), and with some ties to the Amun (Zeus) of Egyptian Thebes (2.42.3–6); (2) the Heracles of Phoenician Tyre whose cult was founded 2,300 years before Herodotus or 2750 B.C. and the related Heracles of Thasos whose cult was established by these same Phoenicians circa 1500 B.C.; (3) the son of Amphitryon and Alcmene, born in Greece circa 1350 B.C. This last "Heracles," as Herodotus says occasionally happened (2.145–146), took the Egyptian deity's name, lived his life, died, and became a hero. The Egyptian, Tyrian, and Thasian Heracleses were gods (θεοί), the Greek Heracles a hero (ἥρως). Two Heracleses, one a god and one a hero, are thus appropriately, according to Herodotus, worshiped by some Greeks in separate sanctuaries, one with "Olympian" ritual and epithet, the other, the son of Amphitryon and Alcmene, with "heroic" ritual. Both owe their names ultimately to the Egyptians, but they are distinct, generically different deities. And Herodotus comes to these conclusions, as would a modern scholar of Greek religion, by considerations of chronology, localities, and differences of ritual.

## Pan

Mendes, Pan in Greek,[83] was one of the original eight Egyptian gods, dating back at least about 17,450 years (2.43.4 and 145.1–2).

(The Egyptian) painters and sculptors paint and sculpt the statue of Pan just as the Greeks do, with the face and legs of a goat, but they do not believe him to be such but like their other gods.[84] And why they represent him like this I would rather not say. The Egyptians of the Mende district respect (σέβονται) all goats, males more than females, and their goatherds have rather high honors. One of the goats, when he dies, especially causes great grief for the whole district of Mende. Both the goat and Pan are called, in Egyptian, Mendes. (2.46.2–4)

For Herodotus the one point of comparison of Mendes and Pan is the goat features.[85] For the Greeks, Pan was one of the youngest gods, introduced about 1250 B.C., just after the Trojan War (2.145.4). His cult was not, however, everywhere in Greece in these early times. It was brought to Athens first in 490 B.C. (6.105 and Paus. 1.28.4).

## Hephaestus, Hermes, and Ares

The gods Hephaestus, Hermes, and Ares each had a major cult in Egypt, but the shared feature of interest to us is that Herodotus gives to each only a Greek name. The statue of Egyptian Hephaestus in Memphis looked like a pygmy (3.37.2); the sanctuary of Egyptian Hermes was in Bubastis (2.138.4); and the Egyptian Ares had an oracle at Pampremis (2.59.3 and 83) and his cult included a ritual battle between partisans of an Oedipean Ares and the defenders of his mother (2.63).[86] There is little or nothing in Herodotus' account to suggest why he associated these Egyptian deities with the Greek gods. The Scythians also had a major cult of Ares, one obviously involved with war (4.62), and here, too, Herodotus, although carefully giving the other gods Scythian names (4.59), calls this god only Ares. The reason here, however, and also for the Thracian Ares (5.7), may be that the Greek, Scythian, and Thracian Ares were all forms of the same god with, in fact, the same name.[87]

## Athena

Herodotus gives the name Athena to the Egyptian goddess whose cult was centered at Sais with its (male) priests and oracle (2.28.1, 59.3, and 83).[88] Egyptian kings from Sais had their tombs in her sanctuary (2.169.4).[89] Again our historian does not give the goddess's Egyptian name (Neit) or any explicit or implicit reason for likening her to Athena. Bernal (1987.51–53) asserts a direct linkage between the Egyptian Neit and Greek Athena through etymology (Athena = "Temple or House of Neit" in Egyptian) and function. His etymology and claims of similarity of function have been widely and virtually unanimously rejected by other scholars,[90] but this Neit/Athena has won at least ephemeral notoriety as "Black Athena." The case against Bernal's claims has been made, many times over, and Black Athena should now be allowed to pass from ancient religious history and find her rightful place in the history of twentieth-century scholarly and cultural history.[91]

Of greater religious interest is the "Athena" whose cult was practiced by nomadic Libyans living in the area of Lake Tritonis.

The Libyans sacrifice to the sun and moon alone. All Libyans sacrifice to these, but those living around Lake Tritonis sacrifice especially to Athena, and secondly to Triton and Poseidon. The Greeks made the clothing and aegises of the statues of Athena from (those of) the Libyan women. For except that the clothing of the Libyan women is leather and the tassels from the aegises are not snakes but straps, all the other things have been fitted out in the same way. Furthermore, the name indicates that the dress of the statues of Pallas has come from Libya. The Libyan women wear around their clothes shaved goatskins (αἰγέας) with tassels, colored with a red dye, and the Greeks changed the name from goatskins (αἰγέων) to aegises (αἰγίδας). (4.188–189.2)

In the annual festival of (the Libyan) Athena the maidens divide up into two teams and fight one another with stones and clubs, saying that they are performing the ancestral rites for their native goddess whom we call Athena. They call those of the maidens who die from wounds "false maidens." And before they set the girls loose to fight, they do the following. Each time they all together adorn the most beautiful maiden with a Corinthian helmet and a full set of Greek armor, and they mount her on a chariot and lead her around the lake. I cannot say with what armor, long ago before the Greeks settled around them, they used to adorn the maidens, but I think they were adorned with Egyptian armor, because I say that the shield and helmet came to the Greeks from Egypt. They say that Athena is a daughter of Poseidon and Lake Tritonis, but that she found fault with her father and gave herself to Zeus. And Zeus made her his own daughter. (4.180.2–5)

One tribe of the nomadic Libyans (*not* Ethiopians)[92] had a locally born (αὐθιγε-νέι) deity whom the Greeks called Athena. The Libyans must have called her something else. The salient features of her cult were the annual battle of the maidens and the tour of the select maiden dressed in armor. These alone would have been sufficient for Herodotus to identify this goddess with Athena.[93] Whether the Libyan Athena wore the aegis we are not told, but Libyan women did and from them, with minor variations, the Greeks had their statues of Athena do the same.[94] It is the aegis and other garments alone that, in Herodotus' account, the Greeks took from the Libyans. Furthermore, there were significant Greek influences, no doubt from neighboring Greeks, on the cult.[95] The select maiden in the festival wore Greek (originally perhaps Egyptian) armor, and the goddess's genealogy was adjusted (Zeus made her father) to fit the Greek model.

For those nomadic Libyans in the region of Lake Tritonis a native-born goddess had an annual festival that, unlike any Greek Athena festival, featured a maiden in armor and a battle of girls. The maiden in armor, in the Greek tradition as defined by Homer and Hesiod, would certainly bring to mind only Athena. We do not know the goddess's Libyan name, but the Greeks called her Athena. Libyan women wore tasseled goatskins similar in some respects to the aegis commonly worn by the Greek Athena. The "borrowings" from Libya are the tasseled aegis and, as we saw earlier, the "wail" of Libyan women over sacrifices (4.189.3).

In the context of what we have hitherto seen of Herodotus' treatments of Greek religious borrowings, I would suspect that Herodotus has again focused on some rather superficial similarities at the expense of some major differences and has then employed the *post hoc ergo propter hoc* argument for the borrowings. As with the goat-legged and -faced Pan, he has moved quickly from external similarities to identification and has left aside the broader context (which he probably did not know) of the foreign deity's cultic functions and mythology. In short, the Libyan Athena may have differed as fundamentally from the Greek Athena as the Egyptian "Pan" did from the Pan that the Athenians introduced in 490. There was enough—and perhaps only what Herodotus tells us—for the Greeks to call this deity Athena, but beyond this all is speculation.

## Poseidon

Poseidon was, as we have just seen, the original father of the Libyan Athena (4.180.5). His name was one of the few gods' names not to come from Egypt, but "the Greeks learned of him from the Libyans, because no peoples except the Libyans possessed the name of Poseidon from the beginning, and the Libyans have always honored this god" (2.50.2–3).[96] This brings us back again to Lake Tritonis, and Libyan Poseidon fits, with Triton and Tritonis, into a cluster of "water" deities. Here, I think, the Herodotean logic is fairly transparent. The Egyptians had no Poseidon and hence could not have been the source for the name of the Greek god. The Libyans from their very beginnings had and worshiped a deity named Poseidon. All Greek gods' names were imported and came to Greece relatively late. And hence, *post hoc ergo propter hoc*, the name Poseidon must have been imported from Libya.

## Aphrodite

At Ascalon of Syria there was a sanctuary of Aphrodite Ourania.

This sanctuary, as I discover in my inquiries, is the oldest of all the sanctuaries of this goddess. Her sanctuary on Cyprus came from there, as the Cyprians themselves say, and Phoenicians, being from Syria, founded her sanctuary on Cythera. (1.105.3)

The Persians later learned also to sacrifice to Ourania, having learned of her from the Assyrians and Arabians. The Assyrians call Aphrodite Mylitta, the Arabians Alilat, and the Persians Mithra.[97] (1.131.3. Cf. 1.199.3 and 3.8.3)

Elsewhere Herodotus adds that the Scythians called Aphrodite Ourania Argimpasa (4.59).

In this, our last deity to be considered, we have our best and most detailed account of cult transference, and here, importantly, the emphasis is on the similarity of the deity despite the variation of names, and not vice versa. All of these deities, despite their varying names, are the goddess that the Greeks call Aphrodite Ourania, and Herodotus makes explicit the Phoenician foundings of the cult of Aphrodite on both Cyprus and Cythera. The cult of Aphrodite Xeinia at Egyptian Memphis was also, in all probability, Phoenician (2.112).[98] There are, as well, in at least one case, explicitly designated similarities of cult practice, with a form of ritual prostitution (of which Herodotus does not approve) for Mylitta at Babylon and for, presumably, Aphrodite at various Cyprian sites (1.199). If Herodotus had had the occasion to discuss them all, he probably would have traced back all these cults to the original at Ascalon.[99]

Herodotus' treatment of Aphrodite Ourania invites discussion of an important topic that has been somewhat neglected in the scholarly literature. How did foreign cults find their way to Greece and how did Greek cults move within the Greek world? And why did they move? Given the complexities of the ancient world and of Greek religion itself, we should not expect the process to be simple or uniform, and it was not. Again drawing from just Herodotus, we find whole peoples, or families, or individuals as the agents. As to the purposes, we can draw only from hints in Herodotus' narrative.

## Peoples

The Phoenicians, as Herodotus expressly states, founded the cult of their Aphrodite on Cythera, and they too probably founded her cult on Cyprus (1.105.3). Herodotus gives no reason, but a fragment of Solon (19 West) strongly suggests that in the sixth century among the concerns of the Cyprian Aphrodite was the protection of sailors. If this was the case, it would go far in explaining the Phoenicians' export of this deity to their trading outposts. Presumably the sanctuaries were originally established to allow Phoenician sailors (not the local Greeks) to maintain their deity's protection. The cult, sooner or later, found acceptance among the Greeks.

## City-States

In his account of Greeks in Egypt at the time of King Amasis (579–ca. 525), Herodotus offers some insight into the founding of Greek cults in foreign lands:

Amasis granted to those Greeks coming to Egypt to settle in the city Naucratis, and to those who did not wish to settle there but were just making voyages he gave lands on which to set up altars and sanctuaries. The largest, most famous, and most used of these sanctuaries is the one called the Hellenion, and the following cities jointly set it up: of the Ionians, Chios, Teos, Phocaea, and Clazomenae; of the Dorians, Rhodes, Cnidus, Halicarnassus, and Phaselis; and of the Aeolians only the city of the Mytilenaeans. . . . The Aeginetans separately on their own set up a sanctuary of Zeus, the Samians another of Hera, and the Milesians one of Apollo. (2.178)

The critical point here is that the Greek cities, either as a consortium or individually, established these sanctuaries of their gods for the use of their own citizens, whether they were residents or travelers. And for the Samians and the Milesians the sanctuaries were of the most prominent god in the homeland.[100]

Other Samians, rebels defeated by Polycrates, wandered the Aegean for a time, finally settled on Crete, and founded the city Cydonia there. During their five years at Cydonia they built sanctuaries, one with a temple of Dictyna (3.59.1–2). If Herodotus' text is not corrupt here,[101] these Samians apparently adopted the local Dictyna as a major deity for their new city.[102]

When the Phocaeans evacuated their city in Asia Minor in 540 rather than submit to Persian domination, they took with them their cult statues and precious dedications. They refounded their cults in their new homes, first in Alalia on Cyrnus (Corsica) and later at Hyele (Elea) in South Italy (1.164–167). The Teians probably did the same at Abdera (1.168). Here cults follow the migrations of residents of Greek cities. A city might also actively pursue a cult of a nearby city. In the *Histories* this is usually a hero cult and is done at the instigation of an oracle. So the Athenians established a sanctuary of the Aeginetan Aeacus (5.89) and the Spartans recovered the bones of their Orestes from Tegea (1.67–68), both at Delphi's recommendation. In both cases the two cities were at war with another, and this was a factor. The Aeginetans in their turn and on their own initiative, also amid hostilities, stole the cult of the fertility goddesses Damia and Auxesia from Epidaurus (5.82–88).

Shortly after 490 the Athenians imported from Arcadia the cult of Pan, as Philippides reported the god virtually ordered them to do. The god complained that he was "well intentioned" and was and would be "useful" to them but had no cult in Athens. The Athenians built his cave sanctuary on the slope of the Acropolis "when their affairs were again in good order," and that was probably before 488. Miltiades died that year, but before his death he had dedicated a statue and a poem to the goat-legged deity. Herodotus' and Pausanias' accounts together (6.105 and Paus. 1.28.4) would suggest that the Athenians' purpose was not only to maintain the god's immediate help (at Marathon) and future help but also to appease him for past neglect.

## Families

Immigrating families might bring with them their own cults. The Athenian Gephyraioi, originally from Boeotia, set up their own sanctuaries in Athens (including that of Demeter Achaia) and kept them for their exclusive use (5.61.2). Similarly, that the kinsmen of the Athenian Isagoras sacrificed to the Carian Zeus was a factor in assessing Isagoras' Athenian lineage (5.66.1). Here, as with the movement of citizen groups, the family brought the cult for its own use and maintained control of it.

In remote times the daughters of Danaus brought the rituals of the Thesmophoria from Egypt and "taught" them to the Pelasgian women (2.171.2–3). These same Danaids were said to have founded, while passing by in their travels, the sanctuary of Athena in Lindus on Rhodes (2.182.2).[103]

## Individuals

Apostolic-style founders of cults lay, like the Danaids, in the remote past. In the time of Cadmus of Thebes and Tyre, the seer Melampus taught Greeks Dionysiac-type rituals (2.48–49). The shaman-like Aristeas of Proconnesus in very mysterious circumstances introduced Apollo to Metapontum, the god's early cult in Italy (4.15.2–4). In the context of colonization and not individual mission Philistus of Athens, in the time of King Codrus, helped settle Miletus and founded the sanctuary of Demeter Eleusinia at Mycale (9.97). Colonization was probably the single most important factor in the spread of Greek cults to scattered places on the shores of the Aegean and Mediterranean, but Herodotus offers us nothing except the account of Philistus and occasional reports of cults of *oikistai* like Miltiades of the Chersonesitae (6.38.1).[104]

In the historical period, circa 600–570, the Sicyonian tyrant Cleisthenes, in a tangled web of politics, legend, and religion, imported the Theban hero Melanippus to annoy and displace from Sicyon Melanippus' bitter enemy, the Argive hero Adrastus. After establishing Melanippus, Cleisthenes gave to him Adrastus' sacrifices and festivals (5.67). But not all attempts to transplant cults succeeded. In the sixth century the widely traveled and legendary Scythian Anacharsis encountered a festival of Magna Mater at Cyzicus. He prayed to her for a safe return, with a vow that he would establish her cult in his homeland. When he reached home, he introduced her cult with its night festival, drums, and statuettes. For his efforts he was killed by his xenophobic fellow countrymen (4.76).

We save for last the first transference of a foreign cult to Greece in Herodotus' scheme of the origins of Greek religion. It is of value because, given conflicting accounts of the origins of the cult, Herodotus, a man knowledgeable about the history of Greek religion but, even more important, a practitioner of it himself, imagines how this cult was founded. An Egyptian woman, once an attendant of the Egyptian Zeus in Egyptian Thebes, finds herself living as a slave in Thesprotia, a remote corner of northwestern Greece. "Serving as a slave there she founded under a live oak tree a sanctuary of Zeus. It was natural for her to remember him in the place she had come to because she had been an attendant in the sanctuary of Zeus in Thebes. Afterward, when she had learned the Greek language, she introduced an oracle" (2.56–57). From this simple and natural act, a lone slave woman recreating for her own use a remembered cult of her homeland and of her personal devotion, a major Greek cult developed, and this cult, as we have seen, became the linchpin in the importation, as Herodotus saw it, of further major Egyptian influences on Greek religion.

In the midst of whatever social, economic, and political forces were at work, religious cults were imported into Greece and moved around the Greek world by humans, either in groups or as individuals.[105] Even these few examples from Herodotus indicate that the reasons were complex and varied significantly from case to case, no less varied and complex than Greek religion itself or its deities. If we are not again overinterpreting our meager bits of evidence, the establishment of cults and rites in "heroic" times, like those of the Danaids and those commonly credited to itinerant heroes in epic and tragedy, seems different from the foundations of the historical period. The latter are for the benefit, often exclusive, of the founders and are intimately tied to their cultural traditions; the former appear less locally distinct, more generic, and more Panhellenic. One suspects that the historical foundings better reflect cult realities, and that it is such cult realities that are in the mind of Herodotus when he gives his version of the founding of the cult of the "first" truly Greek god, Zeus of Dodona.

Herodotus never, of course, intended his *Histories* to be a history of Greek religion. He raises the subject only sporadically and in passing, always in regard to some other historical, ethnographic, or topographical topic he is pursuing.[106] Herodotus also did not have the interest in explicit statements of methodology that characterize the writings of Thucydides and modern scholars. The lack of an explicit methodology and the occasional format of his comments on Greek religion can lead one to underestimate or disregard him as a source for Greek religion, to treat him equally unmethodologically and occasionally as a source only for the miscellaneous detail. But quite to the contrary, he does have a comprehensive and, given his circumstances, reasonable view of the development of Greek religion. The methodology that emerges is quite sophisticated, with several elements that have become canons of modern studies of ancient religions.[107] Finally, he was a "believer" himself and had wide personal experience in the cults of many Greek cities and foreign peoples.

Modern students of Greek religion widely use, sometimes quite unknowingly, Herodotean strategies such as the separation of deity and ritual, differences between rituals, chronological sequence, *post hoc ergo propter hoc* assumptions, individuals and events to serve as intermediaries for movements of deities and cults, and even etymologies, and they have, of course, developed far further the theory behind them.[108] But we modern scholars cannot have, and can never remotely approximate, the breadth of experience Herodotus had as a participant in and observer of the religion of early classical Greece. I would also add that Herodotus was aware of and was not unaffected by the poetic conventions concerning Greek religion. Indeed, he was the first to point to them in 2.53. But the bulk of his discussions of religion was not shaped by these poetic conventions as was that of the epic, lyric, and tragic poets whom modern scholars occasionally and often unwarily use as their prime sources for archaic and classical "Greek religion."

Herodotus' major limitation as a historian of Greek religion is not his mind or methodology; it is the quality, nature, and even quantity of his own sources. He was, necessarily at his time, engulfed in a sea of heterogeneous sources. Most were oral, a few were written. Some were monuments: inscriptions, tombs, buildings, and sculptures. Some were Greek. Many were foreign, and for these he was dependent on priests, tourist guides, dinner party companions, and interpreters, all probably equally unreliable. These sources described for him three continents and nearly eighteen millennia of history. The sources were often hard to understand and impossible to validate. Erroneous, incomplete, and unintelligible sources may on occasion have misled him, but this problem he shares with modern scholars whose sources are far fewer and often no better. But in reporting and interpreting such sources, Herodotus had the considerable advantage of judging them in relation to the religion he practiced and to the culture in which he lived. Herodotus is our best single source — ancient or modern — for the religion of his time, and his view of its history deserves serious consideration, not just as an antiquarian piece of theory but as a *logos* that reflects the Greeks' own beliefs about their religious history and that may even contain some historical realities.

# ❧ NOTES ❧

## Introduction

1. When in 2000 a version of this book was virtually complete, Thomas Harrison published his *Divinity and History: The Religion of Herodotus*. Harrison's purpose is to describe and judge "the variety of religious beliefs of one man, the variety of beliefs, most importantly, that can be held *in combination* with one another" (17). He provides essentially a study of Herodotus in intellectual history terms (16–18), with ample parallels in the notes to earlier and contemporary poetic literature. Much of his discussion focuses on how Herodotus (and Greeks in general) could, "in the real world," still believe that prayers were answered, propitiations worked, the gods punished impious actions, heroes actually "appeared" to men, oracles and omens were accurate, and so forth. My purpose is quite different, to collect and discuss Herodotus' descriptions and comments on the cultic, practiced side of Greek religion and to place them into a religious and historical context. Our two approaches have several areas of overlap, of course, and Harrison has caused me to rethink a number of significant points and to eliminate some rather elaborate discussions on matters in which I find myself in essential agreement with him. These include the relationship of religion to the study of ancient history, the nature of the "miraculous" and the "divine" in Herodotus' *Histories*, the varieties of divination, questions of whether Herodotus "believed" in the religious phenomena he described, and a number of smaller topics. I, of course, refer to Harrison's discussions of these topics and also note minor and some major points of disagreement in interpretation, particularly in Chapter 3, "Some Religious Beliefs and Attitudes of Herodotus." Before Harrison the best general study of religion in Herodotus' *Histories* was G. Lachenaud's wide-ranging *Mythologies, religion et philosophie de l'histoire dans Herodote* (1978). It offers many valuable insights into religious aspects of Herodotus' thought and thoughtful interpretations of several individual episodes. It is particularly helpful in matters of the oracles and of Herodotus' approach to religious history. Harrison tends to focus on the inconsistencies in Herodotus' views, but Lachenaud, also concentrating almost exclusively on the *Histories*, stresses the consistency of Herodotus' religious views and attitudes. Lachenaud, unlike Harrison, makes some important distinctions (sometimes explicitly, sometimes implicitly) among the popular, poetic, and philosophic layers of "religion" in the *Histories*, and these contribute to understanding the inconsistencies Harrison details.

2. There are those who claim that Herodotus pervasively and intentionally falsified events, his sources and his use of them, and his travels and experiences. They have been dubbed "the Liar School of Herodotus," and their own history from ancient times to the

present has been set forth by Momigliano (1958), Evans (1968), and Pritchett (1993). I am neither a member of nor a sympathizer with the Liar School, in part from my own reading of Herodotus and study of his treatment of religious matters, but more importantly from the arguments raised by Marincola (26–33 in Dewald and Marincola, 1987) and Pritchett (1993) against the most recent proponents of the thesis. Pritchett, with his usual vigor, makes a full-scale assault from many directions on the modern Liar School, including historiography; epigraphical, archaeological, and topographical verifications of Herodotus' claims; and quotations of positive assessments of Herodotus by modern archaeologists, ethnographers, and historians.

There are, of course, errors, misrepresentations, inconsistencies, and illogicalities in the nearly 800 OCT pages of Herodotus' *Histories* that range over 12,000 years of human history and three continents, but given the geographical, topographical, ethnological, and historical knowledge and methods of his time, the oral sources upon which he had almost exclusively to depend (Evans, 1991; Gould, 1989), the "storytelling" tradition in which he and his sources apparently worked (Gould, 1989), the difficulties of understanding foreign cultures near and far with languages unknown to him (Gould, 19–28), and even the difficulties of referring to what he himself had written on papyrus rolls (Lattimore, 1958.9–10), the overall accuracy of the *Histories*, when it is judged on the basis of independent evidence (as from Egypt by A. B. Lloyd, 1975, 1976, 1988, or Scythia by Pritchett, 1993.191–226), is astonishing and deserving of the highest respect and admiration. See also Dover, 1998; Burkert, 1990; and Lewis, 1985.

In this study I share the approach of those who, with an awareness of the "historical" and literary conventions of his time, are inclined to trust Herodotus except in those relatively few cases where he can be proved wrong by independent evidence. As John Gould (1989.67. Cf. 114) states, "the likelihood is that Herodotus is giving us the true feel of what men said, of how contemporaries perceived and accounted for the major happenings of their experience." And, to reveal further my biases, it is precisely "what men said" and "how contemporaries perceived and accounted for major happenings of their experience" that I as a historian of practiced Greek religion try to cull from ancient authors.

3. For a brief survey of how ancient historians after Herodotus did or did not introduce "the divine" into their narratives, see Price, 1999.131–133.

4. Harrison (2000.1–30) describes and critiques at length ways in which modern historians justify excluding from their histories the religious material in Herodotus' *Histories*. Among them are arguments that Herodotus introduced religious elements only to entertain or not alienate his less well educated and less historically minded audience; that he was simply repeating, more or less as unconscious assumptions, "traditional ideas"; that as a rational historian he could not possibly have believed in miracles and oracles and in various ways demonstrated his disbelief by "distancing" himself from them in his presentations; and that Herodotus' relatively rare skeptical comments on specific religious events should be extended to cover all matters of religion. The most aggressive recent attempts to disparage the "religious" element in the *Histories* in the endeavor to show Herodotus' political sophistication are Lateiner (1989) and Shimron (1989), both of whose arguments Harrison addresses directly throughout his book.

5. D. Lateiner (1989.196–210) offers a concise, lucid, and thoughtful summary of "Five

Systems of Explanation" found in Herodotus' *Histories*. These include immoral and divine jealousy (φθόνος); fate; divine intervention; a "vengeance" that maintains a natural, dynamic equilibrium in historical events; and "a historicist, down-to-earth, political analysis, the sort of explanation expected from a modern historian." Lateiner has much of value to say of each of the five systems, and I strongly agree with him that Herodotus often offers two or more of these causes for single events. I also agree that Herodotus gives historical causes for major events and that religious causation or fate "sometimes supplement" but "never prevent human motives and political causes from appearing."

Lateiner's preference (as also Shimron's [1989]) as a historian for Herodotus' "historical" explanations is matched, however, by a pervasive hostility to the historian's "divine" explanations, in fear, apparently, that a "naive" Herodotus may be "dismissed as a cracker-barrel apologist for popular religion." Lateiner puts each of the first three systems of explanation (divine jealousy, fate, and divinities) into the worst possible light, systematically attempting to minimize Herodotus' own belief and confidence in them. Here I object. Religious and "metaphysical" causes are, of course, not as "observable," verifiable, and certain as some of the "historical causes," and some might be recognized only retrospectively. Herodotus understood this and expressed himself accordingly, but that certainly does not mean that religious elements were, to him, irrelevant or bogus. As I trust Chapter 1 alone shows, in the *Histories* the "realm of the divine" is not, as Lateiner claims, "largely dismissed." Nor is it the case that, as Shimron (1989.75) claims, "in the second part of the *Histories* . . . the supernatural—apart from a few oracles—all but disappears, and what there is of it, refers almost completely to signs that happened to the Persians." And that is undeniably true if we include, as Herodotus does, not just what "gods do" but also what "humans do" in prayer, sacrifice, dedication, and divination. For a critique of Lateiner's views of religion in Herodotus, see Harrison, 2000, and Gould, 1994.92–98.

For what I consider more balanced views of "supernatural causation" in Herodotus' *Histories*, see Harrison, 2000; Romm, 1998.142–147; Gould, 1989.70–82 and 1994; Pritchett, 1979.147–148; Pelling, 1991.137–140; Burkert, 1990; Fornara, 1990; Lachenaud, 1978; Ste. Croix, 1977.138–147; Pohlenz, 1973.96–119; Romilly, 1971; Starr, 1962.324; Immerwahr, 1954 and 1966.

6. See, for example, Harrison, 2000.234–238, but his idea that a large number or chain of causes for a single incident indicates that Herodotus thought the event was "fated" is not compelling.

7. Cf. Romm, 1998.74–75.

8. 7.233.2, 6.91.1, 9.73.3, and 7.137.3.

9. 8.65 and 9.16.

10. Tölle-Kastenbein, 1976.63–71.

11. I recognize that the use of "account" is not without consequences. In particular it submerges the insight (see esp. Gould, 1989) that Herodotean *logoi* are fundamentally "stories" told to and by Herodotus and that one should be aware of "storytelling" narrative structures, dynamics, and purposes in evaluating them. Cf. Romm, 1998.114–131.

12. Humphreys, 1987.

13. Frost (1997.70–72) uses, for the same purposes, similar conversions at the same rate.

## Chapter 1

1. Cf. Thuc. 1.20.2, 6.56–58, and *Ath.Pol.* 18.

2. Herodotus serves as a dream interpreter himself for Cyrus' dream about Darius (1.210.1) and for the dream of Polycrates' daughter (3.124.1–125.4). In numerous other instances the recipients themselves (e.g., Hippias, 6.107–108; Croesus, 1.45.2; and Cambyses, 3.65.4) or others (e.g., Artabanus and dream interpreters for Xerxes, 7.12–18) give the proper interpretation of the dream.

3. For one attempt to explain the "riddling" words, see Frisch, 1968.33–34.

4. κίβδηλος is used elsewhere by Herodotus not of false oracles but of misleading ones: on "measuring Tegea" to the Spartans (1.66.3) and on "crossing the Halys River" to Croesus (1.75.2). On the term, see Harrison, 2000.152 n. 106, and Flower, 1991.71 n. 96.

5. Cf. Plut. *Mor.* 860C–D; *Ath.Pol.* 19; Pind. *Pyth.* 7.10 and schol. to *Pyth.* 7.9; Dem. 21.144. For more sources and bibliography, see Fontenrose Q124. On this account see Kirchberg, 1965.71–72.

6. Harrison, 2000.143 n. 77. Pausanias, following Herodotus and writing some 600 years later about the same event, claimed to know of "no one else except Cleomenes who dared in any way to corrupt the oracle" (3.4.3–6).

7. Two examples from outside the context of the Persian Wars also illustrate the point. Herodotus has the Spartan tyrant Euryleon on Sicily beset by his subjects, the Selinusians. Euryleon fled for safety to an altar of Zeus Agoraios, but the Selinusians nonetheless killed him (5.46.2). Similarly Hecataeus recommends to the Milesians, just before the Ionian Revolt, that they seize Croesus' dedications at Didyma and use the revenue to finance their naval effort against the Persians. Hecataeus wanted also, according to Herodotus, to prevent the Persians from stealing the dedications (5.36.3–4), but this is a lame excuse for expropriating a god's property. Rather we see here and in the case of the Selinusians that Herodotus does not decry apparent impieties when they are directed against oppressive tyrants.

8. In this context a *xenos* was a personal friend who was a citizen of another Greek city-state. The two friends were bound by the obligations of *xenia*.

9. On the pollution of the Alcmaeonidae, see Parker, 1983.16–17. Other instances of the violation, through murder, of asylum in a sanctuary include the Persian killing of the defenders of the Athenian Acropolis (Hdt. 8.51–55); Cleomenes' massacre of Argive suppliants (6.75 and 79); and the Aeginetans' killing of one of their own (6.91). When the Cymaeans were considering surrendering a suppliant, Apollo reasserted for them the sanctity of suppliants (1.157–160). The Spartans attempted by complicated and ultimately unsuccessful measures to avoid violating the asylum of their Persian War commander and hero Pausanias just after the Persian Wars (Thuc. 1.134 and D.S. 11.45.5–9).

10. On the archaic and classical belief in inherited pollution, especially in reference to the Alcmaeonidae, "If it was through hostility to tyrants that the Alcmeonids incurred pollution, it was surely their carefully nurtured reputation for the same quality that helped to cleanse it," see Parker, 1983.203–206. The pollution of the Alcmaeonidae could still, eighty years later, be raised against the Alcmaeonid Pericles (Thuc. 1.126–127).

11. For varying accounts of these episodes, see Thuc. 1.126, Plut. *Solon* 12, and *Ath.Pol.* 20.2–3.

12. The scene is surely the "old" temple of Athena, the goddess Athena Polias. An *adyton*, a place "not to be entered," is not otherwise known for this temple.

13. The import of Cleisthenes' approach to Athena Polias and of his claim to be an "Achaean, not a Dorian," is not surely known. For various possibilities, see Parker, 1998a.4–6 and 24–26, and Boedeker, 1993.166.

14. On the *megaron* here as part of the "old" temple of Athena, see Hurwit, 1999.144.

15. Fragments of the original of this inscription and of a later post-Persian version were found on the Acropolis (ML 15 = *IG* I³ 501). On the text and on the order of the lines of the original version, see Page, *FGE*, 191–193. See also Clairmont, 1983.91–92, and, for the site of the monument, Hurwit, 1999.129, 144, 146, and Pritchett, 1993.150–159. Cf. D.S. 10.24.3; Paus. 1.28.2; *Anth.Pal.* 6.343; and Aristides 2.512 (Dindorf) and scholia ad loc.

16. Chains were similarly dedicated by the Tegeans to their Athena after a victory over the Spartans, but these were chains the Spartans had brought with them to use on the Tegeans (Hdt. 1.66.4).

17. On ἀκροθίνια versus δέκαται, see Lonis, 1979.151–153, and Gauer, 1968.33–34. On the general practice of giving "firstfruits," see Burkert, 1979.52–54. For a different kind of "tithe," see Hdt. 7.132 and the Oath of Plataea.

18. For the general paucity in Greek for expressions of gratitude, particularly in prayers and dedications, see Pulleyn, 1997.39–55; Bremmer, 1994.39; and Versnel, 1981.42–62. Herodotus has only two formal expressions of owing thanks to the gods: of the Abderitae for being spared from providing both lunch and dinner for Xerxes' army (7.120), and when the Scythians advise the Ionians "to be grateful to the gods and to them for their freedom" (4.136.4). Neither is in a cult context.

Bremer (1998), however, rightly notes that in dedications and hymns Greeks usually expressed their gratitude indirectly, either by praising the deity or by describing the good services received. The latter is more common in private dedications and seems noticeably lacking in the dedications related to the Persian Wars.

19. On the function of public and private dedications to memorialize human accomplishment, see Lonis, 1979.271–277, and Van Straten, 1981.76. On this in Herodotus in particular, see Gould, 1991.13–14.

20. Fontenrose Q63. According to the scholiast on Aristides 46.187 (Dindorf, p. 598), Damia and Auxesia were Demeter and Persephone. On these deities, see Crahay, 1956.76, and HW, 2.46.

21. For the site, see Müller, 1987.742.

22. On τὸ δαιμόνιον in this passage, see Linforth, 1928.236–237. Cf. Paus. 2.30.4 and 32.2. On the historicity of this whole account and on Herodotus' sources for it, see Figueira, 1985.

23. Fontenrose Q130.

24. On this episode, see Pritchett, 1979.15–16.

25. On this account, see Kearns, 1989.47, and Kirchberg, 1965.78–79.

26. For an extensive and effective argument that Herodotus does not distinguish between "mythical" and "historical periods" but rather sees the past as a "continuous whole," and that he does not separate his *logoi* into "mythical" and "historical" categories but treats them all in the same way, "historical" to him, see Harrison, 2000.196–207.

27. Harrison (2000.206–207) argues, unsuccessfully I think, that Herodotus' use of μῦθος in these two passages "cannot safely be taken as 'implying disbelief.'" The first passage (2.23) might be open to doubt in this regard; the second (2.43–45) is not.

28. Further examples of *logoi* of very ancient events and situations that we might call "mythological" but were introduced by Herodotus as historical precedent or cause for actions in or about the time of the Persian Wars include the the genealogy of Perses and Perseus (7.61.3 and 148–152); the death of Minos on Crete (7.169–171); and the invasion of the Peloponnesus by the Heraclidae, the Seven against Thebes, and the Amazon attack on Greece (9.26–28.1).

29. On heroes in general, see Whitley, 1994.218–222; Kearns, 1989 and 1992; Burkert, *GR*, 203–208; Visser, 1982; Nock, 1944 = 1972.2.575–602; and Farnell, 1921. Specifically on Herodotus' treatment of heroes, see Linforth, 1928.209–211.

30. Fontenrose Q131.

31. On the cult of Aeacus on Aegina and in Athens and on the Anakeion in Athens, see Stroud, 1998. esp. 85–104.

32. See Immerwahr, 1966.212 n. 65. On this Athenian-Aeginetan war, see Figueira, 1991.104–113. Parker (1985.317) sees this oracle as simply "referring the issue back to Athens undecided," whereas others see it as Delphi's "attempt to protect Aegina from attack" or as "a helpful warning to the Athenians not to tangle with the mighty Aeginetan fleet too soon."

33. As Figueira (1991.104) puts it, "Just as the Eurysakeion, a hero shrine of the Athenian *genos* of the Salaminioi, solidified an Athenian claim to the ownership of the island Salamis, the Aiakeion expressed a similar claim to Aegina." Cf. Kearns, 1989.47.

34. Stroud, 1998.85–87.

35. Among these oracles may have been the one described in Hdt. 8.141.1.

36. Almost certainly the "old" temple of Athena.

37. For a recent account of the history of the Ionian Revolt, see Balcer, 1995.169–191.

38. On the cult of the goddess Cybebe, probably a protectress of cities and particularly associated with royalty, in archaic Sardis, see Roller, 1999. esp. 44–46 and 128–131. For musings on why Herodotus calls her a "local goddess" despite "her established identification with Demeter, the Great Mother and Aphrodite," see Harrison, 2000.216.

39. The Persian Zeus was "the vault of the sky" and was worshiped on mountaintops (1.131). As the father of Perseus he was the ultimate ancestor of all Persians (7.61.3). He gave to the Persians hegemony over other men and to the king rule over the Persians (9.122.2. Cf. 1.89.3 and 1.207.1). The "chariot of Zeus" with its eight horses accompanied Xerxes on the Greek campaign (7.40.4).

40. Cf. 6.94.1.

41. Fontenrose Q134. This was originally a double oracle, given to the Argives some years earlier. For the Argive part of this oracle, see 6.77.2. See also Fontenrose, p. 169.

42. On this account, see Kirchberg, 1965.41–43. For the earlier, pro-Persian history of the oracle at Didyma, see Balcer, 1995.85–86. On the variant ancient accounts of its history after the Ionian Revolt, see Bigwood, 1978.36–39.

43. On the questions involved, see Meiggs, 1972.505.

44. Cf. Plut. *Mor.* 869B. For a map, photographs, and bibliography on Naxos, see Müller, 1987.984–986.

45. For problems reconciling Thuc. 2.8.3 and his claim about the first earthquake on Delos with Herodotus' account, see Pritchett, 1993.88–90, and HW, 2.104. On the site, see Müller, 1987.934–942.

46. On this account, see Kirchberg, 1965.84–86.

47. For a map and photographs of Eretria, see Müller, 1987.401–405.

48. For the site of Marathon, see Müller, 1987.655–673.

49. On the name as Philippides, not Pheidippides, see HW, 2.107.

50. On the god Pan, his arrival in Athens, his cave, and his development in the Athenian context, see Parker, 1996, 163–168; Garland, 1992.47–63; and Lonis, 1979.182–183. For speculation on how Pan might have assisted the Athenians in the Persian Wars, see Immerwahr, 1966.253–254.

51. Cf. Paus. 8.54.6.

52. On this epigram, its date, and its ascription to Simonides, see Page, *FGE*, 194–195.

53. Plutarch describes how Zeus Eleutherios was to receive, on his new altar with its fresh, unpolluted Delphic fire, the Greek sacrifices after the victory at Plataea (*Arist.* 20.4–5).

54. Plutarch is the source for the sacrifices to the Sphragitid Nymphs of Plataea by the Athenian Aiantis tribe (*Arist.* 11.3–5 and 19.5).

55. The exception here is the Athenian sacrifice to the Twelve Gods.

56. On *nomos* as "tradition" or "law," see Introduction.

57. On these questions, see Bowen, 1992.26; Hereward, 1958.241–244; and HW, 2.108–109. On the date of the Artemis Agrotera festival in relation to this battle, see my subsequent discussion of that festival. On the Spartans' "scrupulous" respect for festivals in times of warfare ("She was devout, but not to the point of extinction"), see Holladay and Goodman, 1986.156–160.

58. Only one prayer explicitly for "victory" is reported, and that by a *phantom* (8.94).

59. Cf. D.S. 11.31.1. Cf. Immerwahr, 1966.252 and 265–266.

60. An owl as a good omen may also have flown over the Athenian army before the battle began at Marathon (Ar. *Vesp.* 1086). Cf. Plut. *Them.* 12.1.

61. The scholiast to Ar. *Eq.* 660 attributes this vow to Callimachus. Aelian (*VH* 2.25) gives it to Miltiades but is mistaken in the number of victims (300) and the day of the battle (Thargelion 6).

62. Mikalson, 1975.18 and 50.

63. *Ath. Pol.* 58.1; Plut. *Mor.* 862A–C; and Mikalson, 1998.243, 248, and 253. On this vow and festival, see Pritchett, 1979.173–175 and 232. For Plutarch's dating of the battle to Boedromion 6, see my earlier discussion of Plut. *Mor.* 861E–F.

64. Cf. Thuc. 2.34.5.

65. For the memorial of Miltiades, see Clairmont, 1983.112–113. For fragments of, possibly, a state dedication on the Athenian Acropolis to honor their polemarch Callimachus, who died in the battle (6.114), see ML 18 (*IG* I³ 784) and Hurwit, 1999.130–131.

66. On this episode, see Hdt. 6.132–136.

67. Fontenrose Q142. On the hero Echetlaeus, see Kearns, 1989.45–46 and 165.

68. Vanderpool (1966) has identified fragments of a large marble column and Ionic capital with this trophy monument. The column would have been about ten meters tall and surmounted with a sculptured figure. For the numerous ancient references to it, see Vanderpool, 1966. On this trophy, see also Clairmont, 1983.111–112.

69. For the possible discovery of a mass of Persian bones in Marathon in the late nineteenth century, see Vanderpool, 1966.101.

Before the battle of Marathon the Athenians camped in a sanctuary of Heracles (6.108 and 116), and Vanderpool (1942.333–337) suggests that soon after the battle the Athenians remodeled the local Marathonian Heraclea into a Panathenian agonistic festival that attracted even some regional, non-Athenian competitors (Pind. *Ol.* 9.89–90 and 13.110 and *Pyth.* 8.79).

70. For the site, appearance, and excavations of this famous *soros* in Marathon, see Pritchett, 1985.126–127; Clairmont, 1983.95–99; and Müller, 1987.655–673. For the funeral rites of the Marathonian dead, see Vanderpool, 1942.333–337. On the *soros* and for the claim that its form was an attempt to assimilate the Marathon dead to the epic heroes, see Whitley, 1994. esp. 215–217 and 227–230.

71. For a review of the various arguments concerning these epigrams, see Page, *FGE*, 225–230.

72. Jacoby (1945.160) asserts that this was *not* an epitaph and "even in Lycurgan times it can hardly have stood on a stele at the Soros in the Marathonian plain." He is unsure whether it is a fifth-century poem or was ever engraved on a stone. He admits, though, that "Lycurgus palms it off on his hearers as an epitaph." Jacoby flatly denies that there was any poetic epitaph on the *soros* at Marathon (176–177). For the possibility that it may have stood beneath the Marathon painting in the Stoa Poicile (Paus. 1.15.3) and may not date to the fifth century, see W. C. West, 1970.278.

73. Some would have this second epigram on the tomb of the Athenians at Plataea (Clairmont, 1983.105).

74. For a now excavated tomb often identified with that of the Plataeans, see Hammond, 1992.147–150; Pritchett, 1985.126–129; and Clairmont, 1983.99–100.

75. After Delphi ordered it in 476/5 (Fontenrose Q164), Cimon recovered the bones of Theseus from Scyros and brought them home to Athens, probably in 469/8 (Plut. *Th.* 36 and *Cim.* 8.5–6; Paus. 1.17.6 and 3.3.7; D.S. 4.62). On this and for possible association with his appearance at Marathon, see Garland, 1992.82–98.

76. E.g., *IG* II² 1006.69–70 of 122/1. See Mikalson, 1998.245–249. On the war dead as a distinct class of "heroes," see my subsequent comments on Plut. *Arist.* 21.2–5.

77. The statue is now more commonly attributed to Agoracritus (Miles, 1989.138 and 227). For surviving fragments of this statue and its base (also described by Pausanias, 1.33.7–8), see Despinis, 1971. On the cult of Rhamnusian Nemesis and her temple, built circa 430–420, see Miles, 1989. On Pausanias' account and on later versions of this episode, see Asheri, 1998.78–79.

78. On this and the statue in general, see Hurwit, 1999.24–25, 151–153, 228, and 230; Ridgway, 1992.130; Gauer, 1968.38–39 and 103–105; and Niemeyer, 1960. esp. 76–85. Its

height, with the base, was probably about thirty feet, and the statue was probably completed circa 450.

79. The temple of Eukleia is otherwise unknown. Cult foundations for pure personifications ("Good Fame") are rare in this period. Wilamowitz's association (1880.150–151 n. 70) of her with the Artemis Eukleia of Plataea (Plut. *Arist.* 20.4–5) would seem promising, but contradicts Pausanias' association with the battle of Marathon. There is also no later evidence of a cult of Artemis Eukleia in Athens. See Gauer, 1968.24 and 70.

80. Cf. Plut. *Mor.* 604F, Paus. 1.14.5, and Athen. 14.627C. Page (*FGE*, 131–132) strongly argues that this epigram is not by Aeschylus, is not an epitaph, and is Hellenistic in date.

81. On the Stoa Poicile and these paintings, see Camp, 1986.65–72.

82. Paus. 5.11.6; Pliny *NH* 35.57 and 59; Aelian *NA* 7.38; Arrian *Ana.* 7.13.5. On these painters and this painting, see Pollitt, 1990.126–145.

83. On this painting and its partners in the stoa representing as a whole a tableau presenting in historical and mythological terms the Athenian victory over the Persians, see Francis and Vickers, 1985. For the unlikely claim that Herodotus' description of the battle of Marathon was based largely on this painting, see Massaro, 1978.

84. On the heroes depicted in the painting and their roles or nonroles in the battle, see Kearns, 1989.45–46.

85. On the placement of these shields and that they are distinct from the shields dedicated at Delphi from Plataea (Aeschines 3.116), see Gauer, 1968.26–27.

86. This treasury and the dedicatory inscription raise a host of questions concerning the dates of the building, its inscriptions, and its sculpture. For a summary, see Gauer, 1968.45–65, who argues that all can be dated from 490 to 480. See also Miller, 1997.37.

87. Fontenrose Q125.

88. On this monument, see Gauer, 1968.65–70.

89. There was also in the sanctuary of Delphi a sculpted horse, dedicated, Pausanias says, by the Athenian Callias, son of Lysimachides, "after he privately made money from the war against the Persians" (10.18.1).

90. On the sanctuary and cult of Athena Areia, see Schachter, 1981.127–128. For plans and photographs of Plataea, see Müller, 1987.546–570.

91. Gauer, 1968.98–100.

92. See Miller, 1997.42, and Gauer, 1968.22–23, 42, and 135.

93. See Gauer, 1968.23. For the argument that Miltiades dedicated this helmet years before the battle of Marathon, see Clairmont, 1983.93–94.

94. On the Apollo cult at Delion and this account, see Schachter, 1981.44–47. On the site, see Müller, 1987.464–466.

95. For views of Paros, see Müller, 1987.991–999.

96. Fontenrose Q143. For musings on what Timo may or may not have done for Miltiades, see Harrison, 1997.121 n. 39. On Herodotus' account and for varying versions of it in other, later sources, see Kinzel, 1976.

97. Pausanias, as we shall see later, offers another explanation for the death of Miltiades, but one also involving a serious impiety (3.12.7).

98. For the fulfillment of this oracle, once symbolically in 513 and again actually centuries later, see Shapiro, 1990.336–337, and HW, 2.127.

99. On Onomacritus and other *chresmologoi* in Pisistratid Athens, see Shapiro, 1990.

100. The Athenian *chresmologos* Lysistratus, however, by his accurate oracle won Herodotus' respect (8.96).

101. On Artabanus as the "wise adviser," and especially on the limits of his predictions as accurate forecasts but on their value as pointing to greater truths, see Pelling, 1991. esp. 130–143. Evans (1991.14) sees Cassandra as the "ultimate archetype" of Artabanus. "More than a wise adviser, he is almost a seer whose accurate vision of the future introduced a note of dramatic irony."

102. Parallels to these and other statements of Artabanus here may be found in Herodotus' own Solon (1.31.3 and 32.4). For parallels in tragedy, see A. *Ag.* 567–569, *Suppl.* 802–803, *Pr.* 747–754; S. *Ajax* 758–761, *El.* 1170, *Tr.* 1173, *OC* 954–955; Eur. *Suppl.* 1000–1005, *Tr.* 271, 606, 641–642, *Heraclid.* 591–596, *Alc.* 937–938, *Hipp.* 1370–1373, *Or.* 1522, and frag. 964[N].

103. For varying views of *phthonos* in Herodotus' *Histories*, see Cairns, 1996. esp. 13–15, 18–22; Fisher, 1992.361–363; Gould, 1989.79–80; Lateiner, 1989.196–197; Lloyd-Jones, 1983.55–58, 68–70; Ste. Croix, 1977.140, 145; Pohlenz, 1973.110–119; Pötscher, 1958; Dodds, 1951.30–31.

104. On the *phthonos* Polycrates engendered and on the difficulty of finding any "fault" of Polycrates that merited or is explicitly linked with divine *phthonos*, see Fisher, 1992.361–363. Fisher thinks Amasis, as Polycrates' friend, would naturally not allude to any such fault. Fisher also suggests that the Ring Story is a folktale that may have expressed the idea that great success alone begets divine *phthonos*, but that Herodotus "does not necessarily endorse the meaning of folk-tale as a whole." For the view that Polycrates in Amasis' judgment lacked the proper attitude vis-à-vis the divine—which would offend the divine—and should "acknowledge the role of the gods in all human prosperity and manifest a proper perspective with regard to his wealth," see Cairns, 1996.21.

105. On the relationship of "lofty thoughts," *phthonos*, and *hybris* here, see Cairns, 1996.13–14, 18. For further discussion of both *phthonos* and especially *hybris* in Herodotus' *Histories*, see Chapter 3.

106. On Herodotus' use of θεήλατος here, see Chiasson, 1982.159.

107. On these dreams, see Harrison, 2000.132–137, 231; Evans, 1991.15, 28, and 37; Gould, 1989.70–72; Lloyd-Jones, 1983.61–62; Pritchett, 1979.96–98; Ste. Croix, 1977.143–145; and Immerwahr, 1954.33–36. Unlike Linforth (1928.226–227), I do not think that Herodotus imagined any specific Persian god to be sending the dreams. For the claim that these dreams are solely the invention of Herodotus, see Bichler, 1985.140–144.

108. On dreams in Herodotus, see Harrison, 2000.122–157, esp. 132–137; Fornara, 1990.34–39, 43–45; Bichler, 1985; and Frisch, 1968.

109. Frisch, 1968.

110. For the claim that all dreams in the *Histories* would have been thought to have a divine origin, see Fornara, 1990, and Frisch, 1968.47–52.

111. The apparent exceptions are dreams ordering an action of religious expiation (of Datis, 6.118, and of Xerxes, 8.51–55); the dream vision of the Egyptian Hephaestus that

came to his priest Sethos in his sanctuary (2.141.2–6, on which see A. B. Lloyd, 1988.101); the dream of Otanes that apparently bid him to repopulate Samos as a cure for his disease (3.149); and the dream of Agariste, Pericles' mother (6.131.2). The very helpful dream that Plutarch has appear to Arimnestus before the battle of Plataea (*Arist.* 11.5–8) is unparalleled in Herodotus' *Histories*.

112. This is explicitly stated in the case of Cambyses' dream about Smerdis (3.65.3–4). Cf. 1.34.1.

113. On dreams in Greek tragedy, see Mikalson, 1991.101–104, 107–110, 129, and 208.

114. It is true, as J. A. S. Evans has stressed (1991.15, 28, and 37), that the dream apparition did *not* promise Xerxes success of the expedition, only the loss of his throne if he did not pursue it. Or, as Immerwahr (1954.34–35) summarizes it, "The false interpretation of the dream (that it presages the defeat of the Greeks) is given by Artabanus; the dream says only: you *must* go *now*." And, "as a prophecy, the warning is also true: Xerxes went on his campaign and did not become small quickly, but continued to rule after Salamis." All this is true in hindsight, but Xerxes and Artabanus—and no ancients could have thought otherwise—concluded that the expedition was divinely ordered. The comparison is often made to the false dream sent to Agamemnon by Zeus in *Il.* 2.1–71. See also Harrison, 2000.132–137; Evans, 1961; and Pritchett, 1979.96–98.

115. For various aspects of these questions, see Harrison, 2000.132–137 and 231; Evans, 1961 and 1991.15, 28, and 37; Pelling, 1991.139–140; Fornara, 1990.36–37, 43–45; Lloyd-Jones, 1983.61–63; Pritchett, 1979.96–98; Pohlenz, 1973.117–118; and Immerwahr, 1954.33–36.

116. Pelling, 1991.139, and Dodds, 1951.30–31.

117. On the *magoi* and the later associations of them with "magical" practices, see Dickie, 2001.14–16, 28–29, 33–34, 41–43, and 135–136; Graf, 1997.20–35; and G. E. R. Lloyd, 1979.13.

118. On this and on how this dream completes the previous dreams of Xerxes and Artabanus, see Köhnken, 1988.

119. For Herodotus' belief in and use of omens, especially in conjunction with oracles or other forms of divination, see Harrison, 2000.132–157, esp. 137–138.

120. A prime example is the solar eclipse predicted by Thales in 585 that ended the Lydian-Mede war (1.74.2–3). Further examples include 1.59.1–3, 78, and 175; 3.124.1–2; 4.79; 6.27.1–3; 8.104 and 137.2–3; and 9.10.3 and 116–121.

121. The hero Protesilaus, himself now a fish, sent the omen of the revivified fish to Artaüctes (9.116–121).

122. Cf. Linforth (1928.227): "Herodotus is in the habit of referring to signs and omens without any hint of divine agency, and a belief in signs has no necessary theistic implication."

123. For the possible significance of Xerxes' offerings at Troy, in relation both to the Trojan War and to contemporary Greeks of Asia Minor and Athenians, see Georges, 1994.60–65.

124. Harrison (2000.81, 98, and 217) sees in the offerings an attempt by Xerxes "to legitimize his possession of Troy," and the panic attack a sign that Athena and the heroes were displeased both by his entry into Troy and his attempt to claim it.

125. For an attempt to explain Xerxes' actions here on the basis of Persian customs, see Balcer, 1995.235.

Darius' expedition of 492 had suffered serious losses on the cape of Mount Athos (Hdt. 6.44.2–3), and Xerxes avoided the risk by having a channel dug behind Athos (7.22–24). According to Plutarch, Xerxes sent letters to the mountain, saying, "Sir Athos, in my excavations do not make your rocks large and hard to work. Otherwise I will cut you into pieces and throw you into the sea" (*Mor.* 455D–E).

126. E.g., Lateiner, 1989.129, and HW, 2.169. One should note, however, that Cyrus went to elaborate lengths to punish the Gyndes River for carrying off one of his sacred horses (1.189–190.1). On that event, see Fisher, 1992.353–354.

127. Cf. Cleomenes' attempt to get good omens in a sacrifice before crossing the Erasinus River (6.76.1).

128. For a transposition of lines that make 757–759 directly precede 737–741 in Hesiod's poem, see M. L. West, 1978.338.

129. See Burkert, *GR*, 174–175, and Nilsson, *GGR* I³, 236–240.

130. For the contrast between Aeschylus' and Herodotus' treatments of Xerxes' crossing the Hellespont, see Immerwahr, 1954.27–30.

131. Fisher (1992.155) offers this on ἀτάσθαλον: "frequently found in authors writing in the Ionic dialect or with Ionic tendencies . . . , and often indicating rash, outrageous acts leading to disaster; the link with *ate*, if etymologically doubtful, seems to be felt by Greek authors."

132. Herodotus also describes the Corcyraeans' killing of Periander's son as a πρῆγμα ἀτάσθαλον (3.49.2).

133. Prime Herodotean examples of the relationship of "madness" and "impiety" are the Persian king Cambyses (3.27–31 and 37–38.1) and the Spartan king Cleomenes (5.74–75; 6.75, 79–82, and 84).

For a general account of Cambyses, see Balcer, 1995.101–124; Georges, 1994.186–195; Brown, 1982; and Burn, 1962.81–95. On the historicity and possible origins of the stories of Cambyses' various impieties, see Hofmann and Vorbichler, 1980. Cambyses' rule was characterized by madness in secular affairs too (e.g., 3.25.2, 33–37, 61–66). Herodotus speculates that his madness was caused by "the holy disease" (i.e., epilepsy) (3.33). Cambyses was also known to be too devoted to drink (3.34.2–3).

On Cleomenes' madness and impiety, see Immerwahr, 1966.192–193. On Cleomenes' madness and how Herodotus treats it differently from Cambyses', see Friedrich, 1973.119–120. For a treatment of Cleomenes' "mad" acts as "miscellaneous, all purpose anti-tyrant folklore" and for a sometimes quirky comparison of Cleomenes to Cambyses ("Two almost contemporary, deranged, dipsomaniac, priest-flogging, skin-stripping, sacrilegious, sadistic warrior-kings who are misled by place-name oracles and expire in circumstances symbolically retributive of their capricious cruelties"), see Griffiths, 1989. esp. 56 and 70–72.

134. For more discussion of *hybris* in Herodotus' *Histories*, see Chapter 3.

135. On this passage, see Evans, 1991.63.

136. Cf. 1.91.3.

137. Herodotus gives relatively few prayers to his Greeks, and even then seldom designates the recipient: the mother of Cleobis and Biton to Hera at her festival in her sanctuary (1.31); Ladice's prayer to Aphrodite to consummate her marriage (2.181.4); the nurse of Ariston's future wife to Helen that the ugly child she tended become beautiful (6.61.3-5); the deceived Athenians to Pisistratus' bogus Athena (1.60-61); the Greeks to Poseidon Soter at Artemisium (7.191-192); the Delphians to the winds at Thyia (7.178) and the Athenians to Boreas (7.189); and Pausanias to Hera at her Plataean sanctuary (9.61-62). Only Polycrates' daughter's prayer (3.124.1-125.4) was not answered, and that was an unusual prayer in unusual circumstances. On such prayers in Herodotus, see also Harrison, 2000.76-82.

138. Mikalson, 1989.

139. On this passage, see Evans, 1991.63, and Immerwahr, 1954.20-21.

140. For the likely exaggeration of the expense, see Introduction.

141. For the site of Abdera, see Müller, 1987.37-41.

142. For the Strymon River, see Müller, 1987.104-107; for Ennea Hodoi, 57-58.

143. Jameson, 1991.203.

144. Cf. Thuc. 2.67. On the historical circumstances and on possible reasons why Athenians and Spartans may have maltreated the Persian heralds, see Sealey, 1976. For the dispute about the date of the trip of Sperthias and Bulis, see Miller, 1997.110.

145. On this episode, on the inviolability of heralds, and for the claim, based on Plut. *Them.* 6, that the Athenians killed the interpreter of the heralds, not the heralds themselves, see Wéry, 1966.

146. On the improbability of Pausanias' account, see Wéry, 1966.474-475.

147. Cf. D.S. 11.3.3. On the circumstances of the oath and on the nature of the tithe to be paid, see HW, 2.177-178. See also Lonis, 1979.151-153; Pritchett, 1979.232-233; and Siewert, 1972.66-69.

148. On the question of when during the invasion Herodotus has these oracles delivered to the Athenians, that is, how many months before the battle of Thermopylae, see Evans, 1982.

149. Fontenrose Q146.

150. Fontenrose Q147.

151. Cf. Plut. *Them.* 10.2. On Herodotus' account here, see Harrison, 2000.150-152; Fontenrose, 1978.124-128; and Kirchberg, 1965.90-96. Parker (1985.318) notes how the two oracles here "mention the three policies that were discussed in Athens at the time (flight abroad . . . ; standing a siege; evacuation) but not the possibility of Medism, which was not."

For an example of a highly rationalizing account of the origin of these oracles, see Georges, 1986.14-42. Georges (15-16, 25-26, 31, and 38 n. 53) is incorrect in claiming that Plutarch in *Them.* 10.1-3 supports his view that these oracles were inventions of the Athenians themselves, not "genuine pronouncements of Delphi."

152. I treat here only those oracles directly relevant to the Persian Wars and leave aside the many Herodotean oracles that concern disease, colonization, the establishment of cults, and other such matters. On Herodotus' treatment of oracles in general and for all

individual oracles, see Fontenrose, 1978. esp. 111–117; Lachenaud, 1978.244–305; Kirchberg, 1965; Crahay, 1956; and Parke and Wormell, 1956. See also Harrison, 2000.122–157; Parker, 1985; Price, 1985; and Lonis, 1979.69–80, 83–87.

153. In 7.141.2 the *adyton* is apparently the same as the *megaron*. See Lachenaud, 1978.251.

154. 6.132–136; 7.148–152 and 169–171. Cf. 1.19.2; 1.67–68 and 174; 5.79.2. The Spartans had four appointed *theopropoi* who attended the kings (6.57.2).

155. 1.46–49 and 65–66.

156. 6.66 and 125.2.

157. The Pythia: e.g., 7.148–151. Cf. 1.167.4 and 174, 3.57.3, and 4.150–151. The oracle: 1.13 and 46–47, 5.80.1, 6.19.1–2. The god: 1.69.2, 4.155.3–4 and 157.2, and 5.80.1.

158. On ἀναιρεῖν, see Fontenrose, 1978.219–220, and Crahay, 1956.69.

159. E.g., 1.65–68, 85.2, and 91.1; 4.151.1; and 5.79.1.

160. κελεύειν: e.g., 5.82–88 and 3.58.3, 4.15.3, 155–157, and 161.2; 6.36.1, 52, and 139.2. ἀπαγορεύειν: 7.148–152. οὐκ ἐᾶν: 5.82–88; 6.132–136; 8.35–39; and 4.164.3.

161. 6.19; 1.65–66 and 91.4–5; 4.155–157 and 163.2; and 5.92.ε.2.

162. E.g., 4.150–151 and 155–157; 6.80–82 and 86.

163. χρᾶσθαι: e.g., 1.46–49; 3.57.3; 4.163.1; 5.42–45; 6.86. χρηστηρίζεσθαι: 7.178.

164. The point is nicely confirmed by the masculine participles defining the speaker in the Pythia's oracular responses at 4.157.2 and 7.141.3. The Pythia was, of course, the *promantis*, not the *mantis* (6.75). Cf. A. *Eum.* 33.

165. E.g., 7.219–220; 1.46–49, 56.1 and 174; 5.92.β.2; and 6.86.

166. See Fontenrose, 1978.196–228, and Compton, 1994.

167. For the direct (vs. indirect) quotation of this oracle, see Aristotle, *Rh.* 1407a.

168. For this line of interpretation and what follows, see Kirchberg, 1965. esp. 90–96.

169. Fontenrose Q109.

170. Of the oracles we include from the accounts of Plutarch and Pausanias, Fontenrose designates Q125 on the selection of the Athenian eponymous heroes (Paus. 10.10.1), 142 on the identification of the hero Echetlaeus at Marathon (Paus. 1.32.5), and 156 on the establishment of the altar of Zeus Eleutherios at Plataea (Plut. *Arist.* 20.4) as "authentic." Q154, on sacrifices to be made before Plataea (Plut. *Arist.* 11.3), is "partly genuine," and 158 on Themistocles' offering of spoils at Delphi (Paus. 10.14.5) and 164 on the recovery of Theseus' bones (Plut. *Thes.* 36.1 and *Cim.* 8.6) are "not genuine."

171. Evans (1991.133–134) thinks that the oracles had a basis in fact but "had already received a conventional reworking into metric form by *logioi* and *aoidoi* before Herodotus incorporated them into his *Histories.*"

172. On Herodotean oracles in general, Plato has Socrates casually refer to and quote part of Q101 (Hdt. 1.55) without reservation (*Rep.* 8.566c), and Aristotle (*Rhet.* 1407a) similarly refers to Q100 of Hdt. 1.53.3, 69.2, and 91.4. Plutarch, who was intimately familiar with Delphic traditions, raises no questions about the authenticity of Q7 of Hdt. 1.65.3 (*Mor.* 1098A, 1103A, 1116F); 47 and 49 of Hdt. 4.155.3 and 157.2 (*Mor.* 405B–C, 408A); and 152 of Hdt. 7.220.4 (*Pelop.* 21.3). He does, however, consider Q157 of Hdt. 8.121–122 a Herodotean invention (*Mor.* 871C–D). Pindar also knew a version of Q47 of Hdt. 4.155.3

(*Pyth.* 4). Pausanias, no doubt in some cases using local traditions as well as Herodotus, gives versions of or refers to Q63 of Hdt. 2.30.4; 88 of Hdt. 1.66 (3.7.3. and 8.1.6); 89 of Hdt. 1.67.2 (3.11.10); 90 of Hdt. 1.67.4 (3.3.6); 92 of Hdt. 6.86.c.2 (2.18.2 and 8.7.8); 112 of Hdt. 1.174.5 (2.1.5); and 134 of Hdt. 6.77.2 (2.20.10). All of these are labeled "not genuine" by Fontenrose. Finally, Plutarch (*Them.* 10), Aristotle (frag. 399 Rose), Pausanias (1.18.2), and the reliable Philochorus (*FGrHist* 328 F 116) do not question Fontenrose's "doubtful" Q147 on the "wooden wall."

173. Regarding oracles, Crahay (1956.107) puts it well: "[T]out ce que nous pouvons attendre d'Heródote, c'est une idée de ce que l'on croyait de son temps." Cf. Gould, 1985.221 n. 17: "It is the perceived image of the oracle that is crucial (all the more so if it is historically inaccurate), and for that the evidence of Herodotus, for example, is decisive for the fifth century." See also the discussion of Flower, 1991.65–66.

174. For some of the problems, see Habicht, 1961; Podlecki, 1975.147–167; and Georges, 1986. For additional bibliography, see Balcer, 1995.246 n. 79.

175. For ancient quotations of this text, see Plut. *Them.* 10.4; Aristides, 1.225–226 and 2.256 Dindorf. For the numerous other ancient sources that refer to it, see Jameson, 1960, esp. 201–202.

176. Quintilian's comment, as one interpretation among many possible, is noteworthy: "nam Themistocles suasisse existimatur Atheniensibus, ut urbem apud deos deponerent, quia durum erat dicere, ut relinquerent" (9.2.92).

177. On the literary, epic form of this description of Athena, see Jameson, 1960.210: "It is the most emphatically national of her epithets—others may have an Athena Polias but only Athenians have an Ἀθηνᾶ Ἀθηνῶν μεδέουσα." It is unparalleled on inscriptions, and for the implications of that regarding the text, see Habicht, 1961.3–4.

178. Cf. Hdt. 8.51–55. Jameson, 1960.214: "In the event, it seems that the treasurers stayed with the less movable and less holy offerings, while the priestesses fled with the sacred objects."

179. Pancrates seems too to be a literary epithet, as may be Asphaleios of Poseidon here (Jameson, 1960.220). All the recipients of the sacrifice seem to lack specific Athenian cultic associations, and that and Nike as an independent deity here may indicate a later fourth-century rewriting or composition of the decree. See Habicht, 1961.6–7. On the deities in general, see Podlecki, 1975.153–155.

180. See Jameson, 1960.218–219.

181. Fontenrose Q144.

182. On the unusual instance of the Argives apparently being ready to disregard an oracle in these circumstances, see Harrison, 2000.154 n. 114.

183. On Argive-Persian relations in the period, see Georges, 1994.66–71.

184. Fontenrose Q145: "The meaning is, 'Have you not had enough punishment from Minos' anger? Do you want more?'" For the story, see D.S. 4.79 and Strabo 6.2.6 and 3.2.

185. Fontenrose Q148.

186. Thyia was also, by Apollo, the mother of Delphus, the eponym of the Delphians (Paus. 10.6.4 and HW, 2.209). The site of Thyia is unknown, but for two possibilities, see Müller, 1987.590.

187. On Cape Sepias, see Müller, 1987.360–364; on the Euripus, 408–412.

188. On the earlier Persian losses at Athos, see Hdt. 6.44.2–3.

189. Cf. Paus. 8.27.14. On an altar of Boreas in this area, see Plato, *Phdr.* 229C. Boreas' role in these events may have been described in Simonides' elegiac poem on the battle of Artemisium (frag. 3 W²). See M. L. West, 1993.3–4, and Rutherford, 1996.171–172.

On this whole selection, see Pritchett, 1979.24–25; Kirchberg, 1965.98–99; and Linforth, 1928.214.

190. If Herodotus has in mind a specific god here, that "god" is probably Poseidon, and Herodotus is probably aligning himself with the view of the Greeks in general as against that of the Delphians and the Athenians. But see Harrison, 2000.173 n. 63, and Linforth, 1928.225–226.

191. On Herodotus' account of this, see also Linforth, 1928.213–214.

192. On this method for us identifying a deity and for further examples, see Linforth 1928.213–215. For possible other reasons for seeing divine intervention in these events, see Harrison, 2000.93–94.

193. On Artemisium and the sanctuary of Artemis, see Müller, 1987.310–314.

194. Cf. *Mor.* 867F. This epigram has been attributed to Simonides (frag. 109 Diehl). It is probably a simple dedicatory inscription (Jacoby, 1945.157 n. 3). Gauer (1968.117–120) claims that the monument, like the plaques that stood on the graves near Thermopylae (Hdt. 7.228), marked the battlefield and honored those who fought there. The usual battlefield trophy would not have been appropriate because neither battle was, in conventional terms, a victory. On these questions, the text, and the punctuation, see Page, *FGE*, 236–238, and Pritchett, 1985.168.

195. Plutarch (*Them.* 15.2) reports that this incident occurred at the battle of Salamis.

196. For photographs and maps of Thermopylae, see Müller, 1987.369–384.

197. The Spartan Carneia was a nine-day festival celebrating Apollo Karneios. See Burkert, *GR*, 234–236.

198. Some Peloponnesian Greeks did not come even after the Carneia and Olympic Games were over (8.72).

199. Fontenrose Q152 and pp. 77–78. Cf. 7.239.1. See also Kirchberg, 1965.99–100.

200. Clairmont (1983.115–116) thinks that the tombs of Leonidas and Pausanias may have been part of a sacred precinct devoted to the heroes of the Spartan resistance at Thermopylae. On the tombs of Leonidas and Pausanias in Sparta and on cultic activities and celebrations there of the victory over the Persians, see Asheri, 1998.81–85. On all dead Spartan kings, including Leonidas, as heroes or hero-like, see Boedeker, 1993.168.

201. Simonides, frag. 91 Diehl. For difficulties with this epigram, see Pritchett, 1985.169–171. On the likely exaggeration of the number of the enemy, see Introduction.

202. Simonides, frag. 92 Diehl. Cf. Lycurgus, *Leoc.* 109 and Strabo 9.4.16. For the texts of these epigrams, see Page, *FGE*, 231–234.

203. For the text and the role of the Locrians at Thermopylae, see Page, *FGE*, 235–236, and Pritchett, 1985.172.

204. Pritchett, 1985.171–172. For doubts that it was ever inscribed, see Page, *FGE*, 78–79.

205. Frag. 83 Diehl. According to Page (*FGE*, 196), this epitaph "has the peculiar dis-

tinction of being the only extant epigram whose ascription to Simonides may be accepted with fair confidence."

206. Public: Simonides, frags. 87 and 122 Diehl, *Anth. Pal.* 7.258. Private: *IG* I³ 1218, 1231, 1234, 1277–1279, 1357.

207. The only exception is a fragment of the epigram (νέμωσι θεοί) thought to stand on the tomb of the Athenians who died at Salamis, ML 26. For the possible meaning there, see Page, *FGE*, 224. See also Hansen, 1983, no. 2.

208. Some have associated this song with annual rites at Leonidas' tomb in Sparta (e.g., Campbell, 1967.383), but Leonidas' tomb there was established well after Simonides' death (Paus. 3.14.1).

209. On the war dead as heroes, see my earlier comments on Paus. 1.32.3–5.

210. On this account, see Kirchberg, 1965.101–102.

211. Ancient sources knew three figures of the name Bacis—one of Boeotia, one of Attica, and the third an Arcadian. He may in fact have been just the personification of the term βάξις, "prophecy," to whom various oracles without pedigree were attached. He was strongly satirized by Aristophanes (e.g., *Eq.* 123–143, 997–1068; *Pax* 1046–1126; and *Av.* 959–991). On Bacis, see Prandi, 1993, and Asheri, 1993.

212. E.g., 4.150.2–151.2.

213. Abae was the site of one of the oracles tested by Croesus (Hdt. 1.46–49). For Abae and an account of the sanctuary and its ruins after the Persian attack, see Paus. 10.35.1–4. For the site of Abae and its oracle, see Müller, 1987.446–449. For the other destroyed Phocian cities, Drymus, 485; Charadra, 460; Erochus, 489–490; Tethronium, 582; Amphicaea, 452–453; Neon, 527–528; Pedies, 541; Trites, 591; Elateia, 486–487; Hyampolis, 495–498; and Parapotamii, 534–536.

214. For the site of Delphi, see Müller, 1987.467–483.

215. Herodotus offers a full description of Croesus' dedications at Delphi at 1.50–51.

216. Fontenrose Q149.

217. On the Corycian cave above Delphi, see Paus. 10.32.7.

218. The Delphic *prophetes* was, according to Fontenrose (1978.218–219), the priest-prophet who attended the Pythia and presided over the mantic session, "answering all questions except the question put to the Pythia."

219. On this account, see Pritchett, 1993.10–11; Marincola in Dewald and Marincola, 1987.28; Parke and Wormell, 1956.1.171–174. For some historians' claims that this whole episode is a fiction, see Hignett, 1963.445–447.

Plutarch (*Numa* 9.6), apparently mistakenly, claims that the temple at Delphi was burned by the Persians and that the sacred fire was extinguished. A new, pure fire had to be generated by collecting the sun's rays with mirrors.

220. This epigram was also recorded in A.D. 1675–1676 from an inscription found near the spring of Castalia in Delphi but now lost. The date of the inscription is uncertain but may be circa 400. See Meritt, 1947.58–61. On the text, see also Page, *FGE*, 410–412.

221. Public: after Marathon, for treasury of Athenians at Delphi (ML 19) and bronze helmet at Olympia; and, perhaps, in Athens for the Athenian polemarch Callimachus who died in the battle (ML 18 = *IG* I³ 784); after Salamis, Corinthian dedication to Leto

(Plut. *Mor.* 870F); after Plataea, for altar of Zeus Eleutherios at Plataea (Plut. *Arist.* 19.6–7), for gold shields and the Peparethian dedication at Delphi (Aeschines 3.116 and Gauer, 1968.74). Cf. Athenian dedication at Delphi after victory in Cyprus in 449 (D.S. 11.62.3).

Private: Mandrocles' dedication in the Heraion (4.88); three tripod dedications in the Theban sanctuary of Apollo Ismenios (5.59–61, on which see Pritchett, 1993.116–121); Pausanias' inscription on gold tripod monument at Delphi (Thuc. 1.132), and the choregic monument of Themistocles in 476 (Plut. *Them.* 5.4).

Compare the dedications in *IG* I³, esp. 502, 503/4, 507, 508, 511, 517, 518, 521 bis, 522–525, 533, and 597.

222. The clearest exception is the dedication of the Corinthian courtesans after Salamis, as reported by Plutarch and Athenaeus (Plut. *Mor.* 871A–B).

223. On the function of public and private dedications to memorialize human accomplishment, see Lonis, 1979.271–277, and Van Straten, 1981.76. On this in Herodotus in particular, see Gould, 1991.13–14.

224. On this snake and its relationship to Athena, see HW, 2.247–248.

225. In Plut. *Them.* 10.1 these are *daily* offerings.

226. For the modern claim that Themistocles not only assisted the priests here but "manufactured" the whole ominous event, see Podlecki, 1975.19 and 106–107.

227. On this statue of Athena Polias, see Hurwit, 1999.20–21.

228. On these treasurers (*tamiai*) and why they might have stayed on the Acropolis, see Hurwit, 1999.48–50, and Harris, 1995.9–22.

229. The sanctuary of Aglaurus, unexpectedly at the base of the cliff on the northeast end of the Acropolis, has been recently found (Dontas, 1983).

230. Ctesias (*FGrHist* 688 F 13 no. 30), generally an unreliable source, claims that the defenders of the Acropolis escaped in the night.

231. For the extent of the destruction, see Hurwit, 1999.136, 138, 141–142.

232. For the location of these, see Paus. 1.26.5 and 27.2; Philochorus, *FGrHist* 328 F 67; and Hurwit, 1999.144–145, 202–204.

233. Cf. Paus. 1.18.2. Pausanias (1.27.2) claims the olive tree sprouted three feet.

234. For the one exception, the murder of the suppliant Euryleon by his subjects, the Selinusians (5.46.2), another example in which Herodotus describes no punishments and raises no objection to impieties committed against a tyrant, see my previous comments on 5.62–64.

235. Mikalson, 1991.69–77, 166–167, 176, 192–193, 195, and Gould, 1973.

236. For the complicated and ultimately unsuccessful maneuvers by the Spartans to avoid violating the asylum of Pausanias after the war, see Thuc. 1.134 and D.S. 11.45.5–9.

237. On these events on Aegina, see Figueira, 1991.104–106.

238. On the nature of the pollution (ἄγος), see Parker, 1983.8–12. The Alcmaeonidae murdered Cylon and his supporters after they had enticed them from sanctuary in the temple of Athena with the promise that they would not face the death penalty. For this the Alcmaeonidae and their descendants, including Cleisthenes and Pericles, were labeled "polluted" by some (5.70–71). From Herodotus' brief account, however, it is unclear whether the pollution was for murder, violation of asylum, or both. Thucydides (1.126) and Plutarch (*Solon* 12) link the pollution directly to the violation of asylum.

239. Arrian (7.19.2) and Pliny (*NH* 34.69–70) claim Alexander the Great, not Antiochus I, returned these venerable statues to the Athenians. For an attempt to sort out this and on the replacement statues of Harmodius and Aristogiton sculpted by Critias and Nesiotes, see Rackham, 1952.256.

On this whole account, see Balcer, 1995.35–36. On the cult of Harmodius and Aristogiton, see Kearns, 1989.55 and 150; Day, 1985; and Fornara, 1970.

240. The priests at Branchidae surrendered the sanctuary, its property, and themselves to Xerxes. After Xerxes took what he wanted, he burned the temple and sanctuary and resettled the priests in a new location. The oracle fell silent and revived only in the time of Alexander the Great. Alexander killed the descendants of the priests for the impiety of their ancestors, and construction was begun on a magnificent new temple (Strabo, 11.11.4, 14.1.5, and 17.1.43; Plut. *Mor.* 557B; Quintus Curtius, 7.5.28–35; and Suda s.v. Βραγχίδαι). See also Bigwood, 1978.36–39.

241. On this *telesterion* and on Themistocles' connection with the deme and the Lycomidae, see Shapiro, 1989.73; Burkert, *GR*, 278–279; and Podlecki, 1975.173.

242. For a photograph, see Müller, 1987.722–723.

243. This was the cry of the initiants on their procession from Athens to Eleusis for the Mysteries. See Clinton, 1992.64–71.

244. For a detailed but at times quite fanciful discussion of the episode, see Carrière, 1988.220–230.

245. In Xen. *Symp.* 4.80 reference is made to the Eleusinian gods "who campaigned with Iacchos against the barbarian." Plutarch (*Them.* 15.1) has the miraculous events on the Thriasian Plain near Eleusis occur during, not days before, the battle at Salamis. On this and on Plutarch's dating of the battle of Salamis elsewhere to Boedromion 20 and Mounichion 16, see Hignett, 1963.212.

246. Mikalson, 1998.245–247.

247. On Mounichion 16 as an unlikely date for the battle but suitable for later commemorations of it, see Pritchett, 1979.176–178.

248. See also on Xen. *Ana.* 3.2.11–12.

249. For maps and views of Salamis and the immediate area, see Müller, 1987.692–713.

250. On this episode and on whether the Aeacidae arrived as statues, see Pritchett, 1979.15.

251. Koros is here the "insolence" that may attend "satiety" in morally corrupt individuals. Cf. Theognis, 153–154 = Solon no. 6 West with minor variations: "Koros begets Hybris when prosperity attends a man who is evil and whose mind is not right." Pindar (*Ol.* 13.10) like Bacis makes Koros the son of Hybris. On the relationship and significance of Koros and Hybris in this oracle, see Fisher, 1992.375–376.

252. On this oracle and on its relationship to events, see Harrison, 2000.130–131; Immerwahr, 1966.278–279; and Kirchberg, 1965.103–105. On the difficulties of the (metaphorical) "bridge" and of the topography, and that the oracle may be a revised version of an oracle applied to other battles, see Asheri, 1993, and Carrière, 1988.230–236.

253. On usual prebattle sacrifices for omens and the role of the *mantis*, see Lonis, 1979.105–107; Pritchett, 1979.49–90 and 1971.109–115.

254. On a sneeze from the right as a favorable omen, see Pritchett, 1979.126–127.

255. On this ritual of the Athamantidae at Alos of Thessaly, see Hughes, 1991.92–96.

256. On this account, see A. B. Lloyd, 1988.51.

257. For a dramatization of this, see Euripides' *Iphigenia among the Taurians* of 413.

258. On this event, see Jameson, 1991.216–217.

259. For a review of the scholarly discussion of this sacrifice, see Bonnechere, 1994.288–291; Hughes, 1991.111–115; and Henrichs, 1981.208–224. Henrichs raises important objections against Dionysus Omestes as the recipient of the sacrifice. This Dionysus is not otherwise attested for Athens or Attica. He is known for Lesbos, the home of Phanias, Plutarch's source for the event. Despite finding the ritual of the sacrifice appropriate, Henrichs thinks the episode historically improbable. Note, however, Turcan's comment on Henrichs' argument (242). Bonnechere admits the possibility that the sacrifice occurred as does Burkert (1966.113), but Jameson (1991.213 and 216) and Hughes (1991.111–115) reject it.

260. But on the modern low estimation of Phanias as a credible source, see Hignett, 1963.19–20.

261. On the hero Cychreus and his long association with Salamis and snakes, see Kearns, 1989.180.

262. For Adeimantus' epitaph that indicated valor in the Persian Wars, see Plut. *Mor.* 870E.

263. For the argument that this Athenian version is a complete fabrication, see Hignett, 1963.411–414.

264. Later (1.207.1) Croesus holds Zeus responsible for this. Cf. 1.34 and 45.

265. Cairns (1996.20–22) bridges the gap between divine *phthonos* for immoderate human success and, separately, for impieties by arguing that, for Polycrates (3.40–43) and the Solon-Croesus case (1.32.1), "the emphasis is more on the need to manifest the proper attitude in success than on the notion that success in itself provokes the gods to envy." By not exhibiting the proper attitude the individual breaches "the boundary which separates his *time* from that of the gods," and thereby also commits impiety. See also Pohlenz, 1973.110–119.

266. As noted parenthetically by Harrison, 2000.177.

267. Lloyd-Jones, 1983.55–58 and 68–70.

268. On Herodotus' anti-Corinthian bias, see Salmon, 1984.253–256, and Immerwahr, 1966.229 n. 113.

269. The sanctuary of Leto, presumably in Corinth, has not been identified.

270. On whether the dedication was a painting or statues, on the ascription to Simonides, and on the identity ("temple slaves") of the women, see Page, *FGE*, 207–211. On the correct version of the epigram, see Kurke, 1996.73–75. On the temple "courtesans" and the Aphrodite cult at Corinth, see Strabo, 8.6.20; Kurke, 1996; Williams, 1986; and Salmon, 1984.398–400.

271. The ship dedicated at the Isthmus was certainly for Poseidon, as, I think, was the one at Sunium. Gauer (1968.33) and some others would have the Sunium dedication to Athena, who also had a sanctuary there.

272. Ajax was, of course, an Aeacid, one of that "heroic" family that assisted in the battle.

273. On the nature of these stern ornaments, see Miller, 1997.33.

274. Cf. Paus. 10.14.5. On the sculptural motif of the Apollo statue, see Gauer, 1968.71–72. Alexander may have erected the statue of himself from booty he took from the retreating Persians at Amphipolis (Dem. 12.21). See Gauer, 1968.40 and 101.

275. Fontenrose Q157. Plutarch (*Mor.* 871C–D) claims that Herodotus invented this oracle.

276. On such prizes for excellence in battle (*aristeia*), awarded to states here and in Plut. *Arist.* 20.2–3, but also commonly to individuals (7.227; 8.11.2, 17, and 124; 9.71, 74, and 105), and on Herodotus' particular interest in them, see Pritchett, 1974.276–290.

277. On this dedication of the Aeginetans and on the proposed identification of the three stars as the two Dioscuri and Apollo, see Gauer, 1968.73–74.

278. On this epitaph and for arguments for the genuineness of both couplets, see Hansen, 1983, no. 131; Page, *FGE*, 202–204; and Boegehold, 1965.

279. On this epigram, see Page, *FGE*, 204–206, and Pritchett, 1985.174.

280. On this epitaph, see Page, *FGE*, 200–202.

281. Fontenrose Q153. On Xerxes' beheading and impaling of Leonidas after the battle at Thermopylae, see Hdt. 7.238; on the later honors paid to Leonidas in Sparta, see Paus. 3.14.1.

282. King Leonidas had been of the royal family, the twenty-first descendant in the male line from Heracles (7.204).

283. On this account, see Kirchberg, 1965.107–108. Asheri (1998.66–72) treats this episode, based on Spartan sources, extensively in the context of viewing the battle of Plataea as retribution for the loss in the battle of Thermopylae.

284. On the difference in authority between an oracle of Apollo solicited for an event and an existing oracle of Bacis applied to an event, see Parker, 1985.298.

285. On the site of Potidaea, see Müller, 1987.197–200.

286. Trophonius lived underground as an oracular deity in Lebadea of Thessaly, with peculiar rituals of consultation. He had been consulted also by Croesus (Hdt. 1.46–49). See Bonnechere, 1998, and Schachter, 1994.66–89. For the site, see Müller, 1987.520–524.

287. On the oracle of Zeus at Olympia and divination there through observation of sacrificial omens, see Parke, 1967.164–193. For the remains of Apollo's oracle at Thebes, see Müller, 1987.584–586.

288. Herodotus explains why Mys had to follow this unusual procedure: "No one of the Thebans may seek prophecy there for the following reason: Amphiaraus through oracles bid the Thebans to choose which of two things they wished, to use him either as a *mantis* or as an ally in war, but not both. They chose him as an ally, and for this reason no Theban may sleep in his sanctuary" (8.134.1–2). On the "Theban" career of Amphiaraus, see Parke, 1984.212 n. 7, and Schachter, 1981.19–26. His oracle had been validated by Croesus and received dedications from the king (Hdt. 1.46–49).

In Plutarch's account, Mardonius' Lydian agent "slept in the shrine of Amphiaraus and dreamed that an attendant of the god stood by his side and ordered him to leave. When the Lydian refused, the attendant threw a large rock at his head. The man dreamed that, struck by the rock, he died." This "oracle" of Amphiaraus predicted Mardonius' own death from the blow of a rock (*Arist.* 19.1–2. Cf. Hdt. 9.78–79).

289. On Apollo Ptoös and the Ptoön, see Schachter, 1981.52–73, and on the event described here, 66. For photographs of the site, see Müller, 1987.571–576.

290. On the name Mys, on Europus as Euromus of Caria near Mylasa, and on the "Carian" of the oracle of Apollo Ptoös, see Robert, 1950. For warnings against rationalizing the events recorded here, see Daux, 1957. It is worth noting that in 4.155.2 Herodotus assumes the Pythia knew the language of the Libyans. Plutarch (*Arist.* 19.1–2) has Mardonius send a Lydian to Amphiaraus' oracle and a Carian (presumably Mys) to Trophonius'. In his account the Carian received the oracle in Carian from Trophonius, not from Apollo Ptoös. Cf. Paus. 9.23.6.

291. Cf. D.S. 11.28.1.

292. Fontenrose Q155.

293. Parker (1998a.10–24, 27–33) has properly emphasized that by "shared sanctuaries of the gods and sacrifices," Herodotus refers to cultic religion, and that these shared sanctuaries and sacrifices include, in addition to the Panhellenic cults at Delphi and Olympia and elsewhere, cults that were shared by cities, regions, ethnic groups, and amphictyonies.

294. By Zeus Hellenios is undoubtedly meant "the Greek Zeus" in contrast to "barbarian Zeuses," perhaps in particular to the "Persian Zeus" (cf. Hdt. 1.131–132). On θεοὶ Ἑλλήνιοι or Ἑλληνικοί used to create a similar distinction, see 4.108.2 and 5.49.3 and Harrison, 2000.215, and Raaflaub, 1985.141–143. Cf. 5.92.η.5 and 5.93.1. A reference by Athenians to the cult of Zeus Hellenios on Aegina (for which see Raaflaub, 142) would be inappropriate here.

295. Cf. 9.11.1. The Hyacinthia was held annually at Amyclae near Sparta for Apollo. On the festival and the hero Hyacinthus, see Mikalson, 1976.144–152.

296. Simonides' elegiac "mini-epic" on the battle of Plataea has the heroes Dioscuri and Menelaus accompany the Spartans on this expedition (frag. 11.29–31 W²).

297. This statue stood in Megara, and the Megarians erected an identical bronze statue of Artemis near the site of this incident, at their town Pagae near the border with Boeotia (Paus. 1.44.4).

298. For the extent of the destruction, see Shear, 1993.401–406 and 415–417.

299. For the Cabirion near Thebes, see Paus. 9.25.5–10 and Schachter, 1986.66–110.

300. The *taxiarchos* commanded the forces of one Athenian tribe; the *enomotarchos*, one Spartan platoon. See Siewert, 1972.58–59.

301. As in Hdt. 7.132, by "tithe" here is probably meant the depopulation and destruction of the city. See Siewert, 1972.66–69.

302. Cf. Paus. 1.1.5.

303. For the details of this controversy, see my later discussion of Plut. *Arist.* 21.1.

304. Habicht (1961.11–19), Étienne and Piérart (1975.63–68), and Blamire (1989.151–152) reject the historicity of the oath. Siewert (1972) offers a strong defense of it on historical and philological grounds. The issues are well set forth in Meiggs, 1972.504–507 and 597.

305. Siewert, 1972.102–106.

306. Hurwit, 1999.138, 141–145, 157–158, and 160, and Dinsmoor, 1950.150–151. Note also Stadter, 1989.205, and Meiggs, 1963.36–40.

307. For the site, maps, battle plans, and photographs, see Müller, 1987.546–570.

308. On the mantic Iamid family that practiced at Olympia, see Parke, 1967.174–185.

309. Cf. Paus. 3.11.7. For the possibility that Tisamenus was featured as an epic-style *mantis* in Simonides' elegy on the battle of Plataea (frag. 11.39–42 and frag. 14 W²), see M. L. West, 1993.7–9.

310. On the Telliadae, see Fiehn, *RE*, 2nd ser., vol. 5, cols. 405–406.

311. Cf. 9.45.2 and Plut. *Arist.* 11.2, 15.1 and 3. On the whole episode, see Pritchett, 1979.78–79.

312. Mardonius omits the awkward fact that the Persians had months *previously* tried to sack Delphi but failed (Hdt. 8.35–39).

313. For the events to which Herodotus thinks this oracle applies, see Apollod. 3.5.4 and E. *Ba.* 1330–1339.

314. The Thermodon River flows in Boeotia between Tanagra and Glisas (Hdt. 9.43.2). See HW, 2.307.

315. On this group of Plataean heroes, see Schachter, 1986.55–56.

316. Fontenrose Q154.

317. Cf. Plut. *Arist.* 19.4–5 and Paus. 9.3.9.

318. On the sanctuary and cult of this Demeter, see Schachter, 1981.152–154. On the site of Hysiae, see Müller, 1987.499–501.

319. Cf. Hdt. 9.25.3. On the heroön of Androcrates, see Müller, 1987.558.

320. For an attack on the historicity of this whole account, see Hignett, 1963.419–420.

321. On this Hera of Plataea, see Schachter, 1981.242–250, and Müller, 1987.564.

322. On the differences between Herodotus' and Plutarch's accounts, see Jameson, 1991.207–208.

323. On the fundamentally pious, not skeptical, nature of this comment, see Sourdille, 1925.301–302 n. 1.

324. Cf. Hdt. 9.57.2. The *anaktoron* was the initiation hall of the Mysteries. See Clinton, 1992.126–132. On this whole passage, see Linforth, 1928.235–236. Demeter and her sanctuary at Plataea may also have played a role in Simonides' elegy on the battle of Plataea (frag. 17.1 W²). See Boedeker, 1996.236–237, and Rutherford, 1996.187.

325. On Herodotus' intent not to identify a specific god here, see Linforth, 1928.228–229.

326. Cf. Paus. 3.4.10. On Herodotus' account making the battle of Plataea retribution for the loss at Thermopylae, see Asheri, 1998.72–75.

327. On name, sanctuary, cult, and dedications of Alea Athena at Tegea, see Hdt. 1.66; Strabo 8.8.2; and Jost, 1985.145–146, 151–154, 368–386 and plates 36–37.

328. The "three-headed" snake was in fact three intercoiled snakes. On this monument and its interesting later history, see Pritchett, 1993.147–148; Laroche, 1989; and Gauer, 1968.75–96. For a photograph, see Müller, 1987.483.

329. On the sanctuary and cult of Poseidon at Isthmia, see Paus. 2.1.7 and Gebhard, 1993.

330. For the association of tripod dedications with Apollo and victory in war or games, see Krumeich, 1991.52–53, and Lonis, 1979.169.

331. On this epigram and especially its dialect (Ionic or Attic), see Page, *FGE*, 216–217.

332. Cf. [Dem.] 59.97–98.

333. Cf. 8.82.1. For the complete list, see ML 27. On the historical circumstances of the erasure and reinscription, see Hornblower, 1991.218–219, and Fornara, 1967.291–294.

334. See Lonis, 1979.163, and Gauer, 1968.96–98.

335. Although the founding of the cult of Zeus Eleutherios at Plataea is firmly associated with the victory in 479, many scholars claim the Eleutheria and its games were a later, fourth-century innovation. The major point against it is that the Eleutheria is not elsewhere attested until the late fourth century (Posidippus *PCG* 7 F 31). It remains possible, however, that the Eleutheria was founded just as Diodorus and Plutarch describe it, fell into disuse when Plataea was abandoned, but was refounded in the fourth or third century (Boedeker, 1995.222 n. 18). For full discussion, see Étienne and Piérart, 1975.55 and 63–68; Raaflaub, 1985.126–128; Robertson, 1986.94–95; and esp. Schachter, 1994.125–143. On the cult of Zeus Eleutherios at Plataea, see Strabo, 9.2.31; schol. to Pindar *Ol.* 7.154; and Hesychius s.v. Ἐλευθέριος. On the Eleutheria in general, see Pritchett, 1979.178–182. On the "inviolability" of Plataea, see Rigsby, 1996.49–51.

336. Fontenrose Q156.

337. On this Plataean Artemis Eukleia, see Schachter, 1981.102.

338. On the text, see Page, *FGE*, 211–213, and Schachter, 1994.126 n. 8. Raaflaub (1985.126–127) claims this epigram dates from the second half of the fourth century.

339. Plutarch elsewhere (*Cam.* 19.5 and *Mor.* 349F) dates the battle to Boedromion 3. Plutarch may again have confused the date of a battle and religious events celebrating it. The battle may in fact have been fought on Boedromion 3 and the new cult of Zeus Eleutherios founded the next day, on Boedromion 4. The founding of the altar of Zeus, the first and later celebrations of the Eleutheria, or the first and later honors to the Plataean dead (Plut. *Arist.* 21.2–5) may have been occasions of performance of Simonides' elegiac epic on the battle of Plataea. For a survey of the possibilities, see Boedeker, 1995.220–225.

340. Cf. Thuc. 2.71.2 and Strabo 9.2.31. On archaeological finds associated with this altar, see Clairmont, 1983.121–122.

341. On the nature of such vows in wartime, see Lonis, 1979.148–150.

342. Plutarch has also the *heorte* of Artemis Agrotera as χαριστήρια τῆς νίκης (*Mor.* 862A).

343. Cf. D.L. 1.95 and Nic. Dam. *FGrHist* 90 F 59.2–4.

344. This is unmistakably the case of the μιμήματα of the later festival at Sparta described by Plut., *Arist.* 17.8. On festivals commemorating war victories, see Lonis, 1979.270–271.

345. On this nature of *heortai*, see Mikalson, 1982. Herodotus as always is disinclined to give details of religious activities familiar to his audience, but he offers vivid descriptions of *heortai* as the Egyptians celebrated them. A total of 200,000 Egyptian men and women sailed together in boats for the Artemis festival at Bubastis, with women playing castanets and men flutes on the trip (see A. B. Lloyd, 1976.272–276). The other men and women sang songs and clapped their hands. At the landings along the way the music continued, while some women jeered at those on the dock, some danced, and some even, à la Mardi Gras in New Orleans, exposed themselves. When they arrived at Bubastis, they sacrificed, feasted, and drank—drank, in fact, more at this festival than they drank for the rest of the year (2.60). One may compare the similar features in the *heortai* of the Babylonian Belus

(1.183.2 and 191.6) and of the Egyptian Dionysus, Isis, Athena, and Ares (2.40, 47.2–49.3, 61–63, and 3.27–29). There is much here that is not Greek, but for Herodotus these are all ὁρταί, these foreigners ὁρτάζουσι, and the general atmosphere, if not the details, are no doubt characteristic of many Greek *heortai*.

346. On these prizes, see note 276 in Chapter 1 on Hdt. 8.121–122.

347. Diodorus (11.33.1) claims that on Aristides' proposal Sparta and Pausanias received the *aristeia* for Plataea. On the question, see Pritchett, 1974.283–286.

348. Aeschines 3.116 is often taken to mean that these shields were first dedicated circa 340. That may be the case, but it is possible that the shield dedications were much older and had to be "rededicated" for the new temple. It is also possible that they were the original "Marathonian shields" (Paus. 10.19.4), which, being reinstalled, were given a new dedicatory inscription that suited contemporary times in casting a bad light on the Thebans. See Gauer, 1968.26–27, for questions about the date and purposes of this dedication.

349. Fontenrose, Q158.

350. Miller (1997.44), without explanation, terms this account "doubtlessly fabricated."

351. Themistocles also repaired and adorned the *telesterion* at Phlya that had been burned by the Persians (Plut. *Them.* 1.3).

352. On the cult, see Garland, 1992.73–81. On the sanctuary, see Clairmont, 1983.119; Podlecki, 1975.174–176; Gauer, 1968.122; and Threpsiades and Vanderpool, 1964 (1965).

353. In this regard it is interesting to note that Themistocles' children had a portrait of him dedicated *in* the Parthenon (Paus. 1.1.2).

354. Cf. Hdt. 9.64.

355. On Masistius' breastplate and Mardonius' dagger, see Hurwit, 1999.138 and 250; Harris, 1995.204–206 and 217; and Thompson, 1956.283–285. Harris suspects that these were "spurious relics."

356. Cf. Suda s.v. ἀργυρόπους δίφρος. On this δίφρος as a footstool and its later appearance in the Parthenon inventories, see Miller, 1997.54, and Thompson, 1956.285–290. Harris (1995.205 and 207) thinks this too was probably a "spurious relic," but concludes from Dem. 22.13 and Thuc. 2.13.4 that there were numerous genuine but unspecified dedications from Persian War booty adorning the Acropolis and sanctuaries in Attica.

357. Cf. Plut. *Mor.* 628E–F. On this sacrifice, see Pritchett, 1979.182–183.

358. A *proxenos* represented the interests of a foreign city-state, here Aegina, in his own city-state.

359. On the Greek tombs at Plataea, as of now undiscovered, see Müller, 1987.567–569; Pritchett, 1985.174–175; and Clairmont, 1983.103–105. For questions concerning the three Spartan tombs, see HW, 2.325. On the site of the tombs at Plataea, see Müller, 1987.567–570.

360. Zeus and Hermes Chthonios ("of the earth"), in contrast to their *ouranic* ("of the sky") counterparts, were associated with the underworld and hence are appropriate in this prayer on behalf of the dead.

361. Cf. Thuc. 3.58.4, Isoc. 14.61, Plut. *Mor.* 872E–F, and Paus. 9.2.6. On these offerings, see Schachter, 1994.129, 131, 134, and 137–138.

362. On the Greek war dead, see Garland, 1985.89–93, 113.

363. Paus. 1.32.3–5 and 3.14.1, and D.S. 11.33.3.

364. To those inclined to symbolic readings, the three elements (the washing, the perfuming, and the decking with myrtle garlands) might suggest that the tomb represented quite literally the dead, and that the dead were being bathed, perfumed, and garlanded in preparation for their banquet.

365. These gods are quite probably the θεοὶ Ἑλλήνιοι.

366. Cf. 9.92.2.

367. On the sites mentioned here, see HW, 2.330.

368. Codrus was an early king of Athens, and Philistus was no doubt an Athenian also.

369. Diodorus (11.35.1–3) treats the report of the Greek victory at Plataea as a stratagem by Leotychides to encourage his troops. Cf. Polyaen. 1.33. On this whole account, see Pritchett, 1979.134.

370. On how this whole account ties Xerxes' invasion to the Trojan War and appropriately concludes major themes of Herodotus' *Histories*, see Boedeker, 1988. See also Harrison, 1997.105–106, and 2000.68–69 and 120–121.

371. On the cult and myth of the Trojan hero Protesilaus, and on Protesilaus as a "god" at Elaeus, see Boedeker, 1988.

372. Xanthippus was the father of Pericles.

373. Cf. 7.33 and Paus. 3.4.6. One "bridge boat" may have been dedicated on the Acropolis in Athens where two inscribed blocks of a suitable base have been found. See Gauer, 1968.72. For doubts about this "dedication," see Miller, 1997.38.

374. On the tent of Xerxes, its possible use as the *skene* "building" in the Theater of Dionysus at Athens, and on its relationship to the Odeion of Pericles, see Miller, 1997.218–224 and 235–236; Gauer, 1968.44; and Broneer, 1944. On the Odeion of Pericles, see Hurwit, 1999.216–217 and 317, and on Persian influences behind it, Miller, 1997.218–242.

375. Cf. Vitruvius 1.1.6 and see also Gauer, 1968.102–103.

376. On the Carystian group, see Gauer, 1968.113–115. He thinks these animals represented sacrificial victims (106). The Athenian Stoa at Delphi was long thought to have been built circa 470 to display some of the "bridge equipment" seized at Sestus by the Athenians (Hdt. 9.121), but it now appears that this stoa was built circa 450 and never held Persian spoils (Walsh, 1986). See also ML 25.

377. For the monument and probable circumstances of its dedication, see Gauer, 1968.74 and 134.

378. On the Athenian Epitaphia, see Clairmont, 1983.22–28. He would have the early Epitaphia not annual but held only in years when there were war casualties. In the Hellenistic period they were certainly annual (Mikalson, 1998.182–185, 244, 248, and 253). See also Pritchett, 1985.112–124.

379. Cf. D.H. 5.17.4. Those scholars (e.g., Jacoby, 1944, and Clairmont, 1983.24 and 255 n. 4) who for various other reasons wish to have the Athenians introduce funeral orations later, usually in the 460s, dispute Diodorus' association of funeral games and orations with the burials of the Persian Wars. See Garland, 1985.90; Pritchett, 1985.112–124; and W. West, 1970.274.

380. Loraux, 1981.

381. Cf. Hdt. 9.69.

382. The site of "the navel" in Megara is unknown.

383. Nisaea was the seaport of Megara. On the text and its epigraphical history, see Page, *FGE*, 213–215, and Pritchett, 1985.175–176.

## Chapter 2

1. References in italics (e.g., *9.81.1* vs. 9.81.1) henceforth refer to passages treated more extensively in Chapter 1.

2. This temple was being constructed during Herodotus' lifetime. See A. B. Lloyd, 1976.46–47.

3. On Zeus Eleutherios, Zeus Soter, and the Persian Wars, see Raaflaub, 1985.125–147. On the role of this Zeus in warfare, see Lonis, 1979.181–182.

4. Raaflaub, who sees the Zeus Eleutherios of political freedom as a product of the Persian Wars, argues that this account of the origins of the Samian Zeus is fictitious or, at the least, inaccurate or anachronistic (1985.139–140).

5. Compare the founding of the cult of Zeus Eleutherios in Syracuse circa 463 (D.S. 11.71.2).

6. On the possibility that the festival was a later, fourth-century innovation in the cult, see notes to Plut. *Arist. 21.1*.

7. Linforth (1928) does not include this or other oracles in his demonstration of Herodotus' disinterest in what Linforth terms "divine mythology."

8. For Athens's owing its security to Athena and Athena's special relationship to Zeus, compare Solon, frag. 4.1–4 W and A. *Eum.* 996–1002. Cf. A. *Pers.* 345–347.

9. Didymus in Suda, *Etymologicum Magnum*, and Harpocration s.v. ἐλευθέριος. Cf. Hesychius s.v. ἐλευθέριος Ζεύς. On the Stoa of Zeus, see Camp, 1986.105–107. On the cult of this Zeus in Athens, see Raaflaub, 1985.132–133, 135–137, and 144–147.

10. Wycherley, 1957. nos. 29–32.

11. Mikalson, 1998.110–111.

12. On the Poseidon cult at Sunium and his epithet Soter there, see Farnell, *Cults* 4.81. For this being a dedication to Poseidon, not Athena, see note 271 to Chapter 1. For the apparent beginnings or efflorescence of the Poseidon cult on the Athenian Acropolis after the battle of Salamis, see Hurwit, 1999.32, and Binder, 1984.21–22.

13. Cf. Plut. *Them.* 17 and *Mor.* 871D–E.

14. Burn (1962.499) nicely comments, "The whole phenomenon was no doubt caused by an undersea earth-tremor; after their fashion, the Potidaeans were perfectly right in attributing it to their patron god, Poseidon the Earth-Shaker."

15. On the Panionion and Panionia, see Strabo 8.7.2 and 14.1.20 and Hornblower, 1982.

16. On Poseidon Helikonios, known to Homer (*Il.* 20.404), see Farnell, *Cults* 4.29–33.

17. A crater was a large vessel in which wine and water were mixed for drinking.

18. On these craters, see Pritchett, 1993.136.

19. Theodorus made also the ring of Polycrates (Hdt. 3.41.1). That this crater was used for the Delphic Theoxenia (not Theophania), and on other aspects of the crater, see Pritchett, 1993.134–135.

20. Plutarch (*Mor.* 401E–F) records that Croesus' bakeress saved him from a poisoning attempt by Alyattes' second wife and for that reason Croesus made this dedication at Delphi. Parke (1984.219–220) argues that the statue represented Artemis.

21. Diodorus (16.56.6–7) estimates the value of Croesus' gold dedications to have been 4,000 talents ($2.4 billion) in the mid-fourth century. The silver dedications of Croesus and others were then worth 6,000 talents ($3.6 billion).

Parke (1984. esp. 212, 216–217) claims that Croesus' test of the oracles (Hdt. 1.46–49) is "a fiction invented later at Delphi to provide an honourable explanation of Croesus' generosity," and then suggests other occasions on which Croesus may have made some of these dedications. For a nuanced and positive analysis of the relationship among Croesus' dedications, oracles, and "history" as preserved at Delphi, see Flower, 1991.

22. For other ancient sources concerning Cleobis and Biton, see Frazer on Paus. 2.20.3. On the statues, now displayed in the museum at Delphi, see, e.g., Stewart, 1990.1.112. On recent uncertainties concerning their identification, see Pritchett, 1993.184.

23. Cf. Athenaeus 13.596C.

24. According to Pausanias (10.13.7), these statues represented Heracles and Apollo fighting over the tripod, with Leto and Artemis restraining Apollo and Athena restraining Heracles. Chionis sculpted the Athena and Artemis, Diyllus and Amyclaeus together the other figures.

25. According to Pausanias (10.11.2), the Siphnians were ordered by the Delphic oracle to donate this tithe (Fontenrose Q115). On the architecture of this treasury, see Daux and Hansen, 1987; on the sculpture, Stewart, 1990.1.128–129.

26. On this temple, see Bommelaer and Laroche, 1991.181–183.

27. On the problems with dating this oracle, see discussion at Hdt. 5.89.

28. As to when in the course of the invasion the Athenians received these oracles, see note 148 to Chapter 1.

29. Cf. 8.53.1.

30. Cf. 8.60.γ.

31. For the claim that the oracle to the Cnidians (Hdt. 1.174.2–6) was also an example of Delphic defeatism, see Parker, 1985.316.

32. Parker (1985.318) sees these oracles as "confirming the consultants in their own inclinations."

33. Fontenrose Q160.

34. The Athenians probably had too little time to consult Delphi. For the oracle's later identification of Echetlaeus, the mysterious hero who aided the Athenians in battle, see Paus. 1.32.3–5.

35. Note Parker, 1985.317–318: "It is a common modern belief that Delphi 'medized' in 481/0. Indeed, scholars often assert, in bold defiance of the evidence, that it was this humiliating misjudgement that brought the oracle's political influence to an end. But Delphi's prestige was perhaps never higher than in the aftermath of the Persian Wars." As examples of the many modern criticisms of the "Medizing" of the Delphic oracle, see Georges, 1986.28–31; Forrest, 1984.7; Hignett, 1963.439–447; and Parke and Wormell, 1956.1.165–179. For generally positive assessments of Delphic Apollo's role in the Persian Wars, see Price, 1985.152–153; Pritchett, 1979.312; and Immerwahr, 1966.235–236.

36. In Herodotus' account Delphic Apollo gives no oracular advantages to the Persians and their Lydian predecessors in their encounters with the Greeks. The oracles to Gyges (1.13 and 91.1–3) and Croesus (1.46–49 and 53–56.1) concerned largely intrabarbarian af-

fairs. The oracle to Alyattes (1.19–22) reconciled him and the Milesians, and there is no indication that later Persian kings, including Darius and Xerxes, sought or received responses from the oracle.

37. On the nature of this tithe, probably involving the total destruction of the offending city, see discussion of *7.132* in Chapter 1.

38. On the inscriptions of these tripods, see Pritchett, 1993.116–121.

39. The other 2,000 shields and similar statues the Phocians dedicated to Apollo at Delphi (Hdt. 8.27.4–5).

40. For the possibility, unlikely in my judgment, that Athena at Sunium received one of the Phoenician ships dedicated after the victory at Salamis, see note 271 to Chapter 1.

41. This is probably the same statue described in Paus. *9.4.1–2*, sculpted some years after the Persian Wars. See discussion of that passage in Chapter 1.

42. Cf. Polyaenus 1.21.1. Another version had Phye a Thracian woman dwelling in the deme Kollytos and making a living from selling garlands (*Ath. Pol.* 14.4). Cleidemus (*FGrHist* 323 F 15) makes her Greek (the daughter of Socrates) and has Pisistratus wed her to his son Hipparchus, an account that Jacoby (ad loc.) accepts.

43. For a recent study of this account and of the various scholarly discussions of it, see Parker 1996.83–84. See also Georges, 1994.44–45; Sinos, 1993; Connor, 1987.40–47; and Nock, 1942.2.478 = 1972.544.

44. On the Panathenaea in this period and on Pisistratus' possible contributions to its development, see Parker, 1996.68, 75–79, and 89–92.

45. For a recent and full discussion, see Hurwit, 1999.130, 133, and 165.

46. On the sanctuary of Athena Nike, see Mark, 1993.

47. See notes to Lycurg. *Leoc. 80–81* for questions about the historicity of this oath.

48. On the sculpture, see Hurwit, 1999.211–215, and Stewart, 1990.1.165–166.

49. Hurwit, 1999. esp. 222–234.

50. On the various occasions when Demeter avenged impieties in Herodotus' *Histories*, see Boedeker, 1988.46.

51. The Aeginetans were expelled from Aegina in 431 by the Athenians (Thuc. 2.27). On these events, see Figueira, 1991.104–106.

52. For Plutarch's error in dating the battle to Boedromion 6, see discussion of *Mor. 861E–F*.

53. On Artemis Agrotera, in both Athens and Sparta, and on her relationship to these sacrifices, see Jameson, 1991.209–211. On this Artemis' relationship to prebattle sacrifices in general, see Lonis, 1979.109.

54. Mikalson, 1998.247–248, 253.

55. I accept Roscher's emendation of "Hera" for the manuscript's "Hebe" here.

56. On Calami and its relation to the Heraion, see Tölle-Kastenbein, 1976.91.

57. On this temple (which measured 55.2 by 108.6 meters and had 155 columns inside and out), the sanctuary, the cult, and the many surviving dedications of this Heraion, see Kyrieleis, 1993. On Herodotus' account of it, see Tölle-Kastenbein, 1976.53–62.

58. Whitley, 1994.218–222; Kearns, 1989 and 1992; Burkert, *GR*, 203–208; Visser, 1982; Nock, 1944 = 1972.2.575–602; and Farnell, 1921. Specifically on Herodotus' treatment of heroes, see Harrison, 2000.158–162; Boedeker, 1993; and Linforth, 1928.209–211.

59. Herodotus offers valuable accounts of the origins of several hero cults. The Eges-taeans of Sicily gave to Philippus of Croton, an Olympic victor, a hero cult after his death because of his exceptional beauty (5.47). An oracle bid the Amathusians of Cyprus to establish a hero cult for Onesilus who had led the Cyprian revolt against the Persians in 497/6 but was killed and mutilated by the pro-Persian Amathusians (5.114–115.1). On this account and on the common pattern of Greek cities eventually giving a great enemy a hero cult, see Visser, 1982, esp. 405–406. The founders of colonies after their deaths com-monly received hero cult status in the colony they founded (Malkin, 1987.189–266), and Herodotus describes the founding of such a cult for Miltiades, namesake and great-uncle of the general at Marathon, by the Chersonesitae, with equestrian and athletic games (6.36–38.1).

60. On the Athenian eponymous heroes, see Kearns, 1989.80–92, and Kron, 1976.

61. On Ajax' cult in Athens, see Kearns, 1989.141–142.

62. On the Athenian cult of Aeacus, see Kearns, 1989.47 and 141. The establishment in Athens of a shrine of Aeacus, the major Aeginetan hero, would be a claim to Athe-nian ownership of Aegina. As Figueira (1991.104) puts it, "Just as the Eurysakeion, a hero shrine of the Athenian *genos* of the Salaminioi, solidified an Athenian claim to the owner-ship of the island Salamis, the Aiakeion expressed a similar claim to Aegina."

63. Mikalson, 1998.183–184, 248.

64. On the role of heroes in the battles of the Persian invasion, see Kearns, 1989.44–47.

65. On this as another instance of Greeks giving an enemy hero cult, see Visser, 1982.410–411. On the site of Acanthus, see Müller, 1987.140–141.

66. See, e.g., Harrison, 2000.164–181; Mikalson, 1991.18 and 1983.66–68; and Pötscher, 1958.

67. Things that "happen" without human planning and intent may just "happen" (τυγχάνειν) and be manifestations of τύχη ("chance"). Τύχη plays a remarkably small role in Herodotus, especially in comparison to that in Thucydides, but on a few occasions He-rodotus sees a chance happening that is in fact "divine," a θείη τύχη. When Heracles was in Scythia, his horses disappeared, snatched away by "divine chance." In his search for them he went to Hylaea, met up with the Echidna, and, to secure the return of his horses, had sexual intercourse with her. A product of this union was Scythes, the eponym of the Scythians and the founder of their royal house (4.8–10). An oracle came to Eëtion of Corinth that his wife would bear a son who would attack the ruling aristocrats and bring justice to Corinth. The oracle became widely known, and when Cypselus was born the ruling Bacchiadae sent ten men to assassinate the baby. When in their clutches, Cypselus by divine chance (θείη τύχη) smiled at his assassins, softened their hearts, and escaped death (5.92.β–γ). He was later to oust the Bacchiadae and become the tyrant of Corinth from 657 to 627. And, finally, Polycrates' brother Syloson, by divine chance, recovered Polycrates' tyranny over Samos from an encounter with Darius (3.139–149).

The relationship of the θεῖον to τύχη is only twice clarified. Cyrus the Great, founder of the Persian Empire, thought he was born by a divine chance (θείη τύχη) (1.126.6). Harpa-gus, one of his prime supporters, comments on Cyrus' great successes: "Gods watch over you, for otherwise you would not ever have attained such a level of τύχη" (1.124.1). And near the end of the Persian Wars, in 479, the Greek general Leotychides received an omen that incited him to liberate Samos and Ionia from the Persians. It may have happened, according to Herodotus, "by chance (κατὰ συντυχίην), with a god causing it" (9.91.1). "Divine chance" (θείη τύχη) is chance guided by one or more gods, and for Herodotus it may well determine the fate of nations and peoples.

68. Harrison, 2000.179–180, and Lloyd-Jones, 1983.64. It is equally mistaken, I think, to claim that through these terms Herodotus, "in his own belief," rationalizes the gods into a semiabstract "divine," a divine which guarantees the world order through maintaining balance in nature and history (Immerwahr, 1966.311–314). There are occasional traces of this conception of the divine (e.g., 3.108.2), but I think Immerwahr mistakenly combines references to "necessity" (see Chapter 3) with the divine, puts too much programmatic weight on passing references such as 3.108.2, and, in general, gives to the whole a coherence and cosmic and religious significance not warranted by the text of the *Histories*.

69. See Gould, 1985.9, quoted in Chapter 3, note 43.

70. On Herodotus' use of τὸ θεῖον in the context of a *deduction* that an event is a result of divine intervention, see Harrison, 2000.176–178.

71. See note 66.

72. Linforth (1928.219–233) describes how the singular θεός or ὁ θεός may refer to a god previously mentioned, to a particular but unnamed or unknown god, or to the collective of the gods. I share Pötscher's view (1958) that Linforth in several cases overreaches in attempts to identify a specific god and that most such references concern the "collective" of the gods. For a catalog and discussion of Herodotus' uses of θεός, θεοί, and δαίμων, see Lachenaud, 1978.182–187, 202–205.

73. Cf. 9.76.2.

74. On the programmatic nature of this last sentence, see Georges, 1994.201–203.

75. Cf. Hdt. 9.61.2–62.

76. Cf. 5.49.3 and 9.90.2.

77. Cf. Immerwahr, 1966.252 and 265–266.

78. In Herodotus' account, from the Persian perspective, "the gods," "the god," or "the divine" provided, on the favorable side as it at least initially appeared, help in establishing and expanding their empire (7.8.α.1); the birth, rescue, and success of Cyrus, the founder of the empire (1.118.2, 124.1, 204.2, and 209.4); the downfall of Croesus and his "enslavement" to Cyrus (1.89.1); a dream to Cambyses revealing a conspiracy against him (3.65.4); and the dreams that induced Xerxes to continue the expedition (7.12–18). On the negative side the "divine" contributed to the defeat at Plataea (9.16.4) and of the whole expedition against the Greeks (8.109.3). It is noteworthy that the dream sent to Cambyses and those to Xerxes turned out to be erroneous or misleading and destructive. They might well, in retrospect, later have been put down by the Persians to the hostility of the divine.

79. For the occasional problematic Delphic oracles, see the preceding section on Apollo.

80. Not one of the divine epiphanies listed by Harrison (2000.82–86) is by an Olympian god.

81. Burkert, 1990.21–22.

82. Mikalson, 1991.21, 29–31, 64–65, and Pritchett, 1979.11–46. There is scattered evidence for deities "appearing" in battle in the Hellenistic period, though not to Athenians.

Most relevant is Apollo's "appearance" to help his Delphians ward off the Galatians in 280. On these Hellenistic examples, see Garbrah, 1986.

83. Lachenaud, 1978.209–210, 215–216, and 644. So, too, as Gould (1989. esp. 42–85) emphasizes, "revenge" is Herodotus' major narrative and causal device for human actions in the *Histories*.

84. Cf. Hdt. *6.101.3* and *7.8*. As Diodorus puts it succinctly, "The Persians learned the burning of sanctuaries from the Greeks. They were repaying the same *hybris* to those who had first wronged them" (10.25.1).

## Chapter 3

1. For a welcome reassertion of the need to study the beliefs as well as the rituals of Greek religion, and for various methodological concerns in isolating the personal religious beliefs of Herodotus in the *Histories*, see Harrison, 2000.11–30.

2. For the formulation and ancient sources for these three beliefs, see Yunis, 1988.38–58.

3. On the Peneus gorge, see Müller, 1987.273–275.

4. See Harrison (2000.95–97) for a refutation of Herodotean skepticism, which some modern scholars find in this account.

5. Immerwahr, 1966.299: "When Herodotus refers to the sanctuary of Demeter at Plataea, he speaks as if he believed in the goddess, and this belief must be accepted."

6. Lateiner (1989.209) attempts to trivialize the significance of these two passages: "If the Greeks' victory was owed first to the gods (7.139.5; 8.109.3) and then to the Athenians (ibid.), Herodotus' parenthetical piety should not obscure his thorough account of the mundane and complex efforts of all the independent Greeks to repel Xerxes' venture. The weight of the narrative overwhelms the pietistic aside."

7. Mikalson, 1991.139–142, 151–152, 161–162, 179–183, and 197.

8. The search for Herodotean criticisms of Greek religious beliefs and practices has yielded little that is compelling. One method is to assume that Herodotus shares the rare criticisms he has foreigners make of Greeks, as in 1.131–132 and 4.79.3. Another is to note Herodotean expressions that can be paralleled in contemporary "rationalizing" accounts of religion, as of Protagoras and the Hippocratic writings, and then to assume Herodotus shared these views. For both methods and the results, see Burkert, 1990.20–22, 26.

9. On Herodotus' belief in the accuracy of the various forms of divination, given the cautions necessary, see Harrison, 2000.122–157.

10. On Herodotus here being among the first to introduce as a criterion of oracles that they be "clear," see Asheri, 1993. Herodotus *8.77*, however, should not be taken to mean that he rejects all "unclear" oracles, only that "clear" and "clearly fulfilled" oracles cause him to trust oracles in general.

11. To these fulfilled oracles might be added, among others, the oracle to Cleomenes about the capture of Argos (6.79–80) and the oracles predicting that Sparta would suffer at the hands of the Athenians (5.90.2–91.1 and 93).

12. See discussion of *7.12–18* in Chapter 1.

13. On this claim, see A. B. Lloyd, 1976.346–347.

14. Cf. the oracle (?) applied to Pisistratus' situation by the Acarnanian *chresmologos* Amphilytus (1.62.4).

15. For a successful instance of supplication, a form of prayer, see *7.141–142.1*.

16. Mikalson, 1991.178–179.

17. Commonly noted, as by Evans, 1991.142; Burkert, 1990; and Lateiner, 1989.244 n. 118.

18. See A. B. Lloyd, 1976.287–288.

19. On Herodotus' reaction to these *logoi*, see Harrison, 2000.88–90.

20. See Parker, 1983.74–103, and A. B. Lloyd, 1976.289–290.

21. On Herodotus' reluctance to tell "sacred *logoi*" and for the complete list of them, see Harrison, 2000.184–189.

22. On this festival and the sacred *logos*, see A. B. Lloyd, 1976.280–283.

23. Cf. 2.51.4 and 5.83.3.

24. On Herodotus' handling of sacred *logoi*, see A. B. Lloyd, 1976.279, and Linforth, 1924.280–282 and 1928.240–243. Lateiner (1989.65) views Herodotus' reluctance to tell ἱροὶ λόγοι "an elegant excuse for avoiding an excursus into the irrelevant."

25. That τὰ θεῖα of 2.3.2 is balanced by ἀνθρωπήια πρήγματα of 2.4.1 and, in addition, τὰ θεῖα πρήγματα of 2.65.2 justify taking the τὰ θεῖα of 2.3.2 as τὰ θεῖα πρήγματα.

26. Linforth (1924.271) summarizes the contents of these pages: "temples and precincts; statues of the gods; forms of ceremonial; the organization of festivals; the duties and habits of priests; the treatment of sacred animals; the operation of oracles."

27. Linforth, 1924 and 1928. Cf. Lateiner, 1989.65–66.

28. On what θεῖα πρήγματα here were, namely, essentially "mythological" accounts and *not* cult matters, see Burkert, 1990.24–25; A. B. Lloyd, 1976.17–19; Linforth, 1924 and 1928.201–202. Cf. Lateiner, 1989.55–56. But note also Sourdille, 1925. Harrison (2000.182–189) is misled by his insistence on θεῖα πρήγματα as the sacred *logoi*. The two were, I think, separate matters of concern to Herodotus.

29. For exceptions in the Egyptian *logos*, see Harrison, 2000.187–188.

30. A. B. Lloyd, in Burkert, 1990.35, and Linforth, 1924 and 1928.201–204 and 211.

31. On this account, see A. B. Lloyd, 1988.58–59.

32. On the *logos* of the phoenix, see A. B. Lloyd, 1976.317–322.

33. For quite a long list of instances in books 1–4 where Herodotus expresses incredulity in nonreligious matters, see Baldwin, 1964. See also Pearson, 1941.

34. The assumption that, when Herodotus introduces a "source" for an account or reports it in indirect discourse, he is "distancing" himself from the account and questioning its veracity underlies the fairly recent dismissal or belittling of much of the "religious" material in the *Histories*. It attains its fullest application in Lateiner, 1989. esp. 22–23, 34, 66, 78, and in Shimron, 1989, esp. 75–85. Harrison (2000.24–30) effectively refutes the assumptions behind this treatment of "reported" material in the *Histories*.

35. Certain particles and constructions do indicate strong questioning of statements, but particles such as κως and κου are milder, indicating a "hesitant statement" or "approximate truth" (Lateiner, 1989.31–32). κως is naturally used in speculating about the divine ordering of nature, but the same statement can also be termed οἰκός (3.108.2). There, as in 6.27.1, κως and κου express only a touch of uncertainty, not disbelief, and one should not assume that Herodotus by introducing these particles was rejecting or treating with irony the statements that they affect.

36. Cf. 7.152.3.

37. On the value of these "reports" to the study of Greek religion, see Nilsson, *GGR* I³, 759. On Herodotus' relationship to his quoted "sources" and, in more general terms, to his own *logoi*, see Gould, 1989. esp. 19–41, 50–51; Hartog, 1988.260–294; Dewald, 1987; and Pearson, 1941.337–338.

38. Cf. Harrison, 2000.24–30 and 82–83; Pritchett, 1979.20–21, 41; Dodds, 1951.117; and Pearson, 1941.338. For a contrary view, see Lateiner, 1989.23.

39. On Herodotus' use of variant versions (125 cases) as a historical device, see Lateiner, 1989.78–90. On how few of these concern "supernatural" matters and how they do not necessarily indicate Herodotus' disbelief, see Harrison, 2000.29–30.

40. Cf. Herodotus' preference for the Carthaginian version of the disappearance of Amiclas (7.166–167).

41. See also Harrison, 2000.189–192.

42. Cf. Burkert, 1990.28–29.

43. Gould's comments (1985.9) on this in another context are helpful: "How did an ancient Greek *know* that a divine power was at work in the world of his experience? The answer, of course, is that he didn't—outside, say, the fictional worlds of the *Iliad* and *Odyssey*. He had to guess, to wrestle with uncertainty and disagreement, both in discerning the active power of divinity at work in events and, more particularly, in determining what divinity and for what reason. And until these questions could be answered, response was premature and might be misguided and misdirected; it was inhibited by thoughts of the consequences; it might involve irreparable loss in the effective destruction of foodstuffs, in the slaughter of scarce animal resources (or in myth even of sons or daughters), and might even result in an outcome counter to the intentions of the respondent. So these are questions that matter, and our sources (particularly Herodotus) reflect the doubts and anxieties that attend their answering." See also Sourdille, 1925.301–302 n. 1.

44. Cf. Herodotus' explication of the Delphic oracle given to the Siphnians (3.57–58).

45. On such cases, see Harrison, 2000.223–242; Fornara, 1990; Gould, 1989.68–74; Lloyd-Jones, 1983.67–68; and Ste. Croix, 1977.140–143.

46. For further examples of "what had to happen," see 1.120.1 (Cyrus), 2.133.3 (Mycerinus), 2.139.3 (Sebacus), and 9.42.3 (Mardonius). Cf. *7.142.3*. On these and similar expressions, Lachenaud, 1978.96.

47. The Persian Zopyrus thought that, because an oracle about the taking of Babylon had been fulfilled, it was "destined" (μόρσιμον) to happen (3.153.2–154.1). Cf. Cambyses' reaction on understanding the oracle concerning his death from Leto of Buto (3.64.5).

48. *Moira* might be seen a candidate for the force that determines "what will be." In 1.91.1 Herodotus has the Pythia say that "it is impossible for even a god to escape the destined" μοῖρα. The adjective "destined" is inappropriate here, however, if μοῖρα itself is "Destiny" or "Fate." But the Pythia continues to say that in Croesus' case Apollo was not able to turn aside the μοῖραι, but "accomplished and gave as a favor to Croesus what these μοῖραι granted." Here the Pythia, using Homeric and Hesiodic concepts and terminology, seems to be treating the μοῖραι as beings, that is, as the Moirae as defined in Hes. *Th.* 904–906. The language and thought of the Delphic oracle were, however, much more

Homeric than were Herodotus' own, and the lack of other occurrences of the Moirae in this sense throughout the rest of the *Histories* makes this seem like an isolated case conditioned by the oracular setting. Whatever the case here, we should not generalize from it to conclude that for Herodotus the Moirae are what cause all that "will or must happen" in the *Histories*.

For the rarity and use of μοῖρα or μοῖραι in the sense of "Fate," and for its occasional use (3.142.3 and 4.164.4. Cf. 1.121 and 3.64.5) to indicate an individual's "death as fulfilling his μοῖρα" (also Homeric), see Lachenaud, 1978.89–93. See also Pohlenz, 1973.107–109, on *moira* in Herodotus.

49. See Immerwahr, 1954.33.

50. Mikalson, 1983.19, 50, 58–62; 1991.18, 26–28, 114, 205–206.

51. It is the Persian Xerxes who prays to an un-Greek deity, the sun, that he not suffer "reversals" in his expedition (*7.54.2*), and his prayer is one of few not answered in Herodotus' *Histories*.

52. Note parallels cited in Harrison, 2000.38–39 nn. 17–21.

53. Mikalson, 1991.205–206. Harrison (1997.110–111) has noted how genuine catastrophes afflicting Greeks, like those of the Chians recorded in 6.27, are described not as evils but as omens sent by "the god." The same would be true of the earthquake on Delos (*6.98*) if in fact it caused destruction and death.

54. For the contrast with Aeschylus here, see Immerwahr, 1954.27–30. On the lack of a coherent, tidy theology in Herodotus, see Harrison, 1997.101, 111–112 and 2000.116. On the lack of a consistent theology regarding what he calls Herodotus' fatalism, see Harrison, 2000.28 and 241.

55. Mikalson, 1989.

56. Mikalson, 1991.87–114.

57. The major exception here is the dreams of Xerxes and Artabanus in *7.12–18*, but even these can be forced into giving an accurate prediction. See discussion of *7.12–18* in Chapter 1.

58. The differences and separateness of ancient "poetic" (epic and tragic) and "historical" accounts of the past can, however, be overstated. For their numerous affinities, see Walbank, 1960.

59. For this discussion of *hybris* I am much indebted to Fisher, 1992. esp. 86–150 and 343–365, and to Cairns's critique (1996) of Fisher's arguments. See also Romilly, 1977.42–46.

60. In the oracle of Bacis concerning Salamis (*8.77*), Hybris as a personification is tangentially introduced. The dedication celebrating the Athenian victory over the Boeotians and Chalcidians (*5.77.4*) may offer an indirect connection between Athena and the punishment of the enemies' *hybris*. Both, significantly, are in poetic form.

61. This is all the more remarkable given that poets, preceding and contemporaneous with Herodotus, often framed the Persian Wars in terms of *hybris* and punishment for *hybris*, as demonstrated by Asheri, 1998.76–86. In the *Histories* a trace of this may be seen in the oracle of Bacis referring to the battle of Salamis (*8.77*), also poetic in form and content.

62. Romilly (1977.46) makes the distinction between "religious" and "political" *hybris*. See Fisher, 1992.384–385.

63. Mikalson, 1991.182–183. For the three cases where the idea of *hybris* was even raised in such matters, see Fisher, 1992.145–147.

64. For other, nonreligious variations from the Homeric account in this *logos*, see Neville, 1977.

65. Harrison, 2000.31.

66. On this in general terms, see Burkert, 1990.

67. For such an attempt to delineate the principles underlying Herodotus' *graeca interpretatio* of foreign religions, see Mora, 1986.

68. See Burkert, 1990.14–15, 17–18, and Burn, 1962.65–68.

69. Harrison, 2000.213 and n. 16. Cf. Gould, 1989.99: "Herodotus has no key to an understanding of these things that he has often accurately observed." Gould later (1994.98–102) argues that Herodotus concentrated on the rituals and practices of foreign religions because "he, and one might guess, the majority of Greeks, defined their own religion to themselves and understood its significance largely in ritual terms." For him such ritual detail is "central to his perception of religion" and hence dominates his descriptions of foreign religions. For a critique of this argument, see Harrison, 2000.220–222.

Also Bremmer, 1994.2, "For Herodotus, the problem of describing foreign religions could be reduced to the question 'which (other) gods do they worship and how?'" On Herodotus' (mis)representation of Persian religion in general terms, see Georges, 1994.54–58 and 194–195.

70. For a similar statement of belief resulting from observing foreign customs, see 2.64.

71. See Mikalson, 1989.97–98.

72. On this Persian burial practice, see Burn, 1962.66–68.

73. Cf. A. *Pers.* 205–211. The awaited and staged horse whinny to select the king among the conspirators and the confirming thunder and lightning could also be considered Greek-style omens (3.84.3–87).

74. Cf. Xen. *Ana.* 4.5.35 and Tac. *Ann.* 6.37.

75. For other examples from tragedy, see Mikalson, 1991.101–104, 107–110.

76. For the "Greek" nature of the dream of Xerxes in 7.19, see Köhnken, 1988.

77. Cf. the Mede Harpagus' letter to Cyrus, 1.124.1.

78. Cf. 7.8.α.1.

79. For parallels, see discussion of 7.10.ε in Chapter 1.

80. Evans (1991.14) sees Cassandra as the "ultimate archetype" of Artabanus. "More than a wise adviser, he is almost a seer whose accurate vision of the future introduced a note of dramatic irony." On Artabanus as the "wise adviser," and especially on the limits of his predictions as accurate forecasts but on their value as pointing to greater truths, see Pelling, 1991. esp. 130–143.

81. On the sources for Herodotus' account of Croesus and, more important, on Croesus' relationship to Delphi and his reputation for piety, see Flower, 1991.

82. On the χάρις relationship, see Parker, 1998b; Mikalson, 1991.188–190; Yunis, 1988.101–107; and Versnel, 1981.47–49.

83. On the Moirae, see note 48.

84. For another Lydian expressing the same idea, see 1.71.4. For Greek examples, see Dover, 1974.136–137.

85. E.g., *Ag.* 60–62, 355–402.

86. Mikalson, 1983.69–73, and Linforth, 1926.4.

87. Evans, 1991.45 (with bibliography): "The general consensus of scholars is that the Croesus-story is dramatic, tragic, and theatrical, and perhaps even derived, in its outlines, from the Athenian stage." Cf. Romm, 1998.68–72. More generally on the influence of Athenian tragedy on Herodotus, see Chiasson, 1982.

## Appendix

1. For all matters Egyptian I am much indebted, as the notes indicate, to A. B. Lloyd, 1975, 1976, and 1988. For extensive discussions of this selection, see 1976.232–251 and Linforth, 1924.

2. On the cult of the herms, see A. B. Lloyd, 1976.239–241.

3. That Herodotus has confused the Cabiri with the Theoi Megaloi of Samothrace or has used for them a name more familiar to his Greek audience, see Cole, 1984.2, and A. B. Lloyd, 1976.227–231 and 241–243. On the Samothracian cult, see Cole, 1984.

4. On the oracle of Zeus at Dodona, see A. B. Lloyd, 1976.246–247 and 251–264, and Parke, 1967.1–163. Plato has Socrates (*Phdr.* 275b) claim that it was the first oracle. Archaeological evidence indicates habitation from the early Bronze Age (Lloyd, 259–260).

5. "The poets who are said to be earlier" are Orpheus and Musaeus. See A. B. Lloyd, 1976.251.

6. See A. B. Lloyd, 1976.232–234 and 240–241.

7. The Egyptians claimed that in the 11,340 years of their history there had been no anthropomorphic god (θεὸν ἀνθρωποειδέα, 2.142.3). On this claim, see A. B. Lloyd, 1988.106.

8. On all aspects of the oracle of Dodona and the relationship of Zeus of Egyptian Thebes, Zeus Ammon, and Zeus of Dodona, see Pritchett, 1993.71–75; A. B. Lloyd, 1976.51–64; and Parke, 1967.52–59.

9. On Herodotus' "almost obsessive" concern with gods' names, see Gould, 1994.103–105.

10. In similar fashion but at a later date the Greeks learned the names of Heracles, Dionysus, and Pan from the Egyptians and after that created a genealogy for each of them. See subsequent discussion.

11. Rudhardt, 1992.224–236, and Lachenaud, 1978.195.

12. See my subsequent discussion of Poseidon.

13. For others' various attempts to solve this dilemma, see Harrison, 2000.251–264; Hartog, 1988.241–248; Burkert, 1985.125–132; A. B. Lloyd, 1976.203–205; Lattimore, 1939; and Linforth, 1924.274–276, 285–286 and 1926 and 1940.

14. This point was reasserted by Lattimore, 1939; A. B. Lloyd, 1976.203–205; and now Harrison, 2000.251–255. It is doubted by Rudhardt, 1992.227–228; Burkert, 1985.125–132; Parke, 1967.57; and Linforth, 1924.274–276, 285–286 and 1926 and 1940.

15. Or, as Harrison (2000.214) puts it, "Given the lengthy contacts between Greece and Egypt, it is likely that the vast majority of such identifications had been long established by both Greeks and Egyptians for their mutual convenience."

16. Pearson, 1941, and A. B. Lloyd, 1976.204.

17. Burkert, 1985.125–132, and Linforth, 1924.274–276, 285–286 and 1926. On these, see Harrison, 2000.251–255.

18. In 2.4.2 Herodotus has the giving of epithets to gods an Egyptian practice in origin. In 2.82.1 he may be including Hesiod among Greek poets influenced by Egyptian astrology.

19. The common terms are πυνθάνεσθαι and μανθάνειν.

20. Rudhardt, 1992, and Linforth, 1924.275 and 1926.10–25.

21. As Harrison (2000.213) puts it, "The identification of gods takes place . . . in spite of what seem extraordinary obstacles." See also Mora, 1986, and Linforth, 1926.12–17.

22. So, too, Aeschylus "made (ἐποίησε) Artemis a daughter of Demeter" (2.156.6). In 3.115.2 Herodotus complains that Eridanus was a name (wrongly) "made" by some poet (ὑπὸ ποιητέω δέ τινος ποιηθέν).

23. As J. Gould (1994.105) puts it, "The fictional narrative tradition of poetry alone creates a 'world' and 'history' which makes identifiable and describable beings out of the recipients of sacrifice and prayer."

24. ἐξευρίσκειν and cognates as "search out" in 1.67.3–5, 5.33.2, 7.119.2; and, most commonly, as "invent," of board games (1.94.2), refinements of armor (1.171.4), marital customs (1.196.5), and ways to cook sacrifices (4.61.1). Most interesting to contemplate in this regard is Gyges' comment to Candaules, πάλαι δὲ τὰ καλὰ ἀνθρώποισι ἐξεύρηται (1.8.4).

25. Lachenaud, 1978.161–162.

26. Rudhardt, 1992; Evans, 1991.142; Gould, 1989.95; and Linforth, 1926.2. For what evidence, rather weak and subject to other interpretations, one can collect to show Herodotus' "condescension" toward foreign deities and the religious practices of foreigners, see Harrison, 2000.214–220.

27. I henceforth follow the Herodotean chronology as outlined by A. B. Lloyd, 1975.171–194. Two principles are fundamental. Despite his claim in 2.142.2, Herodotus sometimes, as in the Spartan king list, uses generations of 40 years. Second, when Herodotus uses three generations for 100 years, he does *not* take the next step of having one generation equal 33 1/3 years. For his method of calculation here, see A. B. Lloyd, 1975.176–177. More generally on Herodotean chronology, see also Mosshammer, 1979.105–107 and 328 n. 25; Boer, 1967; and Mitchel, 1956.

Lateiner's assault (1989.118–119) on Herodotus' chronology of the "tales" of the gods and heroes seems overwrought. Hdt. 2.53 and 143.1 do not justify the claim that Herodotus "scorns, for the most part, the chronologies that date" such tales, and the accounts given here hardly show "irreconcilable and irresponsible chronological arithmetic." Rather, with one widely accepted emendation, the "dating" of gods and heroes forms a consistent pattern, a pattern all the more noteworthy because pieces of it are scattered throughout the *Histories*. This is not, however, to minimize the Herodotean inconsistencies of "genealogical dating" in other areas of "mythical history," inconsistencies abundantly illustrated by Mitchel, 1956.

28. For problems with the date of Dionysus, see my subsequent discussion.

29. For the reckoning here, see A. B. Lloyd, 1975.178–179. The genealogy of the Spartan king Leotychides (8.131.2) leads to the same date for Heracles.

30. The Trojan War was dated by Herodotus before 1250 (2.145.4). A. B. Lloyd (1975.177–178) finds the terminus post quem for the Trojan War to be circa 1330.

31. Cf. A. B. Lloyd, 1976.18.

32. On this claim, see A. B. Lloyd, 1976.238–239. On Heracles and Egypt, see my subsequent discussion.

33. Cf. Amiclas of Carthage in 480 (7.167).

34. Garland, 1992.93–94.

35. Cf. Burkert, *GR*, x: "Great gods are no longer born, but new heroes can always be raised up from the army of the dead whenever a family, cult association, or city passes an appropriate resolution to accord heroic honors."

36. For full discussion of this selection, see A. B. Lloyd, 1976.12–33.

37. See A. B. Lloyd, 1976, on Egyptian Hephaestus (7–8), Thebes (12–13), Heliopolis (14), and the priests of Heliopolis (16).

38. On this important sentence, see Burkert, 1990.24; A. B. Lloyd, 1976.17–19; Pötscher, 1958.29 n. 80; Linforth, 1924 and 1928; and my earlier comments.

39. On the question whether these were the Greek twelve gods or the Egyptian twelve gods, see A. B. Lloyd, 1976.29.

40. A. B. Lloyd (1976.29) takes ἐπωνυμίας here to be "names," not merely "epithets," but in 2.52.1 Herodotus distinguishes between ἐπωνυμίη and οὔνομα.

41. On the nature of Egyptian altars, see A. B. Lloyd, 1976.29–30, 174.

42. On the pervasiveness of this argument in the *Histories* and its importance to Herodotus' history of Greek religion, see A. B. Lloyd, 1975.147–149.

43. E.g., 1.182.1.

44. On the nature of the Egyptian equivalents of these activities, and especially on προσαγωγάς, see A. B. Lloyd, 1976.264–266.

45. On the question, see A. B. Lloyd, 1976.29.

46. On these restrictions, see Parker, 1983.74–103, and A. B. Lloyd, 1976.287–291.

47. On the ὀλολυγή, see Pulleyn, 1997.178–180.

48. On this Egyptian hemerology, see A. B. Lloyd, 1976.344–345.

49. On the unlikelihood that there was an Egyptian belief in metempsychosis, see A. B. Lloyd, 1975.57–58 and 1988.59–60.

50. In what follows similarities and differences between Greek and foreign deities are based on only what Herodotus reports of them in his *Histories*. More such similarities and differences can be adduced if one introduces evidence from non-Herodotean sources for the foreign deities. For a full application of this second method, see Mora, 1986. esp. 81–101 and 208–222.

51. On differences between the Scythian and Greek pantheon, see Hartog, 1988.174–175.

52. For the strong Carian presence in Herodotus' home country Halicarnassus, see Gould, 1989.6–7.

53. See A. B. Lloyd, 1976.124–125.

54. A. B. Lloyd, 1976.200. On the Egyptian Zeus, see 190.

55. A. B. Lloyd, 1976.195–198.

56. For the inference that Herodotus gives an Egyptian origin to Zeus of Olympia, see A. B. Lloyd, 1976.253.

57. On this selection, see A. B. Lloyd, 1988.139–146, and on Egyptian Leto and the city Buto, A. B. Lloyd, 1976.270.

58. Horus was the last god to rule as king over the Egyptians (2.144).

59. Elsewhere Herodotus gives oracles to the "Egyptian" gods Heracles, Apollo, Athena, Artemis, Ares, and, as we have seen, Zeus. Leto's was most honored (2.83) and is the most widely consulted of the the Egyptian oracles in Herodotus (2.111.2, 133, 152.3–5, and 3.64.4–5).

60. On Bubastis and Busiris, see A. B. Lloyd, 1976.268–269.

61. On this claim, see A. B. Lloyd, 1988.59.

62. On this selection, see A. B. Lloyd, 1988.55–57.

63. On this festival, see A. B. Lloyd, 1976.276–280.

64. On this selection, the Thesmophoria, and the Danaid myth, see A. B. Lloyd, 1975.124–125 and 1988.209–211.

65. For an attempt to date the origins of the Egyptian elements of the Danaus legend, see A. B. Lloyd, 1975.124–125.

66. On this claim, see A. B. Lloyd, 1976.124–125.

67. On the distinction between rituals and deity evident in the following account, see Rudhardt, 1992.227.

68. For all aspects of this selection, see A. B. Lloyd, 1976.220–231. For the usual Egyptian proscriptions against pigs and swineherds, see 2.47.

69. Among such "dances" (χοροί) Herodotus may well have included dithyramb, tragedy, and comedy.

70. On this Melampus, see A. B. Lloyd, 1976.224–225.

71. On Cadmus and his career, see A. B. Lloyd, 1976.226–231.

72. Cf. Burkert, 1985.121–122.

73. On this selection, see A. B. Lloyd, 1988.112–114.

74. For a significantly different interpretation of this very difficult sentence, see A. B. Lloyd, 1988.113–114.

75. See A. B. Lloyd, 1988.112. For a defense of the text as handed down, see Mitchel, 1956.60.

76. Herodotus' description of the Scythian Scyles' participation in the Dionysus cult at (Greek) Borysthenes (4.79) reveals much of the cult there, with its initiation (τὴν τελετήν), μανία, "possession" by the god, thiasoi, and Bacchic revelry (βακχεύοντα). On the sanctuary and the inscribed bone tablets found there, which indicate an Orphic cult at least in the fifth century, see M. L. West, 1982.

77. On all aspects of this selection, see A. B. Lloyd, 1976.200–214.

78. Both Amphitryon and Alcmene were descendants of Perseus.

79. On Heracles as the Phoenician Melquart and the cult there, see A. B. Lloyd, 1976.205–207.

80. On the Heracles cult on Thasos, see A. B. Lloyd, 1976.208–211. On the site and the Herakleion there, see Müller, 1987.108–117.

81. On the "heroic" and "divine" cults of Heracles, see A. B. Lloyd, 1976.208–212.

82. On this closing wish, see Linforth, 1924.289–290.

83. On the Egyptian Mendes, see A. B. Lloyd, 1976.191–192 and 214–215.

84. On this whole selection, see A. B. Lloyd, 1976.214–215.

85. For Plutarch's protest at linking Pan to the Egyptians, see *Mor.* 857D.

86. On this ritual battle, see A. B. Lloyd, 1976.285–286.

87. On this and for speculations on the nature of the Scythian Ares, see Hartog, 1988.188, and Mora, 1986.91–92.

88. On the Egyptian Athena, see A. B. Lloyd, 1976.111 and 280–283.

89. On these tombs, see A. B. Lloyd, 1988.202–206.

90. See for examples and bibliography Jasanoff and Nussbaum, 193–194; Coleman, 300 n. 20; and Tritle, 321, all in Lefkowitz and Rogers, 1996.

91. Herodotus, it must be admitted, left the opening for claims such as Bernal's by his own imprecise and perhaps inconsistent statement of what he meant in writing that "the names of almost all the gods have come to Greece from Egypt" (2.50).

92. Herodotus distinguishes between Libyans and Ethiopians (4.197).

93. It is somewhat surprising that in this discussion of the Libyan Athena, Lake Tritonis, and Triton, Herodotus does not introduce Athena's familiar epithet Tritogeneia ("Triton-born"), found in Homer (e.g., *Il.* 4.515 and 8.39). Herodotus' account offers an implicit explanation of the epithet, but many uncertainties remain. For discussions of the meaning(s) of Tritogeneia, see M. L. West, 1966.404.

94. On the aegis, see C. Sourvinou-Inwood, *OCD*³ s.v. aegis.

95. For Greek cults in Libya, especially Cyrene, before Herodotus' time, see Pritchett, 1993.40–42.

96. On the North African cults of Poseidon, see A. B. Lloyd, 1976.237–238.

97. Herodotus' making the Persian Mithra female and identifying him or her with Aphrodite is widely considered one of his greatest blunders in religious topics. See, e.g., Harrison, 2000.209 n. 9, and Georges, 1994.55.

98. On her cult, see Pritchett, 1993.67–68, and A. B. Lloyd, 1988.44–45. On Herodotus' treatment of Aphrodite Xeinia, see Harrison, 2000.214.

99. For the Aphrodite Ourania cult at Corinth, with ritual prostitution, see discussion of Plut. *Mor. 871A–B* in Chapter 1.

100. In understanding the foundation of a cult by one state in the territory of another, we should recognize the likelihood that the first state was acting only in the interests of its own citizens, not in the interests of the second state. Cf. A. B. Lloyd, 1976.208: "[T]he analogy of Naucratis shows that a Greek state with considerable interests in a foreign city would establish a shrine of its major god in order to serve the religious needs of its citizens without any reference to native cults."

101. HW, 1.272.

102. On the Cretan Dictyna and her cult at Cydonia, see Nilsson, *GGR* I³, 311–312, and Müller, 1987.943–945. On Cydonia, Müller, 966–967.

103. On this account, see A. B. Lloyd, 1988.239–240.

104. The Spartan Dorieus intended to be an *oikistes*, but we learn nothing of the cir-

cumstances of his founding of a sanctuary and temple of Athena Krathia by the Crathis River in southern Italy (5.45.1).

105. Herodotus claims that if the Egyptians had taken over the name of any Greek god, they would have known Poseidon and the Dioscuri because they practiced seafaring and there were Greek sailors in Egypt (2.43.2–3).

106. On Herodotus and the history of religions, see Mora, 1986, and Lachenaud, 1978.115–164 and 194–198. There is much of value also in Rudhardt, 1992, and Pohlenz, 1973.98–110.

107. Cf. A. B. Lloyd, 1975.169: "In the history of extant Greek literature Herodotus is the first to devote his attention in a scientific fashion to the problems of the development of religious phenomena and amply merits the title given him by Burckhardt of 'Gründer der vergleichenden Religions- und Dogmengeschichte.' . . . It is in the discussion of the history of Greek religion and its development in interrelation with foreign cults and the speculations of the poets that the title has its basis." "The results are certainly mistaken but that does not alter the fact that Herodotus has created an ingenious and original synthesis. Given the conditions of his time we must regard it as little short of brilliant."

108. Burkert (1990.3–4) gives Herodotus an "Ehrenplatz" among the founders of the comparative study of religions for, especially, four principles: Herodotus represses religion's claim to truth (i.e., theology) and hence is open to foreign peculiarities; he concentrates on what is immediately describable (i.e., ritual); he employs the concept of *nomos*, which makes what is foreign understandable in its own place and context; and he always demonstrates, even in his descriptions of curiosities, human sympathy and empathy.

Also relevant here is, mutatis mutandis, Lateiner's comment (1989.56) on Herodotus as a political historian: "It is the rare historiographer who recognizes that . . . later historians only elaborated the fundamentals of historical criticism already implicit and sometimes explicit in the *Histories*."

Asheri, D. 1998. "Platea vendetta delle Termopili: Alle origini di un motivo teologico erodoteo." Pp. 65–86 in *Responsibilità perdono e vendetta nel mondo antico*, ed. M. Sordi. *Contributi dell' Istituto di storia antica* 24. Milan.

———. 1993. "Erodoto e Bacide. Considerazioni sulla fede di Erodoto negli oracoli (Hdt. VIII 77)." Pp. 63–76 in *La profezia nel mondo antico*, ed. M. Sordi. *Contributi dell' Istituto di storia antica* 19. Milan.

Balcer, J. M. 1995. *The Persian Conquest of the Greeks: 545–450 B.C.* Constanz.

Baldwin, B. 1964. "How Credulous Was Herodotus?" *G&R* 11:167–177.

Bernal, M. 1987. *Black Athena*. London.

Bichler, R. 1985. "Die 'Reichsträume' bei Herodot." *Chiron* 15:125–147.

Bigwood, J. M. 1978. "Ctesias as Historian of the Persian Wars." *Phoenix* 32:19–41.

Binder, J. 1984. "The West Pediment of the Parthenon: Poseidon." Pp. 15–22 in *Studies Presented to Sterling Dow*, GRBS Monograph 10, ed. K. J. Rigsby. Durham, N.C.

Blamire, A. 1989. *Plutarch: Life of Kimon*. BICS Supplement 56. London.

Boedeker, D. 1996. "Heroic Historiography: Simonides and Herodotus on Plataea." *Arethusa* 29:223–242.

———. 1995. "Simonides on Plataea: Narrative Elegy, Mythodic History." *ZPE* 107:217–229.

———. 1993. "Hero Cult and Politics in Herodotus." Pp. 164–177 in *Cultural Poetics in Archaic Greece: Cult, Performance, Politics*, ed. C. Doughterty and L. Kurke. Cambridge.

———. 1988. "Protesilaos and the End of Herodotus' *Histories*." *CA* 7:30–48.

Boegehold, A. L. 1965. "The Salamis Epigram." *GRBS* 6:179–186.

Boer, W. den. 1967. "Herodot und die Systeme der Chronologie." *Mnemosyne* 20:30–60.

Bommelaer, J.-F., and D. Laroche. 1991. *Guide de Delphes*. Paris.

Bonnechere, P. 1998. "La scène d'initiation des *Nuées* d'Aristophane et Trophonios: Nouvelles lumières sur le culte lébadéen." *REG* 111:436–480.

———. 1994. *Le sacrifice humain en Grèce ancienne. Kernos Supplément* 3. Liège.

Bowen, A. 1992. *Plutarch: The Malice of Herodotus*. Warminster.

Bremer, J.-M. 1998. "The Reciprocity of Giving and Thanksgiving in Greek Worship." Pp. 127–137 in *Reciprocity in Ancient Greece*, ed. C. Gill, N. Postlethwaite, and R. Seaford. Oxford.

Bremmer, J. N. 1994. *Greek Religion*. Oxford.

Broneer, O. 1944. "The Tent of Xerxes and the Greek Theater." *University of California Publications in Classical Archaeology* 1.12:305–311.

Brown, T. S. 1982. "Herodotus' Portrait of Cambyses." *Historia* 31:387–403.

Burkert, W. 1990. "Herodot als Historiker fremder Religionen." Pp. 1–39 in *Hérodote et les peuples non grecs*, ed. E. Nenci. Fondation Hardt, *Entretiens* 35. Geneva.

———. 1985. "Herodot über die Namen der Götter: Polytheismus als historisches Problem." *MH* 42:121–132.

———. 1979. *Structure and History in Greek Mythology and Ritual*. Berkeley.

———. 1966. "Greek Tragedy and Sacrificial Ritual." *GRBS* 7:87–121.

Burn, A. R. 1962. *Persia and the Greeks*. New York.

Cairns, D. L. 1996. "*Hybris*, Dishonour, and Thinking Big." *JHS* 116:1–32.

Camp, J. M. 1986. *The Athenian Agora: Excavations in the Heart of Classical Athens*. New York.

Campbell, D. A. 1967. *Greek Lyric Poetry*. London.

Carrière, J.-C. 1988. "Oracles et prodiges de Salamine: Hérodote et Athènes." *Dialogues d'histoire ancienne* 14:219–275.

Chiasson, C. C. 1982. "Tragic Diction in Herodotus: Some Possibilities." *Phoenix* 36:156–161.

Clairmont, C. W. 1983. *Patrios Nomos: Public Burial in Athens during the Fifth and Fourth Centuries B.C.* Oxford.

Clinton, K. 1992. *Myth and Cult: The Iconography of the Eleusinian Mysteries*. Stockholm.

Cole, S. G. 1984. *Theoi Megaloi: The Cult of the Great Gods at Samothrace*. Leiden.

Coleman, J. E. 1996. "Did Egypt Shape the Glory That Was Greece?" Pp. 280–302 in *Black Athena Revisited*, ed. M. R. Lefkowitz and G. M. Rogers. Chapel Hill.

Compton, T. 1994. "The Herodotean Mantic Session at Delphi." *RhM* 137:217–223.

Connor, W. R. 1987. "Tribes, Festivals and Processions: Civic Ceremonial and Political Manipulation in Archaic Greece." *JHS* 107:40–50.

Crahay, R. 1956. *La littérature oraculaire chez Hérodote*. Paris.

Daux, G. 1957. "Mys au Ptôion." Pp. 157–162 in *Hommages à Waldemar Déonna*. Collection Latomus 28. Brussels.

Daux, G., and E. Hansen. 1987. "Le Trésor de Siphnos." *Fouilles de Delphes* II. Paris.

Day, J. 1985. "Epigrams and History: The Athenian Tyrannicides, a Case in Point." Pp. 25–46 in *The Greek Historians: Literature and History: Papers Presented to A. E. Raubitschek*. Saratoga, Calif.

Despinis, G. 1971. Συμβολὴ στὴ μελέτη τοῦ ἔργου τοῦ Ἀγορακρίτου. Athens.

Dewald, C. 1987. "Narrative Surface and Authorial Voice in Herodotus' *Histories*." *Arethusa* 20:147–170.

Dewald, C., and J. Marincola. 1987. "A Selective Introduction to Herodotean Studies." *Arethusa* 20:9–40.

Dickie, M. W. 2001. *Magic and Magicians in the Greco-Roman World*. London and New York.

Dinsmoor, W. B. 1950. *The Architecture of Ancient Greece*. 3d ed. London.

Dodds, E. R. 1951. *The Greeks and the Irrational*. Berkeley.

Dontas, G. S. 1983. "The True Aglaurion." *Hesperia* 52:48–63.

Dover, K. J. 1998. "Herodotean Plausibilities." Pp. 219–225 in *Modus Operandi: Essays in Honour of Geoffrey Rickman*, ed. M. Austin, J. Harries, and C. Smith. London.

———. 1974. *Greek Popular Morality*. Berkeley.

Étienne, R., and M. Piérart. 1975. "Un décret du koinon des Hellènes à Platées en l'honneur de Glaucon, fils d'Étéoclès, d'Athènes." *BCH* 99:51–75.

Evans, J. A. S. 1991. *Herodotus, Explorer of the Past*. Princeton.

———. 1982. "The Oracle of the 'Wooden Wall.'" *CJ* 78:24–29.

———. 1968. "Father of History or Father of Lies: The Reputation of Herodotus." *CJ* 64:11–17.

———. 1961. "The Dream of Xerxes and the 'Nomoi' of the Persians." *CJ* 57:109–111.

Farnell, L. R. 1921. *Greek Hero Cults and Ideas of Immortality*. Oxford.

Figueira, T. J. 1991. *Athens and Aigina in the Age of Imperial Colonization*. Baltimore.

———. 1985. "Herodotus on the Early Hostilities between Aegina and Athens." *AJP* 106:49–74.

Fisher, N. R. E. 1992. *Hybris: A Study in the Values of Honour and Shame in Ancient Greece*. Warminster.

Flory, S. 1987. *The Archaic Smile of Herodotus*. Detroit.

Flower, H. I. 1991. "Herodotus and Delphic Traditions about Croesus." Pp. 57–77 in *Georgica: Greek Studies in Honour of George Cawkwell*, ed. M. A. Flower and M. Toher. *BICS Supplement* 58. London.

Fontenrose, J. 1978. *The Delphic Oracle*. Berkeley.

Fornara, C. W. 1990. "Human History and the Constraint of Fate in Herodotus." Pp. 25–45 in *Conflict, Antithesis, and the Ancient Historian*, ed. J. W. Allison. Columbus.

———. 1970. "The Cult of Harmodius and Aristogeiton." *Philologus* 114:155–180.

———. 1967. "Two Notes on Thucydides." *Philologus* 111:291–295.

Forrest, W. G. 1984. "Herodotus and Athens." *Phoenix* 38:1–11.

Francis, E. D., and M. Vickers. 1985. "The Oenoe Painting in the Stoa Poikile, and Herodotus' Account of Marathon." *ABSA* 80:99–113.

Friedrich, W. H. 1973. "Der Tod des Tyrannen." *Antike und Abendland* 18:97–129.

Frisch, P. 1968. *Die Träume bei Herodot*. Meisenheim am Glan.

Frost, F. J. 1997. *Greek Society*. 5th ed. Boston.

Garbrah, K. 1986. "On the ΘΕΟΦΑΝΕΙΑ in Chios and the Epiphany of Gods in War." *ZPE* 65:207–210.

Garland, R. 1992. *Introducing New Gods: The Politics of Athenian Religion*. Ithaca.

———. 1985. *The Greek Way of Death*. Ithaca.

Gauer, Werner. 1968. *Weihgeschenke aus den Perserkriegen*. Tübingen.

Gebhard, E. R. 1993. "The Evolution of a Pan-Hellenic Sanctuary: From Archaeology towards History at Isthmia." Pp. 154–177 in *Greek Sanctuaries: New Approaches*, ed. N. Marinatos and R. Hägg. London.

Georges, P. 1994. *Barbarian Asia and the Greek Experience*. Baltimore.

———. 1986. "Saving Herodotus' Phenomena: The Oracles and the Events of 480 B.C." *CA* 5:14–59.

Gould, J. 1994. "Herodotus and Religion." Pp. 91–106 in *Greek Historiography*, ed. S. Hornblower. Oxford.

———. 1991. "Give and Take in Herodotus." *The Fifteenth J. L. Myres Memorial Lecture.* Oxford.

———. 1989. *Herodotus.* London.

———. 1985. "On Making Sense of Greek Religion." Pp. 1–33 in *Greek Religion and Society*, ed. P. E. Easterling and J. V. Muir. Cambridge.

———. 1973. "Hiketeia." *JHS* 93:74–103.

Graf, F. 1997. *Magic in the Ancient World.* Cambridge, Mass.

Griffiths, A. 1989. "Was Kleomenes Mad?" Pp. 51–78 in *Classical Sparta: Techniques behind Her Success*, ed. A. Powell. Norman, Okla.

Habicht, C. 1961. "Falsche Urkunden zur Geschichte Athens im Zeitalter der Perserkriege." *Hermes* 89:1–35.

Hammond, N. G. L. 1992. "Plataea's Relations with Thebes, Sparta and Athens." *JHS* 112:143–150.

Hansen, P. A. 1983. *Carmina Epigraphica Graeca Saeculorum VIII–V a. Chr. N.* Berlin.

Harris, D. 1995. *The Treasures of the Parthenon and Erechtheion.* Oxford.

Harrison, T. 2000. *Divinity and History: The Religion of Herodotus.* Oxford.

———. 1997. "Herodotus and the Certainty of Divine Retribution." Pp. 101–122 in *What Is a God? Studies in the Nature of Greek Divinity*, ed. A. B. Lloyd. London.

Hartog, F. 1988. *The Mirror of Herodotus.* Berkeley.

Henrichs, A. 1981. "Human Sacrifice in Greek Religion: Three Case Studies." Pp. 195–242 in *Le sacrifice dans l'antiquité*, ed. O. Reverdin and J. Rudhardt. Fondation Hardt, *Entretiens* 27. Geneva.

Hereward, D. 1958. "The Flight of Damaratos." *RhM* 101:238–249.

Hignett, C. 1963. *Xerxes' Invasion of Greece.* Oxford.

Hofmann, I., and A. Vorbichler. 1980. "Das Kambysesbild bei Herodot." *Archiv für Orientforschung* 27:86–105.

Holladay, A. J., and M. D. Goodman. 1986. "Religious Scruples in Ancient Warfare." *CQ* 36, n.s.:151–171.

Hornblower, S. 1991. *A Commentary on Thucydides.* Vol. 1. Oxford.

———. 1982. "Thucydides, the Panionian Festival, and the Ephesia (III 104)." *Historia* 31:241–245.

Hughes, D. D. 1991. *Human Sacrifice in Ancient Greece.* London.

Humphreys, S. 1987. "Law, Custom and Culture in Herodotus." *Arethusa* 20:211–220.

Hurwit, J. M. 1999. *The Athenian Acropolis.* Cambridge.

Immerwahr, H. R. 1966. *Form and Thought in Herodotus.* Cleveland.

———. 1954. "Historical Action in Herodotus." *TAPA* 85:16–45.

Jacoby, F. 1945. "Some Athenian Epigrams from the Persian Wars." *Hesperia* 14:157–211.

———. 1944. "*Patrios Nomos*: State Burial in Athens and the Public Cemetery in the Kerameikos." *JHS* 64:37–66.

Jameson, M. H. 1991. "Sacrifice before Battle." Pp. 197–227 in *Hoplites: The Classical Greek Battle Experience*, ed. V. C. Hanson. London.

———. 1960. "A Decree of Themistokles from Troizen." *Hesperia* 29:198–223.

Jasanoff, J. H., and A. Nussbaum. 1996. "Word Games: The Linguistic Evidence in *Black Athena*." Pp. 177–205 in *Black Athena Revisited*, ed. M. R. Lefkowitz and G. M. Rogers. Chapel Hill.

Jost, M. 1985. *Sanctuaires et cults d'Arcadie*. Paris.

Kearns, E. 1992. "Between God and Man: Status and Function of Heroes and Their Sanctuaries." Pp. 65–107 in *Le sanctuaire grec*, ed. A. Schachter. Fondation Hardt, *Entretiens* 37. Geneva.

———. 1989. *The Heroes of Attica*. BICS Supplement 57. London.

Kinzel, K. H. 1976. "Miltiades' Parosexpedition in der Geschichtsschreibung." *Hermes* 104:280–307.

Kirchberg, J. 1965. *Die Funktion der Orakel im Werke Herodots*. Hypomnemata 11. Hamburg.

Köhnken, A. 1988. "Der Dritte Traum des Xerxes bei Herodot." *Hermes* 116:24–40.

Kron, U. 1976. *Die Zehn Attischen Phylenheroen*. Berlin.

Krumeich, R. 1991. "Zu den Goldenen Dreifüssen der Deinomeniden in Delphi." *JDAI* 106:37–62.

Kurke, L. 1996. "Pindar and the Prostitutes, or Reading Ancient 'Pornography.'" *Arion*, ser. 3, 4:49–75.

Kyrieleis, H. 1993. "The Heraion at Samos." Pp. 125–153 in *Greek Sanctuaries: New Approaches*, ed. N. Marinatos and R. Hägg. London.

Lachenaud, G. 1978. *Mythologies, religion et philosophie de l'histoire dans Hérodote*. Paris.

Laroche, D. 1989. "Nouvelles observations sur l'offrande de Platées." *BCH* 113:183–198.

Lateiner, D. 1989. *The Historical Method of Herodotus*. Toronto.

Lattimore, R. 1958. "The Composition of the *History* of Herodotus." *CP* 53:9–21.

———. 1939. "Herodotus and the Names of Egyptian Gods." *CP* 34:357–365.

Lefkowitz, M. R., and G. M. Rogers. 1996. *Black Athena Revisited*. Chapel Hill.

Lewis, D. M. 1985. "Persians in Herodotus." Pp. 101–117 in *The Greek Historians: Literature and History: Papers Presented to A. E. Raubitschek*. Saratoga, Calif.

Linforth, I. M. 1940. "Greek and Egyptian Gods (Herodotus II.50 and 52)." *CP* 35:300–301.

———. 1928. "Named and Unnamed Gods in Herodotus." *University of California Publications in Classical Philology* 9:201–243.

———. 1926. "Greek Gods and Foreign Gods in Herodotus." *University of California Publications in Classical Philology* 9:1–25.

———. 1924. "Herodotus' Avowal of Silence in His Account of Egypt." *University of California Publications in Classical Philology* 7:269–292.

Lloyd, A. B. 1988. *Herodotus Book II: Commentary 99–182*. Leiden.

———. 1976. *Herodotus Book II: Commentary 1–98*. Leiden.

———. 1975. *Herodotus Book II: Introduction*. Leiden.

Lloyd, G. E. R. 1979. *Magic, Reason and Experience*. Cambridge.

Lloyd-Jones, H. 1983. *The Justice of Zeus*. 2d ed. Berkeley.

Lonis, R. 1979. *Guerre et religion en Grèce à l'époque classique*. Paris.

Loraux, N. 1981. *L'invention d'Athènes*. Paris.

Malkin, I. 1987. *Religion and Colonization in Ancient Greece*. Leiden.

Mark, I. S. 1993. *The Sanctuary of Athena Nike in Athens: Architectural Stages and Chronology.* Princeton.

Massaro, V. 1978. "Herodotus' Account of the Battle of Marathon and the Picture in the Stoa Poikile." *AC* 47:458–475.

Meiggs, R. 1972. *The Athenian Empire.* Oxford.

———. 1963. "The Political Implications of the Parthenon." *G&R* Supplement to Vol. 10:36–45.

Meritt, B. D. 1947. "The Persians at Delphi." *Hesperia* 16:58–62.

Mikalson, J. D. 1998. *Religion in Hellenistic Athens.* Berkeley.

———. 1991. *Honor Thy Gods: Popular Religion in Greek Tragedy.* Chapel Hill.

———. 1989. "Unanswered Prayers in Greek Tragedy." *JHS* 109:81–98.

———. 1983. *Athenian Popular Religion.* Chapel Hill.

———. 1982. "The *Heorte* of Heortology." *GRBS* 23:213–221.

———. 1976. "Erechtheus and the Panathenaia." *AJP* 97:141–153.

———. 1975. *The Sacred and Civil Calendar of the Athenian Year.* Princeton.

Miles, M. M. 1989. "A Reconstruction of the Temple of Nemesis at Rhamnous." *Hesperia* 58:133–249.

Miller, M. C. 1997. *Athens and Persia in the Fifth Century B.C.* Cambridge.

Mitchel, F. 1956. "Herodotus' Use of Genealogical Chronology." *Phoenix* 10:48–69.

Momigliano, A. 1958. "The Place of Herodotus in the History of Historiography." *History* 43:1–13.

Mora, F. 1986. *Religione e religioni nelle storie di Erodoto.* Milan.

Mosshammer, A. A. 1979. *The Chronicle of Eusebius and the Greek Chronographic Tradition.* Lewisburg, Pa.

Müller, D. 1987. *Topographischer Bildkommentar zu den Historien Herodots.* Tübingen.

Mylonas, G. E. 1961. *Eleusis and the Eleusinian Mysteries.* Princeton.

Neville, J. W. 1977. "Herodotus on the Trojan War." *G&R* 24:3–12.

Niemeyer, H. G. 1960. *Promachos.* Waldsassen.

Nock, A. D. 1972. *Essays on Religion and the Ancient World.* Ed. Z. Stewart. 2 vols. Cambridge, Mass.

———. 1944. "The Cult of Heroes." *HTR* 37:141–174.

———. 1942. "Religious Attitudes of the Ancient Greeks." *Proceedings of the American Philosophical Society* 85:472–482.

Parke, H. W. 1984. "Croesus and Delphi." *GRBS* 25:209–232.

———. 1967. *The Oracles of Zeus.* Cambridge, Mass.

Parke, H. W., and D. E. W. Wormell. 1956. *A History of the Delphic Oracle.* 2 vols. Oxford.

Parker, R. 1998a. *Cleomenes on the Acropolis: An Inaugural Lecture Delivered before the University of Oxford on 12 May 1997.* Oxford.

———. 1998b. "Pleasing Thighs: Reciprocity in Greek Religion." Pp. 105–125 in *Reciprocity in Ancient Greece,* ed. C. Gill, N. Postlethwaite, and R. Seaford. Oxford.

———. 1996. *Athenian Religion: A History.* Oxford.

————. 1989. "Spartan Religion." Pp. 142–173 in *Classical Sparta: Techniques behind Her Success*, ed. A. Powell. Norman, Okla.

————. 1985. "Greek States and Greek Oracles." Pp. 298–326 in *Crux: Essays Presented to G. E. M. de Ste. Croix*, ed. P. Cartledge and F. D. Harvey. London.

————. 1983. *Miasma: Pollution and Purification in Early Greek Religion*. Oxford.

Pearson, L. 1941. "Credulity and Scepticism in Herodotus." *TAPA* 72:335–355.

Pelling, C. B. R. 1991. "Thucydides' Archidamus and Herodotus' Artabanus." Pp. 120–142 in *Georgica: Greeks Studies in Honour of George Cawkwell*, ed. M. A. Flower and M. Toher. *BICS Supplement* 58. London.

Podlecki, A. J. 1975. *The Life of Themistocles: A Critical Survey of the Literary and Archaeological Evidence*. Montreal.

Pohlenz, M. 1973. *Herodot: Der Erste Geschichtschreiber des Abendlandes*. 3d ed. Stuttgart.

Pollitt, J. J. 1990. *The Art of Ancient Greece: Sources and Documents*. 2d ed. Cambridge.

Pötscher, W. 1958. "Götter und Gottheit bei Herodot." *WS* 71:5–29.

Prandi, L. 1993. "Considerazioni su Bacide e le raccolte oracolari greche." Pp. 51–62 in *La profezia nel mondo antico*, ed. M. Sordi. *Contributi dell' Istituto di storia antica* 19. Milan.

Price, S. 1999. *Religions of the Ancient Greeks*. Cambridge.

————. 1985. "Delphi and Divination." Pp. 128–154 in *Greek Religion and Society*, ed. P. E. Easterling and J. V. Muir. Cambridge.

Pritchett, W. K. 1993. *The Liar School of Herodotus*. Amsterdam.

————. 1985. *The Greek State at War*. Vol. 4. Berkeley.

————. 1979. *The Greek State at War*. Vol. 3. Berkeley.

————. 1974. *The Greek State at War*. Vol. 2. Berkeley.

————. 1971. *The Greek State at War*. Vol. 1. Berkeley.

Pulleyn, S. 1997. *Prayer in Greek Religion*. Oxford.

Raaflaub, K. A. 1985. *Die Entdeckung der Freiheit*. Munich.

Rackham, H. 1952. *Pliny: Natural History*. Vol. 9. Loeb Classical Library. Cambridge, Mass.

Ridgway, B. S. 1992. "Images of Athena on the Akropolis." Pp. 119–142 in *Goddess and Polis: The Panathenaic Festival in Athens*, ed. J. Neils. Princeton.

Rigsby, K. J. 1996. *Asylia: Territorial Inviolability in the Hellenistic World*. Berkeley.

Robert, L. 1950. "Le Carien Mys et l'oracle du Ptôon (Hérodote, VIII, 135)." Pp. 23–38 in *Hellenica*, vol. 8. Paris.

Robertson, N. 1986. "A Point of Precedence at Plataia: The Dispute between Athens and Sparta over Leading the Procession." *Hesperia* 55:88–102.

Roller, L. E. 1999. *In Search of God the Mother*. Berkeley.

Romilly, J. de. 1977. *The Rise and Fall of States According to Greek Authors*. Ann Arbor.

————. 1971. "La vengeance comme explication historique dans l'oeuvre d'Hérodote." *REG* 84:314–337.

Romm, J. S. 1998. *Herodotus*. New Haven.

Rudhardt, J. 1992. "De l'attitude des Grecs à l'égard des religions étrangères." *Revue de l'Histoire des Religions* 209:219–238.

Rutherford, I. 1996. "The New Simonides: Towards a Commentary." *Arethusa* 29:167–
192.

Salmon, J. B. 1984. *Wealthy Corinth*. Oxford.

Schachter, A. 1994. *Cults of Boiotia. BICS Supplement* 38. Vol. 3. London.

———. 1986. *Cults of Boiotia. BICS Supplement* 38. Vol. 2. London.

———. 1981. *Cults of Boiotia. BICS Supplement* 38. Vol. 1. London.

Sealey, R. 1976. *A History of the Greek City States, ca. 700–338 B.C.* Berkeley.

Shapiro, H. A. 1990. "Oracle-Mongers in Peisistratid Athens." *Kernos* 3:335–345.

———. 1989. *Art and Cult under the Tyrants in Athens*. Mainz am Rhein.

Shear, T. L., Jr. 1993. "The Persian Destruction of Athens: Evidence from Agora
Deposits." *Hesperia* 62:383–482.

Shimron, B. 1989. *Politics and Belief in Herodotus*. Stuttgart.

Siewert, P. 1972. *Der Eid von Plataiai*. Munich.

Sinos, R. H. 1993. "Divine Selection: Epiphany and Politics in Archaic Greece." Pp. 73–
91 in *Cultural Poetics in Archaic Greece: Cult, Performance, Politics*, ed.
C. Doughterty and L. Kurke. Cambridge.

Sourdille, C. 1925. "Sur une nouvelle explication de la discrétion d'Hérodote en matière
de religion." *REG* 38:289–305.

Stadter, P. A. 1989. *A Commentary on Plutarch's Pericles*. Chapel Hill.

Starr, C. G. 1962. "Why Did the Greeks Defeat the Persians?" *Parola del Passato* 17:321–
332.

Ste. Croix, G. E. M. de. 1977. "Herodotus." *G&R* 24:130–148.

Stewart, A. F. 1990. *Greek Sculpture*. 2 vols. New Haven.

Stroud, R. S. 1998. *The Athenian Grain-Tax Law of 374/3 B.C. Hesperia* Supplement 29.
Princeton.

Thompson, D. B. 1956. "The Persian Spoils in Athens." Pp. 281–291 in *The Aegean and
the Near East: Studies Presented to Hetty Goldman*, ed. S. S. Weinberg. Locust
Valley.

Threpsiades, J., and E. Vanderpool. 1964 (1965). "Themistokles' Sanctuary of Artemis
Aristoboule." *Arch. Delt.* 19:26–36.

Tölle-Kastenbein, R. 1976. *Herodot und Samos*. Bochum.

Tritle, L. A. 1996. "Black Athena: Vision or Dream of Greek Origins?" Pp. 303–330 in
*Black Athena Revisited*, ed. M. R. Lefkowitz and G. M. Rogers. Chapel Hill.

Van Straten, F. T. 1981. "Gifts for the Gods." Pp. 65–151 in *Faith, Hope, and Worship*, ed.
H. S. Versnel. Leiden.

Vanderpool, E. 1966. "A Monument to the Battle of Marathon." *Hesperia* 35:93–106.

———. 1942. "An Archaic Inscribed Stele from Marathon." *Hesperia* 11:329–337.

Versnel, H. S. 1981. *Faith, Hope, and Worship*. Leiden.

Visser, M. 1982. "Worship Your Enemy: Aspects of the Cult of Heroes in Ancient
Greece." *HTR* 75:403–428.

Walbank, F. W. 1960. "History and Tragedy." *Historia* 9:216–234.

Walsh, J. 1986. "The Date of the Athenian Stoa at Delphi." *AJA* 90:319–336.

Wéry, L.-M. 1966. "Le meurtre des hérauts de Darius en 491 et l'inviolabilité du héraut."
*AC* 35:468–486.

West, M. L. 1993. "Simonides Redivivus." *ZPE* 98:1–14.

———. 1982. "The Orphics of Olbia." *ZPE* 45:17–29.

———. 1978. *Hesiod: Works & Days.* Oxford.

———. 1966. *Hesiod: Theogony.* Oxford.

West, W. C., III. 1970. "Saviors of Greece." *GRBS* 11:271–282.

Whitley, J. 1994. "The Monuments That Stood before Marathon: Tomb Cult and Hero Cult in Archaic Attica." *AJA* 98:213–230.

Wilamowitz-Moellendorff, U. von. 1880. *Aus Kydathen.* Berlin.

Williams, C. K., II. 1986. "Corinth and the Cult of Aphrodite." Pp. 12–24 in *Corinthiaca: Studies in Honor of Darrell A. Amyx*, ed. M. A. Del Chiaro. Columbia.

Wycherley, R. E. 1957. *Literary and Epigraphical Testimonia. The Athenian Agora* 3. Princeton.

Yunis, H. 1988. *A New Creed: Fundamental Religious Beliefs in the Athenian Polis and Euripidean Drama. Hypomnemata* 91. Göttingen.

Citations in italics indicate primary or extensive discussion of the relevant passage.

4.152: 128

4.155–157: 210 (nn. 157, 160–162, 164, 172), 218 (n. 290)

4.161: 210 (n. 160)

4.162: 117

4.163: 210 (nn. 161, 163)

4.164: 210 (n. 160), 231 (n. 48)

4.180: *188–189*

4.181: 180

4.186: 182

4.188–189: 178, *188*, 189

4.198: 125, 137

4.205: 82, 147

5.1: 56

5.7: 183, 188

5.18–21: 143

5.22: 112

5.33: 148, 234 (n. 24)

5.36: 143, 200 (n. 7)

5.42–45: 210 (n. 163), 238 (n. 104)

5.46: 143, 200 (n. 7)

5.47: 176, 226 (n. 59)

5.49: 111, 218 (n. 294), 227 (n. 76)

5.55–56: *15–16*, 41, 124

5.59–61: 122, 192, 214 (n. 221)

5.62–64: *16–17*, 24, 55, 117, 124, 143

5.66: 18, 129, 179, 192

5.67: 176, *193*

5.70–71: *18*, 146, 214 (n. 238)

5.72: *18–19*, 107, 124

5.74–75: 208 (n. 133)

5.77: *19–20*, 71, 124, 231 (n. 60)

5.78: *15*, 117

5.79–81: *21–22*, 56, 77, 118, 148, 176

  5.79: 210 (nn. 154, 159)

  5.80: 130, 210 (n. 157)

5.82–88: *20–21*, 43, 192, 210 (n. 160)

  5.82: *20–21*

  5.83: 101, 229 (n. 23)

  5.85: *21*

  5.86: 145

5.89: *23*, 118, 130, 192

5.90–91: 16, 24, 228 (n. 11)

5.92.β–γ: 210 (n. 165), 226 (n. 67)

5.92.δ: 148

5.92.ε: 56, 210 (n. 161)

5.92.η: 101, 218 (n. 294)

5.93: 218 (n. 294), 228 (n. 11)

5.94: 154

5.97–103: 24

5.101–105: 134–135

  5.102: *24*

  5.105: *24–25*

5.106: 159

5.114–115: 176, 226 (n. 59)

5.119: 179

6.7: 114

6.11: 30, 133

6.18–19: 149

  6.19: *25*, 118, 135, 140, 210 (nn. 157, 161)

6.25: 135

6.27: 140, 146, 207 (n. 120), 229 (n. 35), 231 (n. 53)

6.32: 25

6.34–35: 56

6.36–38: 176, 193, 210 (n. 160), 226 (n. 59)

6.43–45: 26, 208 (n. 125), 212 (n. 188)

6.48: 50

6.52: 210 (n. 160)

6.57: 210 (n. 154)

6.61: 209 (n. 137)

6.62–63: 159

6.64: 148

6.66–67: 18, 210 (n. 156)

6.75: 18, 74, 118, 142, 146, 200 (n. 9), 208 (n. 133), 210 (n. 164)

6.76: 158, 208 (n. 127)

6.77: 211 (n. 172)

6.79–82: 208 (n. 133)

  6.79: 74, 200 (n. 9)

  6.79–80: 228 (n. 11)

6.80–82: 56, 140, 149, 210 (n. 162)

6.84: 118, 146, 208 (n. 133)

6.86: 142–143, 210 (nn. 162, 163, 165), 211 (n. 72)

6.91: 74, *126*, 142, 147, 199 (n. 8), 200 (n. 9)

6.94: 26, 202 (n. 40)

6.96: 26, 135

6.97–98: 26–27, 43, 87, 122, 137, 140, 157, 231 (n. 53)

Suda, s.v.
  ἀργυρόπους δίφρος: 221 (n. 356)
  Βραγχίδαι: 215 (n. 240)
  ἐλευθέριος: 223 (n. 9)

Tacitus
  *Annales*
    6.37: 232 (n. 74)
Theognis
  153–154: 215 (n. 251)
Theopompus
  *FGrHist*: 115 F 153: 92
Thucydides
  1.20.2: 200 (n. 1)
  1.126–127: 200 (nn. 10, 11), 214 (n. 238)
  1.132: *98*, 103, 214 (n. 221)
  1.134: 200 (n. 9), 214 (n. 236)
  2.8.3: 203 (n. 45)
  2.13.4: 221 (n. 356)
  2.27: 225 (n. 51)
  2.34–46: 110
    2.34.5: 204 (n. 64)
  2.67: 209 (n. 144)
  2.71–74: 99
    2.71.2: 220 (n. 340)
  3.58.4: 221 (n. 361)
  6.56–58: 200 (n. 1)
  8.1.1: 38

Vitruvius
  1.1.6: 222 (n. 375)
  5.9.1: 109

Xenophon
  *Anabasis*
    3.2.11–12: 29, *30*, 127
    4.5.35: 232 (n. 74)
  *Hellenica*
    4.2.20: 127
  *Symposium*
    4.80: 215 (n. 245)

*Inscriptions*

*Inscriptiones Graecae*
  I³ 502, 503/4, 507–508, 511, 517–518, 521
    bis, 522–525, 533, 597: 214 (n. 221)
  I³ 1218, 1231, 1234, 1277–1279, 1357: 213
    (n. 206)
  II² 1006: 204 (n. 76)
  VII 53: *110*

Meiggs and Lewis (ML)
  15: 201 (n. 15)
  18: 223 (n. 221), 203 (n. 65)
  19: *34*, 213 (n. 221)
  23: *58–59*
  24: *84–85*
  25: 222 (n. 376)
  26: 213 (n. 207)

Page numbers in italics indicate the most general or important discussions of the topic. Entries for peoples (for example, Plataeans) do not necessarily include all the individuals, gods, heroes, oracles, and festivals of that people. See also the entries for individuals (for example, Arimnestus of Plataea) and the entries for individual gods, along with the following entries: Delphic Oracle, Festivals, Heroes and heroines, and Omens.

Auxesia, goddess of Aegina, *20–21*, 101, 145, 192

Babylonians, 143, 180
Bacchiadae of Corinth, 226 (n. 67)
Bacis, 68, 85–86, 140; oracles about Euboea, 68, 85–86; Plataea, 94; Salamis, *77–78*, 85–86, 112–113, 125, 127, 140, 231 (nn. 60, 61)
Biton of Argos, 116, 209 (n. 137)
Boreas, god of Athens, *61–62*, 114, 119, 209 (n. 137)
Bubastis, goddess of Egypt, 171, 177, *180–181*, 183, 220 (n. 345)
Bulis of Sparta, 51

Cabiri, gods of Boeotia, 90, 167
Cadmus of Thebes, 184–185, 192
Callias of Athens, 205 (n. 89)
Callimachus of Athens, 33, 203 (nn. 61, 65), 213 (n. 221)
Cambyses of Persia; dreams of, 82, 141, 143, 158–159, 200 (n. 2), 207 (n. 112), 227 (n. 78); impieties of, 142–143, 147, 153–154, 160, 164, 208 (n. 133); oracles to, 158, 230 (n. 47)
Candaules of Lydia, 148–149, 234 (n. 24)
Carians, 24, *87*, 110, 122, 179
Carneia of Sparta. *See* Festivals
Carystians, 109–110, 115
Cecrops, hero of Athens, 34, 53
*Charis*, 162
Charites, 167, 171
Chians, 108, 116, 140, 146, 191, 231 (n. 53)
*Chresmologoi*, *38*, 54–55, 68, 86, *141*, 157, 206 (n. 100), 228 (n. 14)
Cimon of Athens, *37*, *72*, 176, *204 (n. 75)*
Cleades of Plataea, 104–105
Cleisthenes of Athens, 15, 18–19, 129, 179, 214 (n. 238)
Cleisthenes of Sicyon, 193
Cleobis of Argos, 116, 209 (n. 137)
Cleomenes of Sparta: Impieties of, 19, 57, 74, 142–143, 146, 153, 200 (n. 9), 208 (n. 133); omens to, 18, 107, 140, 148–149, 208 (n. 127); oracles to, 16, 18–19, 24,

56–57, 118, 124, 148–149, 200 (n. 6), 228 (n. 11)
Cnidians, 191, 224 (n. 31)
Codrus, hero of Athens, 34, 36, 115
Corinthians, 63, *79–80*, *83–85*, 99, 101, 128, 132, 145, 148, 213 (n. 221), 214 (n. 222)
Cretans, 59, 60, 119, 121
Croesus of Lydia: Dedications of, 69, 84, *116*, 122, 161–162, 200 (n. 7); dreams and omens, 163, 200 (n. 2); oracles to, 56–58, 88, 116, 140, 149, 161–162, 200 (n. 4), 224 (n. 36), 230 (n. 48); *Phthonos* and, 39, 150–152; piety of, 48, 141–142, *158–165*; Solon and, 39, 82, 150, 163, 165
Curses, 25, 89, 91
Cybebe, goddess of Lydia, 24, 27, 134
Cychreus, hero of Athens, 79–80
Cylon of Athens, 18, 146, 214 (n. 238)
Cymaeans, 74, 200 (n. 9)
Cypselus, 56, 226 (n. 67)
Cyrenaeans, 182
Cyrnus, hero of Phocaea, 176
Cyrus of Persia: Divine favor of, 160, 226 (n. 67), 227 (n. 78); dreams of, 141, 158, 200 (n. 2), 208 (n. 126); fortune and, 150, 230 (n. 46); oaths and, 159

*Daimones*, 21, 31, 43, 131–132, 141, 154, 163
Damia, goddess of Aegina, *20–21*, 101, 145, 192
Danaids of Egypt, 182, 192–193
Danaus of Egypt, 126, 182, 192
Darius of Persia, 5, 24–26, 37, 39, 46, 50–51, 121–122, 128, 134–135, 140, 153, 157, 159, 200 (n. 2), 208 (n. 125), 226 (n. 67)
Datis, Persians' general: Apollo of Delion and, *36*, 122, 158; Delos and, 26–27, 36, 87, 121–122, 157; dreams of, *36*, 41, 122, 158, 206 (n. 211)
Dead: treatment of, 31, 47, 65–67, 91, 97–98, 104–106, 110, *142–143*, 147, 156–157, 159
Dedications, 5–6, 8, 11–12, 16, 19–20, 52, 62, *70–72*, *141–142*, *147–148*, 151, 164–165, 199 (n. 5); after Artemisium, 63, 71, 127; after Marathon, 28, *32–35*, 102, 115, 123–

124, 213 (n. 221); after Plataea, *98–99, 102–104, 109–111*, 115, 121–122, 124, 128–129, 213 (n. 221); after Salamis, *83–84*, 114–115, 121, 130, 213 (n. 221)
— others: by Greek individuals, 72, 75, 102–103, 116–117, 205 (n. 89), 223 (n. 211); by non-Greeks, 48, 69, *115–116*, 161 (*See also* Croesus of Lydia); by states, 19, 21, 70–71, 116, 177 (*See also* Aeginetans; Argives; Athenians; Delphi and Delphians; Phocians; Siphnians); to Amphiaraus, 122; to Hera of Samos, 128; to Protesilaus, 108

Delos and Delians, 26–27, 36, 43, 87, 121–122, 140, 157, 181, 231 (n. 53)

Delphi and Delphians, 7, 27, 60, *61*, 69–71, 87–88, 93, 100, 114, 117, 130, 133–134, 140, 209 (n. 137); dedications at, 8, 34–35, 84, 98–99, 102–103, 109–110, *115–117*, 123, 161–162, 205 (n. 89), 210 (n. 170), 225 (n. 39) (*See also* Apollo Pythios of Delphi); temple of Apollo, 16, 34, 55, 117

Delphic Oracle, 14, *55–58*, 85–86, *117–121*, 140, 148–150, 153, 209 (n. 152), *210 (n. 172)*, *230 (n. 48)*; to Alyattes, 116, 225 (n. 36); to Argives, 59–60, 118–119, 121; to Aristides, 94–95, 104, 113, 120, 210 (n. 170); to Athenians, 23–24, 31, 77, 79, 118, 130, 148–149, 192, 204 (n. 75), 210 (n. 170); "Wooden Wall," 38, *52–58*, 71–73, 77–78, 118–119, 121, 124, 140–141, 148; to Cleomenes, 56–57, 148–149, 228 (n. 11); to Cnidians, 224 (n. 31); to Cretans, 59–60, 119, 121; to Croesus, 56–58, 116, 140, 161–162, 224 (n. 36), 230 (n. 48); to Cypselus, 56; to Delphians, 58, 60, 62, 69, 119, 140; to Epidaurians, 20; to Glaucus, 142; to Greeks, 58, 84, 99–100, 113, 115, 120, 210 (n. 170); to Gyges, 115, 149, 224 (n. 36); to Milesians, 25, 27, 118, 120, 140, 149; to Miltiades the Elder, 56; to Parians, 37; to Siphnians, 56, 224 (n. 25); to Spartans, 16–17, 56, 64–65, 85–86, 117–121, 140, 148, 192, 200 (n. 6), 228 (n. 11);

to Thebans, 21–22, 36, 56, 118, 149; to Themistocles, 102–103, 210 (n. 170); to Tisamenus, 93, 120, 140

Demaratus of Sparta, 18, *75–76*, 118, 121, 126, 148

Demeter, 54, *125–126*, 133, 137, *181–183*, 234 (n. 22); Achaea of Athens, 192; Eleusinia, 152; Eleusinia of Athens, 43, 76, 92, 126, 129, 138; Eleusinia of Mycale, 107, 126, 193; Eleusinia of Plataea, 94–96, 126, 134, 138, 228 (n. 5); Thesmophoros, 126, 178, 182–183; Thesmophoros of Paros, 36–37, 52; of Aegina, 74, 126; of Egypt (*See* Isis); of Phlya in Athens, 75

Democrates, hero of Plataea, 94

Dicaeus of Athens, *75–76*, 126, 138

Dictyna, goddess of Cydonia, 191

Didyma, 25, 74, 135, 200 (n. 7)

Dike, 127

Diodorus of Corinth, 83

Dionysus, 129, 146, 173, 175, 178, *183–185*; Omestes, 78; of Athens, 109; of Borysthenes, 236 (n. 76); of Egypt (*See* Osiris); of Ethiopia, 180; of Scythia, 173

Dioscuri, 167, 171, 186, 217 (n. 277), 218 (n. 296), 238 (n. 105)

Dodona, 146, 167–168, 171, 180, 193–194. *See also* Zeus of Dodona

Dorieus of Sparta, 237 (n. 104)

Dream interpreters, 16, 38, 43, 200 (n. 2)

Dreams, 5–6, *16*, 41–42, 97, 139, *141*, 143, *152–153*, *158–159*, 165; of Arminestus, 94–95, 97, 113; of Astyages, 158; of Cambyses (*See* Cambyses of Persia); of Croesus (*See* Croesus of Lydia); of Cyrus (*See* Cyrus of Persia); of Datis (*See* Datis); of Hippias, 15–16, 29, 200 (n. 2); of Otanes, 158; of Polycrates' daughter, 141, 146, 200 (n. 2); of Xerxes (*See* Xerxes of Persia)

Echetlaeus, hero of Athens, 23, 31, *33–35*, 130, 133, 210 (n. 170), 224 (n. 34)

Eëtion of Corinth, 148, 226 (n. 67)

Egestaeans, 226 (n. 59)

Egypt and Egyptians, 37, 41, 43, 78, 126, 139, 141, 144–146, 154, *167–193*

Eleans, 112, 153

Eleusinian Mysteries, 75–76, 126

Eleusis, 75–76, 94, 96, 126, 138

Eleutheria of Plataea. *See* Festivals

Epidaurians, 20–21, 109, 115, 192

Epitaphs, *66–67*; from Marathon, 31, 33; from Persian Wars, 110; from Plataea, 100, 105; from Salamis, 84–85; from Thermopylae, 65–67

Erechtheus, hero of Athens, 20, 34, 73

Eretrians, 24, 26–27, 135

Ethiopia and Ethiopians, 32, 41, 180, 185

Euboeans, 68

Euchidas of Plataea, 100

Euelthon of Cyprian Salamis, 117

Euenius of Apollonia, 147

Eukleia, goddess of Athens, 33

Euphrantides, 78

Euryleon of Sparta, 200 (n. 7), 214 (n. 234)

Festivals, 5, *100–101*, 177; Carneia of Sparta, 64, 212 (n. 197); Eleutheria of Plataea, 91–92, 99–101, 106, 113; Hyacinthia of Sparta, 89, 101; Mounichia of Athens, 76, 127; Olympic Games, 18, 64, 68, 112, 120, 153, 176, 212 (n. 198); Panathenaia of Athens, 15–16, 28, 124; Panionia of Ionians, 114; Theophania of Delphi, 116; Thesmophoria, 144, *182–183*, 192; of Adrastus of Argos, 193; of Amun of Egypt, 180; of Artemis Agrotera of Athens, 29–30, 76, 127, 220 (n. 342); of Artemis of Samos, 100–101; of Athena of Egypt, 144; of Athena of Libya, 188–189; of Damia and Auxesia of Aegina, 101; of Dionysus, 183–184; of Hera of Argos, 101; of Hera of Corinth, 101; of Heracles of Marathon, 204 (n. 69); of Isis of Egypt, 144, 177, 181–182; of Magna Mater of Cyzicus, 193; of Osiris of Egypt, 183–184; of war heroes at Sparta, 65, 96

Fire: as deity, 156

Firstfruits, 20, 34–35, 84, 114, 124, 159, 162

Gephyraioi of Athens, 192

Glaucus of Sparta, 142–143

*Graeca interpretatio, 155–165*

Gyges of Lydia, 115–116, 149, 224 (n. 36), 234 (n. 24)

Hades, 168

Halicarnassians, 191

Harmodius, hero of Athens, 16, 74

Hecataeus of Miletus, 175, 200 (n. 7)

Hegesistratus of Elis, 93

Hegesistratus of Samos, 106–107, 140

Helen of Sparta, 78, 147, 154, 175, 209 (n. 137)

Helios: Eleutherios of Troezen, 110; of Egypt, 145. *See also* Sun

Hellenion of Naucratis, 191

Hephaestus, 129, 168, *187*; of Egypt, 176, *187*

Hera, *127–128*, 133, 154, 167–168, 171; Cithaironia of Plataea, 94–96, 209 (n. 137); of Argos, 101, 140, 209 (n. 137); of Athens, 92; of Corinth, 101; of Samos, *128*, 129, 134, 191, 214 (n. 221)

Heracles, 22, 146–147, 175, 178, 180, 184, *185–187*, 224 (n. 24); Sparta and, 65, 85; of Marathon, 33–34, 36, 204 (n. 69); of Egypt, *185–187*; of Scythia, 179, 226 (n. 67); of Thasos and Tyre, *185–187*

Heralds: sanctity of, *50–52*, *137*, 147, 159

Hermes, 167, *187*; Chthonios of Plataea, 105; of Egypt, 187

Heroes and heroines, 5, 22–23, *31–32*, 36, 70, 80–82, 88–89, 111, *129–131*, 132, *133*, 134–135, 138, *139*, 143, 147, 155, 167, *175–176*, *186–187*, 192, 197 (n. 1); of Abdera, 176; of Acanthus, 18, 131, 176; of Aegina, 22–23, 61, 77, 129–130, 175–176, 182, 192; of Amathusia, 176, 226 (n. 59); of Argos, 193; of Athens, 16, 20, 22–23, 30–36, 73–74, 77, 79–80, 84, 106, 114–115, 129–130, 133–134, 175–176, 192, 204 (n. 75), 210 (n. 170), 224 (n. 34); of Athens (eponymous), 34, 36, 115, 129, 210 (n. 170) of Carthage, 230 (n. 40), 235 (n. 33); of Chersonnesus, 176; of Delphi, 23, 70,

106, 130, 133–134; of Egesta, 176, 226 (n. 59); of Elaeus, 22, 47, 108–109, 130, 134, 138, 175, 207 (n. 121); of Phocaeans, 176; of Plataea, 94–96, 120; of Sicyon, 176, 193; of Sparta, 50–52, 137, 175–176, 192; of Tegea, 192; of Thebes, 87, 122, 140, 157, 176, 193, 217 (n. 288); of Troy, 44, 87, 157; War dead as, 31, 67, 106. *See also* Amphiaraus; Heracles

Herse, heroine of Athens, 22

Hesiod, 81, 136, 139, 144, 147, *154–155, 167, 171–179*, 181, 185, 189, 230 (n. 48), 234 (n. 18)

Hipparchus of Athens, 15–16, 19, 38, 41–42, 74, 124, 225 (n. 42)

Hippias of Athens, 15, 24, 27, 29, 41–42, 74, 124

Hippomachus of Leucas, 93

Hippothoön, hero of Athens, 34

Histia, 167, 171; of Scythia, 179

Homer, 6, 81, 136, 139, 144, 147, 153, *154–155, 168, 171–179*, 181, 185, 189, 230 (n. 48)

Horus of Egypt, 171–172, *180–181*, 183

Hyacinthia of Sparta. *See* Festivals

*Hybris*, 19, 32, 39, *47*, 78, *153–154*, 165, 228 (n. 84)

Hypsion, hero of Plataea, 94

Iacchos, god of Athens, 75–76, 126

Impiety, 5, 16, 18–19, 43, *45–50*, 53, 57, *80–82, 134–135, 142–143*, 146–147, *153–155*, 160, 197 (n. 1); of abusing rivers, 45–47, 81; of corrupting oracles, 18–19; of human sacrifice, 78–79; of maltreating dead, 31, 47, 65, 97–98, 142–143, 147; of maltreating heralds, 50–52, 147; of maltreating *xenoi*, 142–143, 146, 155; of violating and destroying sanctuaries, 19, 25, *36–37*, 39, 47, 72–75, 81–82, 86, 89–90, 108–109, 114, 125–126, 130, 134–135, 142–143, 215 (n. 240); of violating asylum, 18, 46, *73–74*, 126, 142–143, 147, 154; of violating oaths, 142–143. See also *Atasthalia; Hybris*

Io of Argos, 22, 181–182

Isagoras of Athens, 18–19, 179, 192

Isis, goddess of Egypt, 144–145, 171, 177, *181–183*, 221 (n. 345)

Isthmia: dedications at, 98, 111. *See also* Poseidon of Isthmia

Kore, goddess; of Athens, 76, 126; of Paros, 36–37; of Plataea, 94–95

Koros, 78

Laodamas of Thebes, 122

Leonidas of Sparta, 47, 64–68, 85, 97–98, 119–121, 147, 156, 175, 213 (n. 208)

Leos, hero of Athens, 34

Leotychides of Sparta, 106–108, 127, 222 (n. 369), 226 (n. 67), 235 (n. 29)

Leto, goddess, *180–181*, 224 (n. 24); of Corinth, 83, 213 (n. 221); of Egypt, 158, *180–181*, 230 (n. 47)

Leucon, hero of Plataea, 94

Libyans, 167, 171, 178, *188–190*

Locrians of Opous, 66

Lycomedes of Athens, 63

Lycurgus, hero of Sparta, 176

Lysistratus of Athens, 141, 206 (n. 100)

Maeandrius of Samos, 112, 128

Magic, 50

Magna Mater, goddess of Cyzicus, 193

*Magoi*, 43–44, 50, 61, 156–159

Mandrocles of Samos, 128, 214 (n. 221)

*Manteis*, 27, 38, 64, 66, 78, 93–97, 120, *141, 152–153*, 157–158, 163–165, 184

Marathon, hero of Athens, 33–34, 36

Mardonius of Persia; impiety of, 90, 95, 135; omens to, 93–95, 97, 157; oracles to, 85, 87–88, 93–95, 97–98, 120, 122, 146, 157–158

Masistius of Persia, 104, 124

Megacles of Athens, 123–124

Megarians, 90, 104, 110, 127

Megistias of Acarnania, 64, 66–67, 141

Melampus, 66, 184, 192

Melanippus, hero of Thebes, 176, 193

Mendes, god of Egypt, 187

Menelaus of Sparta, 60, 78, 142, 218 (n. 296)

Midas of Phrygia, 115

Milesians, 10, 24–25, 27, 74–75, 107, 118, 120, 140, 149, 159, 191, 200 (n. 7)

Miltiades the Elder of Athens, hero of Chersonnesus, 56, 176, 193, 226 (n. 59)

Miltiades the Younger of Athens; dedications of, 28, 35, 192; impieties of, 31, 36–37, 52, 126, 143, 148; memorials of, 31, 33–35, 115; vow of, 203 (n. 61)

Minos of Crete, 60, 202 (n. 28)

Miracles, 5, 12, 70, 198 (n. 4); at Athens, 43, 72–73, 75, 141; at Delos, 26, 121–122; at Delphi, 7, 69–70, 86; at Elaeus, 108–109, 158; at Mycale, 107, 126; at Plataea, 96, 126; at Ptoön, 87; at Salamis, 79–80; at Sardis, 162. See also Omens

Mithra, goddess of Persia, 190

Moirae, 162, 230 (n. 48)

Moon: as deity of Persia, 156, 188

Mounichia of Athens. See Festivals

Musaeus, 38, 94, 140, 233 (n. 5)

Mylitta of Assyria, 190

Mys of Europus, 87, 122, 146, 157

Myth and mythology, 13, 22, 144–145, 151, 154–155, 168, 182–183, 186, 189, 234 (n. 27)


Naxians, 26, 135, 148

Necessity, 148–150, 160, 227 (n. 68)

Neit, goddess of Egypt, 188

Neleus, hero of Athens, 34, 36, 115

Nemesis, 151

Nemesis, goddess of Athens, 32, 35

Nereids, goddesses, 61, 157, 167, 171

Nicolaus of Sparta, 51

Nike, goddess, 78, 100, 112–113, 125, 127; of Athens, 32, 59

Nomoi, 13, 28, 50–51, 65, 143, 162, 174, 238 (n. 108)


Oaths, 52, 90–93, 108, 121, 142–143, 159, 164; of Plataea, 25, 90–93, 104, 125

Oceanus, 22, 174

Oedipus of Thebes, 122

Oenus, hero of Athens, 34

Olympia; dedications at, 35, 98–99, 111, 213

(n. 221); divination at, 87. See also Zeus Olympios of Olympia

Olympic Games. See Festivals

Omens, 5–6, 12, 38, 43, 133, 140–141, 143, 146, 152–153, 164–165, 197 (n. 1), 199 (n. 5); to Artaüctes, 108–109, 140–141, 158; to Athenians, 30, 71, 73, 75–77, 125–126, 138, 141, 203 (n. 60); to Chians, 140, 146, 231 (n. 53); to Cleomenes (See Cleomenes of Sparta); to Delians, 26–27, 43, 148, 231 (n. 53); to Greeks, 43, 75–78, 93–94, 107, 126, 140–141, 146; to Mardonius (See Mardonius of Persia); to Persians, 79; to Spartans, 19, 51, 64, 66, 90, 93, 95–96, 106–107, 124, 140, 209 (n. 137); to Xerxes (See Xerxes of Persia). See also Miracles

Onesilus, hero of Amathusia, 176, 226 (n. 59)

Onomacritus, 38, 141, 157

Oracles, 5–6, 12, 38, 54–58, 85–86, 88, 96, 133, 140, 143, 148–150, 152–153, 157–158, 164–165, 192, 197 (n. 1), 198 (n. 4), 199 (n. 5), 200 (n. 4); of Ammon, 180; of Amphiaraus (See Amphiaraus); of Apollo Abaios (See Abae; Apollo Abaios); of Apollo Ismenios (See Apollo Ismenios of Thebes); of Apollo Ptoös (See Apollo Ptoös of Ptoön); of Apollo Pythios (See Delphic Oracle); of Bacis (See Bacis); of Egyptian gods, 180–181, 186, 188, 236 (n. 59); of Musaeus (See Musaeus); of Trophonius, 87–88, 157; of Zeus Belus, 180; of Zeus of Dodona, 168, 171, 180, 193; of Zeus of Ethiopia, 180; unattributed, 26, 131

Oreithyia, goddess of Athens, 61–62, 114

Orestes, hero of Sparta, 175, 192

Orpheus of Thrace, 233 (n. 5)

Orphics, 144, 178, 236 (n. 76)

Osiris, god of Egypt, 171, 181, 183–185, 221 (n. 345)

Otanes of Persia, 158–159, 207 (n. 111)


Paionians, 56

Pan, god: Greek, 27–28, 94, 145–146, 175–

176, 184–185, 187, 189, 192; Egyptian, 146, 184–185, *187*, 189

Panathenaia. *See* Festivals

Pandion, hero of Athens, 34

Pandrosus, heroine of Athens, 22

Panionia. *See* Festivals

Panionion at Mycale, 114

Parians, 31, 36–37, 52, 126

Pausanias of Sparta; asylum violated, 200 (n. 9); dead and, 97–98; Delphi dedication and, 98–99, 103, 214 (n. 221); memorial of, 65; omens to, 95–96, 209 (n. 137)

Pelasgians, 139, *167–174*, 177, 180, 182, 192

Peleus, hero of Aegina, 22, 61, 130, 176

Peloponnesian War, 38, 51, 110

Peparethians, 110, 115, 214 (n. 221)

Periander of Corinth, 100–101, 208 (n. 132)

Pericles of Athens, 110, 125, 200 (n. 10), 214 (n. 238)

Perses, 60, 202 (n. 28)

Perseus, 60, 202 (nn. 28, 39)

Phanias of Lesbos, 78–79

Phaselians, 191

Pheidon of Argos, 153

Pheretima of Cyrene, 82, 147

Phero of Egypt, 47

Phidias of Athens, 32, 34–35, 102, 115, 124

Philiades of Megara, 66

Philippides of Athens, 27–28, 145, 192

Philippus of Croton, hero of Egesta, 176, 226 (n. 59)

Philistus of Athens, 107, 126, 193

Phocaeans, 56, 191–192

Phocians, 63–64, 69, 99, 117, 122, 135

Phoenecians, 185–186, 190–191

*Phthonos*, *39–40*, 47, *80–83*, 132, *148–152*, *154*, 160, 164–165, 199 (n. 5)

Phye of Athens, 123–124

Phylacus, hero of Delphi, 23, 70, 106, 130, 133–134

Pisander, hero of Plataea, 94

Pisistratidae, 18, 24, 72, 117. *See also* Hipparchus of Athens; Hippias of Athens

Pisistratus, 15, 18, 38, *123–124*, 133, 209 (n. 137), 228 (n. 14)

Plataeans, 28, 31, 33–36, 52, 95, 97–102, 105–106, 109, 113, 115, 123

Pollution, 18, 74, 91, 99–100, 120, 126, 146, 163, 178

Polycrates of Samos, 11, 39, 82, 112, 128, 141, 146, 150–151, 191, 200 (n. 2), 209 (n. 137)

Polyidus, hero of Plataea, 94

Poseidon, 11, 46, 99, *113–114*, 137, 167–168, 171, 186, *189–190*, 238 (n. 105); Asphaleios of Athens, 59; Helikonios of Mycale, 114; Soter, 61–62, 114; of Artemisium, 28, 138, 209 (n. 137); of Athens, 73; of Isthmia, 84, 98, 111, 113–114, 121, 123, 129, 134–135, 152; of Libya, 188–190; of Potidaea, 86, 114, 137; of Scythia, 179; of Sunium, 84, 114, 129, 134

Potidaeans, 86, 114, 137

Prayers, 5, 6, 12, *30*, 45, *48–49*, 62, 72, 77–78, 80, 83, 95–97, *100*, 101, 104–105, 119–120, 124, 130, 139–140, *141–142*, *147–148*, *150–153*, 165, *167–168*, *171–172*, 177, 193, 197 (n. 1), 199 (n. 5), *201 (n. 18)*; of Lydians, 48, 141–142; of Persians, 47–49, *156*

Prophets. See *Manteis*

Protesilaus, hero of Elaeus, 22, 47, 108–109, 130, 134, 138, 175, 207 (n. 121)

Psammetichus of Egypt, 56

Pythia of Delphi, 16, 18, 20–21, 37, 53–54, *55–56*, 59–60, 64, 102, 113, 117–119, 124, 148, 161–162, 213 (n. 218), 230 (n. 48)

Pythius of Lydia, 44

Reversals of fortune, *150–152*

Rhampsinitus of Egypt, 181

Rhodians, 191

Rhodopis of Thrace, 116

Sacrifices, 5, 6, 20, *28*, 30, 35, 51, 61–62, 73–74, 83, 87, *89*, 91, 94, 100–101, 104, 106, 120, 126–127, 139, *141–142*, *147–148*, *150–151*, 162, 165, *167–168*, *171–172*, 177–178, 199 (n. 5); before battle, 30, 64, 66, 78, 93–96, 127; human, 50, *78–79*, 156, 186; by Libyans, 188; by Lydians, *161*; by

Persians, 44–45, 50, 61, 116, 145, 156–158. See also *Aresterion*
Samians, 100–101, 106–108, 112, 128, 135, 158–159, 191, 226 (n. 67)
Samothrace, Mysteries of, 144, 167, 233 (n. 3)
Sandauce of Persia, 78
Scyles of Scythia, 148, 236 (n. 76)
Scythes of Scythia, 226 (n. 67)
Scythians, 78–79, 145, 173, 179, 187–188, 190, 201 (n. 18), 226 (n. 67), 236 (n. 76)
Seleucus of Syria, 75
Semele, goddess of Egypt, 144
Sexual intercourse, 143, 178, 180
Sicyonians, 193
Simonides of Ceos, 14, 31, 63, 65–67, 83, 105, 212 (n. 189), 213 (n. 206), 218 (n. 296), 219 (nn. 309, 324), 220 (n. 339)
Siphnians, 56, 117, 224 (n. 25), 230 (n. 44)
Smerdis of Persia, 158, 207 (n. 112)
Socrates of Athens, 43
Solon of Athens, 39, 82, 150–151, 163, 165
Soothsayers. See *Manteis*
Sophocles of Athens, 6, 42
Spartans, 16, 18–20, 23–24, 27–29, 50–52, 56, 59–60, 63–67, 85, 88–101, 104–109, 117–120, 124, 127, 137, 140, 147–148, 158–159, 192, 200 (nn. 4, 9), 218 (n. 296), 228 (n. 11); dedications of, 109; festivals of (*See* Festivals); heroes of (*See* Heroes and heroines); impieties of, 16, 18, 50–52, 118, 137, 147, 159, 200 (n. 9); omens to (*See* Omens); oracles to (*See* Delphic Oracle); treatment of dead, 65–67, 97–98, 104–105
Sperthias of Sparta, 51
Sphragitid Nymphs of Plataea, 94, 104, 203 (n. 54)
Sulla of Rome, 109
Sun: as deity, 47, 48, 156, 188, *231 (n. 51)*
Supplication, 49, 53, 102, 229 (n. 15)

Talthybius, hero of Sparta, 50–52, 137, 175
Tegeans, 63, 95, 98, 104, 123, 201 (n. 16)
Teians, 191–192

Telamon, hero of Aegina, 22–23, 77, 130, 176
Thales of Miletus, 207 (n. 120)
Thasians, 11, 49, 185–187
Thebans, 9, 20–23, 36, 52, 56, 63, 77, 87, 102, 118, 122, 130, 149
Themis, 167, 171
Themistocles of Athens, 45, 47, 54, 68, 71–72, 75, 80–82, 89, 103, 114, 129, 132, 134; decree of, 58–59, 92; dedications of, 75, 102–103, 127, 170, 214 (n. 221); human sacrifice and, 50, 78–79; omens to, 71, 77; "Wooden Wall" oracle and, 54–55, 72, 77, 119
Theoi Megaloi of Samothrace, 223 (n. 3)
Theophania of Delphi. *See* Festivals
Theseus, hero of Athens, 23, 31, 33–35, 106, 115, 130, 133, 176, 204 (n. 75), 210 (n. 170)
Thesmophoria. *See* Festivals
Thespians, 52, 63, 65–67
Thessalians, 52, 69, 113, 117, 122, 137
Thetis, goddess, 61, 87, 157
Thucydides of Athens, 6, 7, 10–12, 81, 194
Thyia, goddess of Delphi, 60, 62
Timasius, hero of Abdera, 176
Timo of Paros, 36–37
Timon of Delphi, 53
Tisamenus of Elis, 93, 120, 140
Tritantaechmes of Persia, 68, 112
Triton, god of Libya, 188
Troezenians, 110
Trojan War, 22, 142, 146–147, *154–155*, 175–176, 222 (n. 370)
Trophonius, god of Lebadea, 87–88, 157
Troy: Xerxes at, 27, 44, 87, 157. *See also* Trojan War
Twelve Gods of Athens, 28
*Tyche*, 131, 150, 160, 163, *226 (n. 67)*

Vows, 5, 30, 83, 90–92, 99–100, 104, 127, 159, 193

Water: as deity, 156
Winds: as deities, 60–62, 114, 119–120, 140, 156, 209 (n. 137)

Xanthippus of Athens, 109

*Xenia*, 16, 18, 66, 78, *142–143*, 146, 155, 159, 163–164, 190

Xerxes of Persia: Dreams of, *40–43*, 73, 82, 141, 148, 158–159, 200 (n. 2), 206 (n. 111), 227 (n. 78), 231 (n. 57); *Hybris* and, 39, 47, 153–154; impieties of, 27, 31, 39, 44–49, 65, 69, 72–75, 80–82, 88–89, 91–92, 96–97, 102–103, 108, 122, 126, 129, 132, 134–135, 138, 142–143, 147, 153–154, 156, 215 (n. 240); omens to, 26–27, 43–44, 49–50, 73, 97, 125, 140, 157–158; oracles to, 38, 85, 97, 118, 120, 141, 157; *Phthonos* and, 39, 40, 81–82, 150–152, 165; respect for religious conventions, 39, 44, 47–48, 51, 61, 73–74, 87–88, 108, 156–157, 159, 161–164, 231 (n. 51)

Zeus, 43, 49, 53, 65, 70, 78, *111–113*, 124–125, 127, 137, 163, 168, 172, *179–180*, 207 (n. 114); Agoraios of Selinus, 200 (n. 7); Belus of Babylon, 143, 145, 180, 220 (n. 345); Chthonios of Plataea, 105; Eleutherios of Athens, *113*, 125; Eleutherios of Plataea, 94, 99–101, *113*, 120, 123, 203 (n. 53), 210 (n. 170), 214 (n. 221); Eleutherios of Samos, 112; Epistios, 164; Hellenios, 89; Hellenios of Aegina, 218 (n. 294); Hetaireios, 164; Katharsios, 164; [Pancrates] of Athens, 59; Soter, 94–95, 113; Soter of Athens, 113; Stratios of Caria, 179; Olympios of Olympia, 35, 98–99, 111–114, 121, 123, 129, 134–135, 153, 236 (n. 56); Xenios, 164; of Caria, 179, 192; of Dodona, 171, 167–168, 178, 180, 193–194; of Egypt (*See* Amun); of Ethiopia, 180; of Libya, 189; of Naucratis, 191; of Persia, 25, 134, 156, 160, 179; of Scythia, 179

Zopyrus of Persia, 230 (n. 47)